The Way It Was

Eldon E. Hostetler

Dageforde Publishing, Inc.

Copyright 2004 by Eldon Hostetler. All rights reserved. No part of this publication may be reproduced, stored in a retrieval system, or transmitted in any form or by any means, electronic, mechanical, photocopied, recorded, or otherwise, without the prior written permission of the publisher.

ISBN 1-886225-63-X
Cover design by Rebecca Johnson

Dageforde Publishing, Inc.
128 East 13th Street
Crete, Nebraska 68333
1-800-216-8794
www.dageforde.com

Printed in the United States of America
10 9 8 7 6 5 4 3 2 1

Contents

Acknowledgments vii

Preface ix

Introduction 1
   Separating Truth from Fiction 1

Seward County Agriculture 5
   Imaginary Interview with Tommy West 7
   How the Land Changed Hands 9
   How it all Started 11
   Starting Costs One Hundred Years Ago 13
   Choosing Crops 17
   Not all Wheat and Corn 19
   Same Old Song—Earlier Version 22
   Livestock Production in Seward County. 24
   Hazards Raising Livestock 26
   Will Tractors Ever Replace Horses? 28
   Is Bigger Always Better?. 31
   Invasion from Outer Space in 1874 32
   Did We See a Drought in 2002?. 35
   Dairy Cow and Cream Stories 37
   Help from a Wealthy Uncle 38
   Early Restless Farmers 41
   Harvest Nostalgia 43
   The Price of Good Farmland 45
   Farming—A Dangerous Occupation 46
   Hooray for Chickens 50
   Separating Eggs 51
   What Happened to the Fruit Trees?. 53
   Artesian Wells Change a Community 56

Milford's Milling Industry 59
   Roller Loaf, Kolhonna, and Shogo 64

Early Seward County Newspapers 69
   Dare to Tell the Truth about a Rascal 73
   Exciting News from the Blue Valley Record 76

The Way It Was

Seward County Geography 78
    Seward County's Mason-Dixon Line. 78
    Milford's Nebraska City Connection. 80
    The Forgotten City of Camden 90
    A Town Named Grover 94
    How our Towns Were Named. 95
    Is There Gold in Them Hills? 99

Seward County Transportation 104
    When the Railroad Was King. 104
    Dispossession of the Horse 115
    The "Contraption" Comes to Milford 121
    Almost a "Perfect" Automobile. 125
    Building the Perfect Auto 127
    That "Old Tin Lizzie". 129

Recreational Activities in the "Good Old Days". 132
    Milford's Shogo Island & Laura M.. 141
    Celebrating Milford Fun Days in 1889. 143

Early Crime & Law Enforcement 146
    First & Last Seward County Hanging. 150
    Gun Play in Milford. 152
    Who Killed the Leavitt Sisters?. 154
    Mules—Worth More than a Man's Life 156
    Forgotten Seward County Murders 158
    Who Killed Mr. Lana ?. 162
    Nebraska the "Man Burner State" 166
    The Ku Klux Klan in Milford 168

Milford Institutions 172
    Milford's "Shogo" Legend 172
    Early Shogo Water Health Care 176
    Milford's Crowning Institution. 178
    The Milford "Girls" Home 186
    The First Technical School in Milford 196

All About Nebraska Weather 207
    Temperatures 207
    Precipitation. 208
    The "Dirty Thirties" 211

Drought 215
Confessions of a Survivor 218
An "Old-Fashioned Winter" 220
The Blizzard of 1888. 223
"The Big One?". 227
The Clash of Two Cultures 236
Did the old Chief's prophecy come true?. 240
The Prairie Flower Story: Which Version? 250
Will the Real "Council Oak" Please Stand Up? 256

Early Milford Industry. **262**
Milford's Klay Kraft Pottery 268
Milford Role Models. 273
Earning Respect the "Old-Fashioned Way" 275
Why They Give a Red Rose. 277
A Joy to Sacrifice for His Sake 282
Early Milford Missionaries 285
Milford's Number One Family 288
Early Seward County Liquor Struggles. 301
The Methodist Church Tried 307

Miscellaneous Short Stories. **313**
Earning an Oyster Supper 313
Naughty Boys, Good Boys & Watermelons. 317
What Happened to Herbert ? 319
Beautiful—But Deadly 321
Early Hunting & Fishing Stories 325
Changes in Community Mores. 327
Parable of the Tobacco Seed. 329
Deadly World Plagues 331
Before Bathroom Plumbing 334
Folk Medicine and Faith Healing. 336
A Tribute to Pioneer Women 338
Prose or Poetry. 340
The Corset Curse. 342

Bibliography. **345**

Acknowledgments

A special thank you to many of my "historically minded" friends who have helped in numerous ways to make this publication a reality.

To Alta Krasser and Cliff and Joan Kennel, keepers of the Seward County Museum in Goehner, for their assistance in acquiring and copying old pictures of Milford.

To Patricia G. Collister for the use of her very helpful book *First Land Owners in Seward County*.

To Charlotte Moomey for her timely information on the Culver family.

To Jan Stehlik for her willing and super fast research on Saline County.

And to the *Milford Times* staff for their effort to promote a greater appreciation of Milford's historical heritage.

You have all been great! Since many pictures and illustrations reproduced in this book have been in my family for four generations, it is nearly impossible to know the original source or to identify many of the people involved.

Preface

What started out as a quest for information concerning the roots and founding of Milford area churches, uncovered long-forgotten facts pertaining to Milford's early history. Hours of research through early county newspapers on file at the Nebraska State Historical Society in Lincoln, Nebraska, convinced me that half of Milford's history has never been told. This concern resulted in the publication of my first book in 1995 on Milford history, *Early Milford People Stories*.

In an effort to promote greater historical interest in the community, I was asked by the editor of the Milford Times to write short stories dealing with Milford's historical heritage—one story every other week. Later I consented to furnish one 780 word story every week. Trying not to duplicate Milford history already published in my first book, I decided to include stories dealing with a broader range of historical topics. Receiving favorable comments from *Times* readers, I continued to branch out into topics I knew little about. Forced to spend hours on research, I was surprised to discover how little I knew about the "real" world experienced by our forefathers and how little people have changed since the dawn of civilization. This book is the culmination of over two hundred stories written for earlier or eventual publication in the *Milford Times*.

Introduction

Separating Truth from Fiction

A good share of what is known about Seward County history can be attributed to the efforts of local historians W.W. Cox and John Henry Waterman. Mr. Cox arrived in the Salt Creek Basin near Lincoln, Nebraska, in 1861. By 1864 he was living in the vicinity of what is now Seward. This farmer, carpenter, schoolteacher, and newspaper man published his original version of county history in 1888. Criticized by some for mistakes made in that initial volume, he published a revised and enlarged history in 1905. Cox has often been admonished for focusing on Seward while ignoring outlying areas. But because he was active in county government, Cox records valuable details concerning the early organization and leadership of Seward County. For that reason, his 1888 edition was reprinted in 1975 by the Seward Bicentennial Committee. Copies may still be available, although biographies of notable Seward County residents were omitted from the reprint.

John H. Waterman arrived in the Beaver Crossing community in 1870. When ill health forced him to give up farming, John devoted his career to the newspaper business, editing and publishing three Beaver Crossing newspapers. The *Weekly Review,* the *Independent Examiner* and the *Weekly Echo* were all started by Mr. Waterman. His 350-page *Revised History of Seward County* was published in 1920, just seven years before his 1927 death. Mr. Cox and Mr. Waterman, both eye witnesses to most early county events, often disagreed on facts concerning early county history. Waterman attempted to convince his readers that he alone was telling the county story as it really happened, free from the biased "northern county viewpoint" expressed by Mr. Cox. Both writers appeared to have trouble forgetting the intense, north versus south rivalry generated during the early county seat struggle.

Reading either book, one could get the impression both authors assumed they were correct in every detail. Hours of research has convinced me that "historical game rules" have not changed much since 1860. Some supposedly "time tested" foundational facts concerning county history are actually contradictory, while others appear fuzzy. Several times in my short career, I have been forced to recant both written and verbal opinions after new research uncovered additional information. While it is probably true that 99 percent of the people in any given community could care less about the accuracy of local history, both Cox and Waterman were concerned that past events be recorded correctly. Wanting for words to express my feelings regarding the mistakes encountered when one attempts to decipher 140 years of local history, I discovered that Cox had already figured it all out 114 years ago. In the Preface to his 1888 *Seward County History*, he expresses this common sense approach.

"The author would ask the reader to not be unreasonably critical. All historical works are imperfect and subject to criticism, and why should this work be an exception? We have done the best we could with the material at hand. Many incidents herein related are obtained from people now living, and are generally correctly related, but the memories of men are sometimes faulty, and people are sometimes led to see matters from different standpoints. The best authorities frequently conflict, and many matters of importance were never recorded, and we are left dependent on the memory of men for matters that occurred twenty or more years ago. We have searched diligently and patiently, and have given you the results of our efforts."

This truth is mirrored in the accuracy of each story included in my book. While Cox and Waterman provided the core of early Seward County history, other sources are also available. The earliest account is a short history of Seward County written by Seward native O.T.B. Williams. The document was prepared at the request of the Board of County Commissioners on May 17, 1876 and intended to be read at the "celebration of the Fourth of July A.D. 1876." Later, it was filed at

Eldon Hostetler

the County Clerk's office where it was preserved as part of the records of Seward County. Interestingly, this unique glimpse of history was eventually forgotten, only to be rediscovered and read by modern day historians one hundred years later. A Seward High School student researching early County Commissioner meeting records discovered the manuscript tucked inside a seldom-opened cupboard drawer in a vault. This may be one of the most accurate records of Seward County beginnings. That is, up to at least 1876. One early book, *History of the State of Nebraska*, was written and published around 1882. This work devotes more than thirty pages to early Seward County history. Published by the Western Historical Company, owned by A. T. Andreas, the book is usually known as *Andreas's Nebraska History*. Written by complete strangers who zipped into town and began asking questions, the nine pages dealing with early Milford history touches on facts not recorded in any other county history. However, several of Andreas's so-called "basic facts" do not agree with later versions of Milford history. More on this later. Other informative books referring to Milford and Seward County history include *Early Days in Seward County*, published by long-time *Seward Independent* newspaper editor, Wm. H. Smith. This book is a collection of articles and stories written by assorted authors, most of whom were eye witnesses to early Seward County happenings. It offers a good account of what early pioneer life was really like. *Sand In My Eyes*, on the other hand, is written mostly from an Oklahoma perspective by a descendent of the Laune family. It contains several chapters that portray Milford life during the late 1880s. Other interesting books dealing with early Seward County and Milford history include the following: *On a Bend of The River, Seward County 1992, Nebraska Our Town: Central & Southeast Edition, The Fourth of July Book, Seward County Nebraska, Seward County Supplement and Seward Nebraska*.

Books dealing exclusively with Milford history include: *History of Milford Nebraska* 1920-1930 and *The History of Milford* compiled by the Centennial Committee in 1964. Two Saline County history books are excellent supplements: *The Centennial History of Dorchester and Pleasant Hill* and *Saline County History* by J.W. Kaura. The Dorchester book contains valuable information concerning the early West Mills settlement. The Pleasant Dale, Beaver Crossing, Goehner, Utica, and Cordova communities have also published excellent books recording their histories.

The Way It Was

And then, we have what I would consider to be one of the greatest untapped sources of local historical information— newspapers. In the past eight years I have skimmed through an estimated 4,500 plus copies of assorted Seward, Saline, and Lancaster County newspapers published in the county since 1870. Just like writers of early history books, newspaper editors were not immune from making mistakes. Apparently, many county editors enjoyed recording local history and often enlisted early settlers to record their memories for publication. These first-hand accounts are of infinite value. Thirty years ago, I truly enjoyed "picking the brains" of older residents, a privilege no longer as profitable. (Mostly because I could now be numbered among those known to be over "the big mental hill.") Having studied Milford history for a number of years, I would be one of the first to admit it is often difficult to separate fact from biased, long-held traditions.

Seward County Agriculture

*A*lthough there have been many histories of Seward County written and published over the past hundred years, few writers have concentrated on agriculture, the all-time number one industry. In these stories, I hope to portray the stark contrasts and striking similarities experienced by five or six generations of Seward County farmers. At one time the heartbeat of the county economy, twenty-first century farmers no longer carry the prestige or clout of those of one hundred years ago. In most Nebraska communities, rural population peaked between 1890 and 1900, but has experienced a decline every year since. The fact Seward County's overall population has held steady or increased since the "dirty thirties" is somewhat deceptive. Nearly all of this increase can be attributed to the growth of Milford and Seward, where populations have more than doubled in the past fifty years. While the ratio of farmers to city dwellers widens, total farm output continues to grow. In 1840, it required 276 man hours to produce one hundred bushels of corn. By 1960 this figure dropped to ten hours and is probably even less today. In 1840, more than 70 percent of the American labor force was devoted to the production of food, a figure which slipped to less than ten percent by 1960 and still continues to decline.

Since I launched my farming career near Beaver Crossing, Nebraska, in 1948, the number of farms in the state has decreased 50 percent, while average farm size has increased by 50 percent. These figures could only be realized by drastic changes in farming practices, especially mechanization. The greatest jump in farm productivity ever recorded in world history happened between 1930 and 1945. While I

The Way It Was

Hostetler threshing rig in operation in 1924 doing what was known as "stack threshing."

consider it a privilege to have lived through the tail end of what could have been called the "horse and buggy age" of farming, I have also been fortunate enough to witness the dawn of a modern, computer-oriented farming age. I remember the feel of guiding a walking plow or slinging a pitchfork while loading grain bundles for threshing and the thrill of using a team and wagon to husk 7,000 bushels of corn in 1946, one ear at a time.

Although these so-called "slave" jobs were hard work, they were also said to be "character building" (at least for growing teenaged boys). Wonderful as the change to mechanization was, it did carry a huge price tag. Agricultural statistics reveal that since I started farming in 1948, more than 55,000 Nebraska farmers have either given up, or have been forced out of their chosen livelihood. From a high of 130,000 farmers in 1935, numbers dwindled to slightly more than 50,000 still farming by 1995. Meanwhile, the average farm size grew from 156 acres in 1880, to more than 900 acres in 2002.

A short drive through rural Seward County reveals skeletons of deserted farmsteads no longer needed because larger machinery and better technology provided the resources for serious farmers to expand. My 160-acre farm southeast of Beaver Crossing was at one time home to three sets of farm buildings, one Silver Fox farm, one combination feed yard and slaughter house plus two retirement houses.

While many smaller farmers continue to seek other livelihoods, those who really have their hearts set on farming keep getting larger and larger. Meanwhile, grain surpluses continue to pile up and force commodity prices below the cost of production. Today we conveniently blame big corporate farmers, giant agribusiness companies, an uncooperative president, or American dollars funding huge overseas operations where production costs are somewhat cheaper. While this all makes for great twenty-first century farmer coffee shop chatter, was it really any different 100 years ago?

Although the circumstances may have been completely different, today's Seward County farmers struggle with the same set of problems. Low grain prices, mean and unusual weather, hungry insects, and strange diseases are a constant. So is pressure from huge conglomerates that manipulate farm commodity prices while increasing input costs.

One hundred years ago, wealthy eastern businessmen, said to be in "cahoots with the railroad," were often blamed for farmers' financial problems. Having little help from the government, farmers were often forced to organize for protection. The first recorded rebellion took place in 1794 when federal officers, attempting to collect a distillers tax levied by the 1791 Congress, were tarred and feathered. Organizations like the Grange, the Farmers Alliance, the National Farmers Union, and the American Farm Bureau were organized mostly to fight what farmers in that day felt were nasty, greedy business monopolies.

Imaginary Interview with Tommy West

After deciding to drop out of the 1859-60 Colorado gold chase, Tommy West's family left the trail north of present day Seward and headed south along the North Blue River. While traveling through the entire length of what is now known as Seward County, he became captivated by the rich-looking farmland bordering the West Blue River. They decided to make Seward County their permanent home and settled close to where the two rivers joined. While not considered as risky as chasing gold in the Pikes Peak region, their choice of farming for a livelihood presented unknown challenges and unseen hazards. Considered for years as part of the "Great American Desert," experts had long predicted that agriculture this far west would be limited to what was known as marginal farming.

While the West family apparently succeeded in becoming one of the first successful Seward County farming families, Tommy might be shocked to discover what we modern farmers call "twenty-first century progress." Just suppose that by pressing a few magical buttons and letting our imaginations run wild, we could interview Tommy regarding his thoughts concerning the past and current farm picture in Seward County. Imagine his surprise when we brag about the 200-bushel corn yields or the 50-bushel wheat. Would he be awestruck at the workings of a modern fifty-thousand dollar center pivot? Could he truly understand the versatility of today's combines? How would he accept the explanation of present-day farm assistance programs available from the United States Government? Might he wonder whatever happened to several good old pioneer traits like independence and courage? Try explaining to him why you think it would be impossible to farm today without government safeguards. Would he understand the new government farm program lingo like "parity," "support prices," "L.D.P.," "disaster payments," base yields," or "grain loans?" Would he approve of the large amounts of *Roundup*™ and other expensive weed and bug chemicals we pour on the soils? Might he think it strange that we often pay fifty times as much for one bushel of hybrid seed corn as we get for a bushel of corn? Having relied on sweet clover and cow manure for crop nitrogen in his day, Tommy probably wouldn't have the foggiest idea what anhydrous ammonia is all about. Tell him you raise soybeans along with your corn and he might look at you with a rather blank expression and ask, "Now just what are soybeans good for? Do you raise them strictly for your own table use?"

Should the conversation drift to modern day farm finances, would Mr. West be shocked to discover a good John Deere tractor costs about eighty-thousand dollars—assuming you buy a small one. He might even cough, choke, and probably drop his coffee cup when you mention that a medium-sized Case combine would sell for up to one-hundred-thousand dollars. Would he just assume that all modern-day Seward County farmers are millionaires?

To offer proof that this is not always true, you might cite other expenses connected with farming like fertilizers, chemicals, patented and engineered seed, irrigation costs, fuel, repairs, and crop insurance. After watching the pained expression on Tommy's face, you would probably be too embarrassed to mention the dollars you spent overhauling your favorite tractor last year. Later, the conversation could drift to the subject of high land taxes. At this point Tommy would undoubtedly burst out in hearty laughter.

Would he explain to you how he bought top quality Seward County land for less per acre than you pay in taxes each year? Realizing how foolish this may sound, you might squirm in your chair while attempting to defend some of the modern-day farming practices. Would you be willing to open up your record books and explain to him how you *think* you actually made some money one year? (The same year Uncle Sam socked you good for income taxes.) Now, this just might be more than the old man could take since income taxes were unheard of in his day.

By this time, I'm sure Tommy would be ready to admit he loved farming one hundred forty years ago, but if he had to start farming today, he would probably rather stoop to digging ditches. I believe his response would be something like, "Forget it! Give me back the 'good old days.' Sounds to me like your generation of farmers are simply working for the big chemical companies owned by the 'big rich boys' hiding out on Wall Street!"

How the Land Changed Hands

When Nebraska was first opened up for legal settlement in 1854, it was just taken for granted that much of the state was unsuited for dry-land farming. At one time settlers living east of Seward County were told it never rains west of Salt Creek. The opening of the Nebraska City cutoff trails in the early 1860s helped to disprove this legend, and the County was soon teeming with prospective farmers seeking government land. Between 1854 and 1863, settlers were allowed to claim land under the Pre-Emption Act passed in 1841. Any person over twenty-one years of age, head of a family, a U.S. citizen, or having declared intention of becoming a U.S. citizen, was allowed to file a claim on 160 acres of surveyed or unsurveyed land receiving title to the tract after paying a minimum fee of $1.25 an acre. As long as the prospective owner complied with the terms of the agreement, his claim was "pre-empted" against all subsequent claims. Although this law remained in effect until 1891, most Seward County land was claimed under the Homestead Act passed in 1862. The "Timber Culture Act" passed by congress in 1873 allowed settlers to claim farm ground by planting ten acres of trees and taking care of them for eight years. This law probably had little effect on the disposition of Seward County land.

The Homestead Act took effect on Jan 1, 1863, the first claim in the nation entered by U.S. soldier Daniel Freeman. Daniel staked his claim on Cub Creek at the present site of the Homestead National Monument west of Beatrice. Under this law, a settler could choose eighty acres, (ex-soldiers were granted special privileges) pay a $14.00 filing fee, and receive title to the land after living on and improving the land for five years. After 1870, when good homestead land was no longer available, choice land was available from Nebraska Railroads, who, at one time owned over eight million acres of state land. By 1860, the B&M Railroad owned every other section in Seward County, a fact much resented by early settlers. This land was available for five to eight dollars an acre.

Many settlers who arrived after 1870 purchased land owned by the state. Section No. 16 and 36 in every Precinct was deeded to the state for school revenue purposes. The state also owned 3,000 acres in O Precinct set aside for a state penitentiary fund. Civil War veterans were usually given preferential treatment based on the length they served in the military. Land bordering rivers and creeks was always considered first choice for several reasons better access to wood and water. Early settlers reported the level plains west of Seward and Milford towards York and Aurora were absolutely destitute of trees and shrubs, while the hills east of Milford, especially in the Garland area were covered with oak trees. Trees also grew abundantly along most streams in the area, some of them said to be huge specimens.

The first land to be selected in O Precinct was claimed by Thomas West, who chose ground near West Mills in Sections 30 and 31 in 1860. J.L. Davison was the first person to file for Homestead land in the Milford community in 1864. Others filing for Homestead land in the Milford vicinity included: Lewis Laune, William Collier, Wm. C. Reed, David Tift, Ira Gallup, Silas Atwood, Wm. C. Smiley, Alexander Frisbee, Joseph Stockham, Noah Stutzman, Jacob Culver, J. A. Wilsey, Wm. Klein, Frank Busboon, Robert Danekas, and Lewis Welch. Those purchasing land from the State of Nebraska included: John J. Harris, Jacob Rediger, Jacob Neff, Andrew Bachman, Joseph Hauder, Phebe Steckly, Jacob Stauffer, Joseph Stauffer, Christian Erb, and John P. Welsch. In the early 1870s, abandoned Homestead land and state land usually sold for $6.00 to $8.00 per acre. The Homestead Act provided homes for between 400,000 and 600,000 families. But, like many other government programs, abuses were rampant. One historian has estimated that of all the public land passing into private hands between 1862 and 1900, not more than one acre in seven or eight was actually claimed by a Homesteader. Violators of Homestead rules were sometimes dealt with by the public according to this news note: "We hear rumored that a vigilante committee has been formed for the protection of Homesteaders in the vicinity. This is a move in the right direction, and we want to warn all to be careful about jumping claims in Beaver Crossing and Walnut Creek precincts (Milford *Blue Valley Record*, 1871)."

How it all Started

A drive through rural Seward County in the month of October during a normal crop year could remind one of the old Biblical expression "a land flowing with milk and honey" has truly come to pass. Irrigated fields of corn and soybeans growing in super straight weed free rows are being harvested with giant combines capable of harvesting over 10,000 bushels of grain in one short day. Highly polished semi-trailer trucks hauling over 1200 bushels are being loaded from giant augur wagons hitched to $90,000 all-weather air conditioned tractors. A visit to the nearest grain elevator would show long lines of huge trucks piloted by impatient farmers waiting in line to unload heaping loads of corn and soybeans. This alone could convince you that indeed this is "God's country." Now let your imagination wander back 140 years to the day when Tommy West and his contemporaries first started farming in Seward County. This generation of farmers practiced many of the same farming practices used by their fathers and grandfathers for hundreds of years. Little did they realize the revolution that was about to take place in American and Seward County agriculture. Living on corn meal mush and whatever wild game they could harvest, the thought of living in a land of "milk and honey" cushioned with ease and comfort could have only been a dream.

Picture the struggles and hardships encountered by the Anderson family, pioneers who helped to make Seward County agriculture what it is today. In the fall of 1866, James Anderson in company with D. H. Figard left Pennsylvania seeking a better life in the west. Arriving in Nebraska City, the terminus of the stage route at that time, they walked to the spot where Seward is now located. Mr. Anderson selected a farm bordering Lincoln Creek located two miles west of Seward in Section 24 of F Precinct. At this time, only five families lived in the entire precinct. That fall, Mr. Anderson busied himself cutting cottonwood logs, hauling them twenty miles by ox team to the new Camden sawmill for processing. After finishing a small house, Mr. Anderson went home to Pennsylvania, returning to Nebraska City in the spring of 1867 with the rest of his family. Here they purchased a wagon, one yoke of oxen, and other necessities like food, furniture, a cook stove and a sod breaking plow. The trip to their homestead via the old "Steam Wagon Road" required one week of steady travel, the younger children riding and the older children walking. Arriving at their homestead two miles west of Seward, the nearest settlement west was located in the Grand Island vicinity. In 1928, his son Cal Anderson recorded some of his memories associated with his family's early farming career in Seward County.

"During the winter of '66' much snow had fallen, roads became impassable, and when spring came the snow melted quickly, causing the streams to overflow, marooning many settlers, causing much suffering and many were destitute of food; relief being eighty miles distant, all dirt bridges washed out, draws and lowlands impassable. This and many other drawbacks confronted the early settlers. During the years 1868-69 nearly all of the ground was taken with the exception of the railroad sections which the government had transferred to them in order to get railroads through the country. Prairie fires were a great dread to early settlers, columns miles in length rushing over the

Threshing in the 1920s. Aaron Roth's rig.

prairies backed by a strong breeze was a spectacular sight, often breaking through the guards, destroying their hay and grain. Rattlesnakes were plentiful, and a few fatalities have been recorded by their venomous sting. Farming in those days was rather crude as compared with today. One walking plow, two single shovels, one triangle harrow (homemade) constituted our outfit.

"Our harvesting machine consisted of one grain sickle and cradle made by Father. Threshing was done by tramping the grain with oxen and flail on a ground floor, and cleaned by the wind. Prior to our first crop, food, such as flour, bacon and coffee and other trimmings was limited, and was considered as dessert or side dish. Supplies were obtained at Nebraska City at a high price; flour ten cents per pound and other things in proportion. Corn meal and hominy were substituted, with plenty of wild game, wild plums, grapes and sorghum molasses ("A Brief Synopsis of Our Pioneer Settlement of Seward County Nebraska," *Blue Valley Blade*, January 11, 1928)."

Starting Costs One Hundred Years Ago

The sum of money needed to finance farming operations today requires a good credit rating, as well as a friendly and reliable banker. While this has always been true, those of us who started farming before 1950 are somewhat awestruck by the amount of money needed by our children and grandchildren to start farming in the twenty-first century. In 1948, a day when it was still possible to borrow machinery from family and friends, my total investment amounted to about $700.00. While this may have been cheap compared to today, in 1904 it required even less—a fraction of what it would cost today. This news note from the 1904 *Milford Nebraskan* introduces us to the ridiculously low cost of "starter" farming one hundred years ago:

"A big wedding occurred in the Mennonite settlement southwest of Milford when Barbara Burkey, daughter of Valentine Burkey, was married to Jacob Ehrisman of Mclean County, Illinois. About 300 friends and relatives were present to witness the ceremony and partake of the feast." This news note announced the arrival of one more Illinois farmer to the Milford community, who, having found his wife in Milford, decided to try his luck at farming in Nebraska. Jacob and Barbara lived on the Southwest Quarter of Section 16 in O Precinct, now a part of the ground farmed by two of Jacob's grandsons, Leland and Robert Ehrisman. Jacob's father, who farmed near Hudson, Illinois, died sometime in 1896, leaving the estate to his wife,

Jacob Ehrisman and his favorite mule team in 1910. This is the farm where Jacob got his "cheap" start in 1904. Wife Barbara and son Ezra are to the left. The house and several other buildings are still standing. Jacob died in 1914. Two of his grandsons, Leland and Robert Ehrisman live on the farm today.

Veronica Ehrisman. In Jacob's farm record book dated March 5, 1897 we find the following notation: "I bought off Veronica Ehrisman the farming outfit, including all the livestock." First on the list are the names and colors of ten horses; Prince, Floria, Charley, Susen, Kate, Nell, Dick, Maud, Niger, and Queen. The horses, ranging in age from fifteen to one are valued from $65 to $20 a head, or a total of $410.00 Six head of milk cows; Shaggie, Star, Rose, Nellie, Fanny, and Sally are valued from $20 to $35 each, or a grand total of $150.00. Six brood sows and four fat pigs are said to have a combined value of $102.00. Fifty chickens are valued at $15.00, while eight ton of clover hay was worth $40.00.

The farming implement side of the ledger lists the following property and the assessed value. Two wagons valued at $50, one buggy at $20.00, three sets of harnesses are said to be worth $20.00, while the "Sulky" plow and the corn planter are worth $25.00 each. The highest item on the entire list, a "self binder" checked in at $40.00. Two cultivators, one pulverizer and the feed grinder are said to be worth $10.00 each, while the wood pile and a stack of used lumber were worth $17.00. The rest of the list includes many smaller items including seven bushels of ground shelled corn, stalk rake, two harrows, grind stone, big rasp, hog rack, sled and drag, rasps bits and chisels, saw setter, saddle bags, carpenter square, hatchets, hammers, and anvil, saws, harness tools and clevis, forty gallons of vinegar, twenty-four bushels of potatoes, one crock of lard, garden rake and house vise, draw-knives and work bench, one sledge and two corn knives, one long cattle stay chain and dog chain, one post augur, rat traps and twine, screen door, one bushel of cane seed, sulky rake, four forks, two axes, wood in smoke house, two chicken coops and wood in shed, door hinges, old iron and bolts, hog rings, two hog troughs, two double trees and hay knives, ladder and old planks, scoops and wheel borrow, oil can, file and pliers.

According to this record, Jacob paid his mother a total of $677.00 for the livestock which included ten horses, six milk cows, ten hogs and fifty chickens. For the farm implements, plus all of his father's miscellaneous farm tools he paid the sum of $313.90; making a grand total of $990.90 to start farming in 1897.

Other records from that day would suggest this would have been enough equipment to enter into big time farming, since others farmed eighty acres with only one team of horses or several yoke of

The Way It Was

The cradle attached to the scythe place the cut grain in a swath ready to be bound into sheaves.

The first reaper invented in 1831 by Cyrus Hall McCormick. Its basic principles have been retained.

The first self-binder, wire was used to tie the bundles.

The first binder to use twine. The wire-binding reapers were discarded in favor of this binder.

oxen. We have no records to tell us what Jake did with this equipment before he moved to Nebraska. Jake died suddenly in 1914 at the age of 42 years. This record was preserved by Jake's son, the late Ezra Ehrisman.

Choosing Crops

While early settlers arriving in Seward County in the early 1860s found few trees, they did find acres and acres of tough prairie grass. Prairie sod was good for building houses and fences, but very difficult to prepare for growing crops. While several Nebraska Indian tribes were famous for growing corn and assorted vegetables, early Seward County residents found little evidence farming had been practiced in the area prior to their arrival. By 1862, only three families were living in what is now known as Seward County. When J.L. Davison staked out the town of Milford in the spring of 1864, only 30 acres of sod had been broken in the entire county. By 1865 this had increased to 150 acres. Most of that land was broken with "ox power," not horsepower. Before 1870, few settlers could afford the high price of good horses and grain. While oxen could survive on grass alone, hard working horses required grain to stay in top physical condition. One early settler said, "We were all so poor our turkeys had to lean against a stump while gobbling." Some early settlers made their living by specializing in "sod busting" charging anywhere from 75 cents to three dollars per acre. Most sodbusters used a special breaking plow pulled by several yoke of oxen. But the oxen were traded for mules as soon as farmers could afford to buy and feed this favored draft animal. The only other tool required to farm in that day was a smoothing harrow, which was usually made out of wood. "Sod corn" was the first field crop planted by most pioneer farmers. Corn planted by cutting a slit in the sod with an ax required no additional cultivation or fertilizer. Average or above average rainfall was required to produce a good crop.

A few settlers in the 1870s boasted of yields of up to 80 bushels per acre in a good year, while one farmer near Garland claimed his corn made 100 bushels. Due to the lack of a good cash market before the railroad arrived in the early 1870s, most corn raised before 1873 was used for human consumption or livestock feed. For those fortunate enough to live near one of the popular trails used by western-bound homesteaders, surplus corn could be sold for up to $2.50 per bushel, and dry hay for up to six cents a pound.

The United States census of 1860 reported 3,000 farmers were living in the state. The average farm was about 225 acres and valued at $5.82 per acre. In 1860, the U.S. Department of Agriculture reported Nebraska farmers grew 1.5 million bushels of corn, 148,000 bushels of wheat, 162,000 bushels of potatoes, and 75,000 bushels of oats. By 1890, corn production in the state had increased to nearly 216 million bushels. The updated figure represented ten percent of the national total and distinguished Nebraska as fourth in total production.

While corn production increased from 1860 to 1890, wheat acres actually declined. Soft spring wheat found little favor with early Seward County farmers, since Nebraska soil and weather prevented top yields. Native hard winter wheat varieties in use at that time also proved unpopular. The development of a better milling process for hard winter wheat and the introduction of the Russian Turkey Red variety introduced by Ukraine Mennonite settlers in the 1870s eventually helped to generate interest in wheat production.

Russian Turkey Red was a hit with Midwestern growers and millers alike, prompting the Kansas State Millers Association to import 15,000 bushels for seed. Additional breeding by the University of Nebraska's College of Agriculture improved all hard wheat varieties and breathed new life to the Nebraska wheat and flour industry.

Advances in labor-saving harvest equipment helped to make wheat a popular and dependable crop. Up until 1850 to 1860, many American farmers harvested their wheat using practically the same method the ancient Romans used. Improvements in reel and sickle-type machines advanced to the point where self-tying binders came out in the early 1870s. The first record of a horse-powered "vibrator," (early threshing machine) arrived in Milford in the summer of 1872. The first steam- powered threshing rig was purchased by the Stauffer Brothers and arrived in town in the summer of 1887. A news editorial announced the threshing machine, "…has been the center of attention and the topic of gossip by our curbside loungers." By 1900, wheat was a big part of Nebraska's agricultural economy. Producing just 148,000 bushels in 1860, by 1902 Nebraska was one of the top wheat-growing states in the nation.

Not all Wheat and Corn

Bragging about the wonderful farming opportunities available in Seward County, one so called "farm expert" said this in the *Seward County Handbook* from 1882:

"The Seward County farmer may grow in perfection every grain, grass, plant, fruit and vegetable produced between the latitude of Washington and Winnipeg. No country gives higher sanctions to variety farming than this country, as will be clearly attested to by the testimony of half a hundred good farmers in the later portions of this sketch. Wheat, rye, barley, oats, flax, broom corn, sorghum, millet, Hungarian buckwheat, and all the grasses, vegetables fruits and flora of the medium latitudes flourish here in profusion and perfection."

Several crops in the list have been long forgotten, while a few of the current mainstays like alfalfa and soybeans were not even mentioned. Strange as it may seem, alfalfa did not become popular until the 1890s. It had been introduced to Seward County by the railroad almost fifteen years earlier. On the other hand, soybeans were first introduced in the 1940s but were not widely grown before 1950.

The Way It Was

Grain sorghum was first introduced during the dry 1930s, but did not become popular until the introduction of the small, pull-type combine. Flax was grown for a number of years mainly because it did very well on newly broken prairie sod. According to my father's threshing account book, he was paid for threshing flax seed as late as 1923. A news note in an 1888 paper reported corn averaged 55 bushels, with some fields making as much as 75 bushels, while the price averaged 20 cents a bushel. Buckwheat production that year was good, while flax yields fell short. In 1889, ten carloads of flax seed were shipped from the Milford depot. All was grown on contract for a large linseed oil plant located in Omaha.

By 1871, wheat was worth 50 cents and corn 45 cents. While buckwheat's price stood at 80 cents, it did not last long as a cash crop. Sweet Clover, at one time a popular crop in the county, is now practically extinct except for those places where it comes up like a weed. From 1880 to 1900, clover was "big time stuff"—at least in the Milford community.

In 1886 it was reported that Jacob Roth raised 225 bushels of sweet clover seed and Stauffer brothers threshed more than 2,000 bushels during the 1892 season. Sweet clover was still popular in the 1940s, at which time it was plowed under for what was known as "green manure." Evidently broomcorn was grown on a smaller scale by several county growers since both Milford and Seward boasted of broom factories at one time.

Every community usually had several sorghum mills where farmers could bring their cane to have it crushed and made into sorghum syrup. Joseph Gascho and J. D. Stutzman were known as the sorghum makers for the Milford community, each growing about twenty acres of cane. In 1887, Mr. Gascho manufactured 1,400 gallons of sorghum syrup.

At one time, Seward County was also known as a good fruit growing region. Apples and sour cherries did especially well. Many of the trees that managed to survive the "dirty thirties" perished in the deadly Armistice Day freeze of 1940.

While we don't normally think of Seward County as potato country, around 1900, potatoes were grown commercially in the Beaver Crossing community. In 1904, 95 carloads were shipped from the Beaver Crossing depot. I can still remember using my grandfather's potato digger to harvest the few potatoes we raised in the 1930s.

According to this notice from a Crete newspaper, Seward County farmers discussed the possibility of raising sugar beets at one time: "The people of Milford propose to take time by the foretop and make sugar while the sun shines. We have received the following circular which explains itself: 'You need to get 20 cents a bushel for your corn in order to make corn raising profitable. Sugar beets pay a good profit every season, stand the drought better and are a surer crop then corn. There will be a beet sugar convention in Milford, September 1st for Seward and adjoining counties to talk about it. Well posted speakers from beet sugar centers will address the convention. Come and learn without charge how to make farming pay' (*Crete Vidette*, August 19, 1897)."

Since one newspaper editor mentions a pickle factory located in the Grover vicinity at one time, it can be assumed cucumbers were grown in the Milford area. In 1889, a commercial cannery processing both corn and tomatoes was doing business in the Seward community. After the discovery of artesian wells in the Beaver Crossing vicinity in the mid-1890s, commercial truck gardening was very popular. Sweet potatoes, cabbage, horseradish, tomatoes, string beans, and strawberries were all popular. One strawberry patch was said to be more than ten acres in size.

The Farmers Cooperative canning factory processed Beaver brand tomatoes and string beans in the 1940s. My sisters and I soon learned to loathe even the sight of string beans the year we agreed to plant one-half acre. Probably one of the strangest crops ever tried in Seward County was grown on land I now own southeast of Beaver Crossing. In the mid-1940s, the previous owner, Stanley Matzke planted fifteen acres to asparagus. Being a wise man, he had a contract with the state prison system to furnish men to do the actual harvesting. After plowing the field in 1950, volunteer asparagus came up like weeds for many years. Go ahead—long for the "good old days"—but please don't plague yourself by planting an acre of string beans or tomatoes!

The Way It Was

Same Old Song—Earlier Version

Considered worthless desert for many years after the Civil War, farmers from the eastern states and Europe arrived in droves seeking land many experts thought unfarmable. Those arriving from Illinois were accustomed to an average yearly rainfall of 37 inches, while those from Pennsylvania were used to approximately 43 inches annually. Both were ten to sixteen inches above normal for Seward County.

So why did they keep coming? One reason may have been because long-term weather and rainfall patterns had not yet been established, meaning they were actually taking a big chance. Others may have thought older states were becoming too crowded, the land was worn out, or over priced. This excerpt from a letter written by an early settler to his Pennsylvania relatives in 1879 portrays a common attitude prevalent in that day, a position more or less geared at attracting additional settlers to the community. It was taken from a letter written by Samuel Lapp to his relatives in Pennsylvania. The Lapp family bought land near Juniata in Adams County in 1879.

"We have a nice place of 160 acres. We have enough sod broke for wheat next year. The wheat crops are good out here, and so is the corn. We planted about 100 sweet potato plants and people say they do well out here. We planted a good many potatoes and they look nice. My garden does well, I never had any nicer radishes. It seems strange to plant and sow without putting any manure on the ground. Could not be any nicer, and things grow so nice."

Occasionally Milford residents have been known to exaggerate the truth a wee bit when bragging about the great farming conditions. This story from the 1899 *Milford Nebraskan* newspaper gets right to the point. The boys mentioned were real, since we do have pictures of several.

"According to official reports, Willie Dillenback climbed up a corn stalk to check on how the corn is getting on, and now the corn is growing so fast he can not get down. Harry Brown, Vincent Stahl and Willie Snare are trying to cut the stalk down -but it is growing so fast they cannot hit the same spot twice. Willie is now living on raw corn and has already thrown down three bushels of cobs. Now it is hoped the poor boy can be rescued soon, but how is not known, for at this rate of growth, the stalks will soon blot out the sun. In such fertile ground as surrounds Milford, it is even dangerous to climb a wooden fence post!"

By 1881, Samuel Lapp, having already experienced several years of Nebraska weather at its worst in Adams County, wrote a second letter. This time he portrayed far less optimism.

"A long drought prevails in the community, and the harvest is poor. The wheat and the barley are a total failure and the corn is beginning to die off. I sowed forty acres to wheat and did not harvest a single bushel. Hay and pastures are also very poor."

The Lapp family, along with other transplanted Eastern farmers, soon discovered the raw truth about Nebraska weather: It can be very unfriendly at times and contrary to what they had been told by railroad sales people and others, rain does not always follow the plow. This scenario, described by historian Donald R. Hickey, in *Nebraska Moments* (pgs. 159-60) sounds more or less like the crisis faced by present day Seward County farmers:

"The Civil War ushered in an era of agricultural prosperity that lasted for almost a decade. The demand for food both at home and abroad kept prices high and spurred the commercialization, mechanization, and expansion of American agriculture. By the end of the 1860s, however, overproduction had brought prices down and the downward trend continued in the 1870s. Nebraska farmers had to contend not only with sagging commodity prices but also drought and grasshoppers, high taxes and tariffs, and excessive freight charges and interest rates. Most felt they were being victimized by middlemen, bankers and implement dealers. Increased rainfall and higher prices brought prosperity to Nebraska agriculture in the early 1880s but by 1887 conditions had again begun to deteriorate. Lack of rain cut into production, commodity prices sagged again and bank credit dried up. Corn, which sold for 39 cents in 1881, fell to 17 cents in 1889. Many who had gone heavily into debt to expand their operations could not borrow the funds they needed to stay afloat, except at ruinous rates of 20 or even 40 percent. The results were a host of failures. So many, in fact, that in 1891 some 18 thousand Prairie schooners were observed crossing the Missouri River."

The Way It Was

Livestock Production in Seward County

Unlike today, when I started farming in 1948 most farmers did not "put all of their eggs in one basket." We had a few stock cows, raised a few pigs, fed a few steers, and mostly depended on chickens and dairy cows to furnish the grocery money. Having lived through the drought and depression of the 1930s, we knew from past experiences that farmers are often at the mercy of Nebraska weather, as well as other unforeseen tragic circumstances. The introduction of irrigation and the increase in acres farmed due to the availability of larger machinery has changed the old patterns of yesterday to one of specialization, often to the point where many grain farmers no longer own livestock. Intensive research has now convinced me that many Seward County farmers were highly progressive in their grain and livestock operations 120 years ago. Most Seward County residents are quite familiar with the old adage referring to hog production as the ultimate mortgage lifter. While you may think this adage was coined by worried Iowa bankers, historians tell us it is actually 125 years old and was first used by Nebraska native, J. Sterling Morton, who served as Secretary of Agriculture under President Grover Cleveland. Morton said it like this: "We cannot raise too much corn no matter what corn may be worth in the market. It may be worth five cents or nothing at all. But transmuted to beef, pork, or mutton, it will pay the husbandman a handsome and satisfactory return. This should be, and must be, if it will grow a prosperous, stock feeding state. Wheat growing for exportation will not pay. It wears out the soil, the men who till it, and the reputation of the state."

While Mr. Morton wrote this opinion in 1876, one decade before the introduction of better wheat harvesting machinery, by 1899 he had reversed his earlier opinion when he publicly acknowledged "that after all maybe wheat raising was not all that bad for the state."

Nebraska's future as a meat-producing state was enhanced when the Union Stock Yards were established in Omaha in 1884. By 1890, meatpacking accounted for more then one fourth of Nebraska's total industrial output, most of it concentrated in Omaha. One agricultural expert of the late 1880s predicted that Seward County was ripe for development as a top stock raising country, at least according to this opinion published in 1883:

Livestock Production in Seward County

"That Seward County is a superb stock country is no longer room for any doubt. The abundance of pure and wholesome water, the profusion and high quality of the grasses, the shelter now afforded by native and domestic groves, the extent and wealth of the corn fields, the dry and invigorating atmosphere and the high average of health and vitality among all classes of stock, together with the comparative cheapness of the land and transportation, give the stock men of this region a marked advantage over stock growers of older states, whose expensive shelter, higher priced land and feeds and climate disabilities are steadily and surely driving them out of the race for supremacy in this noblest of all rural industries. It is assuring to the visitor to ride for days and days over this beautiful country and note the number and high character of the herds of cattle and swine, and realize the marvelous change that has come over the local husbandry in half a dozen years. I think it safe to say that fully 4,000 horses and mules, 20,000 cattle, 4,500 sheep and 40,000 swine are now owned and kept within the county, and with the exception of sheep, the herds are rapidly increasing (*Seward County Hand-Book*, 1883)."

Early Seward County stockmen who truly believed in and sang the praises of this "corn-hog ratio" 119 years ago would include: Claudius Jones of Seward who owned 600 head of cattle, mostly prime shorthorns plus 500 head of pigs; Henry Bedford who lived six miles north of Seward kept 200 head of high grade stock cattle, fed one carload of steers and raised 200 Berkshire pigs; F. S. Johnson, owner of the Milford Mills fed from 1000 to 1100 head of pigs from the offal of the mill; Frank W. Upton of Beaver Crossing kept 100 head of high grade stock cows, 550 well bred Berkshire-Poland pigs, a good string of brood mares and 900 grade Merino-Cotswold sheep; John Cattle Jr. of Seward kept a herd of 180 high grade cattle, fed 100 prime steers and 150 pigs; True and Brown of Seward fed 240 head of steers and 350 pigs which annually consumed from 18 to 20 thousand bushels of their home-grown corn.

The Way It Was

Hazards Raising Livestock

While many progressive Seward County farmers were apparently making money by raising and feeding livestock in the 1880s, there were also numerous risks and disappointments connected with the game. Disease was one of the biggest threats. By 1850, fewer than two-dozen European-style, trained veterinarians were practicing in the United States. Not until 1875, when a veterinary college was founded in New York City by a French veterinarian, did American farmers take animal health seriously. One of the first tax-supported veterinary schools in the Midwest opened at Iowa State University in 1879. Although early newspapers carried numerous advertisements sponsored by self-proclaimed animal healers offering their expertise, trained veterinarians were as rare as a June snowstorm.

This news note from an 1886 issue of *Milford Nebraskan* explains how some veterinarians qualified in that day:

"B. F. Stutzman has completed a course in Veterinary Medicine and will work in Milford under Lincoln vets." Dr. Clark, one of the first trained vets to arrive in Milford, was practicing in the community by 1904. Early newspaper editors often reported how local swine raisers "paid the price," especially when hog cholera came calling. In the 1884 paper, the editor reported how Joseph Burkey had just hauled in 40 of his fine, fat hogs to the Dorchester market, where he sold them for $3.60. In the 1885 paper he mentioned that "Joseph Burkey lost most of his hogs to cholera."

Evidently the disease returned by 1898 when he reported more losses. "Albert Matzke's hogs are all sick and many of them are dying, seven or eight every day." The editor also reported that Riley Hornaday had recently lost 80 head. In connection with this epidemic he wrote, "The Blue River is becoming a popular hog dumping place and drastic steps will be taken to correct the problem."

By 1916 hogs threatened by cholera were being vaccinated. According to the *Milford Review*, "J. C. Morford of Beaver Crossing had 43 head of hogs that would average 400 pounds vaccinated this week." Disease, plus prices as low as $2.50 per C.W.T. in 1896, kept early swine producers humble. While the loss of pigs worth about $10 a head was tolerable, the death of a good horse could be a shattering and colors, grasshoppers have been around as long as man can remember. Found along public road ditches and fence lines, modern day farmers normally ignore the tobacco-chewing creatures. No serious infestations have occurred in Seward County since the middle 1950s, at which time we were allowed to kill the pests by using a now-banned chemical known as Aldrin.

Since I do remember the "dirty thirties," (1934-1940) I have seen my share of the little pests, and do remember joining the fight to save what little crops the drought did not destroy. The favorite weapon used at that time was bran or sawdust soaked in poison flavored with banana oil. Crop damage, with the exception of 1934-36, was usually limited to fifty or sixty feet around the edges of crop fields. I do remember the sky occasionally being filled with billions of grasshoppers looking for new crops to destroy, although I don't recall them darkening the noon-time sun as reported by earlier settlers. Additional research has convinced me that unless you are more than 138 years old, you have probably never even seen a real grasshopper plague. Now, the rest of the story.

Both 1871 and 1872 had been good crop years, while 1873 was only fair. The spring and summer of 1874 appeared promising for another bountiful crop year. Following a wet June, came a dry and exceedingly hot July. In September 1873, a large New York investment house failed. A financial panic swept across the country like a prairie fire. Agricultural prices tumbled, leaving many farmers with grain hardly worth selling. By the last week in July, Seward County farmers were eagerly looking toward the sky for a much needed rain—a rain some felt would at least insure a decent corn crop.

One day, about lunchtime, some noticed what they thought was an ordinary summer storm brewing in the northwest. Rushing outdoors expecting to see angry rain clouds, many were shocked at what they were seeing. The heavens were being darkened by huge clouds of Rocky Mountain locusts thick enough to blot out the sun to the point where most chickens went to roost.

As far as the human eye could see (some said up to 20 miles) the sky was one vast sea of swarming, hungry, gray grasshoppers. Falling to earth like summer hail, they made short work of growing crops. Trees were stripped of their leaves. Corn foliage and other green vegetation disappeared as if by magic. For dessert they cleaned out gardens, some hastily covered with bedding, ruining cabbage plants, onions, turnips, and even tobacco plants. Clothes left exposed were cut into shreds; harnesses and shovel handles were pocked with teeth marks. Some witnesses said you could actually hear them chewing. About 24 hours later, part of the swarm took wing and departed to parts unknown. (This version is written from an account as told by Seward County farmer A.G. Hartman, an eye witnesses to the occasion.)

Although the ground was covered up to three inches deep in some spots with the grasshoppers, they did not eat the sorghum or broomcorn. Tree limbs broke off due to the weight of parking hoppers, while farmers were forced to tie their pant legs shut with string to keep them from crawling up their pant legs. Afraid of them at first, hogs and turkeys learned to live on the pests for several months. However, most said the meat was hardly edible because of a strange taste. Hoppers actually stalled trains near Fremont and Kearney, often requiring special hopper clearing crews. Encouraged to introduce new insect destroying bird species to Nebraska, Governor Garber ordered several boxes of English sparrows from New York State. The Nebraska Legislature passed a "Grasshopper Act" in 1877 requiring every able bodied citizen between the ages of sixteen and sixty to serve two days a year in pest eradication. Road supervisors were empowered to require up to ten days of service if needed and levy a ten-dollar fine for shirkers. At one "grasshopper" convention held near Utica in 1877, Elder C. E. Phinney admonished farmers to read Malachi 3:10, where God promised to "rebuke the devourer" in response to more generous tithes and offerings. Quarter sections of good land priced from three to four hundred dollars went begging. It has been estimated that 30 percent of Nebraska's farmers left the state at this time. Nebraska railroad officials did their best to cover up the truth from the American public. After all, they still had acres and acres of Nebraska farmland for sale.

Although grasshoppers were feared by most Nebraska natives, Mennonite farmers of Dutch and German origin from Southern Russia that were settling in Kansas and Nebraska at about this time had a different view. Many said American grasshoppers were actually "babies" compared to the locusts they had learned to live with in the Russian Crimea.

Eldon Hostetler

Did We See a Drought in 2002?

While some Seward County citizens nearing sixty may remember the drought years of 1955-56, as well as the one just experienced in 2002, you may be tempted to think you know all about Nebraska drought. Some have asked, "How does our 2002 drought compare with some of the droughts we have read about in Nebraska history books?" The monster from 1934 to 1940 is best known, mostly because of its longevity. However, other less publicized droughts may have caused more devastation in a shorter time period. For example, the droughts of 1879 and 1956-57 and the second worst drought to ever hit our county recorded from 1892-95, would hold runner-up status in my mind. Two eyewitness accounts from that day tell more. Seward County historian, W. W. Cox recorded his memory of weather conditions in the spring of 1880:

"The winter had been a dry one and the earth had become a bed of dust. The freezing and thawing of the fields without any moisture made it into a vast bed of loose dust, and as the wind sometimes blows in the springtime in Nebraska, this proved a favorable time to make a reputation. Most of the spring wheat had been sown (up to this time spring wheat was our most staple production) when the wind began to blow a gale from the north and it kept the atmosphere black with fine dust for some days. It became so terrific that man or beast could hardly withstand it. We were reminded of the sandstorms of the desert. The fine dust found a way into the best of the houses, so that they were almost untenable and would have been deserted if the poor distracted inmates had known where to go, but they just had to grin and bear it. There was no escape. Dust as fine as powder was piled up along hedge rows and other obstructions like great snow-drifts. Some places it was from three to four feet high (some say the drifts were five feet). Thousands of bushels of sown wheat went south, the Lord only knows how far, without bills of lading attached. In many places the fields that had been plowed were stripped of the soil as deep as it had been plowed. This condition did not augur well for a wheat crop. The spring and summer was dry, and all crops were short (*History of Seward County,* second edition, W.W. Cox)."

The Way It Was

What was probably one of the most frightening days in Nebraska history happened on July 25, 1894. The July 26, 1894 *Omaha Evening Bee* newspaper said:

"It was just before midnight on the night of July 25 that the wind began to blow from the south. By 1 o'clock it had freshened to a stiff breeze and by daylight was blowing a stiff gale. It is difficult to write so as to give one who did not experience it an idea of that awful wind. It fairly blistered, scorched, and withered everything endowed with life. All day the sun shone with fierce intensity, and all day that terrible wind bore clouds of dust and bits of rubbish along, making outdoor life unpleasant and existence indoors all but intolerable. At daylight the heat was intense, but it steadily increased until the local record was broken. Government records indicate it was over 100 degrees from noon until sundown. The temperature at 3 p.m. held at 106 degrees, the hottest ever known in Omaha. After that time, the heat slowly receded until shortly before 8 p.m. when the mercury finally dropped below the century mark. But all that night, the dreadful gale continued making the drop in temperature seem so slight it was scarcely noticed. Eyewitnesses tell stories of green vegetation shriveling like it had been through a blast furnace, creating the appearance of a hard frost."

From one end of the state to the other, streams dried up and wells went dry. News items from the *Milford Nebraskan* reported the same conditions in Seward County. Needless to say, farmers and businessmen were devastated in Seward County. Conditions were even worse in central and western Nebraska. Corn was shipped in to Milford from eastern states as were carloads of relief goods. Rainmakers were hired, some by the railroads and some by towns, while prayer meetings were held by the people. Many pioneers from counties farther west left the state for good.

In light of the tense and serious conditions experienced at this time, the *Nebraska Farmer* editor attempted to create a little humor; maybe just by showing off his powerful vocabulary. In the September 1, 1894 edition he wrote, "If a hog could only eat fodder but it seems he is not built that way, only to a limited extent. Perhaps some enterprising genius will spring up next year with a fodder-eating variety of purebred hogs. The great desideratum of the day is a preeminently herbivorous hog."

Eldon Hostetler

Dairy Cow and Cream Stories

The story of Seward County farming would not be complete without recording the role played by dairy cows. While we just expect today's dairymen to possess well bred Holsteins, sixty-five years ago it was a different ball game. Considered great for milk production, Holsteins were the favorite of the professional dairyman. Average farmers, on the other hand, chose dual purpose breeds such as Milking Shorthorn, Brown Swiss, Ayrshire, or Red Polled. If my memory serves me right, the average farmer's dairy herd in the 30s and 40s consisted in what we knew only as milk cows, usually containing a mixture of several different breeds. Guernsey and Jersey cattle were not all that popular due to the worthlessness of the bull calves. In that day it seemed like everyone wanted or needed his own fresh milk and cream. Even retired farmers who had moved to town wanted access to fresh milk. My Grandpa Burkey kept a cow, as well as his own chickens, on a spot located directly east of the Milford High School. Many of these so called "essential" cow and chicken barns are still standing in Milford. Retired farmers moving to town had the idea that fresh, homegrown country milk, butter, and eggs were a far more wholesome and healthy product. While the milk may have been "country fresh," it may have been far from pure and wholesome. I think I can say this from experience, since I have "been there and done that."

The average farmer milked anywhere from five to twelve cows, or just enough to keep his wife and children busy during the busy farming season. While the average farmer's operation was no match for the 4,000-head dairy I toured recently in California, it was enough to keep the family in grocery money. I have vivid memories of our favorite milk cows: Pansy, Daisy, Bessie, Butte, Reddy, Jersey, Brindle, Rose, Goldie, and Spot. I think we named each cow to better facilitate the expression of our anger and frustration when they hit us in the face with their wet dirty tails.

One good thing about the dirty thirties was the fact we were often forced to baby-sit our cows while they grazed along the roadsides—sometimes the only grass available. Several hours of this each day could prove to be a great bonding experience. In fact, we soon learned to know each cow well enough to recognize her by the sound of her particular grassy gas belch. Since milking machines for the average farmer were unknown in that day, farm kids (boys or girls) were just expected to "rise and shine" at milking time, usually before the sun came up. Today, I think several government agencies would classify this as plain and simple child abuse.

Another thing in our favor was the fact that this was the day before Uncle Sam stuck his fingers in trifling farm affairs. Farmers were their own bosses in every aspect of milk production, unless you sold fluid milk to Roberts Dairy for processing. This may be one reason most separated their milk, feeding the skim milk to the pigs and selling the cream for butter. Half-grown pigs, cats, and dogs would go absolutely crazy over the taste of skim milk, although occasionally we turned it into homemade skim milk (cottage cheese).

While quality production standards were not always perfect, most farmers attempted to keep things neat and clean, although I do have some less than wholesome stories on file concerning cream and butter production in that day. Like, for example, the farmer who insisted he would not throw away a whole pail of milk just because Bessie got her foot in the top half of the bucket. Now, his argument even sounds quite reasonable. After all, it is run through a brass strainer before separating it! I'm sure you have all heard the story of the cautious Milford cream buyer who discovered a small cat in the bottom of a can of cream he was testing. Come to think about it, I don't believe I have ever heard the rest of this story. But, I suppose we may just assume the cat was dead—and it probably didn't even suffer too long. Most of all, I bet Mr. Farmer didn't even miss the cat, since he probably had several more litters back on the farm. Then, on second thought, maybe we should have had several sharp-nosed government inspectors snooping around our cow barns sixty years ago. Every time I think about it, I recall the old adage that goes, "What you don't know may never hurt you."

Help from a Wealthy Uncle

A big share of the total net income received by Nebraska farmers in 2001 came from direct government payments, money many outside the agricultural sector say was not truly earned or deserved. Today, the farm game is played pretty much by Uncle Sam's rules, since the majority of the farmers have learned to rely on government protection and support. But this story is not about the pros and cons of government intervention in farm business or the justification of using hard-earned tax money to support individuals who continue to farm, even while losing money. This is the story of why, when, and how it all started. While a large part of America enjoyed material prosperity throughout the 1920s, Nebraska farmers were struggling financially. Demand for food needed to feed our soldiers and our allies during World War I caused farm commodity prices to skyrocket far beyond any that old timers could ever remember. News notes from 1918 *Milford Review* offer a glimpse of how the local economy reacted: "A. J. Kremer bought a new Huber tractor to help bring in the big crop for the Allies."

"At Joe Miller's sale on Monday, one grade Belgian team brought $625.00."

"Joe W. Sutter sold three hogs, which brought him an average of $100.16."

"Springer's sale on Monday had over 1000 in attendance including more than 200 women. People seemed to come from all over. His cows brought the best price ever, one bringing more than $90."

In other words, prosperity ran rampant. At one point in 1918, corn sold for $1.70, wheat $2.02, and hogs $16.75. Buoyed by artificially high prices, many farmers expanded. By mid-1920, the bubble had already burst and by December 1, 1921, wheat was down to 83 cents, corn to 27 cents, while hogs fell to $7.50.

But this was only part of the story. While farm income was coming down, goods and services needed by farmers rose. In 1914, taxes absorbed less than 5 percent of the average farmer's income, a figure that rose to more than 20 percent by 1922. By December of 1932, commodity prices were the lowest in state history, even lower then those experienced in the 1890s. Total cash receipts for Nebraska farmers declined from 489 million in 1929 to 166 million in 1932, or 46 percent less than the average farm income in the 1910-14 period.

However, by 1932 prices paid by farmers for goods and services were 7 percent higher than during the 1910-14 period. Needless to say, most Nebraska citizens were in big financial trouble. Many felt the Hoover administration, (1928-1932) which was more or less committed to free enterprise and stressed voluntary decision-making, failed to take action. Enter the new Democratic administration headed by Franklin D. Roosevelt, who had just won a smashing victory over President Hoover. Mr. Roosevelt is owed the honor of allowing the government to extend its fingers into agriculture. How well I remember our family sitting in front of our 32-volt radio completely spellbound by his famous "fireside chats" while he carefully explained how he proposed to restore order to a reeling American economy. May new programs, including FDIC, T.V.A, R.E.A and W.P.A were begun.

The new Agriculture Adjustment Act (AAA) was implemented with the task of raising farm commodity prices by reducing supplies by forcing farmers to reduce acreage. Complying farmers would be compensated by money from the federal treasury. Declared unconstitutional by the Supreme Court in 1935, a new act was passed in 1938. Thus began a string of government-sponsored support programs for farmers. Many are still offered at the government's Consolidated Farm Service Agency offices.

One of the first actions to be implemented in 1933 was the purchase and disposal of surplus livestock—stock for which farmers had no feed: 470,000 head of cattle, 438,000 pigs, and 36,000 sows were said to have met their fates in Nebraska. In this community, 176 head of cattle were purchased in Beaver Crossing and 228 in the Milford vicinity for which farmers were compensated only $10 to $12 per head. In 1933, Seward County farmers were required to plant 33 percent less wheat in order to qualify for government wheat payments. On December 28, 1933 the first government program checks were mailed to Seward County participants, a total of $58,000 badly needed dollars. Now I realize this narrative touches only the high spots of what has proven to be a very popular program now nearly seventy years old. American citizens evidently loved Roosevelt's "New Deal" programs. So well, in fact, they elected him to four terms— usually by overwhelming majorities.

Eldon Hostetler

Early Restless Farmers

The bulk of the early settlers arriving in the Milford community between 1861 to 1872 came from northeastern states like New York, Pennsylvania, Maryland, Ohio, and Wisconsin. Early Mennonite settlers were mostly from Ohio and Illinois, while those arriving later came from Ontario, Canada. Regardless of their origin, they had one goal in mind: finding good farm ground as cheaply as possible. Those who came early had their pick of the best homestead land, while late arrivals were forced to buy ground from either the railroad or an earlier homesteader who was ready to move on. As early as 1871, the *Blue Valley Record* editor noted that many of the original homesteaded farms were already changing hands. "Moneyed men are now buying out the first settlers, as the latter push on farther west," he reported.

One of the first large migrations from the Milford community took place around 1880 when homestead land in Holt County near O'Neill was opened for settlement. Milford families who took advantage of this golden opportunity included the Banhofs, Brocks, Kissingers, Meyers, and Raymers. Several years later in 1883, more families followed, including the Bosharts, Erbs, Hershbergers, Jantzies, and Schweitzers. Because of the extremely sandy soil found in the area, many suffered untold hardships during the drought of the 1890s. Other large migrations from the community included a dozen families (mostly Stutzmans) to the Chappell vicinity in Duel County in 1888-89 and six families to Washington County, Colorado area near Akron in 1887-88. One of Seward County's original settlers, James West, son of Tommy West, moved on to this community where he died in 1913.

Milford founder, J. L. Davison did not even hang around all that long in the town he founded. The family left Milford in the mid-1880s and settled in New Mexico. They later moved on to San Diego, California.

The Culver family left Milford soon after 1907, the majority ending up in California. Culver City, California, was founded and named after Harry Culver, son of Jacob and Ada Culver.

In 1891, a large group of Mennonite farmers left Milford and purchased land near Shickley in Fillmore County. Others left Milford in the late 1880s and settled in Hamilton County near Aurora. During the drought of 1890, many of these returned to Milford. From 1904-07, a dozen families purchased land in Hall County and moved to the Wood River vicinity. My grandfather, N. N. Hostetler, moved near Lodgepole Nebraska, in 1893, where he lost nearly everything. In 1895, he moved southeast to Clay County in Arkansas, staying there for less than one year.

Milford natives may have sought greener pastures after reading some of the wild, high-powered advertisements sponsored by railroads and land companies.

One land development company guaranteed land in South Dakota that would "practically pay for itself with one wheat crop." Evidently, some took the bait. George Angermeir moved to Hitchcock County in Nebraska. Chris Sutter, Pete Steider, and Dan Roth all moved to Montana. J. R. Eicher tried his luck in Sherman County in Kansas, Henry Burkey moved to Colorado, while Mose Burkey moved to Wisconsin. Nearly all returned to Milford—most within one year. Valentine Burkey moved his family to Hamilton County, near Aurora, saying, "I need more farmland to keep all my boys busy." He, too, returned after several years. A news note in a 1909 *Milford Nebraskan* reported that Alex Stutzman, Ed Smiley, and Noah Rediger were leaving for Aberdeen, South Dakota, to "look at dirt and buy if they like it." Evidently Alex liked what he saw. In 1914, Alex moved to near West Port where he died in 1917.

For a number of years the Milford newspaper carried large ads advertising the wonderful, undeveloped lands available in the Prairie Provinces of Canada. These ads were sponsored by the Blackburn Brothers, who were Milford businessmen and real estate dealers. One full-page ad in the *Milford Nebraskan* about 1905 offered free rail transportation to certain Mennonite farmers if they would just come and take a look.

In 1905, J. L. Stauffer headed up a party who looked and bought. Pleased with what they saw, many purchased good farmland for a fraction of what it was selling for in the Milford community. By 1912, seventy or more former Milford residents were living and farming in Canada, and as far as I know few, if any, ever returned. Many more farmers left the Milford community during the drought years from 1934-1940. While some went to California or Oregon, others ended up in Iowa, Illinois, Pennsylvania, Washington State, Indiana, Idaho, or Florida.

Eldon Hostetler

Harvest Nostalgia

Webster defines the word nostalgia as "a wistful or sentimental longing for places, things acquaintances or conditions belonging to the past." Of all my childhood memories, harvest time stands out as one of the most exciting. Wheat harvest still generates many pleasant memories, maybe because it did not involve weeks and weeks of that much hated, slave-type labor known as corn harvest.

While the majority of the farm kids I knew detested corn-shucking time, most looked forward to the summer harvest. To us, our John Deere grain binder appeared to be a marvelous machine. We often just pretended we knew how and when to move the numerous adjusting levers and even became familiar enough to know the difference between the platform and the upper and lower elevator canvases. One thing we did not appreciate was shocking the wheat after it was cut. It was a job we insisted was just too hot for kids, always hoping Dad would hire someone older. Since Dad owned his own threshing rig, I was usually allowed to ride in the cab of our 28-50 Model Hart Parr tractor when he towed our 36-inch J. I. Case separator. On the designated morning, horses and hayracks would arrive from all directions, usually eight or ten depending on the length of haul. What was known as the "crew" consisted of one man on each rack, plus four men known as "spike pitchers," two or three to unload the grain, two men to "baby-sit" the tractor and thresher, one water boy plus numerous lazy onlookers. My first paying job in 1937 was water boy. I was paid a whopping sum of 15 cents an hour, which included furnishing my own pony. Water was carried in stoneware jugs, usually capped with a broken corncob covered with a rag. I can still hear several of my customers "gurgle and slurgal" and spit as they tried to expel excess tobacco juice from their throat and mouth before taking a drink. Of course, mealtimes were always the highlight of every day. Since this was before the invention of popular one-dish meals created to meet every nutritional need known to mankind, real farmer-style, he-man food was the order of the day. While it was indeed a pleasure for the men folk involved, I'm sure the mothers and sisters usually got the short end of the stick. The climax to the entire season was the "settlement" meeting, a time when everyone involved gathered at the owners to make final settlement.

The Way It Was

One such meeting was mentioned in the August 14, 1919 *Milford Review*: "The threshing club in the district two miles north of town met in the home of C. D. Becker to make settlement for the season. At the close, a lunch of cake and ice cream and cigars was had, intervened with music and singing. Everyone had a good time, and departed home at a late hour."

Occasionally, thresher owners even received much needed recognition for their accomplishments. "Joe Schlegel threshed 1,110 bushels of wheat for Joseph Hauder in six and one half hours (*Milford Review*, August 13, 1913)."

Although harvest was usually a happy occasion, it also presented numerous hazards. This news item from the October 14, 1884 *Seward Reporter* tells the whole gruesome story. "A man who worked with a threshing crew near Lincoln Creek was so unfortunate as to fall in the thresher throat, and was run through the machine. His body was fearfully mangled and every bone crushed. But strange to say his clothing was not at all torn, or so much as one button off. None around there knew who he was. His companions said his clothes were sold by Charles Greenborn of Seward and contacted him. He said the man's name was Charles Schickelfritz, who had bought the suit from him three years ago and has worn it ever since."

Well at least they did identify his clothes and Mr. Greenborn got some very cheap advertising!

While threshing was hard work, occasionally exciting things happened as reported in the August 1, 1919 *Milford Review*. "Quite a bit of excitement occurred at Frank Smiley's farm when a load of bundles was discovered to be on fire. The horses ran away from the thresher, with the entire load on fire, right through a barb wire fence and headed straight for the barn of August Gurtz, which caught on fire and burned down. It also burned his automobile. The horses were not burned seriously, although one did have his tail burned off." Although few retired farmers would want or could stand the kind of excitement portrayed in the above illustrations, the aroma of fresh wheat straw might trigger some pleasant memories in the minds of many "tired old farmers." Although it was hot, demanding work, the aroma of fried chicken, the sight of freshly sliced, homegrown tomatoes, and the taste of fresh apple cream pie seemed to make it all worthwhile.

Eldon Hostetler

The Price of Good Farmland

Although emigration to Seward County slowed down during the Civil War, hundreds of families arrived between 1868 and 1885. By 1869 most of the desirable homestead land had already been claimed. The *Blue Valley Record* editor reported in 1871, "Emigration has commenced once more, and long lines of covered wagons are seen making their way down towards Milford. So far a total of 189 wagons have passed through town during the month of April."

At that time, most citizens felt it was their civic obligation to do everything within their power to persuade strangers to settle in Milford. One way was through the power of the press as exemplified by this letter published in a *Herald of Truth* magazine in 1876: "We have a nice country and the land is cheap, from six to fifteen dollars per acre. We also have good water at thirty to eighty feet and a good market at the capitol at Lincoln. Anyone desiring to visit, Seward and Dorchester are the nearest rail stations (letter from N. J. Petersheim of Milford)."

At this time land prices were relativity cheap and there appeared to be to be plenty of good farm land for sale. In 1874, one Milford native advertised that he would sell three quarter sections of land in Section 6, for four dollars an acre, while Seward County Commissioners announced they had recently purchased a 160-acre "poor farm" southeast of Seward for $1,500. Mirroring the accepted philosophy of the day concerning the poor, the editor wrote: "Taxpayers have always believed that able-bodied poor should be compelled to earn their own living."

Good crop years experienced throughout the 1880s tended to force land prices even higher. In 1881, Daniel Roth purchased eighty acres from William Matzke for fifteen dollars an acre. A good 160-acre farm owned by William Morford in Section 8 of N Township was advertised for sale at $2,500 in 1883. In 1884, Dan Erb bought J. R. Eicher's 120-acre farm for $4,000, while Jacob Stutzman bought an 80-acre farm from J. H. Culver for $1,600. The drought and depression experienced during the 1890s tended to cool prices, especially with corn selling for only 15 cents. In 1896, an 80-acre farm located six miles east of Beaver Crossing boasting a good two-story frame house, an 18' x 20' stable and a good corn crib plus a good bearing young fruit orchard, was said to be a bargain at $1,600. Few sales were reported during this time period. By 1900, the newspaper editor wrote, "Four years ago hogs were selling for $2. 85 per hundred, while today they are worth $4.85. Now this is prosperity for our farmers."

Following better farm prices, by 1902 good land was once more in demand. John Steckly and John Sutter, newly arrived from Lyon County, Kansas, paid $50 an acre for the 240 acres they purchased southeast of Beaver Crossing. By 1905 the editor could report that Dan Eicher paid $81.20 per acre for a quarter section purchased from H. A. Brisby. "This is probably the highest price ever paid for farm land some distance from a town in the country." In 1907, Dan shocked his neighbors one more time, this time paying $16,000 for the adjoining Sharp quarter. By this time, some thought land prices were absolutely out of control, especially after Silas Miller paid George Choop $130 an acre for his 80-acre farm. Miller said, "George bought it from J. Steckly one year ago for $115 and he thought he had paid too much for it. There seems to be no limit to the value of good farmland." During World War I, local land values jumped even higher when Noah Rediger paid Leo Schlegel $191.25 per acre for his quarter section. By 1918, farm prices were artificially high, putting more pressure on the value of farmland. Hogs were bringing up to $16.75, corn $1.70, and cows were selling for up to $90.00. Feeling the pressure to expand, farmers bid land prices up to the point where some was selling for more than $250 per acre, saddling many with huge mortgages.

And then came a drop in prices along with the depression plus the big drought of the dirty thirties. This double-barreled whammy forced many landowners off their farms—some forever because many had purchased farms at prosperity prices. On January 1, 1932 corn was selling for 32 cents, wheat 40 cents, oats 20 cents and eggs 16 cents. One year later on January 1, 1933 corn sold for 11 cents, wheat 30 cents, oats 9 cents, eggs 8 cents, while cream was 14 cents.

Farming—A Dangerous Occupation

Anyone who has lived in Seward County for a number of years probably remembers someone associated with farming, or other agricultural related work, who was either killed or injured in what is considered dangerous work. For years, farming has usually found a spot in the list of top ten most hazardous occupations. Most of the deaths and injuries sustained by farmers today are more or less related to power machinery, including the improper use of tractors, power takeoff shafts, grain augers, farm chemicals, anhydrous ammonia, highway pickup crashes and small three- or four-wheel all-terrain vehicles. Because none of the above mentioned hazards were available a hundred years ago, one might just assume farming was without danger. However, newspaper articles from a century ago tell a far different story.

One of the earliest tragedies reported in the community happened in 1872 when Mr. Jefferson Stephenson was found dead under his overturned wagon several miles east of Milford. Mr. Stephenson, who was returning home from Lincoln with a full load of lumber, upset while crossing Middle Creek. While tractors and power machinery are the main threats today, frightened horses were the number one cause of farm-related accidents a hundred years ago. Here are several examples:

"Fred D. Grant, a young man living in N Township was killed when he was dragged by a runaway horse (June, 1879)."

"A man and a woman on their way home upset their wagon killing him instantly and badly injuring her (1886)."

"Last week Mr. Chris Zehr, who lives five miles west of Milford, met with a painful accident. While shelling corn on his farm the horses on the power unit got excited and, going too fast, the tumbling rod jumped out of the jack striking Mr. Zehr on the forehead, knocking him senseless. He was carried to the house in this condition, and the family physician summoned, who discovered a fractured skull of the outer skull plate (*Milford Nebraskan,* April 30, 1886)."

"Ralph Jantzie, 15-year-old son of Amos Jantzie, is seriously ill at his home after suffering a kick by a horse. His skull is fractured from front to rear, and by last report will hardly survive (1915)."

"Kenneth, the ten-year-old son of Will Kremer, was killed instantly Wednesday evening when the four-horse team he was using to plow struck a stump and he was thrown to the ground breaking his neck. Funeral services were held at East Fairview on Friday (*Milford Review,* 1924)."

The Way It Was

This tragic farm related accident occurred in Beaver Crossing in July of 1896: "About 5:00 p.m. last Friday, this town was shocked as it never was before by the news that H. W. Bently was killed in his blacksmith shop. He was killed instantly when his emery stone exploded while he was polishing a plow share. He had just made the comment that the stone was running too slow, and had just sped up his steam engine."

But horse farming was no match for lightning as these 1900 examples demonstrate:

"Lightning killed Leon Richardson while he was plowing in a field near Beaver Crossing."

"Abner Means was killed about 12 p.m. while threshing on the Whiteny place. A strike hit him in the farm driveway. A doctor was called, but death was instant." (Many more lightning incidents are recorded, including one near Staplehurst in 1898 that killed five boys and one horse.)

"A farmer residing in L Precinct near Beaver Crossing, went to the field about 6 o'clock Friday evening April 3, 1896 to relieve one of his sons who was running a stalk cutter. He took charge of the machine, which was being drawn by a young and spirited team. Soon after starting, a dog chasing a rabbit frightened them and they ran away. Mr. Hubertus was thrown from the cutter and one of his feet caught in the gearing. He was dragged until the leg was mangled in a terrible manner. His family managed to get him to the house and summoned a physician who amputated the shattered limb, but on account of loss of blood and internal injuries the unfortunate man did not regain consciousness, lingering until the next morning when death relieved him of his suffering."

"A most heart rending accident occurred near Goehner Wednesday evening October 30, 1903. F. Shultz went to the field a short distance from his house to mow some cane. Unobserved by him, his nearly infant daughter followed him and thinking to play a joke on him hid in the way of the sickle. Her father was unaware that she was in the field until the mower knives severed both of her feet. Physicians were summoned and did all that was possible to save her life, but the little sufferer passed on to the one who said, 'Suffer little children to come unto me' in the wee hours of the following morning."

Eldon Hostetler

The following two tragedies were reprinted in the May 3, 1883 *Crete Vidette* newspaper as reported earlier by the *Milford Democrat* newspaper:

"On last Friday afternoon at the farm of J. N. Young, near Dorchester, occurred a horrifying accident, the following particulars of which we learn from Doctor Brandon of Milford: In the afternoon Mrs. Young went to the field with her husband to work, taking with her a babe about eighteen months old. A stubble field had been burned off, near which stood a stack of straw. The child going to sleep, Mrs. Young supposing the fire had gone entirely out placed the babe on the edge of the stack out of the wind while she assisted her husband in the absence of the hired man. When but a few rods away, the stiff wind which prevailed that day blew sparks from the field to the stack, which was soon ablaze, and before the child could be rescued the little one was a charred, unrecognizable mass. The right arm and leg being burned off at the body, the left arm at the elbow, the right leg at the knee and the skull burned through until the brains oozed out and the spirit of the little one had flown."

"On last Saturday morning about 8 o'clock, Frank Kubush and wife, living near Camden, went to Crete, leaving at home a 12 year old daughter and two sons aged one and eight. Shortly after the parents left, the children concluded to make a cake. They went to a neighbors and borrowed some flour and proceeded to make the cake, putting therein some berries or seeds she had previously gathered on the prairie. The cake after being baked was divided among the three children. The older boy went out to herd the cows and was joined by a neighbor's boy to whom he gave a piece of the cake. The cake had been eaten but a short time when they all began to feel sick, and the older boy started for home, but died on the way. The girl took the babe and went to a neighbor's house and told the lady she was sick and was given sour and sweet cream which caused her to vomit. The neighbor's boy was also given an emetic. The parents were sent for and arrived home half past one and found the boy dead and the baby at a neighbors, which was taken home, but soon died. It is supposed the berry seeds were Belladonna, or deadly 'night shade' and they produced the poisoning, but as none of them could be procured it is not certain what kind of poison they took, although it is evident that it was a strong poison as several dogs and cats which ate the vomit of the surviving children died shortly afterwards."

The Way It Was

Hooray for Chickens

For years the butt of degrading and humiliating jokes, real live chickens are usually just taken for granted, especially by the younger generations. Today their worth is usually measured by the quality of McDonald's chicken nuggets, or the taste of "finger lick'en good" KFC drumsticks. Many younger people have no idea what an honest to goodness Plymouth Rock hen would look like. Nor do they realize that chickens, as well as pooches and felines, are actually living, breathing animals. And just like other domestic animals, each chicken has a distinct personality. While cats express their happiness and contentment by purring and dogs by wagging their tails, have you ever seen a happy chicken smile, or wag its tail feathers? Now who is responsible for the present state of disrespect for what was at one time considered a very necessary part of God's creation? Maybe we could start by blaming Adam for choosing to call this handsome creature a chicken. One thing for sure, most normal people would react quite negatively should they be addressed as "chicken."

My generation is not perfect, but we actually enjoyed owning and living with chickens and usually tried to treat them with dignity and respect. What a thrill it was when the rural mail carrier drove in our yard packing several boxes of darling little baby chicks. Often times they came by mail from Missouri because they were usually one or two cents a chick cheaper.

Talk about family excitement! Our children just loved to help move them into the cute little brooder house (ask your grandpa what a brooder house was) already heated up to 90 degrees for the occasion. What fun it was to watch them eat and drink and grow into healthy and happy birds. And then came the time when you were just expected to lose all your civilized inhibitions, throw all decency to the wind, and kill and eat your teenage boy chickens. This often proved to be an excruciating experience for young farm wives who were not all that accustomed to the sight of blood. In fact, some were even happy to see that "meddling" mother-in-law arrive to offer her services. I suppose we soothed our consciences by telling ourselves they are only "fryers," not really individual chickens. Now according to community tradition, any wife that was "on the ball" had her fryers ready for eating about the same time you cut your first lettuce from the garden. When you accomplished this, it proved that you had finally arrived and were now entitled to farm wife bragging rights.

With most of the boy chickens out of the way, you were now ready to concentrate on the little girl chicks, known as pullets until they were a year old. After that, they were called laying hens. Then you expected them to work for you by shelling out eggs by the dozens. When I rehash this scenario in my mind today, I must confess we were just a wee bit cruel to these tender, young blossoming ladies. At least we certainly did our best to deny them the privilege of any romantic involvement in their lives by becoming mothers. Yes, we were even ugly at times, sometimes locking them up in our "chicken jail," until they decided laying eggs for us was more important than motherhood. For more on this subject, please ask your grandmother.

Sometimes I blush with shame every time I even think about this cruel practice. If you tried this today, I am sure the A.C.L.U. would quickly be on your case. If in some way I could address the chickens who touched my life in so many different ways for more than seventy years, I think I would surely say, "You were always there when I needed you, although I was not always kind and considerate. Occasionally I think I even had the idea that maybe you were not all that smart; you know— like we humans are.

"However, this still leaves one question unanswered that your species, dumb as you are, could help us smart humans solve. Please be frank and just answer this one question. Who came first, eggs or chickens?" Cheers to both chickens and eggs—and we smart humans— descended from "monkeys."

Separating Eggs

This 1903 letter addressed to my father's youngest sister, Barbara, does a great job of sharing the role played by both chickens and cows in the farm economy of 100 years ago. Born in 1892, Barbara Hostetler died in 1904 shortly after receiving this letter from her cousin, Elma (Troyer) Burkey who lived near Shickley at the time. Later, Elma married John Burkey and became the mother of two sons. Elma and John lived in the Beaver Crossing vicinity, where she died from the flu in 1918 at the age of twenty-six years. One of Elma's surviving sons, Floyd Burkey is well known in the Milford community. Her use of rather crude English may be attributed to the fact that in school she was forced to speak and write in English rather than the "Pennsylvania Dutch" she had been accustomed to.

Shickly, Nebraska, April 30, 1903
Dear Cousin Barbara,
    Will try and let you know we are all well. Hope you are the same. It snowed on the ground and we have got seven fresh cows. We get plenty of milk. How many cows do you milk? Sometimes we get four dozen eggs. We got a snowstorm last night. We have got fifteen hens a setting and two with baby chicks. Have you got any baby chicks? We have a nice garden, but things is now all drifted up with snow. Our school will last three weeks yet, how long will your school last yet? Grandma's house is moved now. How many eggs to you get? I would like to see you. I will close for this time. Write soon and do not wait so long. Good bye. Elma Troyer

    Few farmers today would even consider chickens and egg production as one of their top priorities in farm management decisions. Not so in the late 1940s and early 1950s when we first launched our farming career. The price of eggs, the brand of chicken mash used, the variety and price of baby chicks, the number of eggs gathered, and the general health and condition of your flock were all hot topics for discussion in that day. Every small town had several "produce houses" where farmers as well as city people sold their eggs and cream. Since most egg buyers paid cash for full cases (30 dozen) without inspecting the contents, trickery and deceit was not that uncommon. One Beaver Crossing egg buyer shared with me how several of his producers would fill some of the inside layers with products other than eggs. Small home grown potatoes, and black walnuts were two of the favorites. Milford usually had two or three egg and cream buyers as well as two baby chick hatcheries. Most grocery stores also bought cream and eggs, each one boasting of paying the top dollar. Unlike today, fifty years ago eggs and dairy products were considered wholesome, healthful and nutritious. In fact, everyone was encouraged to eat all they could for their health giving benefits. The question was not if you wanted eggs for breakfasts, but how many and what method of preparation.

Eggs also came in handy for non-eating uses as well. What was known as "fully ripe" and conditioned eggs often proved to be useful tools for other applications. Often, ripe eggs were the end result of cruel and unjust treatment to innocent laying hens, usually administered by greedy, money-loving owners forced to deal with hormone-laden hens. Denied the privilege of attaining motherhood by forming a lasting relationship with a handsome rooster, said hens would often sneak away and hide large nests of eggs. Discovered after setting on these eggs for several weeks while hens harbored dreams of mothering a dozen little peepers, said eggs were said to be "well ripened," or in plain English, *just plain rotten*, or at least half rotten.

These eggs, fortunate enough to escape being eaten for breakfast occasionally ended up being used as offensive weapons by frustrated people. This example that happened in the town of Utica explains how it all worked: In 1908 Utica citizens angered by the bold preaching of a visiting evangelist encouraged him to leave town by pelting him with well cured eggs. Poor Mr. Preacher, was actually forced to seek medical attention. Needless to say —he took the hint, "shook the egg yolk off his feet" and left town in one big hurry. (*Beaver Crossing Times*)

What Happened to the Fruit Trees?

Have you ever wondered why the apples you eat usually come from some other state? A visit to the Nebraska City community, only seventy-five miles east of Milford in September or October will convince one that good apples can be grown in the state. But, most would agree that today they are not all that popular in the Milford community. According to older records, at one time Milford was home to many large orchards, some containing several hundred various kinds of fruit trees. In 1876 the Seward *Blue Valley Blade* editor traveled to Milford to do a story on the community. "We took a trip out to the residence of D.C. Tift. Mr. Tift's farm joins Milford on the northwest corner of town and he has one of the better farms in the state. He is in the grape culture and fruit growing business. We tasted some of his fruit and pronounced it as good as any grown in any state of the Union." Two years later in 1878, the editor of the *Seward Reporter* traveled to Milford to find out for himself if the things he had been hearing about Milford area farmers were true.

"Some of the new German Amish Mennonite farmers are enterprising farmers. Among them we find J. J. Harris [Author note: who lived on the farm where Bruce and Karen Stutzman live]. Mr. Harris has a fine farm of 320 acres, plus 300 apple trees and sixty peach trees, plus cherries and grapes. On section 9 lives J. M. T. Miller, who has a nice place with 100 apple trees, 150 peach trees, 80 Berkshire hogs, 70 acres of grain and 44 acres of corn." In 1877, a survey taken by the, B&M railroad reported 30,500 apple, 300 pear, 26,450 peach, 8,000 plum, 16,000 cherry trees and 33,000 grape vines in the county. The same survey reported only 46,594 acres of corn planted in the entire county. For most of the early pioneers, a good orchard of 30 to 100 apple trees was consider a must for normal living. Apples were either crushed for cider, dried, canned, or wrapped in paper and stored in caves for future use. In my younger days, 20 gallons of homemade apple butter from our own trees cooked in a 30-gallon copper kettle and stored in stone crocks sealed with paraffin wax provided the basis for many a winter meal. Dried apples were used to make pies later on—pies we kids never learned to appreciate.

And then, there was the cider business.

"Pioneer farmers would bring apples by the wagonload to Goehner, where Henry Roth had a large cider mill run by a steam engine. Cider was made for a beverage and some was aged for vinegar. What could not be used locally by the families and in the local grocery store was taken to the train depot to be shipped out and sold (*Goehner Centennial History Book*, pg. 43)."

The late Ezra Ehrisman remembered riding along

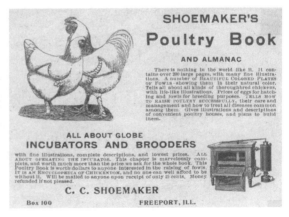

Eldon Hostetler

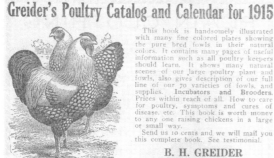

with his dad to deliver triple box loads (about 50 bushels) of apples to W. W. Miller's cider press. He said you usually had to get in line and wait your turn with as many as 40 wagonloads in the line. He remembered bringing the cider home in oak stave barrels and storing it in a cave for future use, but could not recall how they used it.

A news item in the October 22, 1909 Milford paper confirms the fact apple production was big business in this community 92 years ago: "Recently Dan Either shipped one carload of apples to Alliance, Nebraska." Dan's daughter, the late Mary Schlegel, said, "Dad had fruit trees all over the place."

Several things happened to alter Milford's fruit growing status from bountiful in 1909 to practically zero in 2001. Old-timers blame a savage hailstorm that hit the Milford community on June 16, 1901. This storm is said to have wiped out many of the fruit trees and large orchards in the community. But the storm may not have been as severe seven miles west of Milford where Dan raised most of his apples. From my own observation, a second factor often known as the "1940 Armistice Day" sleet and snowstorm, also played a large role. Rain, sleet, snow, and temperatures that suddenly dropped down to zero killed many of the remaining fruit trees, as well as many Chinese elm trees. Few apple trees killed in this storm were ever replanted.

This storm also played havoc with area turkey farmers. Roy Fosler lost 800 of his 1300-head flock, while Ammon Miller lost 400 out of 1000. A total death loss of 5600 birds took place in the Milford community.

The Way It Was

Artesian Wells Change a Community

The years of 1893 and 1894 were discouraging for Milford community farmers and businessmen alike. Severe drought that started in 1893 appeared to get worse in 1894, reaching a peak in July and August when it did not rain one drop for fifty days. Rainfall that averaged more than 36 inches in eastern Nebraska in 1891 was down to 17 inches in 1893. Hot south winds on July 27, 1894 scorched what little green vegetation was left. In 1895 Milford natives watched as long lines of discouraged settlers passed through town each day on their way back east, many carrying all of their earthly possessions on old, tattered covered wagons pulled by skinny horses. Some water wells were now going dry, while others had to be drilled deeper. "Will we run out of water? Will I have to stop irrigating my garden; what will we eat this winter; will it ever rain again?" many residents asked. But while Milford residents were pondering answers to these questions, unusual rumors from Beaver Crossing began to filter into the city.

"Good morning, Joseph. Did you hear the latest from Beaver Crossing? Fresh, cold water is just shooting up out of the ground."

"Now wait a minute Pete. This sounds like a Mother Goose story to me, surely it can't be true. This I will have to see for myself."

"But it's true! All they have to do is dig a well at least 110 feet deep and water simply comes gushing out of the ground. Why, they tell me one well pushed water up to 28 feet above ground level."

"Wow! Let's get our wives, hitch up the horses, and go see for ourselves."

Although the above conversation is purely hypothetical, similar conversations probably happened many times. A news item from the October 12, edition of the *Milford Nebraskan* reports more.

"Beaver Crossing is finally on the map, as well as the hot topic of café gossip from Omaha to Chadron. So much has been said about the artesian wells, and there being a rush from all parts of the state to see them, we accepted the offer of Captain Culver and his wife to inspect the Legion Post there. It is truly wonderful to see the water boiling up, throwing a stream four or five inches square to a height of 18 feet. There are now six wells in the vicinity, and more are being bored every week. Chris Clem has one that throws 260 gal a minute."

Eldon Hostetler

"Living springs" or water boiling out of the ground, has been a common occurrence in the Beaver Crossing vicinity since 1874. These springs were only about 25-30 feet deep and were usually dug with a posthole digger. In 1895, Mercantile Store owner Dwight Eager experienced a shortage of water from his shallow well and hired a Utica well driller to deepen it. At about 100 feet, the bottom appeared to drop out and water and sand rushed out with such force that it practically filled his store.

Mr. Eager's well touched off a mad race for artesian wells. No one knows for sure how many wells were drilled from 1895 to 1960 when the last ones were drilled, but by 1900, M Precinct alone had 400. The wells were available as far east as the Goehner Road, and then west about fourteen miles throughout the width of the West Blue Valley. At one time on my farm one mile southeast of Beaver Crossing I had twelve wells. Today my 8-inch irrigation well is raised 12 feet above the ground level and usually before the irrigation season starts each summer, water runs through the pump head. The discovery of artesian wells completely changed the face and image of the town of Beaver Crossing. In 1894 the town had a population of slightly more than 400 people, by 1909, some records say this had increased to nearly 900.

For years and years I remember Milford's population sign reading 799. Truck gardening and other specialty crops became the rage. In 1904, ninety-six carloads of potatoes were shipped from the railroad station. Strawberries, sweet potatoes, cabbage, tomatoes, and other berry and fruit crops were grown in abundance. "C. H. Hoyt has grown unusually large strawberries this year. So large that 22 berries filled a quart box. One berry measured five inches in circumference (*Beaver Crossing Times,* July 1, 1915)."

By 1908, the town owned one of the few swimming pools (a sand bottom lake filled by artesian wells) outside of Omaha. The July 2, 1908 newspaper announced to the public, "My bath house is now open to the public and the rules are as follows: No one allowed in the lake without a swimming suit. No profane language allowed. Wednesday will be ladies day and no men or boys allowed on Wednesday unless they are accompanied by their wives or daughters. These rules must be obeyed. Anyone violating same will be barred from lake. Season tickets, Gents $1.50, boys and ladies 75 cents."

The Way It Was

Later, a big, steel 45 x 70 open-air pavilion was erected in the park. It had a seating capacity of 2,000 people. In 1917, twenty new bathhouses were added as well as children's playground equipment and a big new dining hall and bandstand. In 1919, a new two-story bathhouse containing ninety rooms and an office was built. Local residents could brag, "our pool is the only one of its kind in the state and since it is filled from several flowing wells which constantly pour fresh water into it, and because of its enormous size, being a round pool measuring 225 feet across." The July 17, 1919 Beaver Crossing newspaper reported, "It is estimated that more than 1,500 people were at the park last Sunday, enjoying the bathing pool, shade and picnic dinners. One party of 60 came from Fairmont."

The availability of artesian wells encouraged Earle Smiley to raise rainbow trout. The 54-degree water provided ideal hatching and growing conditions for the 225,000 trout eggs he ordered. The fish were sold to large hotels and Pullman dining car service after they reached about one and one half pounds.

Later he specialized in goldfish and water lilies. By 1931 he had built a total of fifty concrete ponds featuring thirty-seven varieties of water lilies, two hundred varieties of iris and two hundred varieties of dahlias. Mr. Smiley enjoyed a large commercial trade and shipped bulbs and plants to every state in the union. The gardens brought hundreds of people to Beaver Crossing each summer, and at that time were said to be the second largest botanical gardens in the world.

After Mr. Smiley's sudden death in 1938, the gardens gradually declined. In 1935 you could take the grand tour for 15 cents. According to old Milford newspaper accounts, many local citizens enjoyed picnicking and partying in Beaver Crossing during this time. Believe it or not, I don't know of one artesian well left in the community that flows the year around.

Milford's Milling Industry

Today, we just assume most of the corn grown in Seward County will eventually be consumed by livestock, while the wheat will be processed into flour for the delicious bread and other fattening bakery products so many of us enjoy! One hundred and thirty years ago, things were somewhat turned around. Seward County historian Cox said, "Frequently, cornmeal was our principal diet. Nearly all our first settlers were poor, and consequently times became very hard for many of them. We have known of families to live a whole winter on corn meal and what rabbits they could kill with clubs (*History of Seward County*, Cox, p. 137)."

To avoid eating raw, hard corn similar to what we now know as "pig grub," our ancestors had devised assorted ways to crush or grind this grain to make it more palatable. While natural or shaped stones in the hands of humans served the purpose for thousands of years, as civilization advanced new and better methods were invented to facilitate this crushing process. Stones continued to play an important role in the processing of grain until the introduction of Hungarian-invented steel rollers about 1850. Before the invention and perfection of electric- or petroleum-powered engines, horse, steam, or water was used for most milling jobs. Water-powered stone burr grinders, first used by the Romans, proved to be the most efficient and reliable power source known. From 1910 to 1920, Seward County's Blue River system was known as one of the most used mill streams in the entire nation.

Thomas West built the county's first water-powered grist mill on the West Blue in the summer of 1864. Consisting of a saw mill and one small set of stone burrs, early settlers welcomed the privilege of having a place to process their grain. In 1893, steel rollers and other flour-making equipment was added to manufacture what many considered a good grade of wheat flour. The first, genuine flour mill was erected in Camden by H. W. Parker in 1866.

Other Seward County mills included Seward City Mills, erected in Seward by the Hiram boys in 1867-68. This is the mill often mentioned in the writings of the late Harold Davison who apparently sold Gem Flour and Buddy Boy pancake mix. A second water-powered mill was located several miles southeast of Seward. Known as Heumanns's Mill, it was built by Cooper and Henderson in 1874. Three other Seward County water-powered mills included Mulfinger and Harrison, The Updyke Grain Company, Seward Cereal Mills, and Staplehurst's Flavor Flour Mill built in 1915. The only water-powered mill not using Blue River water was built on Lincoln Creek by Luke Auger in 1870. Beaver Crossing became the proud owner of a new mill built by Smith and Ingress in 1871. Two steam-powered saw or grist mills also served Seward County residents. Kerkham and Hughes erected a saw and grinding mill at Oak Groves (near Garland in H Precinct) in 1868. In 1893, Fred Fosler advertised that he would do custom grain rolling at his new steam mill located four miles northeast of Milford. Since I

This mill dam and trestle on the Blue River was used to transport all finished mill products to the north side of the river for loading on rail cars before the tracks were moved to Milford in 1907.

could find little information on the history of the flour mill and elevator known as "Leahy Mills," I write this strictly from memory. Located several miles east of the northern edge of Seward during the "dirty thirties," I remember dad hauling wheat to this mill to exchange for our yearly flour supply. Firmly convinced that their "*Pride of Seward County*" flour was somewhat inferior to the "*Victor*" brand manufactured by the Crete Mills, my parents usually paid more for the flour made in Crete. J. L. Davison soon realized the ideal location for a dam would be on the limestone bottoms near the ford where the steamwagon train was expected to cross. Although early records do not all agree on the date or the exact details, Davison's April 6, 1916 obituary provides some clues:

Milford's founder, J.L. Davison.

"J. L. Davison was one of Milford's first settlers. In 1857 he came to Weeping Water and built a mill. In 1865 or 1866 he moved the mill to Milford. The first dwelling in the town was a tent. When they finished the mill, they lived there with another family, a relative. The first lumber was hauled from Nebraska City." [Author's Note: The relative mentioned was Davison's brother-in-law, of the Reed family. We have one eye-witness account of the erection of this mill recorded by Marcus Castle who later moved to California.]

"A saw mill was erected at Milford which used water power to saw the logs. I myself worked on the dam. Then a big, three-story grain mill was erected by Mr. Davison. Mr. Hackworth was the contractor and builder. I was present and assisted at the raising of the big buildings. Some heavy timbers were used. Everything was all prepared in advance. Only one mistake was made, in that one hole had to be re-bored to fit the heavy bolt that went there (*Early Days In Seward County* by Wm. H. Smith—information from a letter written in 1937)."

One news note in the 1884 *Milford Ozone* tells the story this way: "The grist mill was built in 1867. The first dam built was a 'brush' dam.

The Way It Was

[Author's Note: This probably meant it was built more or less like a beaver dam.] In 1869 Mr. Davison went to Chicago and bought all new machinery to improve the mill." Another news note describes the first wheat burrs as "primitive" since they may have been the ones moved in from the Weeping Water mill. For several years the mill did a booming business. Customers from Saline, Polk, York, Hamilton, Butler, Lancaster, Fillmore, and Hall counties brought grain to be processed. Some came by ox cart from as far as 110 miles away. At times, wagons—many of them pulled by oxen—were lined up as far as the iron bridge waiting to have their milling done. In the spring of 1874, Davison installed a reading room at the mill for the benefit of his waiting customers, which I suppose would qualify as the first library in town. News items usually kept local citizens informed of mill activities: "Mr. Davison will triple the capacity of the mill (*Blue Valley Record*, June 1, 1872)."

"Everyday farmers from as far as 75 to 80 miles west of town can be found at the mill with grain to grind (*Blue Valley Record*, November 30, 1872)."

"A ton of flour is being shipped to Seward each week by Mr. Davison (*Seward Reporter*, July 21, 1874)."

Photo courtesy Jerry Penray.

Eldon Hostetler

Although J. L. Davison in partnership with his brother-in-law Mr. Reed built the mill, eight other people were involved in its operation or ownership in the fifteen years of its existence. About 1875, J. H. Culver (son-in-law of Mr. Davison) bought a half interest in the mill at which time it was again improved and enlarged. Hard times, dry years, and new competition must have taken their toll on the business making it difficult for its owners to meet their financial obligations. By February of 1875, Mr. Smith had filed suit against Mr. Davison, and the case was in the courts for several years. In October of 1879, Culver sold his half interest to a Mr. Webster for $18,000.

Eventually, eight years of litigation that had attracted the attention of the entire country and many leading citizens of the state was brought to a close in February of 1880. Foreclosure proceedings were finished by the spring of 1880, when Mr. Emerson (an early Milford banker) threatened to take over the property. Culver evidently made a trip to New York and brought a man "with money" to redeem his property. At this time, he also sold off part of his land for new town lots, today known as the "Davison and Culver Addition" in Milford. The "man with money" was the Johnson family from Oswego, New York. Already owners of a prominent New York Milling Company, they became partners for a short time. This family also organized the first bank in the Milford community in 1880.

The mill was again enlarged and improved, and the flour was said "to be as good as any in the state." The name was also changed at this time to the Quenchauqua mills, and the capacity was increased to 900 bushels of wheat per day. A new 24' x 60' flour warehouse with a capacity of 4,500 bags of flour was also erected at this time. That fall, Culver and Davison sold their interest in the mill and the property beneath it to Mr. Perry and E. S. Johnson, a brother of Fred Johnson. Mr. Perry soon died and another Johnson brother, James, bought out his interest.

However tragedy soon struck the mill. On November 3, 1882, the mill burned to the ground, destroying much valuable machinery as well as 5,000 bushels of wheat. So ended Davison and Reed's mill—the business that gave Milford its name—located on the Steam Wagon Road's limestone ford. Jerry Penray was successful in buying a picture of the original mill taken about 1880 on the Internet. Needless to say, the pictures on Milford's light poles do not portray this historical structure as it actually looked. However, this is only part of

Milford's mill story, for out of the ashes of the old structure sprung up a new one that far surpassed the original in every category.

Roller Loaf, Kolhonna, and Shogo

Apparently, the city of Milford was truly blooming and booming in 1888-89. This atmosphere must have given the *Milford Nebraskan* newspaper editor fresh courage to brag about Milford's good fortune to the whole world:

"Milford has five enterprises in which all the people of Nebraska are interested: The Industrial Home, the Sanitarium, the Telegraph School, Shogo Island and the Quenchauqua Mills. In the development of Milford as Nebraska's summer resort and the gaining of such enterprises as do not depend upon local trade for existence, lies all hope of the improvement as a town. Having faith in Milford's future, the editor of the *Milford Nebraskan* has undertaken the work of and expense of getting up a boom edition with the sole hope of benefiting in a general way the town to which he owes much for a generous patronage and a liberal forgiveness for many sins of omission and commission (*Milford Nebraskan*, February 15, 1889)."

Although the editor procrastinated somewhat in producing his promised "boom edition," he was not finished telling the world about what he thought was one of Milford's wonders.

"It is customary for Nebraska towns to point with pride to one or more principal enterprises in their midst, and Milford keeps at the front in any procession that is set moving. We point with pride often and justly to the Quenchauqua Flouring Mill. Because it is the largest in the state; because it is equipped with the best machinery; because it is backed with large capital; because its owners are enterprising and public-spirited; because its products are the very best; and because the enterprise is a credit to the town. The foundation of the mill is built upon solid rock, and upon this rises as substantial a stone, brick and iron structure as one could find anywhere. From bottom to top it is filled with the most improved machinery. No money has been spared in this particular, and it is no wonder that the product of the Quenchauqua is found on sale in Maine, Georgia, Tennessee, Washington D.C., and even in London, England. A large amount of new machinery has just been added for the purpose of manufacturing a self raising flap-jack preparation called "Ryeninjun," which is meeting with a ready sale and promises to become an additional manufacturing industry that will give employment to the heads of half a dozen families in our town. In connection with the mill there is a mammoth elevator with a storage capacity of 125,000 bushels; and a flour warehouse with a capacity of 1,500 barrels (*Milford Nebraskan*, July 26, 1889)."

When the first Milford mill, built by Davison, burned to the ground in November of 1882, the rubble was cleared as soon as it was cold. Everything was razed down to solid limestone and a new and larger dam was erected. A new mill was built and the Johnson family was back in the milling business by February 27, 1884. This mill was also known as the Quenchauqua Mills for a number of years and was later known as "Nebraska Corn Mills." The new dam was fourteen feet high, 260 feet long, and was anchored to the rock bottom with large bolts. The 185,000 feet of hard yellow pine lumber used was rein-

Milford's second dam and mill built in 1883-84 after Davison's first dam burned down in 1882. This dam washed out in 1902 and was replaced by the concrete dam many remember. Photo circa 1895 courtesy Seward County Historical Society in Goehner.

forced with 16,000 pounds of iron. The new main mill house was 50' x 65' at the base, with five full stories which towered 85 feet into the skyline. The roof was of mansard-type design, covered with sheet iron.

The walls of the first floor were built of blue limestone eight feet thick at the base tapering to eighteen inches at the top. Eighty cars of limestone were used in constructing the first floor alone, as well as enough bricks in the rest of the building to reach to Lincoln and back, if laid out in a single row. The first floor was cement and contained all the waterwheel driving equipment with its belts and shafts, while the second floor housed twenty sets of Stevens rollers. The third, fourth, and fifth floors were home to purifiers, bran dusters, magnetic separators, and dust collectors, plus other machinery only a professional miller would be familiar with. The top, or fifth floor, contained all the elevating and conveyor tops, reels, wheat graders, and much belting. The mill boasted one-fourth mile of metal spouting and 1,800 feet of elevators, plus one mile of leather belting.

All this machinery was powered by Blue River water fed to a double turbine waterwheel with three different patterns producing 168 horsepower. In 1899, a huge gasoline engine was installed for standby power if needed. This engine literally "blew her stack" less then one year later. In the spring of 1900, a large steam boiler weighing more than thirteen tons replaced this engine. Later news reports indicate this steam plant was also used to generate electricity when the city was "electrified" about ten years later.

This news item from the February 28, 1884 *Milford Ozone* gives us this optimistic report: "The Quenchauqua Mills started operations yesterday. They will turn out a number one flour, and the mill will be run by Johnson and Company. It is the finest and largest in the west, and has the capacity to grind five carloads of wheat in one day, or three carloads of flour in one day."

Grain was transported from the 85,000 bushel storage elevator by a 24-inch rubber conveyor belt, which was 109 feet long and also transported the power to run the elevator. Before the railroad was moved to the south side of the river in 1907, all processed products to be shipped were hauled across the dam on a four-wheeled wagon pulled by horses running on a narrow gauge railroad. A large flour warehouse, 80 x 24 feet, which was located 100 feet east of the mill, had a capacity of ten cars of flour. A horse barn was located 100 feet

Eldon Hostetler

A sketch of Milford's famous Quenchauqua Mills and Elevator built in 1883-84 after the first mill build by Davison in 1867 burned to the ground in 1882. This mill was said to be one of the largest west of the Mississippi River. Suffering two disastrous fires in 1927 and 1934, the mill was closed and torn down.

north of the warehouse to provide shelter for the mill teams. The main office was built of all brick and stone, and contained everything needed to conduct the business of the company.

The mill was owned by a large milling company from Oswego, New York, said to have strong financial backing. The flour soon gained a wide, favorable reputation and had been introduced into ten different states, as well as London and Liverpool in England. The flour was the very best in the state and the mill was capable of competing with the best mills in Minneapolis and New York.

The title of this story is the name of three brands of flour manufactured and sold by the mill in the 1880s. "Shogo" flour took first premium at the Nebraska State Fair for the best spring wheat made in the state, and the bread from this flour also took the premium. At one time, this mill was said to be the largest one in the entire state, as well as one of the largest between Chicago and the West Coast. This news item from the July 7, 1880 *Blue Valley Blade* would suggest the Johnson Brothers were "on the ball" for that day:

The Way It Was

"Johnson and Perry tried to erect a telephone line to use in the business, but it failed to work so they are back to using bells." This is the first mention of anyone using the new invention known as "telephones" in the town. The Johnson family also raised and fed up to 1,000 head of pure bred hogs, using waste grain and by-products from the mill. This story tells about the early history of the second mill built after the original mill burned in 1882. After 1900, information on the mill is rare, although some of our "senior" residents say they remember playing in the old abandoned building. Those who still remember the dam inform me it was made of concrete rather than the planking mentioned in the 1884 story. This news item from the June 15, 1901 *Milford Nebraskan* may explain when the dam was replaced with concrete: "The Milford mill and dam were washed out in the spring floods."

A few older people still remember when the mill processed only corn, although a later news note dated in 1928 said the mill was again installing flour burrs, and would manufacture flour known as "Tee-Pee" brand, as well as a new pancake flour. Older residents say they never heard of this, so I assume this brand did not last long.

One man died in a disastrous mill fire in 1927. Another fire in 1934 damaged the mill to the point where it was not worth repairing and the mill was eventually abandoned.

This mill probably had a tremendous impact on Milford's early economy and growth. A news item from the 1885 paper mentions the fact that farmers living near Beaver Crossing claimed they could get from five to ten cents more per bushel for their wheat by bringing it to Milford. Other farmers came from Seward, Exeter, Friend, Lincoln, and Garland to sell their wheat in Milford. Newspaper accounts would suggest that during its prime, around 1889, the mill imported a good share of the wheat they needed by rail. In 1888 alone, the mill shipped out 202 carloads of flour, 50 cars of bran, while importing 180 carloads of wheat. The economic impact on the city must have been tremendous. [Author's Note: These mill stories were written from information found in Seward County newspapers published in the 1880s. The foundation of this mill is still standing north of the Co-op elevator and the measurements match the information given in an 1885 newspaper. I have been unable to find anyone who remembers how or when the mill was torn down or what happened to the bricks and blue limestone blocks.]

Early Seward County Newspapers

The first newspaper to be published in Seward County, known as the *Nebraska Atlas* was edited and printed in Seward by O.T.B. Williams. The first edition rolled off the press on March 16, 1870. Records disagree as to how long the paper actually survived. One record says it only lasted four months, while another record says it managed to survive until July, 1874. Several news items from the first edition hint at what life was really like in Seward County in the "good old days."

"Our first frame school-house is to be commenced shortly. We are greatly in need of the building, and hope the committee will prosecute the work with vigor. We trust it will be complete in time for summer school."

"A petition is about to be started for the incorporation of our town. We hope to see every name on it."

"Judge J.D. Maine is credited with having raised on his farm in the Oak Grove settlement one hundred and fourteen bushels of corn to the acre, in the previous summer."

"Plenty of good land to the north and west of us, but none in this immediate vicinity."

"There are nearly seven hundred dollars subscribed for the Baptist church edifice. This is most encouraging."

The second oldest county newspaper, the *Blue Valley Record*, was published and printed in Milford by J. H. Culver and H.G. Parsons. The first edition hit the street December 29, 1870. As was common with most early newspaper editors, Mr. Culver left no doubt in his readers minds as to where he stood politically:

The Way It Was

"Morally we shall labor for what we believe to be truth and justice, and shall act upon what we profess. We shall labor for the best interests of the Republican party, not in a partisan spirit, but in a firm belief that it is the true party of progress and reform."

With every copy on file at the Nebraska Historical Society, the *Blue Valley Record* gives us a good record of early happenings in the Milford community from 1871-72.

"We counted 26 teams on First Street on Saturday afternoon."

"We noticed a motto on a prairie schooner as follows: York County, or bust."

"Fresh buffalo meat is on sale for three cents a pound."

"J. L. Davison, of Milford, has completed the largest and best dwelling house in the county."

"The return of a hunting party consisting of J. W. Hickman, Mr. Davis, Ellis Gandy, Elias France, and others carried three loads of buffalo meat. Their game was caught on the Kansas border, south of the Republican."

Markets prices offered in 1871 included: wheat 50 cents; corn is 45 cent; buckwheat 80 cents and butter is 30 cents.

"In 1870, four thousand acres of prairie sod was broken in the county. Wheat was averaging twenty bushels to the acre, oats forty and corn forty-five."

"Walnut Creek Precinct is being enlivened by a revival under the auspices of the Methodist Church, 25 having already been converted."

"A baseball team known as the Milford Bluebelts was organized in town."

"Two young men just starting out in life would like to correspond with the same number of ladies 17 to 20 years old. Object fun, love or any of the attendant consequences."

"We hear rumored that a Vigilante Committee has been formed for the protection of the Homesteaders in the community. This is a move in the right direction, and we want to warn all to be careful about jumping claims in Beaver and Walnut Creek Precincts."

"A woman from Hamilton County, while fishing in the West Blue near Beaver Crossing caught a fish of the salmon variety, weighing in at ten pounds."

"S.N. Bell reports plenty of deer west of town."

"A Post Office has been established at Weldon on Walnut Creek, ten miles west of Milford."

"A party of buffalo hunters passed through Milford on their way home."

Culver and Parsons published a neat little paper, but evidently made little money for their efforts. The paper was published until April, 1873, at which time they bought interest in a Lincoln paper known as the *Lincoln Leader* and moved to that town. The paper they intended to print in Lincoln also proved unprofitable, and Mr. Culver soon moved back to Milford. Having had his fill of the newspaper business, Culver bought half interest in J. L. Davison's (his father- in-law) Milling business. Milford was without a newspaper until 1882. Until that time, The *Seward Reporter* (founded in 1872) did a great job of reporting news from the Milford community. The *Reporter* was published in Seward until 1899, at which time the plant was sold and moved out of town. The *Seward Reporter* provides us with much needed information on the early history of Milford:

"On Wednesday, December 10, 1874, a sad accident cast a gloomy shadow over Milford. Walter Haverstock, 10, Charles Haverstock, 6 and Oliver Maston, 8, were released from school early and broke through the ice on the mill pond while crossing the river. Oliver and Charlie both drowned, while Walter was rescued and survived. The following Sunday the Congregational Church could not hold all who attended the funeral."

"Mr. Noah Stutzman of Milford set a fire on Section 30 Wednesday evening to burn off some grass instead of plowing. The wind blew it over the plowed ground and it burned 20 acres before it was checked. It destroyed 200 bushels of oats, 125 bushels of barley, four tons of hay, 55 bushels of corn and one acre of new trees for his neighbor, H. M. Hazelwood. Stutzman told Hazelwood to come and take all the property he possesses to satisfy the destruction."

"Persons owning valuable dogs had better keep an eye on them. A patent sausage grinder and stuffer are now in the city (July 21, 1875)."

The fourth paper to be published in the county was the *Seward Advocate*. This paper was started in 1877 by W. S. Walker, who published the paper for two years. After traveling to Milford on several investigative trips, Mr. Walker wrote and published some very interesting stories concerning early Milford history. Several years later, J. H. Betzer bought the paper and changed the name to the *Blue Valley Blade* which survived until my day.

The Way It Was

Milford's second paper, the *Seward County Democrat* was established in 1882, by the Alexander Brothers, who later started one of the first drug stores in Milford. No known copies of this paper are on record. Two years later, in 1884, the paper was sold to Professor George Burkett from Michigan, who renamed the paper the *Milford Ozone*. At first Professor Burkett took Horace Boyle as his partner. Later, Mr. Boyle sold his half to H. C. Hensel of Omaha. After five months in the newspaper business, Professor Burkett dropped out to take charge of the Milford school system. Meanwhile, Mr. Hensel bought out his partner and changed the name of the paper one more time, this time calling it the *Milford Nebraskan*.

Mr. Hensel also published and printed the first successful Beaver Crossing newspaper, the *Beaver Crossing Bugle*, from 1879-1887. Three years later he sold the Nebraskan to H. A. Brainard, who sold it to L. O. Howard in 1893. The *Milford Nebraskan* was printed continually until 1909. At this time, Howard sold the paper to William Ketchum. Mr. Ketchum changed the name of the paper to the *Milford Monitor* and published this paper for one year. In September of 1910, he agreed to sell his subscription list to the publisher of the *Blue Valley Blade,* who had agreed to furnish Milford citizens with the latest in local news.

Meanwhile, Mr. Ketchum moved his printing equipment to Bruning, Nebraska, and started a newspaper there. We have no record of what the *Blue Valley Blade* editor did with his old *Monitor* subscription list, a move that was probably not too profitable. By October 5, of 1910 Mr. O' Neill, a total stranger, had arrived in Milford packing his own printing equipment and had already issued his very first edition of the *Milford Review*. This is the first Milford paper many "old-timers" remember. It was, in fact, the last one before the advent of the present day *Milford Times*. Early editions of the *Milford Review* are poorly printed, so it could be assumed Mr. O'Neill did not have the latest and best printing equipment. Most of the early, county papers consisted of about 70 percent syndicated news articles and advertisements, with limited space devoted to local news coverage.

Eldon Hostetler

Dare to Tell the Truth about a Rascal

One change you may have noticed recently in the *Milford Times* is the publication of police and court records. While this may be new to younger *Times* readers, the practice is actually "old hat" for earlier Milford newspaper editors. Humiliating as it may seem, Milford newspapers have been exposing local citizens who tend to flaunt community mores and laws for more than 100 years. Much bolder than the publishers of today, early editors did more than merely report police and court files, they actually expressed their personal opinions and judgments. We 21st century residents would consider it meddling and preachy.

One good example of this so-called "preachy" attitude is recorded in the August 12, 1892 edition of the *Milford Nebraskan*. "Two boys under twelve burglarized several Milford business places, and it is said four to five dollars were taken. Now these boys are entering the life of sinful pleasure at an early age, and ere long will be behind walls denying them of the sorrow and heartache they will cause their parents. We hope the crime will not be repeated, and they will turn from the error of their ways and seek a higher power found only in the salvation offered by God through Jesus Christ his son. Remember now thy creator in the days of thy youth."

Although the names of the boys are not given, I'm sure every person in town knew who the editor was referring to. A second example can be found in a 1902 edition of the *Blue Valley Blade*. Although the paper was printed in Seward, a Milford correspondent submitted the story in connection with his weekly Milford news. The story mentions the fact that a search warrant had been issued giving the county sheriff permission to search a Milford café for illegal liquor he was known to be selling. It would appear the whole town was well aware of the fact that Mr. Businessman was tipped off via a telephone call from Seward by an informant. With the help of the proprietor of an adjoining butcher shop, his liquor stock was quickly transferred through a secret trap door connecting the two business places and just like magic, no liquor was found. The Milford news correspondent felt not only free to criticize the perpetrator of the crime, but also expressed some pretty disparaging opinions concerning nonaction by the Milford Village Board. The Milford correspondent wrote, "This is not the first time his goods has been moved to the butcher shop to prepare the place for a search. Our people are about to catch on that one place is about as bad as the other and next time a warrant will be prepared for both places. This man came here about one year ago, bought out a small restaurant, purchased a government license for selling liquor and, judging from the crowds of people going in and out of his back room, he is doing a nice business.

"Our Village Board members have been perfectly dormant in regard to these matters, but since groundhog day have commenced to breathe, and if the weather does not get too cold, they may do something about it." Two weeks later he had more to say. "The proprietor has been keeping his stock of liquor at his private residence and carries it up as needed. What an outlook for his young wife; we should think he would blush blisters. A keg of beer was on tap in one of our butcher shops last week." (Milford was supposed to be bone dry in 1902.)

"Our attention has been called to a piece of scandal that has been perpetrated at the Evangelical Convention that is in session. Hereafter we will publish all names in such reports. By doing this, we may detain others from running into the clutches of the law and a bad reputation. Be warned young fellows in time (Milford Review, September 1917)."

This comment published in a July 1887, edition of the *Beaver Crossing Bugle* may be one reason the editors of today have toned down their personal opinions.

"Half a dozen Nebraska editors have been arrested under Nebraska's new libel law. This law reflects the worthlessness of the law when an editor can no longer tell the truth about a rascal."

To me, it would appear that many of our 19th century editors felt it their obligation to report violations of community values, thereby hoping to help younger and less mature persons from following the same downward path. Most of us would have to agree this view point might be considered old fashioned today. [Author's note: The *Beaver Crossing Bugle*, one of the first successful Beaver Crossing papers was published in Milford by the *Nebraskan* editor.]

The 1880 editor printed several stories explaining the bad blood existing between the Bowker and Granger families. The 1884 paper carried the story of a husband and wife who upset their wagon east of Milford while attempting to cross Middle Creek, "they were both highly intoxicated." The 1885 editor moaned on and on about the lawlessness prevailing about this time, writing, "the disgraceful rows, now common in the town are a disgrace to the community and demand immediate action to protect the integrity of our city." He then proceeded to blame the "extreme lawlessness" on the overuse of alcohol.

The 1886 editor printed the name and circumstances surrounding Milford native Peter Zehr who left a Milford saloon one night dead drunk relying strictly on his horses to take him home. When the horses turned off on a side road, he nearly froze to death before a rescue party alerted by his wife found him.

The 1891 editor printed the story and the names of three Milford boys Ben Ficke, Conard Schall, and Herman Johnson who made a nuisance of themselves by entering a church house intent on vandalism. Later, they were charged with laughing, making sport, and spitting tobacco juice over the benches and furniture during their court proceedings. They were all levied a healthy fine for their rebellious attitudes and for desecrating the house of God. The 1891 editor also reported the names and details of those involved in a good old-fashioned fist fight that took place in the local saloon. Eli Emmel and Lon Bacon were each fined $5.20 by the County Judge payable to the county school tax fund. The 1887 paper mentions the facts and name of a "playboy" type husband fetched in by the county sheriff who was said to have "taken up with the hired girl."

One "Hollywood" type love triangle that happened in the Ruby area in 1891 is reported in some detail. Seems like a local wife, Mrs. John Linquest scooted off to Lincoln with her lover, Fred Tracy soon after her husband left for Denver. A want ad in the 1894 paper placed by J. D. Troyer threatened to harm anyone who procured alcohol for a certain Stutzman. The 1900 editor gave full coverage to a local husband and wife struggle featuring Gus Herman and his wife. This incident climaxed with several gun shots being fired and could have ended in tragedy. All names are given as well as the names of the relatives who were forced to play a role in the incident. One year later, another embarrassing follow-up story was published concerning the same incident.

In 1902, the Seward County Sheriff was forced to make a trip to Michigan to bring back a twenty-year-old Milford man, Albert Troyer "to face his responsibility" regarding a young Lincoln girl. Personal details are printed in a 1903 edition involving Rosa (Barth) Wheeler, and a marriage that lasted only several months. Details and dollar amounts concerning the divorce settlement are also documented.

Names and details were often printed concerning community people thought to be "focused slightly off of center in their sanity." The decision reached by the "County Sanity Board" was often reported to the general public, as well as the place to which they would be committed. Other names and details are given concerning the manufacture of illegal booze in the city, one incident as late as 1935. Probably the granddaddy of all exposures by the press occurred in October of 1923 concerning the Vajgrt vs. Anton Lana murder and trial. This murder, committed about five miles southeast of Milford, was well covered by both the Milford and Seward newspapers. During the trial, which was held in Seward, two Seward newspapers filled the entire front page with the proceedings printing every little, lurid detail. The story, and picture of the fifteen-year-old girl involved, now in my possession, came from the *Lincoln Journal Star* newspaper. (More on this incident in a later story.)

Exciting News from the Blue Valley Record

Headline news appearing in the July 20, 1871 issue of the ***Blue Valley Record: Coal Discovered At Milford. 12-ft. vein found at depth of 47 ft.***

"It has been supposed for a number of years that there was a coal deposit beneath the surface at this place. Various reasons have been given, and experienced miners have substantiated this belief. For four miles along the bed of the Blue River can be found a stratum of limestone which extends from three fourth miles north of Milford to Mr. Rhubles farm, three and three fourth miles south. A team can be driven these four miles on a smooth rock service in the bed of the river, except at the rapids where the upper layers of the rock are broken. Why this portion of the Blue River is specially favored remains a mystery to all. Yet, those who are familiar with coal regions have only reported indications of coal within this belt. While there were many strong in the belief that coal existed in this locality, no one had made a move to throw light on the subject until this summer, when Joseph Stockman, aided by Frederick Scheserman, both living one half mile north of this place, commenced sinking a shaft. For three months they have labored persistently, employing from two to five hands. Indications of coal had been noticed from the first, but the parties operating did not want anything published, nor did we desire to mention it until something definite was determined. Mr. Stockman now makes the following statement, which will be gladly received by all: 'We struck a bed of solid coal at a depth of 47 feet from the surface. At a depth of 27 feet we struck a stratum of lime rock through which we bored eleven feet. We then came to a hard gray sand rock eight feet in thickness; below this we struck a thin layer of rock two or three inches in thickness, and below that we found the slate rock so universally overlaying coal beds. We next struck the coal into which we bored four and one half feet. The vein is thought to be twelve or fifteen feet in thickness, and the limestone caption will render it more easy to work and add materially to the value of the mine.' Mr. Stockman's energy and preservation deserve special commendation, not only from the community, but from the entire state. Let their example be followed by others, and one great objection to settlement in Nebraska will be removed and there will be fuel enough for every man's farm."

Mr. Stockman lived on the farm now owned by Richard Hauder. Several older people living in Milford today remember seeing the mouth of the shaft, which they remember as being nailed shut with planks at the time. Public meetings were held in an attempt to raise money to proceed with the mining, but evidently there were no takers. Later reports said the vein was only seven-feet thick, which may be one reason the project was soon dropped. Several years later, after Joseph Stockman failed to return home with his milk cows, a search party found him dead in his pasture. In 1901, it was reported that well-driller Jake Boshart was searching for coal southwest of Milford along the West Blue. He reported, "No coal has been found yet at 96 ft. but the prospects are looking good."

Seward County Geography

Seward County's Mason-Dixon Line

From their earliest school days, most Americans remember the Mason-Dixon line made famous about the time of the Missouri Compromise in 1820. At the time of the Civil War, this line was known as the dividing line between the slave holding and the non-slave-holding states, usually referred to as the division point between the North and the South.

An imaginary line existed in Seward County from about 1860 to 1875, often referred to as Seward County's Mason-Dixon Line. Having no perfectly defined boundary, this line could best be described as a north-south line where Milford's political influence stopped and Seward's influence began. The story of the county's organization is told by O. T. B. Williams, who was asked to prepare a centennial history of the county to be read at the fourth of July celebration in 1876. It was later published in a Seward history book.

"In 1865 under the territorial laws of Nebraska, Seward County was yet unorganized and was attached to Lancaster County for judicial purposes. In October of that year the commissioners called for an election for county officers throughout the territory to be held in Seward at the general election. At this election the following named gentlemen were elected as the Board of Commissioners for Seward County: W. M. Imlay of Seward, W. J. Thompson of Walnut Creek, and H. W. Parker of Camden. J. L. Davison was elected probate judge, W. E. Chapin was elected sheriff, Thomas West was elected clerk, and C. J.

Neihardt was elected treasurer. The northern half of the county was organized into Seward and Oak Precincts, while the southern half was divided into Camden, Milford, and Beaver Crossing Precincts. It was evident even as early as 1866 that the settlers in the northern and southern parts of the county were not going to work together harmoniously in their county organization. They were men of more than average intellect and the jealousies arising from the differences in locality and the aspiring dispositions of many of the sectional leaders were the source of a constant agitation throughout the county (Reprinted in the *Seward Fourth of July Book,* Jane Graff)."

In 1888, W. W. Cox, early Seward County historian wrote, "Milford was founded by Davison in April of 1864, and then the long struggle commenced between the people of the south part of the county and those of the north part as to whom the prize of the County Seat should belong." The southern part of the county had far more people, with settlements at Camden, West Mills, Walnut Creek, Beaver Crossing, and Milford. The south also enjoyed the advantage of the territorial and steam wagon roads located in their backyard, which would have been about as advantageous as having Interstate I-80 near your town today.

Since Camden was the largest city in the county at the time, they dreamed of their city becoming the county seat, but were sadly disappointed in the vote take in November of 1867. The results of this vote left Milford and Seward to fight for the prize. Seward County Clerk, Mr. Reed, (who just happened to be from Milford) manipulated the votes to the point where Milford won by several votes. Camden and Milford soon appeared to be engaged in a little feud of their own, and many Camden residents shifted their loyalty to the Seward camp. One early county resident reported that since both Parker and Davison owned mills, stiff competition may have caused intense friction.

The north vs. south squabble continued for years and reads more or less like the story of two headstrong brothers fighting over their father's estate, or two small children fighting over the same toy. Several versions are recorded by early Seward County historians, and each one tells the story somewhat differently. This story contains accounts of what some felt was vote count fraud, arrests of commissioners, lawsuits and counter suits, surreptitious visits with state legislators, arrests of board members, theft of records from the Milford courthouse, plus general hard feelings between the citizens of all three towns. Northern politicians accused Mr. Reed of "maladministration" in office. Milford may have just assumed that since they were declared "Shiretown," they were in the driver's seat. But northern county residents did not give up in their quest for the prize. One other factor contributing to the defeat of Milford was the fact that many southern county residents supported a wild proposal by the railroad to plat a new county seat town, one in the exact center of the county. For all practical purposes, by 1871 the fight was over and Seward was declared the winner. But Milford had fought a tough battle, and was still not ready to concede defeat. A note in the May 22, 1872 *Blue Valley Record* said, "Steps will be taken to erect a courthouse in Milford this season."

It would appear it took many years for the two towns to make peace and completely bury the hatchet. Milford was rather subdued when they lost out in the early railroad struggles, as well as the county seat fight. By 1872, it was all over and Seward was declared "king of the county hill." Seward County historian, W. W. Cox, spoke to future generations, writing, "Looking backwards through the years, we see many things that were done in haste and anger that were born of prejudice, and that we should all be heartily ashamed of. We were many times misled by unscrupulous lawyers into snares that cost us dearly. Our time and our treasures were sacrificed without stint. In many instances our prejudice and our ambition got away with our better judgment. The county seat cost many of us more money and hard labor than it was worth, while those who lost it were still worse off. It is our advice to the children: never engage in a county seat contest, for when a stubborn fight ensues, it will cost more than it is worth."

Milford's Nebraska City Connection

Many would agree that towns the size of Milford that are lucky enough to be situated on or near Interstate 80 have a distinct advantage over their counterparts. Because of the popularity of one early pioneer trail linking Nebraska City with southern Seward County, Milford holds the honor of being the first town to be organized in Seward County. The majority of the early western emigrants

(1841-1860) destined for Oregon or California came up the Mississippi-Missouri River system to the St. Joseph, Atchison, or Leavenworth vicinity before embarking on a long covered wagon trip to the "promised land" on what was known as the Oregon Trail. Seward County missed out on all of this early action because the county was located nearly fifty miles away from this tremendously popular trail. Thousands of early settlers made the long trip to new homes in the west on this trail, thereby completely bypassing Seward County. However, from 1862 to the completion of the Union Pacific railroad to Grand Island in 1866, early Milford settlers were privileged to experience and profit from what must have been an exciting era in the Nebraska City community. The discovery of gold in Colorado and Montana (1858-62) created a sudden influx of travelers destined west. Alarmed by the numbers of white settlers traveling through and settling on their lands, some Indian groups became hostile, requiring more soldiers for protection. As forts were built to house those soldiers, tons of freight was needed.

Before 1860, most of this freight destined for Colorado, Utah, and Montana came up the Missouri River by steamboat and was transported west by thousands of wagons pulled by mules and ox teams. During the late 1850s, several large freighting companies, looking for a shorter and drier route to Colorado, chose Nebraska City as their home base.

The earliest route to Ft. Kearny from Nebraska City, known as the Ox-Bow Trail, turned north, crossed Salt Creek at Ashland from where it followed the Platte River to a spot near Grand Island before joining the Old Oregon Trail. One of the largest freighting firms in the business, Russell, Majors & Waddell, spent more than $300,000 improving docks and warehouse facilities to meet the expected demand for additional freight.

Before moving his headquarters to Nebraska City, Majors had demanded and was promised that the town lay out and develop a shorter route, one directly west from Nebraska City. When the town failed to do the job as promised, Majors hired Nebraska City engineer, Augustus Harvey to survey a new route. Milford founder, J. L. Davison, who lived near Saltillo on Salt Creek, was one of those hired to help. Using four mules pulling a walking plow, a shorter route was marked by plowing a furrow from Salt Creek to the spot where the new trail intersected the Oregon Trail.

The Way It Was

Somewhat shorter and straighter than the old route, this trail was known by various names. While Nebraska City citizens preferred to call it the "Great Central Airline Route" it was also known as the "Nebraska City Cut-Off," "The Territorial Road," or the "Military Supply Road." This trail entered Seward County about six miles south of Milford near the spot where the town of Camden soon sprang to life. From here it followed the north side of the West Blue to West Mills, crossed Walnut Creek northeast of Beaver Crossing and Beaver Creek several miles northwest of Beaver Crossing before entering York County. Using bold headlines Nebraska City newspapers wasted no time in introducing the new road to the public.

The March 30, 1860 edition of *The People's Press* reported, "THE NEW ROAD TO THE MINES! A STRAIGHT ROAD! SEVENTY-FIVE MILES SAVED."

While some historians feel this claim was somewhat exaggerated, mostly in an effort to humiliate their nearest rival Omaha, it was a busy and well-traveled road. One record mentions that a bridge started in the spring of 1861, was finally finished in 1862, while another source reports early travelers were forced to cross the North Blue on a man-made rock ford for at least a year. The bridge was built and paid for by Otoe County residents by issuing $2,500 in bonds.

When are they ever going to build better roads?

Not only was this the first bridge built in Seward County, it also touched off a period of booming prosperity for the southern half of the county. It has been estimated that 65-70 percent of all the freight destined for Colorado and Utah in 1865-66 passed over this road. In 1865, Nebraska City was headquarters for 18 freighting firms which when combined moved an estimated 8 million pounds of freight west. [Information concerning the Nebraska City freight boom from early newspaper accounts and from the book; *From The Missouri to the Great Salt Lake*, by William E. Lass, p.p 114-143.]

From 1858 to 1865 Nebraska City was well known as a "boom town." With a population equal to Milford of 1,922 residents (29 more than Omaha at the time) it must have been a hustling, bustling city. By 1863, the largest freighting company, the Bryams Brothers, were using 1,357 wagons to move 7.8 million pounds of freight. This job required the help of 1,788 men, 8,912 oxen and 1,156 mules. One man left the city with 850 turkeys headed for Denver. During the early days of the Civil War, freight and mail normally transported on several southern routes was shifted north to the safer conditions found in Nebraska. Before 1864, most of this freight was bypassing Milford by about six miles. But things were about to change. In the summer of 1862, Joseph R. Brown, Indian Agent, fur trader, and member of the Minnesota State Militia, showed up in Nebraska City packing big dreams and still bigger plans. Mr. Brown announced that he was interested in supplying the Colorado mines with freight hauled west by steam power. Brown, who was usually known as "General" Joseph Brown was greeted enthusiastically by Nebraska City residents and newspaper editors. Brown assured local residents that he selected their city and road because he felt it was the best and shortest route to the Colorado gold mines. Sensing a good opportunity to put their town on the map, city officials and local citizens gave him their heartiest blessings. His number one request was for the city to improve their road west, by bridging Salt Creek and the North Blue.

Once more, J. L. Davison was among those chosen to either stake out a new road or improve the old one. Davison, who was living one mile west of the new Camden bridge, was already familiar with the famous limestone bottom Indian ford located about six miles north of Camden. Davison realized that with some modification this would be a good spot for the extra-heavy steam tractor to cross the North Blue without erecting a heavy-duty bridge. Leaving the old trail at Yankee

The Way It Was

The original limestone Indian "ford" across the Blue River. When L. L. Davison built an oak bridge in 1875, the ford was no longer used. This is the "ford" by the mill from which Milford was named.

Hill, this new road went due west on what is now A Street and passed slightly north of what is now Pleasant Dale. From there it more or less followed the same road used today from Pleasant Dale to Grover. Crossing the limestone ford, the road followed First Street through Milford, heading west and slightly north until intersecting the older trail near the Walnut Creek crossing northeast of Beaver Crossing on what is now the Van Dorn Street Road.

It was this limestone ford, located on the proposed Steam Wagon Road, combined with Davison's mill built in 1867 that gave the city of Milford her name. One source would suggest that the huge steam tractor was built in New York and shipped by steamboat to the Missouri River docks. Apparently, early historians are unable to give an exact date Brown tried his bold experiment, although it must have been sometime in early 1863. I can easily believe that all 1,922 Nebraska City residents, plus any strangers in town, dropped whatever they were doing to watch the mammoth steam tractor belch black smoke as it snorted to life. Some probably shook their heads in disbelief as ten large wagons, each loaded with three tons of freight, were hooked in tandem to the tractor. The puffing, snorting machine did make it out of the docks and up the long sloping Main Street. About two miles west of town the giant steamer shuddered and clattered before coming to a complete stop.

Stories vary as to the reason for the early breakdown of the tractor. One account hints that the main drive shaft broke due to weight overload when the wagons hit soft ground. Although Brown left immediately for New York to search for repairs, his plans were drastically altered by the Sioux Indian rebellion in Minnesota about this time. Fearing for the safety of his family, Brown hurried home to find his family unharmed, but he did join the Minnesota State Militia in taking punitive military action. Meanwhile, his associates performed makeshift repairs and succeeded in moving the steam tractor back to Arbor Lodge.

Returning to Nebraska without the parts in 1868, he dismantled the machine for scrap iron in 1869. Brown died one year later in 1870. Although Brown's bold experiment proved to be a complete fiasco, he did leave a lasting legacy. From this time on the trail from Nebraska City, through Milford to Ft. Kearny was known as the "Steam Wagon

This team tractor designed to pull ten loaded freight wagons on the old "Steam Wagon Road" was supposed to cross the Blue River on the limestone ford. It never got within 75 miles of Milford (1863-1864).

Road." Brown probably dropped out of the Colorado freight race because of faster than expected progress being made by the Union Pacific railroad. Although the heavy, noisy steam tractor never did reach the Blue River, Milford owes its very existence to the search for a faster, cheaper way to move freight to the Colorado gold mines. Considered an utter failure for moving freight, it did put Milford on the map, bringing thousands of new settlers through the city. Since many liked what they saw, they took up homesteads in the vicinity.

Although Milford owes its founding to the fame of the old limestone bottom ford, this crossing actually played a secondary role in Milford's early economic growth and history. Few modern day fathers would think it safe to give their wives or children permission to cross the Blue River on the ford using a team and wagon. From what I remember about horses and wagons, it must have been a risky undertaking, especially during high water. Since no newspapers were published in Seward County prior to 1870, we have no "heroic" river crossing stories to share from that era. We could only guess at the number of travelers who used the new "Steam Road" through Milford (before a bridge was erected) compared to the number who used the older trail through Camden, where a bridge was finished by 1862. Businessman that he was, Mr. Davison realized the lack of a bridge was limiting Milford's chances to compete with Camden, Seward, and Beaver Crossing.

In the spring of 1866, Milford citizens decided to build a second bridge in Seward County. Searching up and down the river for several miles, they selected good, straight oak trees for piling. Additional oak logs were used for stringers and oak lumber for crossbracing. The entire deck was then covered with small wooden poles and prairie grass hay, topped off with a thick layer of dirt. One writer observing the bridge in 1870 said, "This bridge was what might be called 'a wild west bridge.'" It was a true representation of pioneer art, calling to mind the adage "necessity is the mother of invention." Believe it or not, this bridge, said to be 160 feet long, lasted until 1875, at which time a new $10,000 iron bridge was erected. Said to be one first of its kind erected in the state, this bridge served the community until 1909. While the old oak bridge was probably not a beautiful structure, it did encourage more travelers to use the new road through Milford. Mr. Davison rode east and west to promote the advantages of traveling through Milford using his shorter and better road. Although

Milford's very own covered bridge was located between Milford and Ruby.

Covered bridge between Milford and Ruby, 1895.

B&M trains were arriving in Crete by 1871, many settlers were still traveling west the "old fashioned way," using oxen and horses. News notes from the 1872 *Blue Valley Record* report more:

"Emigration has commenced once more, and long lines of covered wagons are seen making their way down towards Milford (April, 1871)."

"A total of 64 emigrant wagons passed through Milford during March, and these were only the ones we counted."

The Way It Was

"Actuated by curiosity, one of our citizens, living two miles west of town counted the number of teams passing his residence from morning to night and counted 127."

"We notice large droves of cattle passing through Milford destined for new homes on the West Blue."

"'Where are they all going?' is the question, as Emigrants continue to pass through."

"A drove of 1,600 sheep passed through Milford on their way to Colorado. They are averaging ten miles per day."

"About 200 Omaha Indians passed through Milford on their way to the Republican."

Just like today, living on a good road has its advantages, since travelers always seem to have needs and usually carry cash. It has often been said that from 1864 to 1870, early Milford area settlers had one unified goal—that of attracting additional people to settle in the community. By 1870, nearly every parcel of good government land had already been homesteaded. Settlers arriving after 1870 were forced to buy land from the railroads.

Although we traditionally think of the Milford community as an agricultural community, in 1865 less than 150 acres of prairie sod had been broken in the entire county. Few of the earliest settlers lived on the proceeds they made from farming, since it was next to impossible to haul large amounts of grain to the nearest cash market located in Nebraska City. Consequently, most early Seward County settlers made their living by catering to strangers. Desperate travelers would pay any price for goods and services. Some early settlers sold prairie hay for six cents a pound and corn for as much as four dollars a bushel. Blacksmiths who could repair wagons or shoe horses were in big demand. Those having extra oxen, horses or mules for sale made easy money by selling to emigrants needing replacement animals. In other words, Milford's early "Interstate 80," the Steam Wagon Road was truly Milford's window of opportunity to growth and economic prosperity.

The 1872 editor of the *Blue Valley Record* seemed thrilled to report, "Milford presented a lively appearance Saturday afternoon. We counted 34 teams on the streets." By 1911, Beaver Crossing residents bragged, "There are now 20 autos and 3 motorcycles within the city limits of Beaver Crossing." Reminiscing in 1924, the Milford editor said, "In 1914, the *Review* carried a story of 68 autos and 61 buggies seen on Milford streets. Well, last Saturday night, 265 autos and one buggy were counted on the same street."

In May of 1924 the same Milford editor reported that more than 300 automobiles were parked on the East Fairview Church grounds where the Iowa and Nebraska Conference was in session. In other words, automobiles were taking over, while poor old Dobbin and Nellie were being put out to pasture. But Milford had one major problem. Community roads were not ready for the new "automobile age" in 1923. This news item from a 1923 paper reports more.

"Fifty people, mostly tourists, were delayed in Milford by the muddy roads on the old D.L.D. Many are camped in town and many are in Shogo Park Camp Grounds. Some are taking advantage of the Milford Hotel and Milford cafes, but most are doing their own cooking in the campgrounds. Monday, in spite of the mud, eleven cars put on chains, formed a caravan and started west."

While this little episode of happy misery sounds innocent enough, the editor had previously printed some bragging words.

"The D.L.D., or Harding Memorial Highway, is known as the best dirt road on the earth. Cars from six states were seen recently in Milford."

In other words, while unsuspecting, innocent tourists were stuck in a local mud hole camping on mosquito-infested grass and eating cold beans out of tin cans, Milford City fathers were still proud of their famous road.

Another newspaper item proves just how indifferent town fathers really were.

"From 6 a.m. to 9 p.m., Clinton Tift and Melvin Trabert counted traffic on the old D.L.D. with the count being Monday, 964, Tuesday, 1061, and Wednesday, more than 1200." Well, at least they weren't bragging about their road having just received an Oscar, or even a Triple A rating!

Milford area roads were not all that unusual for that era. From only a few cars in 1910, automobile registration in Nebraska jumped to 205,000 by 1920. In 1909, seventy-seven counties had no improved roads whatsoever. The State Aid Bridge Act passed by the legislature in 1911 shared funds for the construction for more and better bridges. Local taxes also increased from 82 cents per capita in 1904 to $1.51 per capita by 1919, largely due to the demand for better roads. By 1914, only 1.5 percent of Nebraska's roads were graveled.

The Way It Was

The Federal Road Act, passed on July 16, 1916, finally provided funds to upgrade Nebraska roads. By 1921, 5,619 miles had been selected as post roads or roads to be improved. U.S. 38, (now known as Highway No. 6) extending, from Omaha to Lincoln and then on to Colorado, was one of those chosen for development. A two-cents-per-gallon gas tax instituted in 1925 was raised to four cents by 1930 to provide additional funds for road improvement. By 1924, Highway 6 was bricked from Lincoln to Emerald and graveled from Emerald to Milford. One older native remembered that two of the Schlegel Brothers were hired to keep the road smooth. They used a primitive type tractor and a road grader.

Before 1924, the road was known as the O.L.D. (Omaha, Lincoln to Denver). After the federal government took charge, it was known as the D. L. D. (Detroit, Lincoln Denver). Before the road was paved, (1930-32) many improvements were made in and around Milford. Milford citizens, protesting plans to reroute the road around Milford, were convinced by a visit from the governor to drop their opposition. Other improvements included the bricking of Main Street in 1919, plus additional concrete pavement in 1927. Milford, your roads have come a long way since 1900.

What a thrill it must have been for local residents traveling to Lincoln for the first time on the new, four lane concrete road known as Interstate 80! Reaching Milford in 1964, you could drive to York, Aurora, Grand Island, or even to Colorado just two years later. The first thought that comes to mind is the tobacco advertisement aimed at "liberated" females popular about that time, "You have come a long way baby." Milford roads have improved about a thousand percent since the first motor cars were seen on Milford streets around 1904.

The Forgotten City of Camden

Merchants in the town of Camden, a small town located four miles south and 2.5 miles east of Milford, were literally doing a "land office" business in 1866. Founded several years before Seward or even Lincoln, the town was located on what could have been considered "Interstate 80" of that day, or the Nebraska City to Fort Kearney

Milford Post Office, 1890.

Oregon Trail Cutoff Route. In 1858, one of the largest freight hauling establishments at that time, Russell, Majors & Waddell, decided to move their headquarters to Nebraska City. In 1863, 75 percent of all the freight unloaded at Nebraska City docks destined for Denver, Salt Lake, and other points west was transported over this new "cutoff" road. The discovery of gold in the Colorado Pikes Peak area about this time provided the impetus for the transportation and freight boom which followed. In 1860 the firm employed 602 men, who used 5,687 oxen to move 3 million pounds of freight west. By 1863, Nebraska City was said to be home base for 18 freighting companies.

This route entered Seward County four miles south of Milford, passed through West Mills and crossed Walnut Creek near Beaver Crossing before entering York County. The new route was much closer than the old route through Ashland, which more or less followed the Platte Valley. Located on the only bridge crossing the North Blue one mile above the spot where the North Blue and West Blue join, Camden appeared to be a booming place during the 1860s. Built by Nebraska City Enterprises in 1860, this bridge became an important link in moving freight west, at least until the Union Pacific railroad was completed in the late 1860s. The Camden bridge was soon known as a popular stopping off point for weary travelers, at times having as many as a hundred wagons camped for the night.

The Way It Was

Milford's first schoolhouse built in 1867.

In 1862, A. J. Wallingford settled near the bridge, while J. L. Davison (who helped to mark out the new trail) opened his ranch one mile west of the bridge site. In 1864, Mr. Davison sensed greater economic opportunity available four miles upstream at the limestone ford, where the new Steam Wagon Road would soon cross the river. Davison moved his ranch to the present spot of Milford.

In 1865, Hiram H. Parker left Beatrice and moved to the bridge site where he proceeded to erect a $15,000 grist and sawmill. He also staked out a new 160-lot town he named Camden. Customers from as far west as Hall County patronized the new mill. In 1866, Vose and Buchanan open a General Store, a Mr. Thompson opened a blacksmith shop and Fordyce Roper (partner of Mr. Parker) built a new hotel.

In 1863, mail routes were established between Columbus and Camden, from Brownsville and Plattsmouth to Camden, and in 1868, from Beatrice to Milford through Camden. For several years, settlers from several counties west received their mail at Camden. In 1863, (some records say 1865) a post office was opened with James Johnson as Postmaster. In the winter of 1866-67, the town opened the first public school in the county, District No. 1, which had an enrollment of

Eldon Hostetler

A rare photo of Milford's first railroad depot located in what was known in 1879 as "East Milford." In 1885, the town petitioned the government to change their name to Grover. All trains arrived in this depot until 1907 at which time the tracks were relocated in Milford and a new depot was built.

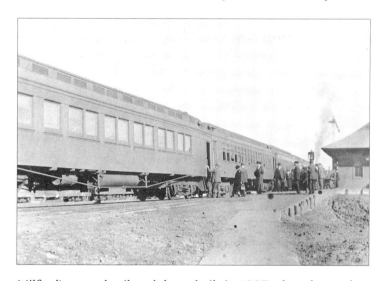

Milford's second railroad depot built in 1907 when the tracks were moved into Milford. Before the move, all Milford rail business was handled in Grover. Photo dated 1916.
Photo courtesy of the Seward County Historical Society in Goehner.

twenty-seven pupils in 1866. Said at one time to have had over fifty residents, today the spot of the town is remembered by few, and the site is marked only by a small stone marker erected on the spot where the first school house stood. Another early landmark, the Camden Cemetery, is located one-half mile north and one-forth mile east of the original town site.

The town's demise could be mostly attributed to some of the "high handed" tactics exercised by the B&M Railroad people. Although the main line tracks west towards Denver were promised to Camden at one time, the railroad decided at the last moment to build the line six miles south in Saline County, thereby completely bypassing Seward County. The loss of traffic on the cutoff trail and the loss of mill business after Mr. Davison erected his saw and gristmill in Milford all helped to take the "boom" out of Camden. Rejected as the county seat, plus the loss of the new railroad to Crete completely isolated Camden from her neighbors. The town soon suffered a slow, painful death.

A Town Named Grover

Most Milford residents know where "Grover" is located, but few know why it was given that name or the reason another town was located on the east side of the river. From an early 1876 news story we discover in that year the spot was just an empty prairie. The new town was first platted in 1879 by L. D. Chaddoch, who offered to lay out thirty acres for town lots and give them free to anyone who would build a house or a business on the property. The town, at first called East Milford, was built after 1879 when the new railroad came to Milford. Since the first tracks did not cross the river into Milford, all early railroad business was taken care of on the east side of the river. One early story tells us the first railroad depot was located one half mile from town. Grover applied for and was granted a post office on November 9, 1885. This office served the town until October 31, 1908, at which time all mail was directed to the Milford post office.

The first train depot, as well as early grain elevators were all located in or near what was Grover. The towns were connected by two bridges. Quoting early Milford resident D. F. Todd: "Before the year 1899 and a little while after, there were two bridges over the river. Many people think and say that there has always just been one bridge, but I have pictures to prove that there was two, both one way, one to go, and one to come back." In 1907 when the tracks were rerouted into Milford, the elevators were moved across the river on rail ties stacked in the river bed. Many houses were also moved from this section to new locations in the southwest part of town (from an interview with Todd by Milford High School seniors in 1932).

Before 1886 the town of Grover was always referred to as "East Milford" and even had its own school system, plus a tub factory, and two grocery stores. Several early churches also met in various buildings located in Grover, usually in the school house. About 1885 the town citizens decided they no longer wanted to be known as "East Milford" and filed a petition with the U.S. Government to have their town renamed "Cleveland" in honor of Grover Cleveland. This name was rejected by the government. The reason given for the denial was Nebraska already had the name Cleveland registered. A later note in the June 19, 1885 paper informs "East Milford has now changed its name to 'Grover' by petition." This name was evidently accepted and today we could say this may have been a rare case where the first choice of a last name was rejected, while the second choice of a first name was accepted. From this time on, Milford continued to grow, while Grover appeared to shrink. After the depot and the grain elevators were moved to Milford, the town gradually declined in importance. The *Milford Nebraskan* editor hinted there may have been some hard feelings between the two towns: "Some of our citizens are now clamoring to annex the town of Grover." Milford was soon "king of the hill," while Grover citizens, although not everyone was happy to submit to their older brother, Milford had at least honored their favorite politician.

How our Towns Were Named

Most Milford natives are well aware of the fact that Milford was named by J. L. Davison soon after he built his saw and gristmill near the old limestone bottom ford in 1866 or 1867. What is now known as "Grover" originally known as "East Milford" was named "Grover" in honor of President Grover Cleveland.

Contrary to what many Seward County residents have heard, Beaver Crossing was not named after that "proverbial" four-legged animal attempting to cross the state. The town was named after the spot where pioneer wagons crossed Beaver Creek, where a post office named Beaver Crossing was opened in 1867. However, the crossing and the post office were actually located four miles west of the present location of the town. In 1871 the town was moved to its present site soon after Ross Nicholas erected a dam and flour mill on the present site of the town. T. H. Tisdale, the postmaster, moved his store and the post office to the new site, bringing the original name of the crossing with him.

Seward was named in honor of William Henry Seward who served as Secretary of State under President Abraham Lincoln from 1861 to 1869.

Goehner was named after John F. Goehner, prominent Seward merchant and state senator. Mr. Goehner was very helpful in securing a second railroad for the county in 1887.

The town we now know as Cordova was first named "Hunkins" after the Benjamin Hunkins family. This name was ruled unacceptable by the post office people, feeling it could easily be confused with Hoskins in Wayne County. Denied their first choice, early natives chose a name similar to Cordoba, the name of a city in Spain, not used by any other town in the United States.

Said to be the only town by this name in the United States, Staplehurst was named by a family that came from Staplehurst, England. This name was chosen by the daughter of the man who established the first post office in 1878. There appears to be no rhyme or reason for selecting the name Tamora for the new town born when the B&M Railroad decided to extend its tracks from Seward to York in 1876. The original post office site was known as "Lafayette." Some say the four land contributors each wanted the town to be named for themselves. Unable to come to a consensus, the parting words were usually, "Let's talk about it tomorrow." Using a frontier pronunciation, this name stuck.

Some county historians say the name Pleasant Dale was suggested by Milford native, Captain J. H. Culver. Culver and his men often stopped near the site while marching to Lincoln on their way to a training camp located near old Capitol Beach. Other suggested names included "Bestville," named after early settler Thomas Best, and "Spiritdale," a name suggested by evangelist James Lier.

Needing a spot for a railroad depot south of the "Oak Grove" settlement in 1872-73, the Midland Pacific Railroad people platted a new town we know today as Garland. Originally named "Germantown," because many of the natives were originally from Germany, the name was officially changed to Garland on November 11, 1918. The name Germantown proved so unpopular during World War I, that the town council decided to rename the town after the first resident to die in the war. Raymond Garland, who died from the flu while on his way to France, was the recipient of this honor.

Bee was platted as a depot stop by the railroad in 1887 to 1888, and was given this name because it is located in B Precinct.

While most historians say Utica was either named after the city in New York, or the famous Mohawk Indian Chief, the name actually goes back to the early days of the Roman Empire, when a city named Utica was located on the North African coast.

A post office, first established north of Milford in 1883, was named Ruby in honor of Ruby Holdrege, daughter of the first railroad depot agent.

Most Seward County historians agree the town of Camden was named after the city in New Jersey.

Three other towns, located in the Milford and Beaver Crossing vicinity, that at one time boasted having post offices are now extinct. West Mills, home of the first grist mill in the county was named after the mills owner, Thomas West. A post office was established on January 22, 1868 and discontinued on December 3, 1884. On March 13, 1882 the name West Mills was changed to Norval, named in honor of T.L. Norval, a prominent member of the State Supreme Court.

State and local historians disagree on two more so called "paper towns," both located on Walnut Creek about nine miles west of Milford. A news note from the July 20, 1871 *Blue Valley Record* newspaper mentions that a post office was established at Weldon located ten miles west of Milford (on what is now Van Dorn Street) and that William G. Keen was recommended as the new postmaster. Elton A. Perky, author of *Nebraska Place Names* mentions a town named Neldon where a post office was established on February 13, 1871, and discon-

The Way It Was

Gold mining in 1895. Some of the machinery used in an attempt to separate the gold from the gravel. All methods failed and the gold rush was over by 1900.

tinued on October 13, 1871. Early Seward County historians, Cox and Waterman shed little light on the subject.

A second "paper town" located at one time several miles south of Weldon is also mentioned by the *Blue Valley Record* newspaper editor in 1872. "Pittsburgh is the name of the now proposed city to be built at the mouth of Walnut Creek by Bradford and Scott for Beardsly and Roggen. They will sell season contracts for peat for fuel at $3.00 per ton and lime at 15 cents a bushel to all actual residents." Said to be the brainchild of early Beaver Crossing area settler, Chris Lazenby after he discovered peat, silicon, and other minerals present in the community, dreamed of his new city becoming a second glass manufacturing center similar to Pittsburgh, Pennsylvania. Perky reports the city received a post office on May 2, 1873, and at one time boasted having twenty-five residents. The post office was discontinued on April 23, 1875. Beaver Crossing historian, John Henry Waterman declares the city never had a post office and was actually named "Peetsburgh." Seward County land records show that Mr. Lazenby's land was laid out in town lots in 1872.

Eldon Hostetler

Is There Gold in Them Hills?

Just mentioning the four-letter word "gold" is often enough to evoke intense excitement in some people, while precipitating frustration and heartache in others. Kings, priests, generals, millionaires, and plain, ordinary citizens have often lost their sanity, as well as their lives by lusting after the precious metal. It was the pursuit of gold that convinced Columbus to embark on what many considered a foolhardy journey for that day. Propelling Columbus was the fact that he had been promised ten percent of all the gold and silver he could carry back to Spain. To Spanish explorer Francisco Pizarro, gold was more valuable than the lives of thousands of innocent women and children. Pizarro demanded a room full of gold in ransom for Inca ruler, Atahualpa. After the gold was faithfully delivered, Atahualpa was brutally killed resulting in the near extinction of the Inca civilization. Pizarro proved just one more time that to many humans, gold is more precious than human life. The search for gold in the Pikes Peak region in 1859, prompted what is usually considered the first permanent European settlement in Seward County. The West family initially set out to pan for gold in Colorado, but changed their plans after meeting numerous disappointed prospectors returning home empty handed. After viewing the fertile West Blue River Valley, the West family decided that farming for "cash grain" in Seward County was a safer bet than panning for Colorado gold. News released to the public that "gold has been discovered" often results in mass hysteria and what could be described as a period of disorderly chaos. Most American history books record some "wild" stories from the California rush in the 1840s, the Pikes Peak rush in 1857, The Black Hills rush in 1876, the Cripple Creek, Colorado rush in the 1890s, and the Yukon rush in 1896. Yet, few Nebraska history books even bother to report the Milford, Nebraska, gold rush of 1895.

In 1878, J. S. Dillenbeck, along with his invalid wife and two small children, decided to leave the state of New York and seek their fortune in the "wild and woolly west," his destination being Lincoln, Nebraska. Through a land promoter he met in Lincoln, they were steered towards Seward County, where he filed claim on what is said to be the last available parcel of government homestead land in the

County. Land records say the Dillenbecks filed for an 80-acre farm in Sec. 8 of P Precinct, about three miles east of Milford.

While excavating dirt preparing to build a bank barn, Mr. Dillenbeck uncovered some very unusual looking dirt. His wife, who was ironing clothes with an iron heated by a hot coke fire, suggested they toss some in the fire. To their utter amazement a small stream of metal began to flow into the ash pan. To them it appeared to be silver.

Three sample bags of this strange looking dirt were rushed to Denver for testing. The results were startling and indicated the dirt was loaded with gold and worth anywhere from $54 to $196 per ton. The sample melted in the coke fire was sent to the University of Nebraska for analysis. Again, the report said gold and silver. The Milford community could no longer hide the discovery. Local and Lincoln newspapers displayed the headlines, "Gold has been discovered in Seward County." To prove the discovery was for real, the *Lincoln Journal* carried this news story: "All together it is equal in extent and vaster in value than any in the world." People living in the Milford, Pleasant Dale, and Crete communities nearly went berserk with joy.

Was good fortune about to smile on a distressed community? The year 1894 had been terrible for businessman and farmers alike.

Action from the Milford-Pleasant Dale "gold" rush of 1895. Several different methods of extracting the gold was tried, all ending in failure. The excitement reached from three miles east of Milford to a few miles north of Crete.

Eldon Hostetler

During that summer, it failed to rain for nearly two months. On July 27 and 28, blast furnace-type winds burned everything green, completely destroying any hope for a corn crop. The local butter factory had just called it quits, leaving many who depended on dairy cows for their livelihood stranded high and dry. Milford area farmers were forced to buy ear corn shipped in for livestock feed. More than three hundred rail cars of relief goods were eventually shipped into the state, averaging four cars for each county.

Many former Milford area farmers who had recently homesteaded land further west were now returning home, some completely bankrupt. News of the gold find sounded great for the troubled economy. It was anticipated that as some got rich, others would find good-paying jobs in the mine fields. Forget drought and hot south winds, Milford would soon be one of the wealthiest communities on the face of the earth, accomplishing something farming never could—bringing prosperity and happiness. But while gold ore was actually present in the soil, one problem remained— how would it be mined and processed? Most people responded about the way we would expect them to react today, as this excerpt from the Beaver Crossing newspaper indicates.

"A large number of Seward county people visited the Pleasant Dale gold fields over the weekend. They reported over ,1000 people there Saturday. Some of the wealthier ones were buying up surrounding farmland, and were paying a good price for it too. A company has been formed in Milford called 'The Middle Creek Gold Mining Company'."

Mining experts showed up in droves hoping to prove their knowledge and skill. All agreed it was an iron-coated flour gold, which was considered very difficult to process. A cyanide process was tried at first, but this was not successful. A smelter was brought in, which did process some gold, but proved far too costly to operate. Sluice boxes also proved unsuccessful. And then, along comes Professor Bartlett who was sure he could find an economical way to retrieve the precious gold. Bartlett proposed using artesian water, which he declared could be found at a depth of 700 to 800 feet. Wells would be dug west of the homestead and the water fed down Middle Creek which would then be used to wash the gold from the gravel. Eight surrounding landowners and Milford businessmen were supporting the project. This ambitious idea floundered before it hardly even got started. One reason mentioned for the failure was the inability of the partners to work and plan together in harmony. The good old professor soon got tired of waiting for his first paycheck and returned home empty-handed, still convinced "there was valuable gold in them hills."

For several years, the search for a profitable way to mine the gold came to a standstill. Finally in September of 1899, Scott Newcommer, a miner from Colorado Springs, announced to the public that he had discovered a new method to mine the gold. Newcomer said, "I found by chemical analysis that there is sufficient gold to pay up to $15 a ton for the ore, and once it is all processed, it will be a fabulous amount of money. I will use a chemical process that will cost up to $1.50 per ton, while the average value of the ore will be $6.50 per ton. This is a large field and beneath the surface of this part of the country it is impregnated with large quantities of placer gold in flour form."

A later news note in the *Milford Nebraskan* reported that Mr. Newcommer had located an engine and a smelter and would commence mining operations.

"Mr. Newcommer is an experienced miner and says there is enough platinum here to pay for all of the expenses, even if no gold is found. We will wait to see what statement he has to make next week." Mr. Newcommer never did make another statement for the press, so we may just assume his plans bombed. And so the gold, the silver, and the platinum are still hiding somewhere in the Middle Creek Hills. And Milford area people were forced to make their fortunes other ways. So, who did cash in on the Milford Gold Rush? None other then the railroad people. It was said that no fewer than fifty people visited the mine daily. On October 18, 1895, 228 people visited the mine site coming on a special train. Others said that at least four times that many came by foot or by horse and carriage.

Lydia (Dillenbeck) Barnes remembered the excitement. She said, "Long sight-seeing trains were run from as far as Chicago. People overran the land between the tracks and our farm. Great crowds came stomping over the hills carrying all kinds of containers to carry away gold. There were tons, dare say, of rocks and earth carried away to Chicago and other places en route. There went with them pieces of the house barn or corncrib, or whatever they fancied as souvenirs. I have no doubt that there are some of our pictures even now to be seen in homes far away." (*Early Days in Seward County*, Henry Smith, 1937.) By the way, Mr. Dillenbeck did get his name inscribed on the county courthouse cornerstone. Not because of his famous gold mine, but because he was elected as one of Seward County's commissioners. In 1895, Mr. Dillenbeck was offered $1,000 per acre for his farm. He turned down the offer. The Dillenbeck farm was not the only place that gold was found. A news note from the November 7, 1895 *Crete Vidette* newspaper said, "John Stehlik is sinking a shaft for gold seven miles north of Crete (two miles south of the Dillenbeck farm). He has not only found pyrites of iron, but flakes of gold and other mineral substances. The most remarkable find, however, is a piece of metallic instrument, about one inch long, which was found 24 ft. below the surface. It is the handiwork of a human and the engraving plainly seen denotes the fact that the maker was of an aesthetic nature. Here is a case for the archeologists."

Another news note from the January 21, 1897 edition said, "Mr. Stehlik has confidence in the gold fields. At least he keeps prospecting and recently reported quite a chunk of gold on an old iron ladle (information from Jan Stehlik of Dorchester)."

Seward County Transportation

When the Railroad Was King

Have you ever wondered why we have two mainline (Burlington Northern and Santa Fe) railroad tracks going east and west so close together; (one through Milford and one through Dorchester) or who decided the names and the locations of towns, or how Doane College got its name and location in Crete, or why Dorchester had rail service eight years before Milford or why Camden, the first town founded in this area, died before reaching adolescence?

Our early Milford railroad story holds the keys to answering all the above questions. Most Seward County residents are familiar with the county seat struggle engaged in by Seward, Camden and Milford from 1868-1872. It was a bitter fight that generated hard feelings for many years. However, few are familiar with the railroad struggles that involved the entire county from 1869-1887. Early Beaver Crossing newspaper editor and Seward County Historian, John Henry Waterman said: "The greatest public question that confronted us in the pioneer period was the railroad bond issue. We are met with thoughts of a triple headed monster in the interests of which certain localities were arranged against others in bitter strife (Waterman's *Revised History of Seward County*)."

Today, most Milford area citizens pay little attention to the rail service. We usually just assume the long, noisy coal trains passing through town are a modern day necessity. No longer forced to depend on railroad transportation for connections to the outside world as our forefathers of a hundred years ago, we pay little attention to what the railroad companies are doing. But from 1864-1910, Milford and other Seward County towns were strictly at the mercy of what they called "the big, ugly, greedy railroad monopoly."

Early railroads controlled the founding as well as the destiny of many Seward County towns. In most cases the advancement and well being of the railroad was of the highest priority. The 1858 discovery of gold in the Rocky Mountain region spurred renewed interest in finding a better land route to western states. After the Civil War, tremendous amounts of freight needed transportation west to supply people moving to Colorado, California, and Oregon. Army personnel, along with their equipment, required tons of freight to maintain the numerous military forts being built to protect early pioneers. Before the completion of the first Union Pacific railroad from Omaha to California in 1869, most of this freight came up the Mississippi- Missouri River system from St. Louis to either Omaha or Nebraska City. Here it was reloaded and transported by wagon train to Denver, Salt Lake City, California, or Oregon.

Although Milford was located on one of the busiest freight roads in the nation from 1864-70, the town was very much handicapped without a rail connection. Before the railroad reached Lincoln, Milford area residents were forced to sell their grain in either Nebraska City or Plattsmouth seventy-five miles to the east. Lumber for several of the early church buildings erected in Milford around 1870 was hauled by team and wagon from one of the towns mentioned. Our first area settler and West Mills businessman Tommy West, who had opened a supply store in 1864, would send a team to Nebraska City for needed supplies monthly. A typical load included two kegs of powder, several hundred pounds of lead, one or two hundred boxes of percussion cap, one barrel of whisky, flour, bacon, 100 pounds of tobacco, 50 to 100 steel traps, as well as other miscellaneous items. Milford citizens needed as well as longed for a railroad. At a meeting held in Camden in June of 1871, angry Milford, Beaver Crossing, and Camden citizens gathered to vent their frustrations upon the Burlington and Missouri Railroad Company (B&M). After a long and heated discussion, the following resolutions were adopted by unanimous voice:

"Whereas, We, citizens of Seward, Saline, York, Hamilton and Hall counties have been fraudulently deprived of the benefits that might have arisen out of the construction of the B&M railroad on the original survey; and Whereas, We settled along the line with the full understanding that the road should be built on said survey, according to an act of congress donating to them one half of our national inheritance; and Whereas said corporation is assisted by Nebraska politicians, in its schemes to plunder the people; Be it resolved that we pledge our sacred honors, without any regards to party ties, to send to oblivion by the strength of our ballots any man that comes before us for office who is in any way connected with said corporation. That we authorize S.M. Boyd to commence proceedings in Nebraska and at Washington against said B&M Railroad Co. for the purpose of compelling them to build a line of railway on their original survey, or that they be deprived of land received under this pledge. Resolved, That the people of the United States, looking for locations in Nebraska are hereby notified that we hold the purchase of said railroad lands to be a dangerous bargain for the purchaser. —Resolved, That these resolutions be published in all Nebraska papers, and three in Iowa, and two in Illinois."

This was only one of several meetings held in southern Seward county to protest the "high-handed tactics" being exercised by the powerful railroad lobby of that day. While local citizens may have felt better after venting their feelings and wrath, apparently the B&M boys

HOMES FOR MENNONITES
— IN —
IOWA AND NEBRASKA,
WHERE THE
BURLINGTON & MISSOURI RIVER RAILROAD COMPANY
OFFERS FOR SALE
MILLIONS OF **ACRES** OF **LAND**
On **Long Credit**, at **Low Prices**, and only **Six Per Cent Interest.**

Large Discounts For Cash!

These **Lands** lie in **Southwestern Iowa** and in the **Magnificent Valleys** of the **Platte** and **Republican Rivers** in **Nebraska**, a region **Celebrated** for the **Healthfulness** of its **Climate** and the **Fertility** of its **Soil**.

FREE FARE FOR PURCHASERS.
And **LOW RATES** on **FREIGHT** and **FARE** for their **FAMILIES.**

Send for Circulars containing full Description of the Land, Terms and Inducements to Purchasers, &c.

A. E. TOUZALIN, Land Commissioner
BURLINGTON, IOWA.

took the whole thing rather lightly. Why were Milford people so bitter and angry? Why had they apparently lost all respect for the B&M Railroad people? To make sense out of the story, we need to backtrack several years to 1869. Early Seward County people needed a railroad for several reasons. The first, of course, was to transport farm produce to market. Without competitive markets, grain and livestock prices were usually low. In 1872, corn prices were down to 10 cents, low enough to force many farmers to burn ear corn for fuel. A second reason was the fact that new and struggling towns rarely survived if they failed to attract a rail line; Camden being one good example. Plans for a railroad through Seward County go back to 1870 when the Burlington and Missouri Railroad was busy building the first track through Western Iowa. A man named Thielsen was hired to survey a tentative route west from Plattsmouth. The new line would run west from Lincoln, enter Seward County at Camden, and more or less follow the route of the old Territorial Road to Ft. Kearny. In 1869, Seward County residents had voted on a bond proposal offered by the Midland Pacific Railroad to build a road from Lincoln to the west bank of the Blue River for $50,000 in ten percent bonds. Although the bond issue passed, the railroad was never built. As an extra inducement the government offered the railroad companies every alternate section extending 20 miles on either side of the track, or 20-square miles of land for every mile of track built. The Union Pacific claimed 4,846,000 acres of Nebraska land while the Burlington and Missouri accumulated 2,374,000 acres between the years 1868 and 1883.

    Early Seward County residents hailed the railroad's decision to build the road through southern Seward County. This route would have certainly been a boon to Camden, West Mills, and Beaver Crossing. Maybe, just because they were big enough and had the political clout to get by with whatever they wanted to do, about the time they were ready to start grading at Plattsmouth, B&M officials decided to change the route and build the road through northern Saline County. On May 6, the House and Senate approved the change in plans allowing the railroad to completely bypass Seward County. Mean while, D. H. Ainsworth was surveying a new line, which would cross the Blue River seven miles south of Camden, near Crete. President Grant signed the bill allowing the railroad to proceed with the changed route in April of 1869. Congressional approval was needed since the railroad had already been granted right of way through

Seward County. Many Seward County residents felt the railroad changed their plans simply to get title to more government land.

Ground was broken on July 4, 1869 under the direction of B&M's chief engineer, Thomas Doane. The new track reached Lincoln on July 26, 1870, Crete on June 12, 1871, Dorchester on July 4, 1871, Harvard on December of 1871, and Denver in 1882.

Guests on the first train arriving in Crete included officials from the Congregational Church Association who had come to Crete looking for a site for a new college. One year later, the railroad granted the church 600 acres of land assuring the city it would have a college. It was said that at this time the city of Crete was home to nine saloons and no churches. A town was founded eight miles west in 1871 and was named Dorchester.

Meanwhile, back in Seward County, Milford and Camden citizens were frustrated and angry, blaming the B&M railroad people for deceiving them by changing the original route. Some felt the B&M boys deliberately moved the line south to collect more government land and force southern Seward County to issue more bonds to pay for a second rail line. War was declared on railroads, in general. While Milford and Camden citizens were still simmering, there appeared one Dr. J. W. Converse, representing the Midland Pacific Railroad. Mr. Converse informed Seward County residents that his company was ready to develop a new rail line between Lincoln and Seward— provided they received $150,000 in 10 percent, twenty-year bonds.

What followed could be classified as the second north versus south "Seward County Civil War." The bond election held on February 22, 1872 was defeated 624 votes to 547. Voting in favor of the bond issue were the Seward, North Blue, and Lincoln Creek communities while Milford, Camden, Walnut Creek, Beaver Crossing, and Oak Groves voted against the bonds. The sentiments of area people regarding railroad bond issues in that day is best expressed in excerpts from this news note published in the January 12, 1871 Crete newspaper.

"We are agitated in this county; and justly too! For the mountain has not brought forth a mouse, but an elephant. That Midland Pacific railroad has induced our noble County Commissioners to submit to the county the issuing of $150,000 in Bonds to aid in building that railroad through the country. We are moved; for it is, or will be, if voted, a mortgage upon the property in the county. The interest we shall pay

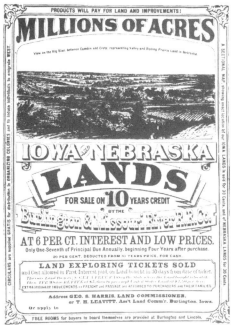

Nebraska land for sale in 1874. Land between Camden and Crete in the Big Blue River Valley is pictured.

on the Bonds at the end of twenty years, at 10 percent interest will amount to $300,000, making principal and interest $510,000 for said road. $150,000 is nearly enough to build the road and if we furnish the capital, we want to own the road, and not build it, and then give it away. The Company then offered to give the county $150,000 in Stock as an offset for the Bonds. What is the value of the stock? The Midland road is already mortgaged for its entire value (as we believe). The history of all railroads built without railroad grants, with few exceptions, is the stock. The original Stock is not of any value, until it has passed into second hands, having been sold for a few cents on the dollar. The original Stock of the Midland railroad, is not as we have been informed worth one cent on the dollar. How much then will the $150,000 be worth to Seward County? Just one hundred and fifty dollars. But that is not all. If the officers should fail in anything, in giving proper notices, meetings of stockholders, or anything the law requires, than the stockholders would be liable for all debts of the company... (Correspondence from Milford to the Crete newspaper by T. N. Skinner)."

Not willing to accept defeat, the railroad offered a third bond proposal which was submitted for a vote in June, this time a less expensive bond for taxpayers. The railroad offered to build tracks within one-half mile of Milford, if southern county citizens would withdraw their opposition. Sensing the stubbornness of Milford and Camden citizens, the railroad made loving overtures to the Oak Grove community. Partly because of Seward's growing population, as well as the promise to build the new railroad through the Oak Groves community (near Garland), the bond carried by a 123-vote margin. At last, Seward County had a railroad from Lincoln to Seward, although Milford was completely bypassed by more than ten miles. The first train rolled into Seward on March 1, 1873. From this time on, Seward was in the driver's seat and Milford was left to bring up the rear. For four years, Seward was home to the railroad's ending. Consequently, everyone within several counties west brought their grain to sell at one of the many grain markets that quickly sprang up around the new railroad. In other words, Seward boomed while Milford pouted.

Seward County historian, W. W. Cox explained Milford's disappointment and bitterness this way: "Victory perched upon Seward's banner again, and Milford was in deep distress and refused to be comforted. She had made a fatal mistake. In her fit of anger she had seriously blundered, and it well nigh cost her life."

Milford area residents now had a king-sized problem on their hands. Without a rail connection, the town could die on the vine. About this time the town lost the county seat prize and desperately needed a railroad to restore the town's image as a good place to settle. Truly, Milford residents were caught between a rock and a hard place. Someone needed to give. Would it be the railroad—or Milford citizens?

Although Seward had a railroad by 1873, local residents were deceived one more time. The road was quickly taken over by the very familiar B&M boys. Controlling both the north and the south main lines, the B&M had no competition, allowing the company to charge any rates they chose. This caused Seward area residents to grumble. Steps were taken immediately to secure a competing line. Both the Union Pacific and the Atchison & Nebraska Railroads were contacted and both appeared slightly interested. A great mass meeting was called in the spring of 1879 to determine which one would be willing to build a new road.

Evidently, the gentleman representing the Union Pacific line did not appeal to county residents. In fact one early citizen reported, "there were some scenes enacted that were not very credible to our people." The A&N offered to build a road from Lincoln through the Middle Creek Valley to Milford, and then up the Blue Valley to Seward, Ulysses, David City, and ending in Columbus. Seward County was asked to put up $75,000 in county bonds for the project. This offer was eagerly accepted and carried by a good majority. The road was quickly built, although not without opposition and more "hanky panky" as well as the threat of several lawsuits. W. W. Cox said this about Milford citizens at the time: "Our Milford friends had suddenly been converted, and were no longer opposed to railroad bonds from principle, and like all new converts were very enthusiastic for the A&N and they were manfully backed by the dwellers of the Blue Valley."

The first train arrived in what is now Grover in early November, 1879. This new railroad completely changed the Seward County map. East Milford was platted about this time as well as Ruby, Staplehurst, and Pleasant Dale. While Milford finally had her railroad, the first train did not arrive in the town proper until November 29, 1907. From 1905 to 1907, the railroad spent more than five million dollars leveling the grade between Milford and Lincoln. The dirt was cut out of the high spots by steam shovel, loaded on dirt cars and dumped in the low spots. Before the new track was built, it required several locomotives to pull the trains out of Milford. Prior to 1907, all railroad business was conducted from Grover. You guessed it. "The oldest town in Seward County, the lovely town of Camden, died on the vine, never to breathe again. Nor was she ever given a proper burial or a decent tombstone (W.W. Cox)."

Was Seward happy now that she had two railroads, supposedly one to compete with the B&M boys? Due to some fancy maneuvering, even before the dirt in the grades had firmly settled, Milford and Seward residents discovered that their new railroad was actually owned by the "hated" B&M boys. So, Milford was forced to deal with people they had decided they didn't like all that well in 1871. In fact, they had even said some pretty ugly things about their new railroad owners while Seward folks were still complaining about extremely high freight rates. In some instances, the railroad took half the value of the wheat to pay shipping charges. Milford area farmers were fortunate to have the mill in town to buy most of the local wheat.

By 1884, the town boasted of four competitive grain markets. The Quenchauqua mills were shipping flour not only to other states, but also as far away as England. Farmers, livestock dealers, and feeders could now lease a car to sell their produce wherever they got the best bid.

The Way It Was

A news note from the January 8, 1904 *Omaha Journal Stockman* reported how one prosperous Milford farmer took advantage of rail service to market his livestock.

"A. H. Vance of Milford, an old settler of considerable note, was on yesterday's market with a load of hogs of his own raising and feeding that averaged 380 pounds and sold at $4.80, the high point of the day. In breeding the hogs were a cross between Poland-Chinas and Duroc-Jerseys. He also brought in a load of cattle."

Those moving to other places obtained special rates by leasing a so-called "emigrant car." You could even lease an entire coach for a special rate if your group was large enough. Several news accounts could give one the impression that occasionally, price cuts were even involved if the travelers persisted.

By 1884, it was reported the Milford depot had shipped out 1,100 cars of grain and 180 cars of livestock in slightly more than one year. It was said to be one of the best shipping points between Lincoln and Columbus. Special trains pulled into Grover carrying up to 500 people, some to attend special conventions and some to just have a good time on Milford's Shogo Island.

Ice cut from Lake Quenchauqua was shipped by the trainload to destinations as far as Denver and St. Louis. The ice company had the capacity to load up to seventy cars per day. Milford citizens were now traveling to far-off places, many to visit friends and relatives they had not seen for years. The arrival of the railroad in Milford in 1879, appeared to give the town new vigor, as well as a fresh hope for the future. Yet Seward and Saline County citizens alike were leaving no stones unturned in their attempt to lure a competing road. The popular cry of the day appeared to be, "With no competition, our freight rates are still too high."

Were early railroad people really as "ugly and greedy" as portrayed by many of the early settlers ? Maybe yes and maybe no. During the height of the great drought and depression Nebraska pioneers experienced in 1874-75 and again in the middle 1890s, the railroads responded by shipping the majority of the aid contributed by other states free of charge. In several instances, Nebraska railroads appeared to bend over backwards in their effort to get new emigrants comfortably settled on recently purchased lands. In one rare incident they all but gave their land free as an inducement to attract new settlers. The editor of the *Daily State Journal* was thoroughly impressed with the benevolent attitude expressed by the B&M boys in an incident that took place in Lincoln in September of 1874.

"The B&M Railroad Company is earning its land grant by a magnanimous public service to the state and the whole country—magnanimous even though it is a trading operation and looks forward to gain, in as much as immediate profit is not the sole object, more especially because it is wise and liberal, as well as large.... The old Immigrant's Home at the B&M depot has furnished welcome rest and shelter for hundreds of families while their homes are being built on the prairies. But this building was altogether too small to accommodate the strangers now coming to us. The company, therefore erected another frame structure in the Fair Grounds. This building is comfortable internally, and sanitary requirements have received due attention. The recent arrivals are now lodged here, and are well satisfied with the accommodations provided. There are now about 1,000 of the Russians immigrants in Lincoln. [Author's Note: Some Mennonite historians feel this figure is too high, and was actually more like 600.]."

The recipients of the railroad's affections were German/Russian Mennonite families from Southern Russia. While many had already set their sights on settling on Kansas land owned by the Santa Fe Railroad, B&M people were hoping to lure many into purchasing land in Nebraska. What followed could probably be considered as a pure and simple "People Auction." B&M representative A. E. Touzalin and Santa Fe representative C. B. Schmidt engaged in a spirited bidding war at the state fairgrounds, each trying to convince the Mennonites to buy their respective lands. Before the session ended, Touzalin had made offers Mennonite leaders called "fantastic."

Touzalin offered to drill a well and install a windmill on every quarter section, furnish enough hay for the first winter, build plank roads wherever needed, build an immigrant house for up to 200 families, later deeding the house to the settlers, furnish lumber for homes at the cheaper Chicago price, sell land supposedly worth $3 to $4 an acre for $2 to $2.50, and ship all belongings and other needed items free of charge for a period of time. In fact, in his final offer, he agreed to give the land free of charge if the entire group would agree to settle on Burlington land. Meanwhile, Santa Fe's agent Schmidt agreed to match every offer except the final one, saying later that he really had no need to match his final offer.

The Way It Was

In spite of Mr. Touzalin's fantastic offers, eighty-nine families chose Kansas as their future home, while only thirty-five families agreed to settle in Nebraska. This may be one reason that today, 21,570 Mennonites call Kansas home, while only 3,506 are presently living in Nebraska. The descendants of the recipients of Mr. Touzalin's generous offer now live in York and Hamilton Counties in and around the city of Henderson (*Lincoln Journal*, several issues, September, 1874).

Seward County residents never gave up trying to induce more rail lines to build tracks through the county. The B&M boys appeared to have a monopoly on Seward County freight rates until 1887-88. At that time a strong competitor, the Fremont, Elkhorn, and Missouri Valley Railroad, later known as the Chicago & Northwestern, offered to build a new rail line through Seward County from Fremont to Superior. Prominent Seward businessman and state senator, J. F. Goehner was chosen as spokesman for a five-man committee to make arrangements. Seward County residents passed a 20-year $60,000 Bond proposal required by the railroad.

Three new towns, Goehner, Bee, and Cordova were born along the new railroad. Beaver Crossing was now on a railroad for the first time in history. Yes, county freight rates were now said to be somewhat lower. Passenger service on this line was discontinued in 1942, and freight service in 1972. Local investors attempted to operate the line for several years after the C&N received permission to abandon the track. Known as the Great Plains Railroad, service continued for several years before ending in 1975. The line was later sold for salvage.

One more railroad that "just about was" was a proposed line from Milford to Crete known as the Crete Milford and Western (CM&W). This line also died on the vine before the tracks were ever laid, although the grade work started in 1887 was practically completed. Scars from the cuts and fills are still visible in many spots throughout the North Blue Valley from Milford to Crete. This proposed line was to run from Crete through Milford, Seward, and York, and end in Aurora where it would connect with another Burlington branch. Burlington records show that the final meeting of the Board of Directors was held on June 5, 1912.

Eldon Hostetler

Dispossession of the Horse

"The horse has made a greater contribution to civilization than any other animal. In terms of service the horse, rather than the dog, has been man's best friend more than the centuries as soldier, hunter, field hand, mail carrier, and until the late 1800s the world's major means of land transportation." This quote by Joseph Casida sets the stage for the investigation into the origin and development of the modern-day automobile, known a hundred years ago as the "horseless carriage." According to an early news note published in the *Milford Nebraskan*, Milford citizens experienced first sight of an automobile when Gus Babson arrived in town in June of 1900. Mr. Babson was driving one of those new horse frightening contraptions known as a horseless carriage. The ten-mile trip from Seward required slightly more than one hour of steady driving time. Mr. Babson, a talented Seward machinist and buggy maker, fitted a gasoline engine to a buggy chassis, a process that helped to name the new hybrid beast. Since this was said to be one of only two autos in the state at that time, we could just assume Milford business probably came to a complete standstill until the powerful 3-horsepower engine roared to life and the Babsons blasted off their launch pad and headed back to Seward. Mr. Babson's trip to Milford may have signaled the beginning of the end for many horse-human relationships.

Many maintained the new greasy, noisy contraption would never replace their horses. What few people realized in 1900 was that by 1922, a good team of driving horses would be a novelty on Milford's Main Street, just like this weird-looking contraption was in 1900. Who was responsible for this motorized contraption, and was it really a new idea? This is the sad story of why and how faithful old driving horses lost their jobs as well as years of respect. Unlike other modern day inventions, the horseless carriage was not the product of any one individual person. In fact, not even the brainchild of any one particular generation. For hundreds of years mechanically minded men had been experimenting with three- or four-wheel horseless carriages. A wind-powered vehicle was invented and built about 1420. Leonardo da Vinci spent some time dreaming and sketching his ideas of future power-driven carriages. Although Isaac Newton proposed a steam-powered vehicle, the first one was actually built by a Frenchman Nicholas Joseph Cugnot in 1769. This vehicle is reported to have carried several passengers at slightly more than two miles per hour. While this machine was not considered a great success, his ground-work did pave the way for later inventors.

Englishman William Murdock (who formerly worked for Isaac Watts) built a steam powered three-wheel vehicle that actually worked as early as 1784.

French car builder, Armand Peugeot also designed and built a steam-powered carriage around 1890, but later decided to concentrate on gasoline-powered machines. By 1800, both the English and the French were experimenting with steam-powered buses and coaches to be used in taxi service. Because of their extreme noise and the ever-present threat of explosions, English people were so aroused, they supported the Locomotive Act of 1865. This legislation required that steam coaches hold their speed down to no more than two miles per hour in cities and four miles per hour in rural areas. In addition, a man carrying a red flag was ordered to proceed the engine by sixty yards to warn bystanders of the approach of this speedy, yet dangerous animal. This legislation was not repealed until the late 1800s.

In United States, Nathan Reed of Massachusetts experimented with steam-driven vehicles as early as 1790. Not financially successful, his vehicles soon disappeared from the scene. The development of smaller, lighter steam-powered vehicles capable of carrying up to four passengers at up to twenty miles per hour appeared in Europe about 1865. A practical version of a steam-powered vehicle did not appear in America until 1896 with the introduction of the world famous Stanley Steamer.

From 1839 to 1885 several attempts were made to power carriages with electricity, one of the first inventors being Robert Anderson of Scotland. In 1886, an electric cab powered by twenty-eight storage batteries was introduced into London. It was capable of traveling eight miles per hour. Later, Walter Bersey designed and built electric cabs powered by forty batteries capable of traveling fifty miles before recharging. The London Electric Cab Company staked their future on the machine and ordered seventy-seven vehicles. But because heavy construction was needed to carry the weight of the batteries, the cabs proved impractical. London Electric Cab Company was out of business in less than 3 years.

Improvement in the gasoline engine by many different individuals around the turn of the century would prove to be a replacement for old Dobbin. Etienne Lenoir of France, Siegfried Marcus of Austria, Karl Benz and Gottlieb Daimler of Germany were all working to design better gasoline engines. Lenoir designed and built a two-cylinder engine powered by an explosive mixture of illuminating gas and air as early as 1865. A later model built in 1882 was capable of speeds up to four miles per hour. Marcus built his first vehicle in 1864 but failed to install a clutch. This made the unit very difficult to start and drive. In 1875, he built a newer, more powerful version capable of speeds up to three miles per hour.

Benz and Daimler are generally given credit for designing and building the first successful cars designed for commercial use, probably around 1886. While they both worked to accomplish the same goal, it has been said the men never met during their lifetimes, although the two companies merged in 1926. Benz was one of the first manufacturers to design a completely new vehicle, not just an adapted version of the old horse buggy. By 1895, he was building lightweight, four-wheel vehicles of 2.5 horsepower capable of speeds up to 15 miles per hour. His machine was also inexpensive and simple to operate. Daimler worked to improve the 4-stroke engine and succeeded in building one that generated one horsepower at 900 rpm. His earliest machine was simply a horse-drawn buggy fitted with this engine.

In 1889, Daimler completely redesigned his engine and introduced a V-type, two-cylinder engine capable of producing more than three-horse power. When his partner, Wilhelm Maybach designed the new jet- and float-type carburetor around 1892, his engine was capable of producing up to six-horse power. Three other Frenchmen, Rene Panhard, Armand Peugeot and Lewis Renault were also in on the early action. One of the first practical autos was produced by Panhard and Emile Levassor around 1900. This auto featured a friction clutch coupled with a three-speed sliding gear transmission and a steering wheel rather than the usual tiller, an arrangement that soon became standard for the industry. For several years, Renault designed and built autos using an air-cooled engine operating at 1500 rpm. Meanwhile, American engineers were also working feverishly in their attempt to dump old Dobbin—or at least to give him a long-deserved vacation.

The Way It Was

In America, as well as in Europe, it is difficult to ascribe the invention of the automobile to any one individual. Working steam carriages had been built by Thomas Blanchard in 1825, by Stephen H. H. Roper in 1865, and by J. W. Carhart in 1871. Other inventors also experimented with various types of horseless conveyances, but no one in particular appeared to hit the magic formula. Around 1890, bicycle builders J. Frank and Charles E. Duryea introduced their first horseless carriage, a high-wheeled buggy with a small single cylinder gasoline fitted in the rear end for power. This vehicle, which the Duryea boys called their "buggyaut" operated quite successfully on a Springfield, Massachusetts street in 1893.

Several years later they designed and built an improved model which they entered in the first-ever American road race held in Chicago in November of 1895. Only two autos finished the fifty-five mile race; the Duryea auto, and one entered by German carmaker Benz. The Duryea auto won the race with an average speed of 7.5 miles per hour. Some auto authorities also consider the Duryea brothers as the first successful American auto manufactures. Thirteen autos of this design were built and sold. About 1894, another machine designed by Elwood Haynes, manufactured by the Apperson Brothers, proved to be quite successful. It has been estimated that as many as 2,000 men worked to design or build horseless carriages between 1890 and 1900. Most labored in small, private work shops.

Charles B. King is credited with inventing, building, and driving the first auto seen in Detroit. Charles was showing off his new machine by March of 1896. Three months later Henry Ford, the man often credited with bringing the horseless carriage to the masses, was showing his new vehicle in Detroit. In September of same year, another famous automobile designer, Ransom E. Olds, introduced his first vehicle to the people of Lansing, Michigan, while Alexander Winton also operated his first successful vehicle. What many feel was the first successful commercially built auto was introduced and sold in 1901 by Ransom E. Olds. It was the three-horse power auto that inspired Gus Edwards to write a popular hit songs of that era, "In My Merry Oldsmobile." The Olds Motor Works sold 600 cars in 1901, 2,500 in 1902, 4,000 in 1903, and 5,000 in 1904. More concerned with profits than hit songs, Olds' stockholders demanded the company build a larger, higher-priced automobile. Olds left the company to manufacture another well-known vehicle, one named after his initials

Eldon Hostetler

R-E-O. As far as I have been able to determine, the majority of the early autos driven and sold in Milford and Seward were REOs. Mr. Olds was also the only auto inventor to have two mass-produced vehicles named after him.

Other well-known manufacturers who got their start about this time included James W. Packard in 1899, Studebaker Brothers in 1900, David D. Buick in 1902, Thomas B. Jeffery in 1902, and William C. Durant in 1904. In 1902, the Cadillac Automobile Company, successor to the reorganized Henry Ford Motor Company, was formed. In 1906 Cadillac sold more than 4,000 cars wresting sales leadership away from Olds. John and Horace Dodge, who had previously been with the Ford organization, started their own company in 1914. The Overland car, first built in 1902, was taken over by John North Willys in 1908. The Oakland-Pontiac Auto Company was founded in 1907.

Chevrolet was organized in 1909 and Hudson in 1911. General Motors, now one of the largest corporations in the world, was organized in 1908 by William C. Durant. Walter Chrysler, retired president and general manager of Buick, also worked for the Willys Overland Company before reorganizing the old Maxwell Motor Corporation. Chrysler produced his first automobile in 1924. Later Dodge, Plymouth, and DeSoto lines were added. Detroit native Henry Ford, often considered the genius who made the new horseless carriage available and affordable for the average wage earner, was actually a latecomer to the industry. Although his first hand-made car appeared in 1896, his early attempts to produce a successful auto ended in failures. His first Model A appeared in 1903 (not to be confused with his 1920 version). Among his early stockholders were the likes of John and Horace Dodge, who designed and built some of his first engines.

By 1906, Ford was building a six-cylinder Model K which sold for $2,700—$2,000 more than Henry Leland's new Cadillac. Because his early machines were costly and did not sell all that well, production was soon discontinued. Meanwhile, Henry Ford also achieved much needed fame and notoriety by winning several early auto races. In 1908, Henry Ford built his first Model T. It was the first auto built on a moving assembly line. The new system allowed him to build up to 250,000 units per year. This method also cut costs, allowing Ford to realize his dream of producing an automobile for less than $500. In

The Way It Was

Little is known about this picture or the date it was taken. The caption reads: "Milford's Rambler dealer. Estimated date 1912-1915. Photo courtesy Seward County Historical Society at Goehner.

fifteen years of production, millions of Model Ts were sold. One model carried a price tag of less than $300.

Unchallenged for several years among low-cost car manufacturers, Ford completely dominated the American market in the early 1920s commanding from 40 to 57 percent of total sales. In 1926, Ford was forced to abandon the outdated Model T in favor of better built machines. His second Model A was introduced to the public in late 1927. By 1929, the Model A was leading the nation in total sales. Many from my generation, including me, started driving with one of these popular Ford machines. Although it may have been the car that put the average American worker in the driver's seat, many were soon demanding a higher quality, more expensive automobile. Ford solved part of his problem by acquiring the Lincoln Motor Company plant in 1922. Other manufacturers were also in the business and provided strong competition that forced many to merge. Now defunct brands of automobiles that were driven on Milford streets during my youth included the Austin, De Soto, Essex, Huppmobile, Hudson, Frazer, Graham Paige, Kaiser, Packard, Rambler, Studebaker, Terriplane Willys Knight, and Whippet. While most early cars built before 1906 were open top, two-seat roadsters, the public soon demanded more size and comfort as well as additional safety features. The first starter was designed by Cadillac engineers in 1911. By 1904, Cadillac,

1903 Oldsmobile

1910 Stanley Steamer

Locomobile and Peerless were offering closed bodies. Ford provided safety plate glass windshields by 1928, while the 1902 Marmon had the first all-metal body made of aluminum. The 1914 Dodge was the first mass-produced auto to be made entirely of steel while the 1923 Model had the first enclosed steel body.

The first six-cylinder engine was introduced by Ford in 1906, the first V-8 by Coyote of California in 1906, the first straight 8 by Winton in 1903. Four wheel expanding brakes were made available by Duryea in 1898. Duesenberg enhanced the brakes by adding hydraulics in 1920. Hydraulic valve lifters made an appearance in 1932 thanks to Pierce Arrow. Synchro-mesh transmissions were developed by Cadillac in 1928, followed by the development of fluid coupling by Chrysler in 1938. Oldsmobile introduced the first hydramatic transmission in 1938.

The "Contraption" Comes to Milford

While I realize most Milford residents may be far too sophisticated to believe that horses ever talk to each other, just pretend for a moment that they do exchange horse-chat occasionally, or at least that they did back in the "good old days." Let your mature imagination wander back to your "Mother Goose" years and just pretend you heard this conversation on the streets of Seward in 1900.

"Hey Dobbin, did you hear what happened to that new so-called horseless carriage? You know, that new contraption invented by Mr. Babson? How it just disappeared in a cloud of black smoke last week?"

The Way It Was

"Sure did Maude. Wow! Was that ever a fire. Can't really say I'm all that sorry though. Old Roan, president of the Horse Teamsters Union has been warning us for some time that this 'smoking monster' could eventually throw us out of work."

"Well, at least in Seward County the jobs should be safe for some time. And get this, Dobbin. They blamed us for starting the fire! Now I heard this directly from my harness mate 'Gossipy Nell.' She said that it started when the engine backfired. What a laugh. Nellie and I have backfired hundreds of times and believe me, we still have our first carriage to set on fire. At least, this should help clear the way for better Horse-Union contracts from the city of Seward when our current contract expires next month."

Yes it was true. The first auto built in Seward County did dissolve in a hot fire generated by the backfiring of the engine. But this incident in no way helped stem the onslaught of new autos in the county. A news item in a September 1905 *Beaver Crossing Bugle* reported this news, "A fine, two-seated automobile was the center of attention in Beaver Crossing Thursday. Two gentleman and two ladies drove over from Milford, the trip taking them thirty five minutes."

Who owned Milford's first automobile? Some say a Mr. Danekas, some say Dr. Wertman and others say Wriley Wright. The postcard mailed to my uncle Floyd Hostetler isn't dated but the postmark reads March 30, 1909.

Eldon Hostetler

My uncle, Aaron Roth purchased this 1915 Studebaker from the Gard Studebaker Agency in Goehner. In 1918 they took a trip to Oregon. With all dirt roads, the trip took two weeks. At places they were forced to open and close wire gates. Pictured are Melvin Hostetler, Elbert Hostetler, Aaron Roth and Floyd Hostetler.

This is the first mention of an auto in the city of Milford. From what I have heard from many "old-timers" (including my father), this auto was probably owned by Riley Wright, long-time owner of the Milford Jewelry store. Other early autos were owned by Dr. Wertman, Dr. Loughbrige, Aaron Roth, L. C. Trabert, Ray Trabert, Joe Hershberger, W. C. Klein, Pete Schlegel, John Jantze, Phil Reil, Jake Kremer, Jake Teucher, James Church, and Mose Schweitzer. By September of 1908, the editor could write, "There are now 16 autos in Milford."

What were most driving at this time? Dr. Wertman and L. M. Trabert were driving new twenty-horsepower Buicks, while Joe Hershberger, James Church, and Aaron Roth were driving shiny new ten-horsepower REOs. Ninety-one-year-old Oliver Roth said that at first his grandmother referred to his dad's new one-cylinder REO as the devil's wagon. We may just assume W. C. Klein was driving a "Jackson" since this was the brand he was selling, while Dr. Loughbrige was driving a Rambler. As far as I am able to determine W. C. Klein, local hardware and farm supply dealer, was the first auto dealer in Milford.

The Way It Was

One 1908 news note tells us that Mr. Klein sold a new Jackson to Dr. Doty of Beaver Crossing in the summer of 1908. Later he also sold the Maxwell and Paige line of autos. Other early buyers may have purchased their first autos from Hershberger and Jantzi of Seward. Milford native Harvey A. Hershberger started one of the first Auto Agencies in Seward about 1907. In 1908, the partnership of Hershberger and Jantzi advertised your choice of a ten-horsepower Maxwell Runabout for $525, or a twenty-two horsepower REO Gentlemen's Roadster for $1,050. Mr. Hershberger was also the first Buick dealer in Seward County.

About 1910, Milford Livery Stable owners, Chamberlin and Cox built an addition to their Milford stables to cash in on the craze for this new, hot-selling toy. They were soon satisfying customers with either new Buicks, REOs or Marathon autos.

Another forgotten auto dealer, Abbey Miller, offered the new Star lineup. Around 1911-12, Mose Schweitzer received the Ford franchise, and proceeded to sell Fords like mad. Later he sold his Ford business to Whitaker and Roth and switched to Durant autos.

In 1934, Jake Kremer bought out Chamberlin Buick and for a short time was said to be the one of the only Buick dealers in Seward County. Jake also sold the Chrysler, DeSoto-Plymouth line in Milford. Since 1950, Rediger's Chevrolet, TeSell's Ford, and Subway Motors appear to have sold most of the cars and trucks in the Milford vicinity.

Just like old Dobbin always suspected, early autos were a true hazard on the streets of Milford. One of the first road rules a new horseless carriage driver learned was that you had to stop in your tracks, pull off to the side of the road, shut off your engine and wait until any horsedrawn conveyance passed.

Milford businessman, Ben Burkey was one of the first buggy drivers to experience the reality of this danger. "Ben Burkey's horse became frightened while meeting an auto and ran away completely smashed his buggy (*Milford Nebraskan*, September 1907)."

The second wreck happened in Milford in October of 1908, when Doc Wertman hit a large dog that was evidently out to investigate this strange looking, noisy creature. Poor Shep paid for his inquisitiveness with his life, while one wheel on Doc's new 20 hp Buick was completely destroyed.

What was probably the first serious auto accident happened west of Milford in 1911. "Near the Andy Welsh farm, Chris Stahly was coming out of town with his buggy and was run into by a car driven by Rev. J. R. Hunter. Chris was hurt badly, while another auto driven by Philip Reil, coming over the hill, ran into the wreck."

An innocent dog was blamed for another serious accident in 1916. "While Harry Stahly and Ralph Rogers were returning home in their auto truck, a dog jumped out and struck a wheel, jerking the steering wheel out of Stahly's hand, causing the truck to lurch and tip over, throwing out both (*Milford Review,* August 10, 1916)."

From this news note published in the October 6, 1932 *Milford Review*, it would appear that horses usually lost the battle when hit by an auto. "Two horses belonging to John P. Roth had to be shot as a result of injuries suffered when crashed into by an auto driven by Lloyd Stutzman."

Most new Milford car owners needed some education in regard to handling their new machines. In July of 1922, Mr. John Wohlgemuth's auto jumped the curb and broke off a city lamp pole while he was standing in front of the machine and attempting to get it started. In December of 1919, Fred Gake's new beast shot through the garage breaking the leg of his brother who was standing on the opposite end. All Fred had done was to innocently turn the starting crank. In spite of the many hazards associated with owning a new horseless carriage, Milford citizens decided they were here to stay—meaning horses were destined to be put out to pasture.

Almost a "Perfect" Automobile

For more than a hundred years, car manufacturers have tried to build what they thought would be "the world's *perfect* automobile." Although many tried, few have succeeded. A word coined in the early 1930s and now accepted in the English dictionary introduces us to the story of what some feel may have been one of the best automobiles ever built. Webster says the word means "something remarkable" so modern day Americans are correct when they use the word "doozie" to describe something extraordinary. This is the story of an automobile that was said to be almost perfect and famous enough to coin a new English word (*The People's Almanac # 2*, p. 665).

The Way It Was

One auto expert said it like this: "It was a combination of imagination, magnitude, and magnificence; It was fantastic; A legend; The best machine in the world. No car ever made anywhere has matched the Duesenberg for its rare combined qualities of meticulous craftsmanship, or its enormous power and great beauty."

Named after German brothers, Fred and August Duesenberg who emigrated to America in 1885, the car was manufactured from 1920 to 1937. Well known for their exploits in setting world speed records for both bicycles and motorcycles, the Duesenberg Brothers began designing and building race cars soon after 1900. They also designed engines for boats, farm tractors, and airplanes. In 1919 they opened a small factory in Indianapolis to design and build passenger and race cars, with speed being the number one objective. Duesenberg-built autos and racecars set sixty-six world speed records. Entering twenty-seven races, they placed in twenty-four. Much to the embarrassment of European car builders, an American built Duesenberg was the first non-European built auto to win the French Grand Prix at Le Mans. Duesenberg built autos also finished first in the Indianapolis 500 in 1924, 1925 and 1927.

In 1926, American car manufacturer, Errett Lobban Cord bought out the Duesenberg plant and hired the brothers, commissioning them to "create the best car ever built." In 1929, Cord introduced his first auto, known as the model J, and in 1932, the "spectacular" Model SJ.

The SJ quickly became the most prestigious car in the world. European royalty and wealthy Hollywood movie stars accustomed to driving English Rolls Royces and German Daimlers, actually switched to American-built Duesenbergs. Tyrone Power, Paul Whiteman, Mae West, Clark Gable, and Gary Cooper all bought "Duesies." New York mayor, Jimmy Walker and popular evangelist of the day "Father Divine" were also "Duesie" lovers. As one film critic said, "To own a Duesenberg was almost required of a film star to prove that he had reached the top."

The popularity of the Duesenberg was a combination of factors. They were gorgeous. They were fast. And they were expensive. The E. L. Cord Company built only the chassis, fitted with a Lycoming engine built to the Duesenberg brothers' specifications in a Cord-owned Pennsylvania plant. Bodies were built to the buyer's specifications by one of the world's top nineteen coach builders. This greatly added to the snob appeal since no two cars would look alike. The 7,000 pound car was propelled by an eight cylinder, 420 cubic inch supercharged engine which was said to produce nearly four hundred horsepower. This handcrafted motor moved the car from a complete stop to 100 miles mph in seventeen seconds. Able to cruise at 135 mph without strain, their potential maximum speed was unknown, since the speedometer stopped at 150. Interior finish was a matter of individual choice and often consisted of the world's finest silks, leathers, ivory, pigskin, fur, morocco, or wood. A typical control panel contained the usual gauges as well as a tachometer, brake pressure gauge, split second stop clock, an altimeter, barometer, and compass. Cars also had special controls to adjust the brakes and carburetor. Some of these were duplicated in the rear seat. A Duesenberg could cost anywhere from $19,000 to $50,000 dollars in 1930s money, which meant in some cases the price equaled one hundred Ford cars of that era. Cord discontinued the cars in 1937 when his Auburn-Cord-Duesenberg empire collapsed. An attempt to revive the company in 1947 also failed. Many of the 500 cars manufactured in the 1930s are still around today, some with more than 400 thousand miles on their speedometers. Needless to say, a good Dusenberg is worth far more today than it cost in the 1930s. After all, the car was responsible for the well-known phrase, practically describing perfection, "That's a real doozy." Milford people were privileged see a real "Duesie" in the 1964 Centennial Celebration parade when Governor Frank B. Morrison appeared in town riding in a 1923 Dusenberg auto.

Building the Perfect Auto

Unless you were born in the 1930s, you are probably not all that familiar with the name Preston Tucker. Thanks to a tremendous advertising campaign handled by a famous New York agency, Preston Tucker, owner of a small factory in Ypsilanti, Michigan, became an American household word in the late 1940s.

Preston convinced the American public that he had designed and would soon manufacture an entirely new and revolutionary automobile. One that would quickly make all autos of the day obsolete. For his efforts in designing a better auto, Preston Tucker was presented with the first award at the World Inventors Exposition held in Los Angeles. The new "Tucker" auto premiered in Chicago in June of 1947 and was being touted as the "first completely new car in fifty years." The rear engine designed car was powered by a 5 x 5 six-cylinder engine built largely of aluminum that could be replaced in thirty minutes. Designed to cruise at 100 mph, the car was advertised to get 35 miles to the gallon. Only sixty inches high, yet 2 inches longer than the largest Cadillac of that period, the doors opened in the roof line to facilitate entry.

The front fenders of the car turned with the wheels while the lights followed the curves in the road. A single fixed headlight, controlled by a photoelectric cell, automatically dimmed the lights when another car approached. When the car was actually finished, the fender headlights remained stationary, while the single middle light followed the road. Tucker spent millions in advertising to proclaim the wonders of the new machine. One scenario portrayed "shapely" girls parading down a runway platform tossing replicas of conventional auto parts in a trash cans—parts said to be no longer needed in the new Tucker. At the first showing it was announced that within four months there would be several thousand of these revolutionary cars available at one thousand dollars each. Although the advance publicity was highly effective, several problems surfaced before the so-called "car of the century" hit dealers' show rooms. Problem number one was raising sufficient capital. The Securities and Exchange Commission warned prospective investors about what they felt were some of Tucker's exaggerated claims. Two states, Michigan and California, banned the sale of his stock. Tucker, being the smooth salesman he was, raised 25 million by August of 1948. Some dealers paid up to $80,000 for the Tucker franchise. When the SEC received the first annual statement from the Tucker corporation and discovered that only two million remained out of the original 25 million—and no cars were being built—they started investigating company finances. The handful of cars being paraded around the country for Americans to ogle were actually designed from 1942 Oldsmobile bodies streamlined with additional welded on parts. Contrary to what Tucker had said earlier, the cars could not be purchased for the quoted price.

Eventually, Tucker did manage to set up an assembly line where forty cars were in various stages of assembly were observed. However the car was still being built from Oldsmobile bodies fitted with Cord engines. Tucker did manage to raise four million dollars by selling advance accessories to his franchised dealers, but the Tucker bubble was about to burst. Following 800 pages of testimony and a four month grand jury trial called for by the U.S. Attorney General, the factory was closed in the summer of 1949. Tucker was acquitted of fraud, but the plant never reopened. Today the fifty autos built by Tucker are all in collectors' hands, mostly in the state of Florida. Considering the ratio of manufactured cars to the ratio of capital raised, someone has calculated that each Tucker automobile that was originally supposed to sell for $1,000 actually cost $510, 000 for each unit built.

That "Old Tin Lizzie"

I suppose my dad was quite proud of his new, black 1927 Ford Model T automobile. At least he should have been after having driven a 1923 Model for four years. While this was the last year Ford built his famous Model T, the 1927 Model boasted several new innovative ideas used later on his newer and better Model A. This was the first auto I remember riding in. I thought it was great—at least until I was educated by the "big ugly boys" in school. Seems like they had the opinion that a plain, black Model T Ford was really not considered all that prestigious. For some unknown reason, it appeared everyone else in school was riding in newer, more modern autos like Model A Fords or 1931 Chevrolets. Needless to say I suffered extreme mental anguish from the verbal abuse heaped on me by these boys, who apparently considered those who drove Model T Fords as either very poor or perhaps even second class citizens.

Not receiving any psychiatric counseling at the time, I'm not surprised by those today who believe somewhere, sometime I lost a good share of my normality. One little song I heard over and over was usually directed at me and went something like this:

The Way It Was

A little gas, a little oil
A little spark, a little coil
A little nail and a two-inch board,
Nail her together, and you got a Ford.

Now, a few facts concerning the famous Model T, the car that launched Henry Ford off to a great auto-building career and, until the advent of the Volkswagen Beetle, was the most popular car model ever built. Introduced in 1908, boasting a four-cylinder 167 cubic inch engine that generated 22 horsepower, more than fifteen million Model Ts were built and sold. In 1923, one of his better years, Ford sold more than two million units, or as many as all of the other carmakers combined. From 1908 to 1927 Ford sold close to one-half of all the autos purchased by American drivers, allowing him to capture industry leadership. Noted people who drove Model Ts included Sinclair Lewis, Charles Lindbergh, Babe Ruth, and Mexican bandit, Pancho Villa. Ford became a national hero in 1913-14 after he pioneered and switched to the assembly line method of auto building. This enabled him to assemble 1,000 Model Ts per day by 1913. In turn, he increased factory wages from an industry average of $2.41 to $5.00 per day and cut the work day from nine to eight hours.

By increasing plant efficiency, Ford was able to cut his car price from $800 in 1908, to as low as $275 in 1924. Some predicted he would have won the presidential election in 1924, had he entered the race. A poll of 258,000 readers conducted by *Colliers Weekly*, (a national news magazine) predicted he would have defeated Warren Harding by 37,000 votes. The popularity of the car started to decline soon after 1925. Ford resisted making improvements to accommodate buyers' changing tastes and improving road conditions. In 1909 he made a vow to the public which soon became a national joke: "No new models, no new motors, no new bodies or colors. In fact you can have any color you want as long as it is black."

Some historians say this was not really the true picture, since many of his earliest cars were painted "Brewster green" with red striping. The Model T did have several bad faults, like no fuel gauge. To check your fuel level you were forced to remove the front seat and use a stick to measure the depth in the tank. In addition, because it had no battery the headlamps usually dimmed when the motor slowed down.

Eldon Hostetler

For Ford, a company that started with a capital of $28,000 in 1903 and quickly zoomed to industry leadership, refusal to replace a model that was approaching obsolescence was bad news. In late 1927, Ford introduced his new Model A, a classic auto styled by Henry's son Edsel. The new model also proved to be an American favorite. Although Ford sold 4.5 million units in five years, General Motors emerged as sales leader in 1927 and 1928. Ford regained sales leadership in 1929-30, but has not led the industry since.

Recreational Activities in the "Good Old Days"

*H*ow did American citizens spend their leisure time in the "good old days?" How did they manage without movies, radios, television, video games, golf, junior and senior high school sports, Big Red football and many of the water sports we just take for granted today? Imagine how your spare time activities and social life would change should you be deprived of your numerous automobiles. While the majority of the early settlers may have engaged in tougher, physical-oriented jobs, some statistics would indicate they may have kept a less demanding schedule than the average family of today. This could mean that they may have had as much, or even more time for recreational activities.

By 1871 Milford citizens had already organized a baseball team known as the "Milford Blue Belts" and were playing local teams like Dorchester, Seward, Crete, and Beaver Crossing. In fact, they were so "hooked" on the game that by 1913, they actually petitioned the Seward County Board of Supervisors for permission to engage in the sport on the Sabbath. For years, questionable recreational activities were banned by the so-called "Blue Laws" in effect at that time. The board granted permission only if a law officer was present at each game. So far I have been unable to determine why this was a requirement.

Horseracing was just as popular as auto racing is today, at least the 1872 Milford *Blue Valley Record* editor called it "the hottest new item in town." Running, trotting and pacing were all featured on the

Eldon Hostetler

This bandshell erected in the Milford City Park soon after World War II is no longer a fixture of Milford life.

new track west of town, usually on Saturday afternoon. Of course there was always the unresolved question as to who had the fastest horse in the community. In 1905, Ben Rediger challenged the local veterinarian, Doc Clark to "put up, or shut up." A race was arranged from the Stauffer School house to the Amish Church (a mile and a half) with John M. Stahly acting as referee. After Clark won the race, Rediger complained Clark's horse had some kind of an unfair advantage.

    Hunting and fishing were just as popular with men as today, in fact it may have been even more rewarding. Some traveled as far west as the Republican River where buffalo were still fair game as late as 1875. Deer and elk were still present in the county in 1870, as well as prairie chicken, grouse, and turkeys. Early in the 1870s ducks and geese were shot with ten gauge shot guns, packed in barrels of salt, and shipped east with no season or limit. A new law passed in 1880 made it illegal to ship wild game across state lines, which soon put a stop to this activity. In 1917 the Stauffer Brothers were forced to run this ad in the *Milford Review:* "We have been compelled to forbid any hunting on our property, because of acts of depredation to fences and the fact we had to destroy a valuable colt due to gunshot wounds."

The Way It Was

According to this early news note, hunting was quite competitive, and at times maybe just a wee bit naughty: "A lot of rowdies from Seward County went to Bruce Park's sale Thursday the 14th, and made fools of themselves. Last week David Nokes beat the record on the West Blue. His score for the week was 115 cottontail rabbits, 18 jack rabbits, 3 turkeys, 30 squirrels, and three bee trees. But the boys outscored him on high five and seven up. He also caught a number of fish by cutting a hole in the ice to fish through (*Milford Nebraskan*, February 1888).

Lake Quenchauqua was a popular spot to spend many hours boating and picnicking, or as one newspaper editor reported "just lolling away a day." Blue River water was also used for swimming as well as to take your weekend bath.

Being a veteran news reporter, the *Milford Nebraskan* editor was quite familiar with the differing approaches used by men and women seeking personal, relaxing quiet time: "We never saw a woman around town in her shirt sleeves with a cigar between her teeth slipping into every saloon she saw. We never saw one go fishing with a

The circus comes to town about 1896. Two of the buildings in this picture are still standing and are now used as the Milford NAPA store on the north side of Main Street. Photo courtesy Keith Boshart family.

bottle in each pocket, sit on the damp ground all day, and go home at night drunk. Neither have we seen a woman yank off her coat, spit out her 'hawds' and say; 'I can lick anybody in town.' God bless her! She just ain't made that way (May 1, 1891)."

Another early, popular recreational activity was dancing, especially a step known as the "Lite fanta toe," also known as the "Light Fantastic Toe." This news note from the May 7, 1913 *Milford Review* tells more: "Last Saturday night friends of Mr. & Mrs. Simon Yordy sprang a farewell party on them. Games and skipping the 'lite fanta toe' were indulged in up to a late hour." Late night dancing was always an important part of these celebrations.

Fourth of July was usually considered a time to leave the farm, pull out all the stops and celebrate with patriotic gusto. "From the large number of people at the fourth of July celebration, we decided Milford has the largest number of people in the Blue River valley (*Blue Valley Record*, July 13, 1872)." We may even be considered "sissies" when it comes to the size of legal fireworks allowed today. In June of 1904, the Milford Board of Trustees met and passed a resolution "that no longer than three inch firecrackers will be allowed within the city limits of Milford."

The Seward County Fair was a welcome diversion for many hard working farmers. According to the editor of the *Seward Advocate*, the Seward County Agricultural Society was organized in 1871 and the fourth annual county fair was held in 1879. Many Seward County towns also held special celebrations during the summer months. This news note from an August 2, 1911 Seward newspaper reports one such celebration: "A jolly crowd of 100 Milford Boosters came gliding into Seward riding in 25 autos. They were accompanied by waving flags and their Cornet Band. They were promoting the up coming festivities to be held in Milford."

The April 16, 1909 *Milford Nebraskan* reports how some local wrestling fans attempted to enjoy their favorite pastime: "Joe Hershberger, Ray Trabert and Pete Schlegel each took a load of our sports to Crete to see a wrestling match, which they thought would be held in Crete. When they arrived there they found out the match was being held in Minnesota. Occasionally good, lively entertainment was provided on the street free of charge, especially when local citizens ironed out their differences using their fists: In October of 1909, two local men retired to the back end of the street to 'repair their differ-

Happy fishermen and 49 fish back in the "good old days."

ences'. The editor reports it was spirited and gamy for about three rounds but the decision was given to Rediger after Hemsath announced he had had enough. Some say the men had brushed at the picnic in August and had been looking for satisfaction."

Other Milford citizens enjoyed somewhat more cultured activities than those just mentioned. One activity considered educational as well as cultural was the Chautauqua program. This news item from the June 24, 1908 *Milford Nebraskan* reports more: "The first annual Chautauqua was held in Milford July 8 to 14; Now if you are looking for recreational amusement, or intellectual attainment, plan to be with us. On the program: "Ministers' round table: The place of the pulpit in moral reform." For farmers there was "How to promote the social and intellectual life of the farmer" with Clarence Wertman presiding."

A 1900 newspaper ad urged readers to purchase reserved tickets for the Milford Minstrel Show to be held Saturday night. "Tickets will be on sale under the Opera Hall (top floor of what is now Schlegel's grocery store). "Ten Nights In a Bar Room. The play will be rendered along with the balancing act and other new feats. Admission 10 cents."

The first library in town was the "reading room" installed by J. L. Davison for the benefit of his waiting mill customers in 1874. The first attempt to establish a Milford public library was made in 1894. "Our circulating library of over 300 books has arrived and is being put in order at the newspaper office. Come in and see the books." Finally by 1912 some action was taken: "A public library is now assured through the efforts of the Congregational brotherhood. The first consignment was 30 volumes, all they needed to do was pay the freight, which the brotherhood will pay. At present the library will be housed in the 'Peoples Variety Store' under the supervision of Fred T. Sullivan, owner of the store. In all we now have 87 volumes, including good heavy reading for those who indulge in this line, and lighter reading for those who love stories."

Milford citizens absorbed additional culture when William Jennings Bryan spoke in the city October 10, 1922 at 10:00 P.M.

Maybe due to the lack of television and today's other electronic gadgets, the meaning of the word "couch potato" was probably unknown in 1900. In January of 1899, Fred Borden, Albert Troyer, and Ira Young skated to Seward on the Blue River, a distance of fourteen miles.

Touch football and boxing was also popular with the boys. One good example of how community entertainment has changed since "the good old days" would be this example from 1900: "Hon. C. E. Bently addressed our people Monday evening on 'Temperance.' Our business men and saloon keepers very kindly closed their doors and the hall was packed with an eager audience who gave close attention to the end. The address was pronounced to be one of the best ever given here on the subject (*Milford Nebraskan*, April 7, 1899)."

I'm quite sure that most modern day residents of Seward County would tend to agree that a good lecture on temperance might be considered just a wee bit dull.

The Nebraska State Fair was also a popular destination for many early Milford residents: "Agent Pumphery reports the sale of rail tickets to the state fair as follows; Monday 33, Tuesday 293, and Wednesday 135 (*Blue Valley Blade*, September 4, 1904)."

A July 6, 1916 newspaper note mentions that a new opera house 100' x 40' was being built in the city. An older building often mentioned in early newspapers was located above Erb's grocery (now Schlegel's) store. Milford, like most small towns in Nebraska supported opera houses at one time in their history. Here all types of so-called culture-oriented activities took place.

The Way It Was

In February of 1885 the city boasted of yet another recreational opportunity when this announcement appeared: "Milford's roller skating rink is finished, and the new craze promises to be both long and profitable." This building soon burned down and was never rebuilt. Movies were first mentioned in Milford about 1912 with this notice in the newspaper: "We will run a good clean reel of comedy *With The Seven People* on Monday night, making the best show you ever saw for a nickel." Free movies sponsored by the Milford merchants were first shown in January of 1922.

Another new trend was started in the summer of 1922 when several people in the town installed radio sets for the first time. The editor commented, "Imagine, some can now get the markets directly from Omaha." Even the invention of the automobile and airplane was exciting entertainment for many local residents: "Tuesday evening three airplanes passed over Milford. They are now becoming quite common (*Milford Review*, June 1922)."

The *Milford Review* editor wrote in September of 1915: "We counted 13 autos go by our office in fifteen minutes." Talk about excitement!

One notable change in leisure time management from a hundred years ago would be the amount of time spent in church-sponsored activities. Activities far removed from the so-called "caring and sharing will meet your every need" category so popular today. Before the Revolutionary War about nine out of ten people were said to be at least "nominal Protestants, although less than 7% belonged to an organized church when the war ended. As thousands moved west, many unaffiliated with an organized. Church, church leaders decided drastic steps must be taken to win them for Christ. Revivalism provided a partial answer. Starting about 1790, camp meetings and revival meetings spread like wildfire throughout the south and west spurring what is often known as the *Second Great Awakening*.

"The noise was like that of Niagara...Some of the people were singing, others praying, some crying for mercy in the most piteous accents... I saw at least five hundred swept down in a moment as if a battery of a thousand guns had been opened upon them, and then immediately followed shrieks and shouts that rent the very heavens. In the excitement, some people spoke in unknown tongues." This testimony from *Reader's Digest*'s *The Story of America* (p. 95) introduces us an early American revival meeting. From 1890 to 1930 special revival meetings were the "in thing" in Seward County. While most lasted a week or ten days, some lasted three weeks and one over six weeks. Some local citizens would drive to other towns quite some distance (over 100 miles) from Milford to attend meetings being held there. One of the earliest revivals recorded in Seward County happened in the Beaver Crossing community in 1872: "Walnut Creek Precinct is being enlivened by a revival under the auspices of the Methodist Church. Twenty five have already been converted (*Blue Valley Record*)."

In June of 1884, the *Milford Ozone* editor said this: "Harrison the boy preacher, is waking up all the old sinners around town, including newspaper scribes." Let the reader be the judge; was he complaining or did he have a guilty conscience?

The editor of the *Seward Reporter* newspaper appeared to be somewhat skeptical of the meetings and expressed a slightly different opinion: "The *Lincoln Journal* reported a man by the name of Severs, attended a camp meeting on Monday, and seemed much elated having received the Holy Ghost, and remarked to his mother on Tuesday he would jump in the well. He did so, and was considerably bruised and injured for his foolishness. He is said to be in a perfect frenzy of excitement (*Seward Reporter*, July 9, 1874)."

Evidently he had not changed his mind one year later: "From the large number of insanity cases caused by protracted Camp Meetings, it is a serious question as to whether they are more damaging than beneficial to man kind. Certainly those unfortunates who become bereft of all reason, and become 'mad' are to be pitied (*Seward Reporter*, September 20, 1875)."

Apparently disagreeing with the opinion of the *Seward Reporter* editor, meetings continued for many years in the Milford vicinity, reaching a peak about 1919. "Revival meetings will be held every night at the 'Egly' church. Special music every night. Good old time gospel preaching, conducted by Evan E. White. J. C. Rediger pastor."

This notice appeared in the June 13, 1919 *Milford Review*. "There will be a tent meeting held in what is known as the 'Pleasant View' grove three miles west and three miles south of Milford. For information on tents and cots, write evangelist Evan White of Milford."

"The camp meetings held by the Pentecostal Assembly, five miles southwest of town, is being well attended. Much interest is being shown. people are being saved and filled with the Spirit in every service. The following ministers are present: Clyde Baily, Mr. and Mrs. Albers of Sterling, Kansas, John Brown and Harry Van-Loon. (September 17, 1916)."

For reasons unknown today, certain preachers were more popular then others, according to this notice in the *Milford Review* on May 16, 1917. "Next Sunday will mark the return of N. W. Rich, that 'Godly' man who was with us one year ago, and did so much good in the vicinity. Mr. Rich is not the type that pulls off his coat as if he is 'going after you' with a hammer, nor does he 'rip' the other churches and declare 'they are all on their way to Hell'."

Occasionally the services would continue until late at night, and many times meetings were held on weekday mornings as well as in the evening. Not all Milford churches followed this intense pattern, but most churches scheduled far more meetings of this type than today. This was also the day when "camp meetings" were quite popular. Camp meetings would usually last a week, and many were held south of Milford along the West Blue, usually designed for the entire family. While not recreation, these meetings must have consumed hours of spare, as well as so-called "working" time.

And then just like today, early Milford natives loved to travel. The September 15, 1899 *Milford Nebraskan* reports this journey by one of the town's leading citizens: "David Bender and wife returned home from their trip on Friday. They visited in Canada and Iowa for four weeks. They enjoyed the trip very much and reported the people are generally prosperous and in good health and have good crops. But then he thinks our crops are just a little better, and is glad to get back to Nebraska. A visit away from home always makes one appreciate Nebraska." Maybe if the same prices were available today as 100 years ago, Milford natives would travel just a bit more.

This news note from the September 7, 1888 *Milford Nebraskan* proves the point: "Jake Stutzman, David E. Stutzman and Joseph Kuhns left for a reunion in Holmes County, Ohio. The round trip tickets cost $16.50."

Or this ad in the May 25, 1904 *Milford Nebraskan*, "From June 3, to June 20th, the railroad will sell round trip tickets to the Worlds Fair in St. Louis for $10.00."

Hotel rooms were also very affordable according to this ad appearing in the 1899 *Milford Nebraskan:* "Visit the Victoria Hotel located at 1308 Dodge Street in Omaha. Newly remodeled rooms with modern furnishings large airy rooms. Rates $1 and $1.50 per day."

Café food was also a bargain: "E. E. Hostetler purchased Sam Unzingers Restaurant and is also an agent for fine woolens. He will sell you a large bowl of soup for a nickel (*Milford Nebraskan*, September, 15, 1898)."

Meanwhile, over at Longford's fine bakery, Mr. Longford was advertising seven loaves of his delicious, home baked bread for 25 cents.

Milford's Shogo Island & Laura M.

Although the Island was often referred to by early Milford newspaper editors, we have few detailed accounts to explain what "Shogo" Island was all about. The best information I have found so far is contained in a letter written to the *Milford Review* editor in 1920 by a former editor of the *Milford Nebraskan*, Mr. Brainard. Mr. Brainard wrote, "Shogo Island consisted of a small island of two to three acres, located north of Milford. It included a ferry boat operated by cable that would haul 50 to 100 people. It also included a large dance hall, as well as facilities for serving lunches and soft drinks. Forty boats were on and for rental at 25 cents an hour, and were usually rented out."

Realizing the raw, natural beauty of Milford, coupled with the availability of Lake Quenchauqua water, several moneyed developers were evidently ready to take the plunge. The Milford correspondent for the *Seward Reporter* newspaper reveals this bit of news in the May 6, 1884 edition: "Mr. Trimbleth of Michigan leased the beautiful island above the mill, and intends to fit it up as a 'pleasure grounds' for excursions, picnicking and boating. Boating is just splendid there now."

In the July 2, 1884 edition he reports more: "A Mr. Westover of Lincoln was in town yesterday looking at the feasibility of putting a steamboat on the Blue to run between Milford and Brown's Lake. Heretofore people have been coming here of their own accord without any special effort on the part of Milford citizens." So far I have been unable to discover which body of water was referred to as Brown's Lake.

An apparently excited *Milford Ozone* editor reported this news to his June 12, 1885 readers: "At last, some enterprising man has secured possession of the island. Four hundred people enjoyed a leisure day under the shade trees of the island." The new owners and developers appeared to be a group of assorted investors, one being the above mentioned Mr. Brainard.

Additional news notes in the July 10, and July 17 editions tell more exciting news: "The Laura M. is the name of the new steamer on which negations are pending. The money has all been subscribed, and the boat is ordered, and if it is up to specks will be shipped at once."

"The new steamer arrived here Saturday morning and has already been tested. She will steam through the waters at 10 miles per hour. Next week she will make regular runs between docks and Shogo Island, leaving the docks at 3:00, 4:00, and 5:00 p.m. Round trip fares are 25 cents. From this time on, very little information concerning the Laura M., or the Shogo entertainment complex is available."

According to this news item from the 1891 paper, it was a money-losing proposition for the stockholders. "I will sell on Saturday, May 23, 1891 at 2:00 P.M. to the highest bidder, at Hazelwood Imp. Co. the following property: The Steamboat, dance platform, tents, barges, organ and other miscellaneous equipment, lately used for picnics and party excursions on Shogo Island. This sale to cover the whole outfit connected. Call for particulars."

Earlier newspaper items reported the popularity of the so-called Shogo Complex. "A grand excursion from Ashland will be in Milford on Friday, July 24. A special train has been chartered. 500 are expected (*Milford Ozone*, June 19, 1885)."

"Pleasure seekers are now arriving from Lincoln and other places for the express purpose of spending the weekend on the Island (*Milford Ozone*, July 18, 1884)."

"A fine party of 500 Sunday school children from David City spent the weekend picnicking and rowing on the river (*Milford Ozone*, June of 1884)."

"What appears to have been one of the last big flings occurred in July of 1887 (*Milford Nebraskan*, July of 1887)."

"500 Japanese lanterns of all colors will be hung from the trees on Shogo Island campgrounds on the Fourth of July celebration. They will also be carried on all the boats. A dance will be held until after midnight."

Closure of the Shogo Island complex did not appear to stop people from taking advantage of Milford's natural beauty. According to the *Milford Nebraskan* editor in a May 13, 1904 edition, visitors kept on coming. "A special train was run out from Lincoln to bring a party of University students for a day of picnicking along the Blue."

"Three Presbyterian churches from Lincoln have united for a picnic along the Blue June 31st. A special train has been chartered. About 600 will attend (*Milford Nebraskan*)."

Realizing Milford's recreational popularity and profitability depended on more visitors, by 1892, Milford businessmen were spearheading a drive to build a recreational electric rail connection directly to Lincoln. However, difficult financial times experienced during the early 1890s helped to cool this dream. What could we say more about the Great Pleasure Resort of Nebraska? At least it was fun while it lasted!

Celebrating Milford Fun Days in 1889

"The most popular of the many groves here has been the one on Shogo Island, not only because it is a pretty place, but because it is surrounded by deep still water that makes most enjoyable boating. For several years it has been under the management of enterprising men who have gone to great expense to keep the weeds and brush off and the grass mowed and to provide facilities to amuse the crowds drawn thither. An average of almost one excursion each week during the summer is normal, and the participants always go away satisfied with the pleasures found here. A small steamer, the Laura M., is kept running all the time when parties are on the island, and the ride up the river is a pleasant part of the day. The steamer has gone as far as seven miles up the river, and there are few more delightful rides to be had in the west than such a trip. Refreshments are always served on the Island, a large dancing pavilion is erected, swings put up and numerous rowboats are available at reasonable prices. One day last summer the managers of Shogo Island gave a 'Harvest Home' picnic.

The Way It Was

After speaking of the baseball game, trotting and running races, rope walking, etc.; all of which passed off nicely, the Nebraskan said: 'In the evening the largest crowd ever assembled was on the Island and the display of fireworks opened with sky rockets, pinwheels etc. upon the small barge on the water west of the island.' A gun boat carrying the rebel flag came down the river and opened fire upon the barge and in turn it was attacked by the Laura M, a continuous firing being kept up for over half an hour with ten and fifteen ball Roman candles. The Island looked beautiful with the hundreds of Japanese lanterns hanging from the trees and the barge also lighted, moving back and forth. The music, lights, magnificent display of fireworks and naval battle made a scene more beautiful than has ever been presented in this part of the state. The large crowd then engaged in dancing until midnight, when those from the country drove home by the light of a full moon. The whole day was a tremendous success, and the managers of Shogo Island are entitled to a great deal of credit for it. (*Milford Nebraskan*, June 1888)."

"The opening picnic on Shogo Island last Saturday was one of the most enjoyable events it has ever been the pleasure of our people to attend. The number coming from Lincoln and Seward was not nearly so great as hoped for, and yet considering the lateness of the season was fair…At 2 P.M. there was a trotting race between the Lincoln horse sent here for training by Wilson and Cosford and John Prossers' stallion and was won by the former. Dr. Brandon's ponies trotted as pretty a race as one could care to see; they are little darlings. The race was won by the mare. Joe Spelts' horse and Noah Stutzman's trotter made a nice race, Joe's winning. Of course the trot between Pennington and Blackburn Bros. mare was the great race of the day. They are both pretty steppers. Pennington won the race fairly, though the mare did not disappoint her friends. At about 3 o'clock the Special arrived from Lincoln and Governor Thayer was escorted to the grounds by Troop A, and was an interested observer of the racing and the drill of the Cavalry Company. The ball game between nines from Seward and Lincoln was a splendid game, resulting in Lincoln's favor by a score of 11 to 5. The football contest and the tub races came off as advertised. In the evening the Island was illuminated, and the meeting was called to order by Professor Paterson, who spoke enthusiastically of Milford's surroundings and possibilities for the future. The Choral Union rendered two choice selections (and by the way,

A typical Seward livery stable about 1895. William Rosborough and his help say good-bye to a traveling peddler starting on his route for the day. Evidently, his kind were a dime a dozen in that era. Identified men on the picture are Ed Meyers and Frank Newton Sr. Later Frank moved to Milford and operated a blacksmith shop and built Newton's café.
Photo courtesy of Marguerite Newton.

good music sounds sweeter on Shogo Island than any other place) and the Quartet helped to make the evenings entertainment delightful with a couple of excellent songs. Governor Thayer congratulated the people of Milford upon having such lovely groves and excellent boating. Hon. J.W. Small of York, also spoke of the pleasure it had been to him to see what Milford has to offer to summer visitors. He had been through the Sanitarium grounds and on Shogo Island in the afternoon and evening and believed we have the nicest place of any town in the state for the development of the summer resort idea. The display of fireworks followed these exercises (*Milford Nebraskan*, June 1889)."

Early Crime & Law Enforcement

"*It* is complained that loud and obscene language is becoming quite common and such a nuisance that ladies frequently pass by on the other side of the sidewalks during the daytime. It is difficult to believe there are men in our town who make such nuisances of themselves. If there is any truth in these charges, they must be taught that our citizens are determined this will be a respectable town (*Milford Ozone*, August 20, 1885, submitted by the Beaver Crossing correspondent)."

"A vigilante committee should be organized at once! The depredation of horse thieves has proven costly, and measures should be taken to stop such activity; let a dozen men agree to be ready to start in pursuit at once. We are glad to know that our Marshal has determined to arrest disturbers of our peace, and that people will uphold him. This is not a frontier town where rows are expected, but a community that prides itself on respectability. Something should be done to prevent any more disgraceful fights, as they are becoming all too frequent for the good name of the town."

While this may sound like a news editorial from a wild frontier town after the fashion of 1865 Dodge City, Kansas, these are all news items recorded in *Milford Ozone* newspapers published from 1884 to 1886.

One problem a hundred twenty years ago was keeping the peace. The editor in that day called these ugly incidents "rows," while today we might call them "altercations." From my interpretation of the editor's comments, many were caused by alcohol pickled brains in a few "fun loving" citizens.

The town had voted out the saloon several times the first time being in 1892. But it usually returned, sometimes within one year. In 1904 the saloon was finally voted out of town, this time until the early thirties, or until prohibition ended. In 1904 the fixtures were even sold from the building. With no saloon in the town the editor could write in September of 1917 "There was no need for a town Marshal during the picnic, as "John Barley Corn" was not once in evidence."

The closing of the saloon did not appear to solve all of the liquor-related incidents requiring the attention of Milford lawmen. Several times the county sheriff was called in to arrest local citizens for alcohol violations (even during prohibition). Charges filed included illegal sale of liquor, possession of, and too much use of "white mule booze."

One incident relating to liquor use happened in Seward on August 12, 1920. This scrape also revealed the "tough caliber" of one Milford lawman. "Last night while at the Seward ball game, a couple of men and a woman became so boisterous that a fight was the outcome and they were swearing up and down that no sheriff could arrest them. Deputy George Runty stepped up and shoved all three in his car and locked them in the county jail. He also found one and one-half gallons of the stuff that started the row, which he appropriated, along with their car (*Milford Review*)."

A second "heroic deed" executed by Marshal Runty happened in May of 1913 when the editor of the *Milford Review* tells us he hauled a big Negro into Lincoln and deposited him in the State Pen charging him with "making himself 'obstreperous'." Each reader can decide for himself what the sin really was.

An important job of law officers today is to enforce existing traffic laws, as well as investigate traffic accidents. Believe it or not, this was also important a hundred years ago. On February 24, 1893 this notice was posted in the local newspaper: "Anyone driving faster than a walk over our bridges will be prosecuted." Yes, even unruly horses caused traffic problems one hundred years ago.

This incident happened in 1898: "Charles Runty's team ran away from the Creamery and across the bridge before stopping in a telephone pole in front of Mrs. Funk's store. The buggy was completely 'used up' and one horse was cut up some. Frank Pumphery and Clarence Sample climbed the bridge railings and not very slowly when they saw the team coming (*Milford Nebraskan*)."

The Way It Was

T e July 26, 1917 *Milford Review* tells about this accident: "Paul Martin, who was driving a buggy, and Henry Eicher was driving an auto, and they both drive fast and ran into each other. Martin broke his collarbone, while Eicher got a good mouth full of glass."

In September of the same year the *Milford Review* reports this entertaining drama: "We did have an exciting time in town when Henry Stutzman's team hitched to a lumber wagon ran away. Many corners were turned, many small trees were run over, and one electric pole was broken off before they finally stopped."

Just like today, Milford police were often forced to intervene in domestic disputes. This exciting moment occurred in September of 1885. "On a Monday morning Philip Gammell, who lived in what is now known as Grover, began beating his wife. He is a big, burly man, while his wife is small and frail. The neighbors soon intervened, calling the Milford Marshal, who appeared and arrested Mr. Gammell. Mr. Gammell said 'it is his business if he feels like beating his wife because she is his property' (*Milford Ozone*, September, 1885)."

The reason he gave for beating her was her failure to put watermelon on the table for his breakfast. The Marshal informed the neighbors all he could do was take him to Seward where the Judge would probably only fine him $10 or give him a short jail sentence. Mr. Gammell said he "would love to stay in jail as that would be better than working. At noon he was able to raise the $5 bail money and was soon released from the Milford City Jail. Before he got home he was met by five angry men with horse whips (*Milford Ozone*, September, 1885)."

The editor said it this way, "who applied lashes with 'cheerful' energy and then he only got half of what he deserved." By September of 1886 the *Ozone* editor could write "The fact that every newspaper that carried the horse whipping story of Mr. Gammell comments favorably. The popular feeling is there should be more severe punishment for wife abusers."

In 1916, Milford city fathers passed this ordinance: "Anyone under 18 years of age shall be off the street by 8:00 P.M." The reason given to justify this law was "some parents who allow their girls out at night are not worthy of the name." Women were evidently blamed for the moral decay in society—even in that day. However, the ladies of Milford soon proved that their men folks were more "hot wind" than action in this incident happening in October of 1884: "A band of horse thieves was seen hanging around the livery barn, looking in on certain stables. Several bold, fearless men of the town volunteered to capture them, but on learning the number and character of the party refrained from making an attack. However, a valiant band of ladies soon formed and drove the thieves out of town (*Milford Ozone*, October, 1885)."

Milford citizens were rather disappointed after reading this news item in the September 30, 1898 *Milford Nebraskan*: "After all the excellent work of our citizens in capturing six robbers, four were dismissed for lack of evidence, while two others sawed their way out of jail taking another prisoner along. They were followed by blood hounds as far as York." "Late flash! before press time: The latest word is they were captured in Kansas."

Another *Ozone* news item tells of the arrest of two horse thieves in December of 1884: "Two horse thieves were captured in Milford. They had stolen two horses from a Presbyterian minister. One mistake they made was they were playing pool and trying to sell the horses, and one had made a down payment on a $6,000 farm in the vicinity."

Not all Milford crime happened one hundred years ago. This excitement took place in the city on April 20, 1935. "Faith Rahe, ten year old daughter of Guy H. Rake, was kidnapped from her home, and taken to Camp Kiwanis. Milford police and the Seward County Sheriff, who had been alerted by her parents when they heard her screams, captured the suspect after a high speed chase near Dorchester."

Eina Alhof of Scotia, Nebraska was sentenced to twelve years in the state penitentiary for the crime. Mr. Alhof told the court this story: He was driving through Milford about 8:00 when he noticed Faith Raye disrobing for bed in her window. He drove to Lincoln, rented a hotel room, returned to Milford about 1:00 and kidnapped her through the bedroom window.

Milford has also suffered from burglars several times. On October 1, 1939 Mrs. E. E. Hart was hit in the head with a fruit jar thrown by a burglar she surprised in her basement. On May 4, 1897 Dave Bender's house was robbed and he lost $40 in cash. A note in the 1935 newspaper says that a suspect is being held in the county jail on charges of stealing $10,000 from Real Estate dealer J.M. Bender." The Milford Review article mentions no further details, although the name of the perpetrator is given.

Evidently some citizens were hard to please and quick to complain and occasionally took the law into their own hands. This note from a woman in Grover appeared in the August 27, 1884 *Ozone*: "Notice is hereby given that on and after the twenty-ninth of August all persons found trespassing on my property will lay themselves liable to a good dose of buckshot!" Others were very gentle and evidently easy to get along with, like good old Walter Selby who posted this notice in the September 10, 1909 *Milford Nebraskan* paper: "If the party or parties who stole my fly nets, pitch forks and grain from my barn will kindly come to me, I will donate to them sufficient money as they need."

The wise old editor of the *Milford Nebraskan* at least thought he had it all figured out when he included this statement in an editorial published in 1900: "Almost any fellow can be a bum, or a tough if he so chooses to be. But it takes a really smart man to be an honest decent fellow good and respectable."

Evidently he was not too shocked by the high incidence of youthful crime according an earlier comment he had published in an 1891 editorial: "No one is surprised to see the number of young men trying to make a living without working. Most have parents, who feed and clothe them now, but when they are left alone to "root hog or die" the state of things will grow only worse from year to year. There are entirely too many young people looking for a soft, easy job with big pay, or for something just to turn up." Sounds like human nature has not changed all that much in the past 100 years! Has our generation determined to make Milford a respectable city?

First & Last Seward County Hanging

Nothing stirs the human emotion more than the news of a murder, especially if a hanging or lynching is involved. While we would like to think Seward County people have always been great law-abiding citizens, history tells us that many of our ancestors were actually made of ordinary clay. Our story begins near Beaver Crossing in 1874 when a Civil War veteran named Orlando Casler moved to the community to join his brother and sister, who had homesteaded in the vicinity several years earlier. Casler supported himself on a government pension of $14 per month earned when he suffered severe shoulder wounds in the war. Pardoned by the Governor of Wisconsin from the state penitentiary for horse theft, Casler was no stranger to crime. His father had served time in New York State for killing a neighbor with a land stake during a quarrel. Living alternately with his brother and sister for some time, eventually he moved in with a young, unmarried homesteader named Gilbert White, who at the time was in the process of selling his land. Unable to provide a clear title, White was forced to relinquish his claim. Hearing of the pending deal, Casler quickly slipped off to the land office and homesteaded the land ahead of the prospective buyer, evidently suffering no consequences for his deceit.

In July of 1878, a Civil War veteran from Missouri, George L. Monroe, appeared in the Beaver Crossing vicinity driving a team of horses and pulling an old wagon. The entire outfit was said to be worth not over $100. Still nursing a mania for horses and realizing that Monroe wanted to sell his team, Casler hatched up a devilish plan.

After inviting Mr. Monroe to move in with him for several days, Casler agreed to buy the team, explaining how it was necessary for them to drive to Seward to get the money. They left for Seward early on the morning of July 7. The rest of the story is somewhat shrouded in mystery. But it was the last time anyone ever saw Mr. Monroe alive.

Three days later, several boys fishing in the North Blue south of Seward reported seeing the body of a man lodged in some driftwood. T. J. Foster, a neighbor to Casler who happened to be in Seward that day, quickly identified the body. Foster recognized the body as the man who he had seen recently in company with Casler. Meanwhile, Casler came driving home with Mr. Monroe's team and wagon telling every one he met he bought the team from Monroe, who was now on his way to California. As you might suspect, all evidence pointed to Casler as the killer.

Seward County Sheriff Sullivan tricked Casler into driving to Seward with his newly acquired team where he was promptly arrested and charged with murder. The evidence against him was overwhelming. Camping along the Blue River for the night, it appeared that Casler shot Monroe with his own revolver while he was sleeping in the wagon box. Monroe's revolver was found hidden in Casler's horse stable, his pocketbook containing many of his private papers was found hidden in his bed while his suitcase containing most of his personal belongings was found hidden in a hedge row north of Beaver Crossing.

Evidently, Casler had shared the whole sordid story with his wife, who in turn confessed the details to the authorities—including where the incriminating evidence was hidden. At the trial held in February of 1879, Casler was quickly convicted of murder and sentenced to death by Judge Post of York, and the hanging date set for Friday, May 20, 1879. A large crowd, consisting of men, women and school children said to number between five and six thousand was on hand the morning of the 20th to witness the first, as well as the last, hanging to ever take place in Seward County. Realizing the carnival-type atmosphere might breed trouble, Sheriff Sullivan had taken the precaution of hiring extra deputies and erected a high board fence reinforced with barbed wire. Before the sheriff could spring the trap, the surging, restless mob rushed forward breaking down the fence, demanding to see some action. Had the sheriff failed to perform the hanging, most witnesses agreed the mob would have done the job for him. Many in the crowd appeared happy to just get a piece of the scaffolding for a souvenir. In 1879, a public execution was said to be contrary to Nebraska state law, although most would agree he had no other choice. It was reported the last words spoken by Casler were, "Before God and man, I am innocent."

Incidentally, Orlando Casler homesteaded the east one half of the northwest quarter of Section 34 in L Precinct, land now owned by the Charles Miller family.

Gun Play in Milford

Being enamored with guns and stories of "gun play" is as American as apple pie. This could be because most older Americans grew up feeding on violent, pioneer-Indian, good guy-bad guy, Lone Range and Jessie James stories. Gunslingers and those who settled disagreements with deadly lead are sometimes worshipped as heroes, while one popular, but deadly revolver was usually known as the "peacekeeper." Is it any wonder that our nation is still the world's number one maker of guns, tanks, warplanes, munitions, and other types of destructive weapons?

While some say our world is getting more violent and wicked to fulfill Biblical end-of-time prophecy, history tells us violence has been a way of life for thousands of years. Certain individuals in every generation have insisted on having their way regardless of the cost, often using a gun to back up their demands. One stranger visiting Nebraska City in 1866 said, "While boarding in a first class hotel, with few exceptions, the men eating in the dining hall were all armed with pistols, and it was not safe for a man to venture outdoors at night."

In late November of 1878, an angry mob battered down the jail door and forcibly hung two men accused of shooting a prominent Nebraska City resident. As late as 1882, the editor of the *Seward Reporter* wrote, "It is surprising how many people in Seward County still carry pistols." One visitor checking into a Milford hotel in 1885 shot himself in the hand while unpacking his valise, requiring Dr. Brandon to perform surgery to remove the bullet.

While the majority of early Milford residents were law-abiding citizens, the town did experience one deadly "gunslinger," Dodge City-style shooting. It took place in March, 1880 in East Milford. It is also interesting to note that four out of the five homicides happening in the Milford community since 1880 were committed by an acquaintance. The first homicide, recorded in 1880, was no exception. In Milford's infancy, a small grocery store was built and operated by brothers Milton and John Granger. Their father Ben Granger and their sister (name not given) lived on a farm southwest of Milford which was said at that time to be in the West Mills community.

"Old Man Granger" (as he is described in the newspapers) got into a good argument over some family-related business being transacted with Samuel Bowker of Grover. It appears Bowker was related to the Grangers through marriage. Using some pretty disrespectful words aimed at Granger's recently married daughter, Bowker lost his temper. Big and muscular enough to settle most arguments with his fists, Bowker swung at Granger and knocked him to the ground.

Several days later, while Bowker was crossing the bridge connecting Grover and Milford, he chanced to meet John Granger who promptly invited him to stop at the store. Immediately Bowker threatened to "have it out" with the Granger family. Shedding his coat, he stepped out of his wagon spoiling for a fight. Pulling a borrowed revolver out of his pocket, John Granger told him he would be hurt if he did not back off.

About this time, Milton Granger made his appearance from around the corner of the store and fired one shot striking Bowker in the lip. The bullet lodged in his cheekbone. John Granger then fired two shots. One passed through Bowker's tenth rib and entered a vital part of his body, a wound which resulted in his death 48 hours later. Milton and John Granger barricaded themselves in their store. Deputy Sheriff Joe Keithly of Milford and Charles Lowe, backed by other Milford citizens, eventually arrested the duo. While the boys did not deny the shooting, they did pass it off as a not too serious offense. The revolver used in the killing had been purchased by one of the Granger brothers at Shupp and Sheiber Hardware in Milford that morning. While paying for the gun the buyer said, "There will be a man in Milford who might get a bullet if he doesn't take care."

Unable to post $1,000 bond, the boys were held in jail until their May 12th trial. Appearing before Judge Post on charges of killing Samuel Bowker, both pleaded guilty to manslaughter and were sentenced to ten years in the Nebraska State Penitentiary. One record says they served only half of their sentence, while another record says they served the full sentence. Mr. Granger homesteaded the east half of the southwest quarter in Section 14 in N Precinct, land now owned by Richard and Mary Roth. After the killing, the Granger family moved to southwest Nebraska.

Who Killed the Leavitt Sisters?

For the benefit of those who feel society has suddenly slipped into decay compared to the standards in vogue in years past, the facts concerning the murder of the Leavitt girls 113 years ago may bring us back to reality. While the news of a murder in any community is terrifying enough, homicides involving defenseless young children tend to bring out the worst traits in the neighbors, often arousing the public's wrath towards the suspected perpetrators. Of the sixteen (possibly 17) known homicides committed in Seward County since 1874, all of the victims have been adults with the exception of the Leavitt sisters.

This murder, committed in 1889, also uncovered and publicized some of the hateful grudges that sometimes prevailed in close-knit farm communities.

Our story is set in Section 18 of D Precinct, located about five miles east of Gresham in Seward County. It was there that a family from Maine by the name of Leavitt had homesteaded 160 acres. The Leavitts were the parents of seven girls ranging in age from eighteen months to four older, married daughters. On Sunday evening, June 20, 1889 the parents returned home from a trip to Gresham and found thirteen-year-old Bessie and eleven-year-old Caroline with their throats cut lying in the yard in a pool of blood. Early Seward County historian John Waterman remembered the occasion. He said it was "The most brutal of all Seward County murders or we will say the most horrible and heartless murder ever known in Nebraska, or any other state." A hastily summoned grand jury—in session for ten days—uncovered some startling evidence. The Leavitt family had many enemies in the neighborhood, some ready to accuse Mrs. Leavitt of murdering her own daughters. Seward County historian Cox, who was also a member of the grand jury said, "Some of the neighbors seemed very little concerned in the matter, according to their own testimony." Some who lived as neighbors to the family did not even bother to visit the family saying it was none of their business. When asked why he did not go down to see the murdered children one neighbor replied, "I didn't care, and I was busy at work."

One neighbor, known to have quarreled over fence lines and unruly livestock with the Leavitt family on several occasions was called to the witness stand. Living less than one half mile away he too admitted he did not visit the family in its hour of tragedy saying that "it was no concern of his." When sharply cross-examined he became very excited and "danced like a chicken on a hot griddle." On the witness stand for nearly half a day, he became so irritated he promptly went home and hanged himself in his own barn.

Some jury members felt he held the key to solving the murders, although the jury never did arrive at an unanimous decision. Fixing blame for the crime became more complicated because a heavy rain washed away helpful evidence. It would appear that many of the local residents had already made up their minds as to who actually killed the girls, many agreeing it was "old woman Leavitt." Inquiring about a motive, local residents answered, "the infanticide theory is based on her violent temper. She did not need a motive. She had an ungovernable temper and was crazed by passion when she committed the deed. In a fit of blind rage created by something done by Bessie, (the eldest victim) the mother picked up the first weapon at hand, which happened to be a knife, and either threw it at the child with deadly aim or thrust it into her neck. That little Caroline ran screaming from the house and that she was silenced forever by the same hand. That the husband to save his wife's life and his own, returned to town and told a far different story."

So who killed the Leavitt children? We may never know. While some blame the angry neighbor who hanged himself, some local residents continued to blame the mother. "Mrs. Leavitt's conduct at the funeral of the murdered ones was so strange as to shock Gresham. She did not exhibit the grief expected but rather a shrinking fear of her neighbors and sympathizers. She has openly a suspicion that her children were killed by the angry neighbor with whom she quarreled over the division of the land and she says threatened her life. This suspicion is derided by the community of whom he was said to be a respected member...The family came to Nebraska from Maine and showed an utter lack of culture as one of its most prominent characteristics (Most information taken from a June 28, 1889 article in the *Omaha Herald*)."

Mules—Worth More than a Man's Life

Remember when the "Little Boy Blue" story from Chester was making national headlines? I for one was interested in knowing if these Stutzmans had any connections with my Stutzman relatives living in Milford and Ohio. After reading an account in a 1879 Seward newspaper telling about the murder of a certain Henry Stutzman in Adams County, I determined to find and read the rest of the story. I soon discovered this Henry Stutzman was famous for being the first proven murder victim in Adams County. This little story also helps to prove the fact that not all of the world's "wicked" men are living in the 21st century, but that there were some around one hundred twenty years ago.

"On Saturday last, just like wildfire spread the news throughout our community that within her confines had been committed the biggest crime known to God and man 'murder.' The news spread from tongue to tongue, and flashed over the wires, and an investigation proved the awful fact that the news was true (Juniata Nebraska newspaper, 1879)."

In 1872 a young man by the name of Henry Stutzman arrived in Adams County from Pennsylvania. Settling on a homestead about five miles southwest of Hastings, it was said by his neighbors that he possessed those rare qualities of truth and honesty in all things and was highly respected by all who knew him. The second person to figure in the story was John McElvoy, a young man who usually made his home in Red Cloud some thirty miles southwest of Hastings. During the year preceding Stutzman's murder, McElvoy did odd jobs wherever he could find work and occasionally for Stutzman or his neighbors.

On the evening of February 7, 1879 John McElvoy left Hastings afoot carrying a rifle and a pistol heading south telling everyone he met he was headed for Red Cloud. On Sunday morning about 6 A.M., one of Stutzman's neighbors was awakened by McElroy who said he wanted to trade his rifle in on a saddle, saying he was on his way to Red Cloud.

Turning down the offer, the neighbor noticed that he was riding one of Stutzman's mules. Suspecting foul play, several neighbors hurried over to Stutzman's house and opened the door to discover a ghastly scene. Although dead, Henry was sitting upright in his favorite chair, his head resting on the table a tin pan placed under his battered face to catch the blood flowing from some terrible wounds. Organizing a posse of one hundred persons, authorities followed in hot pursuit, which was not difficult because there was a layer of newly fallen snow. Overtaken after a thirteen-mile chase, McElvoy admitted that he had killed Stutzman, but only in self-defense. His admission incensed the populace to the point where the crowd talked freely of a lynching party. It was only through the efforts of Presbyterian pastor Rev. D. Schley Schaff that the mob was dispersed. From his buggy, Schaff pleaded with the crowd to let the law take its course. Sheriff Martin tricked the crowd by exiting McElvoy through a window, rushing him to Kearney for safe keeping.

The Way It Was

A grand jury indicted McElvoy on two counts—murder in the first degree for shooting Stutzman with a rifle and for shooting him with a pistol. A jury trial lasting one day declared him guilty and sentenced him to hang on May 29, 1879. An appeal to the Superior Court remanded the case back for a new trial at which time he pled guilty of murder in the second degree and was sentenced to life in prison. Ten years later he was pardoned by Governor Thayer. All sorts of wild rumors were afloat as to the cause of the "hellish" deed, some alleging that Stutzman had just received money from the east, a fact known to McElvoy. McElvoy did admit that after he had killed Stutzman he felt he might as well take the mule team.

Authorities eventually pieced the puzzle together. Leaving Hastings Friday night, McElvoy intended to spend the night with a neighbor, but seeing a light in Stutzman's window decided to spend the night with him. Getting up during the night, he commenced a search of the house hoping to find cash. Seeing his actions were being observed, McElvoy fired a small revolver at Stutzman, the bullet striking Henry below the eye. A struggle ensued in which the deceased was thrown violently against the stove after which he was struck in the back of the head, badly crushing his skull. McElvoy finished the dastardly deed by firing another shot directly into Stutzman's head. One Hastings newspaper editor had this to say: "Whether the whole truth shall ever be told, time alone will tell, but one of the most unprovoked, cruel murders ever perpetrated in the state was committed. From the numbers of murders committed in our young state the past year, it would seem human life is of no more value than a bullock."

After publishing a version of this story in the Nebraska Mennonite Historical Newsletter, a man from Pennsylvania agreed Stutzman would have been a distant relative to the Milford Stutzmans. Stutzman's mules brought $100 each on his farm sale.

Forgotten Seward County Murders

A recent murder committed south of Milford has evidently spurred a renewed interest in previous homicides in the county. With help from early Seward County historians Cox and Waterman, plus news notes from my own files, I will attempt to clarify what appears to be some confusion regarding the number and circumstances leading up to several nearly-forgotten early killings in the county.

According to Cox, the two earliest killings probably happened on the North Blue near the present site of Ruby in 1858. He reported, "Tradition tells us that a Mr. McKinley and a Mr. Morton lived on the North Blue for a short time, but after killing two Native Americans were compelled to vacate." He also mentions the fact that the graves were often pointed out to him, as well as to other early settlers. Early records would suggest that no known white settlers were ever killed in Seward County by Native Americans, although Tommy West is said to have had several narrow escapes.

Both Cox and Waterman agree the first murder happened in Seward in May of 1874, when Nathan Clough's body was found near his home. His brother Warren was eventually charged with the crime. Due to the extreme publicity generated by the killing, the trial was moved to York County where Warren was found guilty and sentenced to hang. On the evening before the hanging Governor Garber pardoned Warren and reduced his sentence to life in prison. Clough served less than half of the sentence. The second recorded murder happened in July of 1878 when Beaver Crossing native, Orlando Casler, killed a stranger he had befriended named G. L. Monroe, a story told in more detail elsewhere in this book.

In March of 1880, William Bates and Hillard Thomas died in B Precinct as a result of an altercation instigated during a revival meeting service being held in a local schoolhouse. Three others were also injured in the fracas attributed to "bad blood" between several families. No one was ever prosecuted for the crime. About one week later a shooting occurred in East Milford (later Grover) resulting in the death of Samuel Bowker. Once more, "bad family blood" triggered an accidental killing in B Precinct. In April of 1882, a mother was killed by a bullet from her husband's revolver—fired at their son during a family quarrel. At his trial he was sentenced to life imprisonment, but was pardoned after serving only several years. The 1889 murder of the two Leavitt sisters near Gresham would have been Seward County murder numbers seven and eight.

On June 25, 1902, a Seward native shot and killed a friend and neighbor he said was "too friendly" with his wife. After committing the crime he promptly went home and shot himself. "Family trouble" was also blamed for a Seward killing on January 9, 1913, when a jealous husband shot and killed his wife of less than five weeks. Pleading guilty to the crime, he was sentenced to twenty-five years, but served less than three.

As far as I can determine, the only murder ever committed where the victim was not acquainted with his killer happened near Milford in 1906. On October 29, Jacob Votava, better known in Milford as "Bohemian Jake" was found dead in his small shack east of town. Eventually the crime was charged to two transient railroad workers who went looking for cash because they were well aware of the fact that he had just sold some hogs. Jake had no known relatives in the county.

One of the least publicized murders on record happened several miles southwest of Milford on December 16, 1908, when a wife and mother was killed by a family member. The person accused of the killing ended up hanging himself. Ninety-eight-year-old Mary Schlegel, who remembered the occasion, said many in the community felt that the guilty party went unpunished, while the innocent, but accused person killed himself.

In December of 1921, Patrick McFarland murdered Seward Mayor George Merriam. Maybe Seward County newspaper publisher and historian, John Waterman said it right in 1913: "It seems our office has more sympathy for criminals than for the victims in their graves."

A killing near Utica in late 1923, also proved to be the result of two brothers who apparently hated each other. This 1923 homicide was probably the last killing in Seward County until the 1998 murder southwest of Milford.*

Note: Many local citizens still question the circumstances surrounding the death of a young wife in Milford several years ago. Was this also "bad family blood?" Oral tradition handed down for several generations in the Van Andel family of Pleasant Dale tells of foreign and transient workers being killed by construction foremen during the railroad renovation project in 1905-07 all in the name of "maintaining order in the camp." (This story can not be verified by documented sources.)

While we would like to think of Seward County citizens as good law abiding people, 125 years ago one newspaper editor was raising questions : "What's the matter with the air which gives the breath of rural life to Seward in this state, that murder should succeed upon murder and tragedy follow tragedy in such close succession? Little news reaches us from the town and country of Seward that does not contain accounts of violence and murder. On Saturday another horrible occurrence added to the infamous notoriety of both town and country for bloody deeds and crimes, wherein two men, John Dobson a man named Ward, met each other in angry collision on the streets. Hard words soon led to something much worse than an ordinary muscular interchange between a pair of brutes. The account of the affair tells how Dobson struck Ward in the face with an iron bar, laying open his cheek, breaking his lower jaw, and closing both eyes. Not satisfied with this frightful performance the enraged beast…stabbed Ward three times with a dirk knife, turning the knife in the wound as if to mutilate his victim whilst he was yet alive. The last news about this ninety-ninth atrocity in the Seward county is that 'Ward will die.' A few more hangings for murder in that section of the state would now seem to be in order to illustrate the beauty of barbarous means of preventing that crime. But what ails the social airs of the Seward district? With what moral poisons are they permeated that murder and violence should riot there as they do? It is not an unusually drunken community, is it? On the contrary, our information it is quite the reverse, and yet scarcely a week passes that does not blacken that particular locality with a fresh record of murderous violence and crime (*Omaha Herald*, June 19, 1879)."[Author's Note: The above incident did not result in any deaths.]

Who Killed Mr. Lana ?

Area citizens may have been thoroughly shaken by an incident that happened on a farm southeast of Milford early Monday morning, October 8, 1923. Although the community had experienced three previous murders, the trial associated with this homicide served to put Milford on the crime map. "Not since the early history of the County dating back to the 'Casler' trial has there been an action in criminal court creating wider or more intense interest than the Vajgrt trial now before Judge Carcaran in the Seward County Court (*Seward Journal*, December 6, 1923)."

While some say it may be of doubtful value to recall and rehash unpleasant experiences happening in small communities, the ensuing trial held in Seward brought to light the morbid feelings inherent in many ordinary, law-abiding citizens. The editor of the *Seward Journal* said it like this: "Every single day the courtroom was crowded-some days more than others. Frequently those determined upon hearing all of the evidence brought noonday lunches and remained patiently, some of them from as early as 8 o'clock in the morning until 5:30 in the afternoon. All drank in the testimony with an avidity that, if it had been water would have been refreshing."

Maybe it had something to do with their lack of modern day "reality" television, or "tell it all" magazines available in grocery stores today. This is the story of a murder that managed to capture the rapt attention of many Seward County citizens in 1923.

"MILFORD, NEB. OCT 9—Antone Lana, thirty five year old farm hand is dead and Alby Vajgrt, fifteen year old daughter of farmer Adolph Vajgrt, living six miles southeast of Milford says that she accidentally killed him. Two shots from a 32 caliber pistol had taken effect in his stomach and one blast from a shotgun under his arm. The father of the girl said 'that he was feeding his stock Monday morning when he saw his wife running towards the straw shed where she picked up Alby Vajgrt who had fainted.' The girl said 'she shot Lana because he had betrayed her.' The father 'said he buried the body in a straw pile and in the afternoon hitched up and went to Crete to inform Dr. A. A. Conrad.' The doctor was brought to the farm where he ascertained the details of the case and notified the county attorney at Seward. The county attorney and the sheriff came to the farm and found the gun belonging to Lana in a wheat drill (*Seward County Journal*)."

Alby Vajgrt, fifteen year old daughter of Adolph said "she went to the straw shed about 5:30 Monday morning and encountered Lana who said that he was going to leave and would not marry her. She claimed that she struggled with Lana before she accidentally pulled the trigger. The body of Lana was considerably bruised about the head. Neighbors said there was considerable dissension between Mr. Vajgrt and Lana and they were both in the habit of carrying guns." A Coroner's jury, consisting of John Vance, Walter Stoltz, Jacob Brong, Bert Vance, John Andelt, and William Kammerer verified the story as

The above reproduction shows Alva Vajgrt, 15, (insert) and the straw shed on the Vajgrt farm six miles southeast of Milford, where Antone Lana, bachelor farm hand, was found slain Monday afternoon. The coroner's jury returned a verdict finding that Lana came to his death from gunshot wounds sustained in a struggle with the girl. The girl, in her testimony before the jury, named Lana as her betrayer. County attorney McKillip has announced that the girl will not be prosecuted.
Photo courtesy Lincoln Journal Star.

told by Alby Vajgrt. However, Seward County authorities as well as members of the Vajgrt family from Bellevue, Kansas disagreed with the findings of the jury. After intensive quizzing by Milford lawman George Runty, who claims to be a detective after the order of "Sherlock Holmes, Mr. and Mrs. Vajgrt and Alby broke down and admitted that they had all taken part in the killing. According to the confession said to have been made to Runty by Vajgrt, the mother and her daughter, both armed went to the straw shed where Lana spent Sunday night, and an argument ensued over his threat to leave

The Way It Was

"The girl, according to Vajgrt's statement shot Lana with a pistol. The mother then struggled with the farm hand. Finally freeing himself from her grasp, Lana made an attempt to leave the straw shed. The mother and daughter then picked up a 16 ft. 2 x 6 and beat Lana over the head, the alleged statement says. At this juncture the father appeared on the scene and aided in the assault upon Lana. After Lana fell under the terrific blows, another shot was fired in his body by either the mother, or the girl according to Vajgrt's testimony." The same story with some variation was also published in the October 9, 1923 Seward *Blue Valley Blade*, *Milford Review*, The *Seward Independent*, *The Seward Leader*, The *Omaha Bee*, and the *Lincoln Journal Star*.

I first learned of the murder from a *Lincoln Journal* clipping, including a picture of Alba and the notorious straw shed found in my grandmother's papers after she died in 1935. Two Seward newspapers, the *Independent* and the *Blue Valley Blade* devoted the entire front page to the story of the trial held in December.

Hearing the details concerning the confessions offered by the Vajgrt family, county authorities moved quickly to arrest the three suspects and confined them to the Seward County jail. The Vajgrts were released on October 24, when friends, relatives and neighbors cooperated to raise $18,000 bail money. Those signing the bail note were Frank Topik, Frank Vajrat, John Vajgrt, Frank Frolik, James Shaw, John Andelt, and Matt Forst. The trial was set for the first week in December to be held in the Seward County Courthouse. Lawyers for the state's prosecution were Barth and McKillip and for the defense Thomas, Vail, and Stoner, along with Barton Brothers of Wilber.

What followed may best be described as a three-ring circus more or less patterned after the notorious O. J. Simpson trial held several years ago in California. Due to the wide publicity generated by the local press, truthful jurors were hard to come by. This prior judgment was carried in one Seward County newspaper on December 6:

"The family of the girl are hard working respectable people, while the hired man seems to be an unprincipled villain, whose habit of drinking hooch intemperately intensifies his disposition. The youth of the girl—his employer's daughter, whom he ruined, shows him to be a beast that one shudders to even think of. [One-hundred-and-thirty-nine potential jurors were examined before twelve men were chosen.]

"From the time the prosecution began examining witnesses until it closed its side of the case at 5 o'clock Wednesday afternoon, twenty witnesses had testified. Some of these were on the stand for hours, while for others a few minutes were required. And every word of the evidence was impressively waited for. All spectators had their anticipation well baited. They were after the juicy parts of the trial and determined to get them, no matter if they had to stand in the aisles, or clutter the passage ways and otherwise make themselves conspicuous to the annoyance of the court. But the court officials were very lenient with the impetuous crowd, and this leniency had a tendency to subdue the noise so usual in such a place.

"The first witness was Mrs. Julia Vajgrt, wife of Adolph and mother of Alby. She related the very numerous incidents connected with the tragedy from ten days prior to and immediately surrounding it. She described scenes enacted on the morning of Lana's death, entering graphically into details of the trip she and Alby made to the straw shed at about daylight, where Lana was found, he not having slept in his usual room in the house that night. She described the struggle, and wept most of the time while doing so. She also told of the anguish she felt when she learned what had happened to Alby and many other things connected with the movements of the family. The same curious crowds characterizing the more than one week of hearings continued to jam the audience room of the court. Several times the Judge was obliged to reprimand the auditors to observe order, and once the merriment assumed such a stage of hilarity that he threatened to have the officers clear the room of all spectators. An order was also issued prohibiting the presence of during court hours of pupils from the city schools. Superintendent Williams having complained that many students were absent from the school rooms and it was his opinion they were sneaking off in order to be at the court (*Seward Journal,* December 6, 1923)."

The twelve man jury was housed and fed in the courthouse until the trial was finished, at which time they reached a verdict in several hours. When a "not guilty" verdict was announced to the audience, the crowd stood up and applauded wildly. In reality, all three Vajgrts were set free. In an editorial the following week, one *Seward Journal* editor said it like this: "Who killed Tony Lana? Now don't all answer at once. A jury is an unknown quality like the Irishman's flea you can never tell which way it will jump. All of the people who heard Deputy

Attorney Charles Barth argue for the state were impressed. He said 'that 14,000 murders were committed in the country last year, but due the employment of clever lawyers by the defense only 1000 were convicted' (*Seward Journal*)."

Evidently many in that day felt the Vajgrts were as guilty as sin and should have served time for manslaughter. After the trial, one "arm chair quarterback" said "the entire truth was never told" and suggested all of the evidence pointed to an earlier killing. His theory: Lana did not spend Sunday night in the straw shed, but was confronted and killed by the family late Sunday night when he returned home. After killing him they dragged the body to the straw shed and attempted to bury it.

Nebraska the "Man Burner State"

Shortly after the Civil War, hundreds of new settlers were arriving daily to claim their future in Nebraska. Having already exhausted most of the good land in eastern Nebraska before 1880, new immigrants were now claiming land west of Grand Island, especially in the southwest and Sandhills regions.

Due to favorable weather conditions experienced at the time, many were willing to risk dryland farming as far west as Broken Bow, although many experts still considered it better "cattle country." Meanwhile, numerous Texas cattle barons were looking north for better pasture, many hoping to expand and take advantage of better beef markets created by the completion of the Union Pacific Railroad. In 1875-76, the Olive family left Texas and moved to Nebraska. Bringing their huge cow herd with them, the Olive boys, Prentice (nicknamed Print), Ira, and Bob took up ranching along the Dismal River in the vicinity of Callaway.

Although their cattle spread was located in the Callaway area, the boys all built houses near Plum Creek or what is now known as Lexington. Having one of the largest cattle herds in the state at the time, the Olive boys were famous for their "gun-play" and usually succeeded in getting anything they wanted. By this time numerous homesteaders had already discovered that good corn crops could be raised in the vicinity. Two homesteaders, the Luther Mitchell family and bachelor Ami Ketchum, formerly from Merrick County moved in and staked out claims. Building sod houses they proceeded to "bust sod" and plant corn.

To the Olive family, fenced corn fields were a threat to the free, open range they just assumed they were entitled to and even the thought of barbed wire fences irritated them to no end. Olive family longhorns soon trampled the helpless corn fields into oblivion and after inspection, the farmers discovered the wires had been deliberately cut. Having nowhere to go and no way to support themselves, Mitchell and Ketchum occasionally helped themselves to "free Olive beef" which they intended to sell in Kearney. Catching them red-handed, Print Olive persuaded Sheriff Anderson to deputize him to arrest the two men.

On November 17, 1878, Print and Bob Olive, along with several of their cowhands attempted to arrest Mitchell and Ketchum. In the ensuing fracas, Ketchum shot and wounded Bob Olive, a wound that resulted in his death several days later. Realizing the gravity of their situation, the men abandoned their homesteads and quickly returned to Merrick county.

Arrested in Loup City by the Merrick County Sheriff, they were quickly hustled off to the Buffalo County jail in Kearney for safe keeping. Not entirely satisfied with this arrangement, Print Olive offered a $1,000 reward to anyone bold enough to deliver Mitchell and Ketchum to his home in Custer County.

Anxious to claim the reward money as well as sympathy for the Olive family induced several area lawmen to take him up on his offer, the two men were eventually delivered to Print Olive. Taking possession of the men about ten miles southwest of Broken Bow on December 10, 1878, Olive and his men promptly hanged the men on a cottonwood tree. From here on the true facts are a wee bit hazy. One version reports that two drunken cowboys packing a jug of "potent" whiskey for whatever reason succeeded in burning the bodies beyond recognition. Print Olive and his accomplices were arrested and sent to Lincoln for safekeeping. Money being no object, Olive was able to assemble a team of top notch attorneys to defend him. Knowing that Olive had numerous friends in "high places" in his home community, the trial was transferred to Hastings in Adams County. Held in the largest building in Hastings the trial got under way on April 1, 1879. Fearful of threatened outside intervention, the Adams County Sheriff requested and received National Guard troops from Omaha to help keep the peace.

To make a long story short: Olive and one of his buddies were found guilty of manslaughter and sentenced to life in prison where they served little time. Olive appealed the verdict and requested a new trial, this time to be held in Custer County. One source says the trial was never held and they were both set free. Olive left Nebraska in 1882 and soon owned large cattle operations in both Kansas and Colorado. Late in the summer of 1886, Print was shot to death in Trail City, Colorado, while quarreling over an unpaid $10 debt.

Our state has been designated by assorted nicknames, including: "Tree Planters" state, (1895), while today we are widely known as the "Cornhusker" state. Given this name to honor the UN-L football team, this name was officially adopted by the 1945 Nebraska State Legislature. Picked up by the national news media in 1878, this less then noble incident made great headlines and for several years after 1880, Nebraska was known as the "The Man Burner" state.

The Ku Klux Klan in Milford

Most Americans are quite familiar with the organization known as the Ku Klux Klan or KKK (also known as the Knights of the White Camellia in Louisiana). One similar organization was known as the White League and the Invisible Circle. These organizations were organized chiefly to reduce the power of the Negro vote after the Civil War. Other objectives of the organization included expelling undesirable carpetbaggers and nullifying Congressional laws that might have placed Southern whites under the control of a party largely supported by newly enfranchised Negro voters.

Organized in the fall of 1865, the Klan and other similar organizations were soon powerful enough to openly defy and flaunt federal laws designed to give Negroes their civil rights. This meant "keeping the Southern Negro in his place." The pointed cardboard hats, masks, long white flowing robes, and secretive rituals were especially designed to frighten and humiliate former slaves. The Klan reached its height of power from 1868 to 1871 during the confusing aftermath of the Civil War, especially during the so-called Reconstruction Years. By 1877, the Klan had succeeded in accomplishing many of its goals, and gradually became a lesser force in southern politics. Those old enough to remember civil rights and school segregation struggles lead by Martin Luther King from 1955 to 1963, may remember the nasty role played by the Klan. While not completely dead today, Klan members prefer to play a less visible role in race relations and politics than they did from 1865 to 1965.

From interviews with the late Ezra Ehrisman, I was told the following story.

In the summer of 1924 or 1925, dozens of unfamiliar automobiles, mostly sporting Lancaster County license plates, turned into the east end of Main Street. We do know that at least one of the marchers was a Milford native, because a friendly Milford dog known by many in the neighborhood trotted out to welcome his master.

Sample of the literature the Lincoln Klan handed out in Milford in 1924-25.

Soon a long line of marchers, all clad in white robes and pointed cardboard hats carrying a huge wooden cross, were marching through the center of town. They did not stop until they reached the west end of town, at which time they turned north into a pasture and burned the cross in a huge bonfire. You might ask what the Ku Klux Klan was doing in Milford in the early 1920s. Organized to frighten and harass African Americans, there was certainly no need to demonstrate in Milford at the time. What was going on?

The Way It Was

The original, exclusive "Negro hating" Klan that was organized in 1865 had completely accomplished its goals. The KKK was assisted by strict Jim Crow policies that were practiced in the South from 1865 to the time of Martin Luther King. The original Klan had practically been disbanded but the Rev. William Joseph Simmons from near Atlanta, Georgia, organized the second, modern day Klan in 1915. The Rev. Simmons said, "This is a high class, mystic, social, patriotic, society devoted to the protection of womanhood and the supremacy of white Protestants. Devoted to the principle that the purity and values of native-born White Anglo-Saxon Americans must be protected at all costs, the Klan found eager supporters throughout United States."

Many so called "Bible toting Christians" joined Klan ranks to enforce this "higher God directed morality" on foreign born whites, Native Americans, Negroes, Jews, and Catholics. By 1920, the Klan had nearly five million members from New Jersey to Oregon. Methods of inciting the fear of God in non-complying individuals included whippings, tar and feathering, branding, mutilating, and lynchings.

We have few documented records to prove when the Klan first arrived in Milford or what effect it had on local church life or Milford politics. One *Seward Independent* news note published in connection with the Antone Lana murder trial (November, 1923) reported that a Milford Law officer threatened the Vajgrt family with speedy intervention by KKK members if confessions were not obtained. The Milford Klan was powerful enough to erect its own building, where regularly scheduled rallies were held. This building was located somewhere in the brick complex now occupied by Milford's Pizza Kitchen. Deed records show that a building was registered in the name of the Milford Ku Klux Klan, but no Milford names are signed in the records. This would be in keeping with the Klan's strict policy of keeping names of members in utmost confidence. However since this story was first written, I have discovered the names of five prominent citizens in another court document connected with the building. Ezra said the Klan soon lost its appeal to Milford people, many after witnessing the before-mentioned, scary march.

The new Klan was very powerful in Oklahoma, Oregon, and Indiana. One Klan leader was soon exposed for the hypocrite he truly was when David Stepheson, "Grand Dragon" of Indiana, was convicted of raping a young woman. This violent act eventually caused her death. This was ironic indeed since the groups' "God breathed" hatred of adultery was one of the great sins the organization was supposed to root out and punish.

What good common sense could not do, dollars helped to accomplish. The Klan was finally put on the defensive in 1944 when the United States Government ruled it owed a huge amount in unpaid taxes. From this time on, the power of the Klan gradually declined. The KKK appeared to be popular in the area for a very short period, mostly supported by Milford church people of the "fundamentalist" slant.

What happened in Milford was typical for that era. Other small towns in the state experienced the same scenario and the movement soon faded out.

Milford Institutions

Milford's "Shogo" Legend

According to Webster a legend is a non-historical or unverifiable story handed down by tradition from earlier times and popularly accepted as historical, the "Shogo Indian Princess" legend being one good example in Milford's history. The name "Shogo" has been used in Milford to designate a famous mineral springs, a city park, a café, a brand of mineral water and soda pop, a High School publication, and a famous recreational island. A large flour and corn mill and a lake famous for its recreational and ice-cutting possibilities was named after Chief Quenchauqua, a second hero in the legend. A popular brand of flour manufactured by the Milford mill was named for a third hero in the story Kolhanna. The first brickyard in Milford, known as the Popotone Brick Yards was named after another hero in the legend. Like all good "red blooded" American legends, this tale contains romance, jealously, intrigue, magic, and murder, all popular present day literary themes. This is the "Shogo Legend" as reported in the September 5, 1890 *Milford Nebraskan*:

"The frequent visits of Omaha, Otoe and Pawnee Indians to Milford with their sick, during the early days of that borough, and their encampment in a picturesque bend of the river just opposite Lithium springs, give rise to many inquiries on the part of many Milfordites. Supposing that there was some good reason for these regular visits of the savages, persistent inquiry and investigation was made by a representative of the *Omaha Republican*, and the following

Logo on early bottle.

Indian tale was elicited. It has never before been published, and is now contributed for the first time to the legendary lore of Nebraska. Added interest is given to the story by the fact that Lincoln and Milford are inferentially connected with it.

"Many years ago the Otoes and Pawnees were united under one tribal organization and presided over by a wise chieftain by the rhythmical name of Quenchauqua. Under his leadership happiness and prosperity reigned. The Omahas in time became strong allies of the united tribes, and together they waged successive war on the murderous Sioux and Cheyenne when occasion required or permitted, and that was not infrequently, for the braves of the Cheyenne who occupied vast tracts of the west and northwest territory inhabited by the Otoes and Pawnees, gave chase whenever opportunity offered, to the herds of buffalo, as they journeyed by their stronger brothers on their regular visits to the Salt Licks (near west Lincoln). Quenchauqua had a daughter, who was called Shogo, the fairest and 'best' of the prairie flowers. Trophies of the chase ordained her wigwam, and she was known and honored for her beauty far and wide. Among the young chieftains of the tribe alliance none was more assiduous in their attentions to the young princess than Kolhanna, of the Pawnees, and Popotone of the Otoes.

"Both of these youthful warriors were brave and noble as warriors go, and for a long time Shogo was unable to make any distinction in her affections between them. At last, however, she decided in her comparative judgment that while Popotone was 'Good' Kolhanna was 'Better.' In this comparative judgment the aged chieftain Quenchauqua coincided. As is ever the case, the course of true love did not run smoothly, and trouble ensued between these hitherto friendly tribes very soon after the espousal of Kolhanna. A division of the territory became necessary, and the Otoes were given the land east of the river, whose waters flowed to the northward, and the Pawnees were given a broad expanse of territory west of the river.

The prairie between these two allotments remained neutral. Experience promptly proved the folly of separation, and while maintaining individual organizations, the two tribes came to amicable understanding, whereby in case of an invasion, a union of forces was assured.

"This treaty continued in effect until the death of Quenchauqua, which according to the most authentic accounts must have occurred sometime prior to the time when the Spanish General Coronado entered the territory known as Nebraska in quest of the seven cities of Cibalo and the magnificent capital of the far famed King Tartarrax. The death of the chieftain Quenchauqua was followed by several years of estrangement. Finally Popotone sent a swift messenger to the camp of Kolhanna and requested him to meet the Otoes in council at the Salt Licks for the purpose of an amicable adjustment of the difficulty. The Pawnee chieftain, ever ready to form a union with his powerful brother, obeyed the request, and taking a few of his wise counselors wended his way towards the rising sun to the appointed place of meeting, buoyed on by the lithesome Shogo whose queenly bravery, as she rode her spotted pony towards the scene of her early childhood, dispelled any dark foreboding that might have lurked in the breast of Kolhanna as he though of meeting his old rival. Arriving at the designated spot, the weary travelers quenched their thirst at the babbling springs and exchanged greetings with their brother braves. The presence of the beauteous Shogo aroused a doormat feeling of jealously in the Otoe chieftain, and despite his good intentions, the preponderance of native treachery inspired him to deal a stealthy blow to Kolhanna, who succumbed to the surprise attack. The avenging spirit of the aged Quenchauqua arose from the spring and slew Popotone, and put to flight his warriors who were about to follow the example of their leader in waging war of annihilation on their defenseless guests. The spirit of Quenchauqua, seizing the tomahawk of the dead slayer, washed the blood stains away in the water, which were immediately turned to bitterness.

"It was decreed by the outraged spirit that the waters should be unfit for man or beast until many summers and winters had come and passed away. Then, turning with the weeping Shogo and her followers, the party sorrowfully departed in the direction of the setting sun. One half day's travel brought them to a rapidly flowing stream where the waters sparkled over rocky beds, shadowed by gigantic trees and winding vines. Proceeding to the western banks of the river the spirit of Quenchauqua smote the rock under a large elm tree and out sprang a crystal fountain of pure water, over which the sad hearted Shogo presided, healing the wounded and curing the sick of her nation until the Big Medicine Water came to be regarded by the savages as a panacea for all ills. Shogo was now the acknowledged queen of the Blue Valley. Her good deeds and self sacrificing devotion to her people resounded throughout the nation, and she was the recipient of many honors and worshipped as one who had direct communication with the Great Spirit. A high promontory situated a few hundred yards south of Big Medicine Water, adorned by stately oaks and overlooking Keego rapids, where the waters of the river lashed the sepulchered banks, was the quiet retreat of Shogo as she watched the rising sun, and appeared to hold secret communion with the departed prince, Kolhanna. This habit gave prominence to her supposed supernatural powers, and this picturesque elevation was held sacred by her dusky followers.

"Years elapsed, and a strange people clad in helmets and armor of brass came from the south (a portion of Coronado's army) and hearing, the sad story of the Indian queen, persuaded her that the one she mourned now inhabited the happy hunting grounds, situated many hundreds of miles to the southwest, beyond the mountains and streams. They told her that they were sent as special messengers to carry her to this land of delight. Their language and gorgeous array, unknown but in mythical traditions of her people added plausibility to their representations, and coincided with her dreams of the future. She was willing to undergo the hardships of a dreary march and camp for the sake of joining the companions of her youth.

"Thus allured, she was persuaded to accompany the cavaliers with a few trusted followers, and after the sacrifice of a spotted fawn on the promontory, and the dedication of the springs to the afflicted of her nation, she bade them farewell nevermore to be seen, but ever worshipped as a guardian spirit. Thus endeth the legend. The Big Medicine Water, as is already apparent, is the well known Lithium Springs at Milford, and the later place where the rudely awakened spirit of Quenchauqua turned the waters into bitterness was the site upon which the city of Lincoln now stands. Invalids and others who take daily drafts of the medicinal water at the artesian well in the government square have little thought that the sulfuric water had its origin in the sequel to an Indian love affair in prehistoric times of ancient Nebraska. It is that even in this day straggling Indians never miss an opportunity, when in the locality, of paying a silent visit to the former abode of Queen Shogo near Milford."

Early Shogo Water Health Care

The beginnings of Milford's early health care connection goes back many years to an unknown date. In 1885, the new editor of the *Milford Ozone* newspaper, Mr. Hansel wrote: "It has been reported to me that around 1840-50, up to five thousand Omaha and Otto Indians were camping on the south side of the Blue River using Shogo Springs water in an attempt to cure various types of illnesses. This fact can not be documented, especially since Mr. Hansel reported that he had only heard this. For myself, I would tend to believe the fact, but I would have some doubts as to the total numbers. Five thousand Indians living in what is now Milford would have been a 'heap of bodies'." It would seem these facts may have come from older Indians who remembered back to 1850. Around 1885, Milford streets were occasionally full of Native Americans passing through town, so I just assume the editor would have had ample opportunity to communicate with friendly Indians, some who may have remembered the occasion. Other early records, although not giving details, would hint that Shogo Springs water was widely used for medicinal purposes by various tribes, including the Pawnees. Not all that impressive looking today, at one time the springs were said to flow at the rate of 1,500 gallons per hour—certainly enough water to supply any and all needs. We do have documented evidence that the water was considered highly medicinal for several types of illnesses even before the early settlers discovered the springs.

A news item published in the 1907 *Milford Nebraskan* reported the importance of the water to early-day Indians.

"Shogo Springs water is the only mineral water discovered in the state up to this date, and are found on the west bank of the Blue River at the highest spot on the rock formation of five miles that crosses the stream. An interesting legend of the Indian girl Shogo was related to the residents of the Blue valley by the Indians in connection with the curative powers of the spring water, and from whence the spring drew its name. The water is carefully guarded by the old soldiers, many of whom have been cured from kidney, rheumatism and other diseases. The Indians discovered this years ago when they brought their sick to partake of the healing waters."

Maybe Milford people were just as skeptical of "Indian medicine as some Beaver Crossing women were in 1893." A big, pug-nosed doctor, calling himself Dr. Gunn, made his appearance along with some Indians:

"The Doctor lecturing for the sale of some Indian remedies, and tried to create in the minds of the ladies the idea that he could cure them of any and all ailments. His lectures were partially successful, but his consultations were conducted in rather a peculiar manner which enraged the ladies to such an extent that Dr. Gunn barely escaped a good dose of ripe hen's eggs. It is strange how the human family is inclined to run after strange gods, especially any kind of medicine with an Indian name or picture on the label of it, when in fact the Indians know the least about medical science of any race on earth… (*Beaver Crossing Weekly Review*, 1893)."

A Shogo Springs advertisement in the *Lincoln Journal* newspaper proclaimed the wonders of their healing water. "From the beautiful mineral water springs at Milford, only a short drive from Lincoln, pours forth waters rich in salts and mineral content that are helpful in keeping folks in good health and condition…Many physicians and leading health experts pronounce the Shogo Lithia Waters equal to many widely advertised American and most favorably known European mineral waters."

The owners made no attempt to hide the fact that lithium was considered as the most important property in the water, although it consisted of only 0.0234 gram in one gallon of water. Calcium bicarbonate, on the other hand, accounted for 14.9655 grams and sodium bicarbonate at 9.2048 gram provided the bulk of the mineral content. This being the heyday of the "patent medicine era," Shogo Springs water was probably as good a cure is many other so-called wonder medicines of that day. Convinced that they had a wonderful curative product at their disposal, I can just about hear and see the excitement generated.

The Way It Was

By December 1886, plans were taking shape. A headline in the *Milford Nebraskan* said, "It's a go! —MILFORD WILL HAVE HER SANITARIUM! J. V. Consaul has captured the bid for $11, 500." An investment company was organized, money raised, and the building started in 1887. The city of Milford would soon be in the 'healing business.' Shogo Springs water, made famous by Native Americans for many years, would now be put to work by new landowners. Would Shogo Springs water soon be world famous for attracting hurting and ill people in need of healing?"

There was one small problem: patent medicine was still the first choice for treating most illnesses of the day. Did Shogo Springs water really have a future? A news item in the 1906 *Milford Nebraskan* newspaper, reported a rosy outlook for the future of Milford's Shogo Springs water. "Shogo water is fast becoming world famous and may soon put 'Patent' medicine out of business."

Few college-trained pharmacists of today could tell you what patent medicine was, how it worked, or for what illnesses it would have been prescribed. As most of us know by now, both Shogo Springs water and patent medicines soon faded out of the picture. Although widely used for its curative powers in Milford's early days, the water was soon forgotten. It probably made more headlines after it was used in soft drinks. But was it good for what ailed you? Evidently many in that day thought so. One thing for sure, it was probably just as effective for most diseases as any patent medicine of that day.

Milford's Crowning Institution

What could be considered one of Milford's greatest achievements of the twentieth century took place in the winter of 1941. This momentous moment in Milford history was recorded in the Feb. 15, 1941 edition of *Seward Independent* newspaper.

"The bill to establish a State Trade School in the buildings formerly occupied by the Milford Soldiers and Sailors Home was reported to general file by the Appropriation Committee without a dissenting vote Tuesday afternoon. A hometown boy, Senator Stanley

Eldon Hostetler

Milford Trade School soon after its beginning.

Matzke, introduced the bill. The bill provides for an appropriation of $32,000 to carry the school through to the end of the biennium July, 1941. This money will be used to pay instructors and remodel buildings. According to other information, this $32,000 will be matched by $70,000 in federal funds."

Without one dissenting vote (38 to 0) LB148 was approved by the Nebraska State Legislature on March 27, 1941. The bill was signed immediately by Governor Griswold and the Nebraska State Trade School was born. The school opened in May of 1941 with an enrollment of 24 students selected from 50 applicants. Only four of the initial 24 students were from Milford.

The rest of the Milford Trade School story is history, a story of early struggle as well as tremendous growth that eventually culminated into what we now know as "Southeast Community College at Milford." Since a good history of the school has already been recorded by others more familiar with its beginnings, this narrative will deal mostly with the school's roots and its main reason for being, namely the unused Soldiers and Sailors Home. Both renowned institutions in their own right, the story of either would be incomplete without a short history of Milford's number one "claim to fame" in the late 1800s, Shogo Springs. It all adds up to this: the sanitarium was built to take advantage of Shogo Springs water, the old Soldiers Home opened to take advantage of the sanitarium and a Trade School was started in Milford to take advantage of the unused Soldiers Home.

One 1888 observer said, "These waters have recently been carefully analyzed and found to be equal, if not superior, to those of the famous 'Bethesda' and 'Silurian' springs of Wankesha, Wisconsin, which have caused so many wonderful cures."

The *Seward Blue Valley Blade* newspaper editor, writing about Milford in 1876, referred to Milford as "The Youthful Saratoga of the West." The Milford Saratoga Hotel, located at one time near the spot where the Dental Clinic stands burned down in 1899. Were some comparing the potential of Milford's Shogo Springs to the world famous medicinal mineral water springs near Saratoga, New York? The Saratoga Springs Resort was well known at that time as "Queen of the Spas," having the capacity to handle 3000 health seekers at one time and process six million bottles of mineral water each year." Several in the community, including spring owner John H. Culver, had visions of future greatness for the Milford Springs. Some thought the stream would become the "Saratoga of the West." The Milford newspaper editor said it like this: "Look around you and what do you see? Milford is the 'Saratoga' of the West. Where will you find a more enchanting summer resort? Look at our attractions. Lake Quenchauqua, Lake Keego, the beautiful Blue, Shogo Island, our pure lithium springs and many other things making it the most enchanting place on earth. Plans are now being made to construct an electric railroad to Lincoln to provide a way for Lincoln residents to enjoy Milford's recreational attractions." Being a visionary person as well as a man of action, Mr. Culver instigated proceedings to harvest the potential wealth he saw in Shogo Springs water.

The early 1880s had been good years for most Milford citizens. In fact farmers were actually making money. Crops were excellent and prices were good for most Nebraska farmers, which caused a general feeling of euphoria and prosperity throughout the state. The 1888 and 1889 corn crops were said to be some of the best ever raised in the community, some fields making up to 75 bushels per acre.

The *Milford Nebraskan* newspaper editor reported, "Milford can now boast of the finest springs, the prettiest lakes, and the most healthful and beautiful location of any burg in the state. Then in an everyday sort of way, with ego clear down to zero, we will also mention that we have the largest flouring mills, as well as the best ice fields and some of the best opportunities for investment in the state."

This may have been the incentive needed to convince the Milford Health Resort Stock Company to build their long awaited Health Spa. Many prominent physicians of the day agreed that Milford, being home to Shogo Springs, was the best location in the entire state. John H. Culver sold forty acres of land to the Sanitarium Company, which consisted primarily of Milford citizens. The December 6, 1886 edition of the *Milford Nebraskan* announced the new plans. "It's a go! Milford will have a new Sanitarium! J. V. Consal has captured the bid for $11, 500 dollars. This building is 5 stories high, including a stone basement for kitchens, laundry and engine rooms. It has a dining room 36'x 44' in size, large parlor, offices and two large verandahs 15' wide, with an aggregate size of 412 feet. Each room is well ventilated and is no smaller than 12 x 15 feet in size." Mr. Consal proceeded to erect the original three-story building, but stopped shortly before it was completed due to a lack of funds by the corporation. By 1889, economic conditions were rapidly deteriorating.

Although Nebraska farmers had excellent harvests, prices tumbled, wheat prices falling below fifty cents and corn to as low as fifteen cents. A general feeling of depression engulfed the entire nation. Communities depending on agriculture were especially hard hit. Not only did commodity prices fall, but freight cost by rail rose. In addition, the state was experiencing the second-worst drought ever. From 1892 to 1895, rainfall was scarce and hot south winds played havoc with crops able to survive the drought. By 1894, Milford farmers were forced to buy corn shipped in from other states to feed their livestock. Over 300 cars of relief goods were shipped to Nebraska residents from other states.

Milford's hopes for a "Saratoga of the West" were put on hold in 1890. One source said people were allowed to live in the lower floor of the sanitarium building where much of the finish work was already completed free of cost. Would the huge building stand unfinished as a monument to a few foolish Milford investors who had great dreams of putting Milford on the map? One more time, Milford's number one businessman and promoter, J. H. Culver, came up with a solution. Culver, who had used his charisma and political influence to bring the Industrial Home to Milford several years earlier was no stranger to business or politics.

The Way It Was

In 1884, he had traveled to a Veterans Convention being held in Dayton, Ohio, to "urge upon the Committee the desirability of Milford as the location for a new Veterans Home (*Milford Nebraskan*, 1884)." Although Culver and the city of Milford lost the battle in 1884, he had in no way conceded defeat. Evidently he launched a new campaign aimed directly at the Nebraska State Legislature. We found no available records to reveal his plan of attack but armed with the facts and figures of the wonders of Shogo water and how it would help cure tired old Civil War Veterans as well as the boundless scenic and recreational opportunities available, Culver and the town of Milford won the battle.

The April 20, 1895 *Milford Nebraskan* announced the good news to the public. "Considerable rejoicing was done on Friday afternoon when it was learned that house roll No. 284, for the establishment of a branch of the Soldiers' and Sailors' Home in our midst, had passed the senate by a good majority, and there was still more rejoicing when it was learned on Monday that Governor Holcome had attached his signature to the document." No second Saratoga, but the city of Milford was now going "big time." Although never used as a sanitarium, the state agreed to rent the facility for an old Soldiers and Sailors Home. Once more, carpenters got busy finishing the building. While the *Milford Nebraskan* editor appeared to be thrilled at the prospects of having a second state institution in Milford, many local citizens were still undecided:

"This in our opinion, is one of the most fortunate things that has yet befallen to the lot of the good people of our city, both in its present and future prospects, as the support of such an Institution necessarily involved the expenditure of a large amount of money, which in these times of financial depression, will come as a great boon to our citizens. In all probability the building to be used for the purpose, now called the Sanitarium, will be ready for occupancy by the first of July (*Milford Nebraskan*)."

This "good news" also released funds to complete the final finish work on the building. Initially, the state signed a ten-year contract to lease the building, a lease that provided for two years of free rent and an additional eight years at $800 per year, plus an option to buy the building at any time. In June of 1899, the State of Nebraska purchased the building for $13,000. Contrary to what the *Milford Nebraskan* editor had predicted, the unfinished sanitarium building was not ready for occupancy by July 1st. What one newspaper editor called "The greatest day Milford has ever seen" happened on dedication day in late September of 1895.

"Visitors began arriving as early as 9 a.m. and the stream kept up until after noon. The governor and other state officers arrived on a special train about 2:30 p.m. and were escorted to the Home by Troop A.N.N.G., various G.A.R. posts and the W.R.C. The exercises began soon after their arrival, and consisted of the building being tendered to the department commander of the G.A.R. and by him to the Governor who in turn placed it in the care of Capt. Culver, the commandant. Patriotic music for the occasion was furnished by Lincoln, Dorchester, and Seward drum corps and appropriate vocal music by a Milford quartet under the direction of Mr. Warner, editor of the *Milford Nebraskan*, and the veterans quartet of Lincoln. This was followed by speeches by one Congressman, two Judges and other visiting dignitaries. An enthusiastic camp fire, representing the camp fires of the Civil War, around which the boys would gather to renew their courage by sharing in songs and stories, was held in the evening, the hall being well filled with veterans and their friends. Thus ended the greatest day Milford has ever seen. The crowd was said to be the largest ever here at one time, being estimated at 1,000 to 4,000, but probably numbered more like 1,500. Everybody seemed happy and appeared to have a good time."

The first residents moved in on October 1, 1895. To gain admission, it was necessary to show an honorable discharge from either the Civil, Indian, or Spanish American Wars, or the Philippine Insurrection and prove that you were either physically or financially unable to care for yourself. Guests were not required to do any work except care for their own rooms, although some were paid to do extra chores around the grounds. In case of sickness, guests were cared for in a well-equipped hospital staffed by excellent nurses and a good doctor. Excellent food and a comfortable bed to sleep in was provided at an average cost of $4,000 per month to the state.

J. H. Culver served as first Commandant at which time the institution housed only ten guests. Culver resigned before 1900 at which time Commander Fowler took over. Starting with a capacity to house 125 guests, the home was enlarged several times to the point where they were able to accommodate 200. In 1908, 183 guests were living in the home, plus 35 staff persons. In 1923, (probably one of the peak years) 125 men and 110 women were living in the home. Staff members included the commander, adjutant, matron, surgeon, and home engineer. The home was always under the watchful eyes of the State Board of Control. Whenever possible, local people were hired to fill positions. Milford natives Thomas Swearingen and local physician James Muir were both long time employees.

Religious services conducted by the home chaplain were held every Sunday at 3 P.M. Additional buildings were added as needed, including a hospital building in 1904 and a new administration building in 1910. One newspaper editor wrote, "the new Administration Building is built strong enough to survive for 1000 years." The original hospital building was used for rooms after a new one was built on the west side of the street in 1926. The only original building used today is known as Nebraska Hall. The stone administration building that was said to be capable of standing for ten centuries succumbed to the wrecking ball many years ago.

Few records are available to tell us what life was really like in the Soldiers and Sailors Home a hundred years ago, although the editor of the *Crete Vidette* newspaper visited the home in 1901 and gives us his version of what he observed.

"There are 80 inmates at present, and carpenters are at work on the 4th floor fitting it up with 20 more rooms. This is a large, clean, commodious building and it makes one feel good to see all the old and crippled comrades so comfortably located. They all speak in highest terms of the new superintendent and everyone seems to be contented and happy. They devote their time to reading, smoking, visiting, playing cards and billiards, walking on the grounds and fishing along the Blue. Those who are able to work do so and are paid from 6 to 12 dollars per month."

Another guest visiting in 1922 reported that he had talked to four former soldiers, aged 88, 86, 84, and 82 years. In 1922, retired veterans received a pension of $50 per month from the U.S. Government. The home did survive one severe mid-life, political crisis in 1925, when bill H.R.106 was introduced in the state legislature by two Grand Island area lawmakers. If passed the measure would have transferred all the old soldiers housed in Milford to the home in Grand Island, thereby providing room to convert the Milford facilities to a state poor farm. Alarmed Milford businessmen, led by Stanley Matzke, appeared before the committee to protest the move.

Eldon Hostetler

Stanley Matzke.

Attorney Matzke called the attention of the committee to the fact that the bill would destroy the community life of the veterans and their wives who offered their lives in service for their country and should not be required to move to Grand Island or be crowded out by an influx of Omaha and Lincoln paupers. J. E. Vance raised the question as to the advisability of making the state responsible for a poor farm instead of leaving it up to the individual counties. He also suggested it would make more sense to use the 640 acres of farm land surrounding the Grand Island institution as a poor farm than the forty-one acres connected with the Milford institution. The battle was heating up! Information from the February 5, 1925 *Seward Independent* newspaper tells the "rest of the story."

"The House, in committee of the whole, considered the bill H.R. 106. Representative McClellan of Hall County defended the bill to the best of his ability and immediately after the killing of his present hope, he is reported as saying as he stood with one hand extended foremost; 'May God forgive you. You know not what you do.' Representative Munn of Lancaster County proposed an amendment which reversed the order of consolidation and named the Grand Island Home as the place for the aged poor instead of Milford. Milford's District Representative, A J. White introduced a motion to indefinitely postpone the bill which carried by a wide margin. The general consensus of opinion is that because of its location, beautiful grounds and convenient arrangement, the Milford home is much better suited for use as a Soldiers home than for a poor farm.

Now back to the question raised at the beginning of this story. Did Milford people really support the Old Soldiers Home as they should have? Testimony given at the 1922 hearing by Pastor Laipply of the Milford Evangelical Church would suggest that there may have been mixed feelings.

"Mr. Laipply briefly reviewed the history of the home saying that while Milford as a community had been <u>negligent</u> in appreciation of the efforts of the late General Culver in establishing the home here, that now, when there is a prospect of its removal, the business men are rallying to its support."

One more quote by the Seward *Blue Valley Blade* editor in 1895 would support this view. "The people of Milford ought to appreciate the efforts of Captain Culver to secure for that place the new Soldiers Home. Culver has done more for them than ten men, and there should be nothing too good for him that the people of Milford can do."

By 1939, attendance at the Soldiers Home was dwindling, as reported in the June 22, 1939 *Milford Review*: "Mrs. Augusta Munger was moved to the Grand Island Home on Saturday, the last hospital patient to be transferred and the local unit was closed. Mrs. Munger, who was moved on her 95th birthday passed away the next morning. Mrs. Sarah Haynes, 87, who had moved on Wednesday died Monday morning at the Grand Island Home.

The Milford "Girls" Home

The Milford community is truly blessed with a rich historical tradition featuring many unusual and important happenings, some very unique to early Seward County history.

All entertaining narratives in their own right, few stories have achieved the notoriety and interest generated by the establishment of the Milford State Industrial Home on the spot now occupied by Sunrise Country Manor. Today, people from all over United States contact Milford authorities, hoping to find information concerning their birth records connected with the home. I have also discovered that many younger citizens have no idea what the home was all about, or why the history of this institution is so vital to persons searching for their identity.

Due to a lack of official records, as well as an aura of silence and secrecy that appeared to surround the home's daily operations, true facts are hard to come by. This story was compiled from information gleaned from bits and pieces of many different newspaper articles written between 1905 and 1987.

It's been happening as long as the world has existed; unprincipled men taking advantage of sometimes unsuspecting females,

No. 9-E. Nebraska Industrial Home, Milford, Neb.

which often results in the conception of unplanned and many times unwanted children. The old tried and proven solution of the father marrying the mother-to-be is usually supposed to provide the most satisfactory answer. But while this simplistic solution sounds great on paper other, more serious factors and circumstances, many times unknown to the public, often prevent this from being the ideal.

Today one needs only to open a newspaper to see ads inviting girls in crisis to dial a certain phone number where she will undoubtedly be assured of all the answers. However, one hundred years ago it was a different ball game, mostly because the so-called "weaker" gender was usually branded as the guilty party. In her initial report to the public the first superintendent of the home, Mrs. E. M. Perkins, echoed her personal sentiments by rebutting what she felt was a widely held misconception: "It is a source of regret that while the state of Nebraska provides so comfortable a home for the unfortunate girls and their children, their partners in guilt are permitted to enjoy freedom while the taxpayer bears the expense...We have reason to believe that the majority of them (inmates) are more sinned against than sinning."

This sentence from an article published in the Nov. 27, 1987 *Journal Star* confirms the social stigma attached to unmarried motherhood in that day: "One century ago, society's treatment of women who were pregnant out of wedlock was almost unimaginably stringent. The institution first was called the Nebraska Industrial Home, so named according to historical data, to disguise its true reason for being."

Other news items appearing in the *Milford Nebraskan* would suggest that the public usually frowned on social "hanky panky," in fact, sometimes even implicating the male species. In 1904, the Seward County Sheriff made a trip to Michigan to bring back a twenty-one-year-old Milford man "to face his responsibility" concerning a Lincoln girl.

Today, I suppose we would consider this government meddling in family affairs. One hundred years ago it must have been a terrifying experience for very young girls to become unmarried mothers. So, has anything really changed in the past one hundred years? News headlines in the Nov. 29, 2001 *Lincoln Journal Star* reported this startling information: "Births to single mothers in Nebraska are at an all time high…unmarried mothers accounted for 27% of all births in the state, up from 24% five years ago." In other words, it would appear people have not changed all that much, although community attitudes and mores certainly have.

The beginning of the story goes back to the year 1887 when the Nebraska State Legislature appropriated fifteen thousand dollars for what was described in an undated pamphlet as a "home for homeless penitent girls who have no specific disease." Nearly 40 acres of land was provided by the city of Milford—land that at one time had been part of the original J. L. Davison Homestead.

The home apparently came to Milford at the urging of J. L. Davisons' son-in-law, J. H. Culver, who appeared to carry plenty of

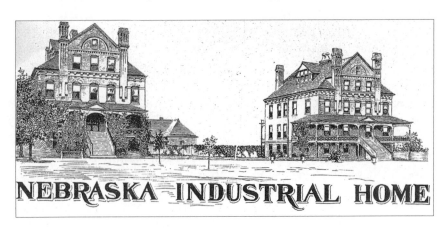

clout with the state government in Lincoln. In 1889, the legislature appropriated an additional thirty-one thousand dollars to build a barn and several other out-buildings. The first girl was admitted on May 1, 1889 to what was said at that time to be the only state-supported maternity home in the nation. Eventually, the campus included two matching four-story dormitories, a cattle barn, a boiler room, a water tower, a huge garden, a laundry room, and later the hospital which is still being used.

Seward County historian Cox, said, "Under the guiding hands of the Board of Public Lands and Buildings, two commodious structures have been erected with all modern appliances for the proper care of the inmates each containing twenty-five neat and thoroughly furnished rooms besides closets, bath rooms, etc. and a fine power house to furnish water, heat and light in every apartment. Beautiful trees furnish ample shade and the place would seem like a little paradise."

The home, having a capacity for fifty girls, was dedicated sometime in 1888. While under the general direction of the Board of Control of State Institutions, the local superintendent had complete control of all day-to-day operations. However, she was always under the watchful eyes of a board of trustees that consisted of sixteen ladies of "high standing" that included Mrs. Thomas Graham of Seward.

In addition to the home superintendent, the mostly female staff included a matron, main cook, sewing teacher, secretary and steward, head gardener, poultry and dairy worker, head laundry woman, and a trained nurse. Dr. William Sandusky of Pleasant Dale, as well as several Milford doctors, were in charge of inmates' medical needs and babies. Two or three men were also on staff; one in charge of the farming and one known as the home engineer. Other short-term male employees were hired as needed. Two Milford men, the late Kenneth Miller and William Stauffer, worked at the home in the mid-1930s. Both were paid $30 a month plus room and board for living space above the laundry building. Stauffer served as a dairy/poultry and garden helper, while Miller worked as the boiler fireman, a job that included unloading some 400 tons of fuel coal annually. The men were not even allowed to say hello to an inmate if they chanced to meet one. Both men worked twelve-hour shifts.

The Way It Was

Early sanitarium photo, circa 1905.

This news item from the March 30, 1895 *Milford Mirror* would suggest that by 1895 state legislatures, as well as local citizens, were thoroughly sold on the new institution.

"It will be very gratifying to the friends of the Industrial Home to know the expression of the house in regard to it on March 12. This was the day set for considering the appropriations for institutions, and every institution in the state was discussed, but with none was there as great enthusiasm and as many complimentary remarks made as with the Industrial Home at Milford. The leading members of the house commented upon the able and economical management. The institution has passed through its struggling and trying times. It is now on a firm basis and will rank with any institution in the state. It has many friends and will receive justice at the hands of our lawmakers. We are pleased to know that the leading citizens of Milford are as a unit with the superintendent of the home, and fully appreciate the high standard she has given this institution."

And from the *Seward Independent* of May 31, 1923: "A spirit of friendly cooperation exists between the girls and officers, and there is a decidedly homelike atmosphere pervading the institution. The object of the home is to protect and shelter the unfortunate girls of Nebraska. Most cases are voluntary admissions, but the courts can now commit girls to the home. Girls from all walks of life, mostly very young come to the institution. At present there is one thirteen year old girl, five fourteen year old girls, nine fifteen year old girls, a large number who are sixteen years of age and seven who are twenty years old. Many of these girls come from broken homes and many are children of over indulgent parents. Mothers of this character often bring their daughters hoping that the home can make them see the light from a different viewpoint. Though often rebellious at first, these girls often come to see that the officers really have their best interests at heart and some of them make the best records."

Girls entering the home were required to stay for one full year, even if their baby was born in only a few weeks. They were not allowed to leave the home to visit with their families during the one-year stay, but were allowed two hours of visiting time each week. Worship services on Sunday consisted of Sunday school in the morning and public worship services in the afternoon. A Protestant minister form Milford and a Catholic priest from Crete conducted the services. Five evenings each week the girls assembled in the chapel, one evening for young people's meeting, one for current events, one for a sacred song service and one for Kensington with Victrola music, and one devoted to listening to a sermon by a pastor. The home kept a splendid library of 800 volumes of fiction and poetry and also books on household arts, popular psychology, and elementary nursing. The girls were encouraged to read the good magazines stocked by the home. In July of 1889, the board of trustees in charge of the home adopted rules that were later known as "our own Ten Commandments."

Type of tract distributed by G. F. Eberspacher for many years.

1. Chapel service and evening prayer will be observed by both inmates and employees.
2. No visitors shall hold interviews with the inmates except in the presence of the superintendent or officer in charge.
3. No visitors shall be allowed to visit the rooms of patients while under ward treatment, except by the consent of the physician.
4. Magazines and religious journals shall be upon the reading tables, accessible to all inmates.
5. Bibles and song books shall be furnished by the Industrial Home.
6. Rooms of the inmates shall be subject to inspection by the superintendent only in cases where there is reasonable grounds.
7. No employees shall exchange department duties with each other, except by the consent of the superintendent or physician.
8. Both inmates and employees shall rise at the ringing of the bell, unless disabled by sickness.
9. Employees who desire to leave the home transiently must obtain permission from the superintendent or resident physician if in their judgment such absence is necessary.
10. The inmates of the home shall be detailed as practicable to perform the household duties of the home (*Milford Times*, July 18, 1984).

One news item suggested that all babies born in the home were either given up for adoption or sent to the Home for the Friendless (one was Whitehall Children's Home in Lincoln). However, a *Seward Independent* story from May 31, 1923 mentioned the fact that over fifty percent of the girls kept their children. "After a home has been investigated the child is placed. If she has relinquished her child and makes good, every time the superintendent hears from the foster parents, a letter is sent to the girl giving her the interesting facts of the child's progress, although she does not know the home into which the child has gone. Within the past three years a number of young men and women who were born here have returned to find out something of their parentage. In every case they were respectable citizens. When a girl leaves, every effort is made to place her in a good environment and secure work for her."

I still have vivid memories of how this Milford institution looked sixty-five years ago, especially in the winter time. It seemed like dark, black smoke was always billowing skyward from the huge smokestack reaching up from the boiler room. The twin dormitories, surrounded by huge shade trees and neatly manicured lawns, created an impressive image in the summer time, at least to a ten-year-old country boy. Like many others in the community, I had no idea of what all was going on behind these high stone-like walls. In fact, I had no idea why it was called the "Industrial Home," instead of what it really was.

Today, after researching through some long hidden and forgotten facts, I feel like I am finally seeing some daylight. An eyewitness account reported in the *Seward Independent* on May 31, 1923 tells:

"Each girl agrees to remain one year, and during this time she is given training in housework, cooking, fancy and plain sewing, laundry work, care of children, and religious training. Those who prove themselves dependable and worthy are given eight weeks of training in hospital work, instruction and practical work in gardening, dairy work and poultry raising is also given. At the present time there are forty girls, thirty babies and ten officers and employees in the house. Mrs. Mary Pritchard has charge of the kitchen and dining rooms. Ten girls are under her supervision for an eight-week period. There is an officer's cook, a girls' cook and one girl in the pastry department and one girl who cares for the milk, the butter and the preparation of food. For the infants; four dining room girls and one girl who prepares the vegetables. The girls are all taught to plan menus and tastily serve what they prepare. They are taught to set the tables in a way fitting to the best of homes. Each girl at some time or another has instruction in this department. Miss Delia Olsen has charge of the sewing department. Here the girls are taught to make her own and her child's clothing. When she leaves the home the state furnishes the material for clothes for her and her child and the girl makes the garments. Mrs. Manderson supervises the laundry department. The large amount of laundry work for an institution of this kind is done here in an unusually efficient manner. Eleven girls are employed; two washing, four mangling and four doing hand ironing, while one girl operates the drying tumbler and hangs up the clothes. There are two nurseries for the babies; one for those from three weeks to eight months and one for the older children. Mrs. Williams teaches each girl how to bathe, clothe feed, and take full care of her child. Miss Townsend as matron, directs the girls in general household arts. They are taught to make beds, care for the rooms and halls and keep the buildings in a very clean and attractive condition. Mrs. McCall supervises the gardening, poultry raising and dairy work. This is a very active department and much practical work is done by the girls. Care of the health and hygiene is also taught, and the health of the girls is always above average in the state, due to the supervision of Dr. Sandusky, who has been physician for the past ten years. One feature of the life we have not stressed, is the punctuality and industry of everyone there. The girls rise early and every minute of the day has its special duty. The work of this home is real missionary work and prepares these unfortunate girls to become useful members of society. They come in contact with refined Christian women as their officers and it is rarely that a girl is not made better by her year at the Nebraska Industrial Home."

W. W. Cox Seward County historian, echoed the true male chauvinistic attitude so in vogue in that day in his 1905 *Revised History of Seward County*: "The Home is truly answering the high object for which it was created; sheltering, protecting and helping to reform the wayward and unfortunate girls that desire a better life. They receive, by moral teaching and training, that uplift that will tend to respectability and usefulness. May the God of love and mercy bless this Home."

The usefulness and popularity of the home appeared to peak in the mid-1920s. From 1907 to 1923, 728 girls entered and graduated from the Home. In 1923 the Home housed a total of 91 girls two in the 10 to 14 age bracket; 59 from 15-17, and 30 from 18 to 30. No figures are available as to determine the total number of girls who passed through the home from 1889 to 1952, although one person familiar with the history of the institution has estimated 4,000.

Children born in the home were allowed to stay, even if the mother decided to leave after her year was finished. However, the family was charged $1.75 per week for board and room. If the family failed to pay for six months, the child automatically became the property of the state and could be put up for adoption. From the first financial report dated November 30, 1890, the home housed 67 residents costing the state an average of $3.72 per week. The home superintendent received $50 per month, the matron and schoolteacher each received $25, while the sewing teacher was only worth $20. In 1950, seventy babies were born in the home costing an average of $104 per month.

In 1950, one state legislator became somewhat perturbed over the rising cost of keeping the home open. A *Lincoln Journal-Star* newspaper article published Jan. 18, 1951 quoted a Legislative Council Executive member who called unwed mothers lawbreakers and referred to the Home "as an encouragement to break the law." One record reported that thirteen expectant girls were living in the home at its closure.

About this time State Fire Marshal, E. C. Iverson found other, even more serious problems, including sagging floors, falling plaster, leaking roofs, structural weaknesses, faulty wiring, and inadequate fire protection. He recommended that several of the buildings be demolished at once. In 1953 the legislature passed a bill to close the home. In 1953 the home, minus some of the farmland, was offered for sale by public auction. Having been appraised at $25,000, the high bid of $18,000 was offered by a group representing the Nebraska Mennonite Mission and Benevolent Board. The board intended to use the plant to start a church school. Governor Crosby rejected the offer. Later, it was sold by private treaty to Wes and Ida Stutzman for an undisclosed sum. The Stutzmans eventually sold the property to the Stauffer family. Most of the original buildings (except the hospital) have now been removed.

"The old home stands as a sentinel to a changing society. If the walls of the remaining dormitory of the Nebraska Maternity Home could talk, they undoubtedly would tell a gripping story. In a small but significant way they do. Scratched on the crumbling plaster in a small fourth-floor room are the words "twenty-four more weeks of this hell hole" and the name Sylvia, another heartbroken girl. It is generally agreed that this attic room was used for solitary confinement to discipline the pregnant women and girls at the home. The room's sloping ceilings provided little space for standing upright. But there may have been hundreds more who found it a haven in their time of need and the first caring place they ever lived. Time is eroding the story, and when the dorm is razed next year, a piece of living history will go down with it (*Maternity Home Fading Into History*, Betty Stevens, *Sunday Journal Star*, Nov. 29, 1987).

The Way It Was

The citizens of Milford, Nebraska, as well as other people scattered all over United States who are so frantically searching for their Milford Industrial Home roots will probably never know many of the "real life stories" behind the story of Milford's number one claim to historical fame. Is it possible that even "dyed in the wool" male chauvinists may have toned down their preachy criticism had they known the real reason why many of these girls were forced to spend one year in the Milford Industrial Home? (Author's Note: I have been told the Industrial Home records are now in possession of the Catholic Social Services Office in Omaha. A court order is required to open a file.)

The First Technical School in Milford

Many Milford residents may remember the billboard erected north of Milford on Highway 6 some years ago calling attention to the fact drivers were about to enter the town made famous as home to the nations' First State Vocational Technical School. Although the sign is long gone, the fame of Southeast Community College continues to grow. Known throughout the Midwest for its top notch teaching program, as well as its good job placement record, the school has few peers. While the school may be one of the oldest of its type in the nation, few realize the State Vocational Technical College started in Milford in 1941 cannot even claim the honor of being the first technical school founded in Milford. A *Milford Nebraskan* editorial dated February 15, 1889 explains.

"Milford has five enterprises in which all the people of Nebraska are interested; Industrial Home, Sanitarium, Telegraph School, Shogo Island and Quenchauqua Mills." While much has been written concerning the other four enterprises, little is mentioned regarding the "Telegraph School."

Founded in late 1887 by Milford depot agents C. F. Wilsey and N. D.

196

Sewell, the school was originally known as the "Milford Telegraph School and Railroad Business College." Dedicated to the philosophy and goals espoused by Southeast Community College today, Mr. Woolsey determined not only to train telegraph workers, but also to see that his graduates found good-paying jobs. "Mr. Woolsey had determined to engage in such an enterprise; but he realized that there is just one difference between the Telegraph Schools that are successful and those that are unsuccessful, and that lies in the ability of the manager to find situations for his pupils after they have learned the trade. Instead of starting the School with a flourish and working with as many pupils as possible without assurance that situations could be found, he quietly took two or three pupils at a time, and now after a year, he having secured good situations for nine pupils, he is justified in opening a regular school and inviting as many to come as desire (*Milford Nebraskan, Feb 28, 1889*)."

The school was held in two large rooms above the post office at that time located in the vacant space west of the Napa Auto Parts store.

"One will be used strictly as a work room with tables, instruments, batteries, railway report books, etc., and the other has a fine parlor set with a library of standard works, magazines, writing materials etc., where the pupils may spend their evenings. During the day sessions, this will be used as the workroom for the lady pupils." The school opened on Monday morning February 4, 1889, with twelve 'gentleman' students and four 'lady' students." Pupils were expected to attend about six months of school paying $50 tuition in advance. Housing was provided by Milford families costing students three dollars per week. While the old post office building was considered headquarters, telegraph lines were installed to eight other Milford locations, including Shogo Island, the Industrial Home, Quenchauqua Mills, and the new Sanitarium. Telegraph messages between the various sites served as practice runs for the students.

A later *Milford Nebraskan* news note reported, "The Telegraph School has met with such encouraging success and such emphatic endorsement from official sources that Mr. Woolsey decided to resign his position at the Milford depot in order to devote full time to the school." Plans were being made to use two rooms in the new Sanitarium building as soon as it was completed.

The Way It Was

This is part of one testimonial letter published in the Jan. 14, 1889 *Milford Nebraskan*:

Smartville, Nebr. C. F. Woosley, manager of the Milford Telegraph School;

Dear Sir; Thought I would write you a letter and let you know how I have been getting along since I left you. Well, I am still holding down my job and don't have any trouble at all. I thank you very much for your past favors and I would say to any young man not having a good trade, learn telegraphy, the best of all trades. Just a little over one year ago I was rustling on a farm for $18 per month, being out in the snow and the rain, and now I have charge of a railroad station at a salary of $40 per month with the probability of a promotion and a better salary when I have been longer at the business."

Must have been the same old song and dance 100 years ago concerning the nastiness, as well as the lack of profitability in the farming business. At this point, I am not sure how long the school was in business, but it was big time stuff while it lasted.

Eldon Hostetler

A "medical miracle" in 1907

Shogo Lithia Springs

The Great Medicine Water of the Pawnee and Otoe Indians for ages past. Located on the west bank of the Big Blue River, has proven such a valuable remedy for kidney disease, stomach trouble and rheumatism, which is evidenced by the cures effected in the Soldiers' Home which was located at Milford on account of this spring. It is sought after by the principal hotels as a table water and by physicians on account of its purity.

Shogo Lithia Springs Company

General Office, 129 N. 14th St.
Lincoln, Nebraska — Milford, Nebraska

1916 ad

"I Can Cure Any Drunkard"

My Golden Specific for the Whiskey Curse will Save Your Husband, Son, Brother, or Father from a Drunkard's Grave

I will Mail Free To All Who Write a Trial Package In Plain Wrapper

I am saving thousands of drunkards every year and restoring them to their loving wives and families. I will save many more as a result of this advertisement. To all who write me, I will send free by

"The Drunkard Can't Save Himself. You Women have to do it for him."

mail, in plain wrapper, so that no one can know what it contains, a trial package of Golden Specific for the Liquor Habit. Though absolutely harmless, it never fails to cure the worst cases of drunkenness, no matter how long standing. It can be administered without the knowledge of the subject, in coffee, tea, soup, milk, etc., and he will be cured in a few days and cured so that he will never drink again.

Golden Specific contains no dangerous drugs or minerals. It does not ruin the digestion or destroy the tissues of the vital organs and endanger life and health. It counteracts and expels from the system all alcoholic poisons and puts an end to all craving or appetite for liquor.

Under its influence the subject regains his health, will-power and self-respect. His eye becomes bright, his brain clear, his step elastic, his vigor returns, and he once more feels and looks like a man.

If you have a beloved husband, son, brother or father who is afflicted, send your name and address to me at once in the coupon below.

More wonderful stuff from 1907.

Blindness Cured

Dr. Milbrandt's Restoratives cure Cataract, Film and all diseases of the eye. Also Cancers, Tumors, Hernia, Rheumatism, Deafness, Female Complaint, Worms, Dropsy, Dyspepsia, Scrofula, and all diseases of the skin, Russian Catarrh, in fact all forms of catarrh, in a remarkably short time.

Price per bottle, $1.00. Postpaid, $1.06

Sample bottle for diseases of women — Prolapus (Falling of the Womb), Leucorrhea (Whites), Backache, Headache, Hemorrhages, etc., free, postpaid

Another 1907 "wonder drug."

The Way It Was

1938 Milford Review.

Depression prices in 1932.

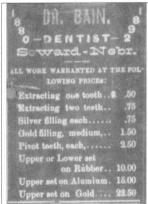

Seward dental prices from 1892.

Lawrence Beckler bought out Milford IHC dealer Floyd Neff in 1949 and operated it until he moved to Seward in 1956. Alfredson Home Improvement Gallery is in the building at present.

1874 advertisement.

1938 *Milford Review*

Eldon Hostetler

Ad from 1938 Milford Review. Tractor sold for about $750.

Carl de Laval of Sweden invented the centrifugal cream separator in 1878. Before the invention of this labor-saving machine, cream was skimmed off the milk by hand. Ad from a 1907 magazine.

```
        THURSDAY, MARCH 23, 1939

              MARKETS
Hens, 5 lbs. and over ............ 14c
Hens under 5 lbs. ................ 12c
Leghorn Hens .................... 10c
Cox ..................................  8c
Cream No. 1 ..................... 19c
Cream No. 2 ..................... 18c
Eggs ............................... 13c
Prices subject to market changes
       REDIGER PRODUCE HOUSE

        Farmers Union Elevator
Wheat ............................. 57c
Yellow Corn ..................... 36c
White Corn ...................... 36c
Oats ............................... 22c
```

To Make Lemon Drops.

Take one ounce of Alcohol, one-half drachm of Oil of Lemon, color with Termeric.

RECEIPT TO MAKE
Cinnamon Drops.

Take one ounce of Alcohol and two drachms of the Oil of Cinnamon, color with Red Sandos.

RECEIPT TO MAKE
Peppermint Drops.

Take one ounce of Alcohol, one drachm of Peppermint, color with Termeric.

RECEIPT TO MAKE
Golden Tincture.

Take one ounce of Alcohol and one ounce of Ether.

For Burns and Scalds.

Take fresh lard, any quantity, and work into it a quantity of powdered soot; about a tablespoonful of soot to an ounce of lard, and apply. This is one of the best applications for burns and scalds that can be made.

RECEIPT TO MAKE
LAUDANUM.

Take two ounces of Alcohol, one half ounce of Opium.

Great Salve for Wounds.

Take one pound of Sheep Tallow, one pound Beeswax, one half pound Rosin, Elder, inside bark, one pound Balm of Gilead, leaves or flowers, put into a pan and fry over a slow fire to a salve, spread thin on a linen rag, apply two or three times a day,

Cure for Bots in Horses.

Mix one pint of Honey, one quart Swee Milk, give as a drench, one hour after dissolve one ounce pulverized Copperas, one pint of water, use as a drench, then give one quart Linseed Oil. This cure is said to be effectual.

RECEIPT TO CURE
Poll Evil and Fistula.

Take one ounce of Aquafortis, one pint good Vinegar, ten cents worth Spirits of Turpentine, one cake Spanish Soap, put in a new jug, let stand for twenty-four hours, use twice a day, when better once. This cure is said to have never failed.

LINIMENT FOR
Sprains and Swellings.

To make this Liniment, which will never fail in curing Sprains, Swellings, &c., take two ounces Hartshorn, two ounces Spirits Camphor, one ounce Oil of Turpentine, one half ounce Laudanum. Mix well together and put into a bottle, being careful to keep it well corked.

1932 advertisement.

It paid to buy in bulk one hundred years ago. 1903.

In 1946, "the Beaver Crossing canning factory completed its fifth year of canning tomatoes. This year's crop produced 6,000 cases of fancy pack. Practically all are sold. There were 55 names on the payroll. The payroll was $4,000. 245 tons of tomatoes were processed and the largest day's pack was 8,500 cans." Beaver Crossing newspaper, November 4, 1946.

The Way It Was

Good traveling prices in 1932.

Before cars and airplanes, most Americans traveled by rail. These prices from 1903 are typical for the era.

The price of a good newspaper subscription in 1932

Newspaper subscription in 1932.

All About Nebraska Weather

Temperatures

- The sun shines 63 percent of the time (daylight hours).
- Average temperature for the entire year is 50.8 degrees.
- The hottest month is July, with an average high of 90 degrees and an average low of 66.3 degrees.
- Number of days 100 degrees or higher is 5.
- The coldest month is January, with an average high of 32.4 degrees and an average low of 10.1 degrees.
- Mean average length of frost free period is 170 days.
- The record high temperature of 115 degrees was recorded on July 25, 1936.
- The Grand Island-Lexington vicinity experienced 118 degrees on July 25.
- The record low of 33 degrees below zero was recorded on Jan. 12, 1974.
- The record low for the state is 47 degrees below zero recorded in the Chadron, Fort Robinson vicinity.
- Average date of the last spring freeze is April 27.
- Average date of first fall freeze is Oct. 7.
- Average number of days with temperatures zero or below is 16 days. Average number of days falling to 32 degrees is 144 days.
- Year with the greatest number of days reaching 100 degrees or above is 41 days recorded in 1936.

The Way It Was

- Hottest years were 1931 and 1934; when temperatures averaged 55.7 degrees.
- Coldest year was 1978 with an average temperature of 47.8 degrees.
- Average number of days reaching 90 degrees or higher is 42.
- The earliest fall freeze ever recorded was on Sept. 11, 1940.
- The latest fall freeze ever recorded was on Nov. 7, 1956.
- The latest spring freeze ever recorded was May 29, 1947.
- The earliest final spring freeze ever recorded was on March 27, 1925.
- Shortest growing season, 118 days was recorded between May 17 and Sept. 11 in 1947.
- The longest growing season, 218 days was recorded between April 2 to Nov. 6, in 1924 (Note! Lincoln records say the shortest growing season was 118 days in 1947 and. W.W. Cox mentions a frost that killed corn in low lying areas in the Salt Creek flats west of Lincoln on August 20, about 1859)
- Longest time below zero, 188 hours, was recorded between Dec. 5 and Dec. 12, in 1983.
- The fastest peak wind speed, 84 mph was recorded on June 23, 1884.
- The average wind speed is 10.4 mph.
- Windiest month is April at 12.1 mph; Calmest month is August at 9.2 mph.

Precipitation

- Average annual precipitation for the Lincoln and Milford vicinity is 28.2 inches.
- The wettest year was 1965 with 41.33 inches. Other above average years would include: 1869, 1875, 1902, 1915, 1944, 1951, and 1973.
- Driest year was 1936 at 14 inches. Other below average years would include: 1890, 1894, 1934, 1937, 1939, 1955 1956, and 1966.
- The wettest summer, was 24.53 inches recorded in 1902.

Eldon Hostetler

Water covers Highway 6 north of Milford. Date unknown.

- The snowiest year was 1948, when 65.2 inches were recorded.
- The snowiest winter was 1914-1915 at 59.4 inches.
- The heaviest rainfall in one 24 hour period would vary from community to community. The Lincoln record is 8.38 inches recorded on August 28, 1910. Some towns in the state have reported as much as 17 inches in one 24-hour period. York recorded over 13 inches on June 8-9 in 1950. The most I ever remember at our farm near Beaver Crossing was 5 inches.
- The heaviest 24 hour snowfall, 19 inches was recorded on Feb. 12, 1965. Feb. of 1965 also holds the record for the snowiest month as well as the most snow on the ground at one time; 21 inches.
- The earliest recorded snowfall was Sept. 20, 1983.
- The latest recorded snow fell on May 28, 1947.
- The least snow ever recorded was 7.2 inches in the winter season of 1967-68.
- The average first snowfall is Nov. 19, while the average winter snowfall is 26.4 inches averaging 6.4 inches a month.
- The wettest month is May with an average of 3.9 inches while the driest month is January, when the averaging is .64 inches.

The Way It Was

- Approximately eleven tornadoes could have been spotted from the city of Milford in the past 130 years since 1877, while they did not all hit Milford.

[Author's Note: Most of the above statistics taken from the *Lincoln Journal* and *Star* newspapers are averages for the Lincoln area and may not indicate a true picture for the Milford community, especially rainfall totals, although temperature and wind records should not vary that much. Average yearly rainfall totals may drop one inch for every 25 miles west of the Missouri River. Local records from my own memory would include: Fourteen inches of rain in the month of August in 1965 and rainy weather in April and May of 1944, whereby Milford area field work came to a complete standstill for five weeks. I also remember snow drifts three feet deep covering non-harvested cornfields, and one fall when corn in the field did drop below 24 percent moisture content.]

Milford people waiting for the crest on the West Fork of the Big Blue following a 14-inch rain in the York vicinity. The river crested higher than anyone ever remembered. Circa June, 1950.

Eldon Hostetler

The "Dirty Thirties"

One of the definitions Webster assigns to the English word frugal is "prudently saving or sparing; and requiring few resources." According to the latest statistics it would appear we Americans love to spend money *now*—many times before it is actually earned. The average balance for credit card debt for Americans jumped from $4,230 in 1995 to $5,610 in 2000. Meanwhile, savings are reported to be at an all-time low, thanks mostly to a rising stock market, easy credit and the unwise use of credit cards. Many old-timers (those born in the 1920s) are urged to get with the program and spend. Occasionally, we are forced to listen to a barrage of trite, pious sounding clichés designed to shame one into changing his spending habits.

"You can't take it with you," "Did you ever see a hearse pulling a u-haul loaded with money?" or "Your kids will just spend it for you, or fight over it," top the list of common remarks. Rare indeed is the parent or grandparent of today who would not agree that the younger generations have more or less lost that frugal, old-fashioned approach to spending money, a practice so cherished by their parents or grandparents. My generation is usually forced to take the offensive in the argument and we quickly counter with, "Haven't I told you before that we are survivors of the dirty thirties?" Even Nebraska's Pulitzer Prize winning author, Willa Cather worried about the negative effects of long-term prosperity on future generations penning these words about 1926 during the height of the great 1920s boom.

"Too much prosperity, too many moving picture shows, too much gaudy fiction have colored the taste and manners of so many of these Nebraskans of the future. There, as elsewhere, one finds the frenzy to be showy; farmer boys who wish to be spenders before they are earners, girls who try to look like the heroines of the cinema screen; a coming generation which try to cheat its aesthetic sense by buying things instead of making things. There is even danger that fine institution, The University of Nebraska, may become a gigantic trade school. The men who control its destiny, the regents and the lawmakers, wish their sons and daughters to study machines, mercantile processes, 'the principles of business.' Everything has to do with the game of getting on in this world (*History of Nebraska*, James C. Olson and Ronald C. Naugle, p. 305).

The Way It Was

While we did suffer through the longest drought ever recorded in Nebraska history, the awfulness of the Depression years was also fueled by other factors. Living on a small farm near Beaver Crossing at the time, I usually had the idea that if it would only rain, our financial problems would all be solved. Additional research on the subject has convinced me it was actually far more complicated than lack of rainfall. In fact, it could be said the roots of the Great Depression were firmly anchored in a few years of unbridled prosperity.

"You can't lick this prosperity thing," said Will Rogers, "even the fellow that hasn't got any is all excited over the idea." Although Rogers made this observation during the boomtimes of the roaring mid-1920s, he may have said the same thing about the present day boom. Following the prosperity connected with World War I, and after weathering a short depression in 1920, the boom that followed caused a general feeling of financial euphoria. It was a feeling that drew more and more Americans with ordinary incomes to the stock market. Brokerage houses opened branches in smaller towns, thereby allowing widows, school teachers, and factory workers to join the professional risk takers in their mad pursuit of a fast, easy buck.

Stock Market quotations soon became ordinary topics of discussion and were sometimes hotter than small town gossip. Secretary of Commerce, Herbert Hoover worried at what he called "this fever of speculation," and warned Americans not to overextend their resources by purchasing stocks on credit. He often criticized the easy credit policies of the Federal Reserve System. Many eagerly joined in on what they hoped would be easy money. At least on paper it looked easy.

Alexander D. Noyes, veteran financial advisor for the *New York Times*, did his best to warn his readers of the danger of assuming that stock prices and prosperity would continue forever. Noyes was quickly denounced as a traitor "trying to discredit or stop American prosperity." Harvard economist William Z. Ripley also attempted to warn the nation's people of what he called the "money fugling, the hornswoggling and the skullduggery taking place in many American corporations." His words, too, fell on deaf ears. Others, like American journalist, Joseph Lincoln Steffens, who just returned home from Russia favorably impressed with the new Socialist takeover of that country, said, "Big business in America is producing what the Socialists held up as their goal—food shelter and clothing for all...It is a great country this; as great as Rome."

By September of 1929, American statistician and economist, Robert Babson was bold enough to predict, "There is a crash coming, and it may be a terrific one involving even a decline of 60 to 80 points in the Dow Jones barometer." Still, others were not convinced. Even Herbert Hoover spoke these reassuring words to the American people during his presidential campaign: "We shall soon, with the help of God, be in sight of the day when poverty shall be banished from this nation."

In his last public message given to the nation on December 4, 1928, outgoing President Calvin Coolidge uttered these reassuring words: "The nation might regard the present with satisfaction and anticipate the future with optimism; no Congress has met with a more pleasing prospect than the one which appears at the present time." On October 16, 1928, Professor Irving Fisher of Yale reported to the Press, "Stock prices have reached what looks like a permanently high plateau."

Maybe Lincoln Steffen's dream was coming true. Times were great, just like Rome at the height of her glory. By Wednesday, October 23, 1929, the booming American Stock market appeared to have a slight belly ache, one that even a good dose of castor oil could not cure. During the last hour of that day's trading a sharp drop occurred. On Thursday October 24, (later known as black Thursday) nearly thirteen million shares changed hands as prices continued to fall. Totaling up their loses many so-called "experts" soothed investors saying, "the worst is now over."

However, on October 28 and 29, stock values were even lower, hitting the bottom on November 13. In the early months of 1930 stocks rose slightly until April, then continued a gradual downfall that hit rock bottom in December of 1932. Several examples of what is meant by "rock bottom" would include: General Electric stock peaked in 1929 at 403, fell to less than 9 in 1932; Remington Rand peaked at 57 in 1929 and fell to a low of 1 in 1932; General Motors reached 91 in 1929 and crashed to 7 in 1932; Electric Bond and Share peaked at 189 in 1929 and dropped to 5 in 1932; Sears Roebuck reached 181 in 1929 and crashed to 9 in 1932; U.S. Steel dropped from 261 in 1929 to 21 in 1932. The Stock Market crash of 1929 did not affect all that many Milford residents because few had surplus cash to have invested. The main concern for most was the accompanying price crash for farm-produced commodities. Wheat, which sold for $2.02 in 1919, fell to a low of 38 cents in 1932. Corn fell from a high of $1.70 in 1919 to a low of 11 cents in 1932-33. Total income for grain raised by Nebraska farmers dropped from a high of 507 million dollars in 1919 to a low of 121 million in 1932. In 1934, Nebraska farm income hit rock bottom, registering only 77 million dollars (*History of Nebraska*, Olsen & Naugle).

By 1932, approximately twelve million American people were out of work—about 25 percent of the total work force. In 1932, factory payrolls dropped more than fifty percent from their 1929 levels. Many large cities were forced to feed unemployed workers in food lines and soup kitchens. Shanty towns sprung up where jobless citizens scrounged through garbage dumps looking for food. Some New York apartment houses offered five-year leases for payment of one year's rent. Entire Pullman trains rolled along without carrying a single passenger. Nebraska farm real estate values decreased from 4.2 billion in 1920 to 2.9 billion in 1930. Land that sold for an average of $165 in 1921 was now worth $115, a decrease of 30.3 percent. In some Nebraska counties it dropped even more. Hard hit were farmers who had purchased land in the early 1920s, during the heat of the war boom. Many tried to refinance through local banks, but credit became increasingly difficult to obtain and many simply surrendered to foreclosure.

Records from nine combined southeastern Nebraska counties reported 472 foreclosures from 1921 to 1930, with 136 of those taking place in 1932, or 8.2 percent of the total land transactions recorded for that year. One Nebraska Sandhills county is said to have recorded 108 farm foreclosures in one year.

Banks with assets tied up in farm real estate were also hard hit. In 1924, 100 banks folded, 23 in 1926, 19 in 1927, 400 in 1928 and 106 in 1929. Business and manufacturing establishments also showed a decrease in numbers from 2,884 in 1920 to 1,491 in 1930. By December of 1932, Nebraska farmers were receiving 80 percent less for corn, 79 percent less for beef cattle, and 72 percent less for their hogs. No, the Depression did not bypass Milford. On November 28, 1929 one of Milford's two banks was forced to close its doors because of what was known in that day as a "run on funds." This meant depositors were getting uneasy about the safety of their savings and bank accounts. The bank was not allowed to proceed without government supervision and restrictions until March of 1933. One Milford bank never did reopen.

When the Milford School Board met in 1932, the 1933 budget was cut $4,800, which reduced teacher salaries by 34 percent. Grade school teachers' pay dropped to $640 for one year's work, while high school teachers would received $750 annually.

On January 1, 1932, farmers were being paid 32 cents for corn, and 40 cents for wheat. One year later, corn was 11 cents, wheat was 30 cents and eggs were 8 cents. Thanks to cheap prices charged by Milford merchants, most natives were able to survive. Down on Main Street at Allison's Meat Market your food dollar would stretch and stretch and stretch. Good pork or beef roast sold for 10 cents per pound, while choice cured ham sold for 12 cents. True's Grocery was selling one gallon cans of choice peaches for 39 cents, corn flakes for 10 cents, and Kirks Castile hard water hand soap 3 bars for 13 cents. Over at the Ford Garage, $460 would buy you a brand new 1932 Ford V-8 two-door Roadster, or if you were one of those more fussy lads, $600 would put you in a new four-door V-8 Victoria—$50 less if you settled for the old-fashioned four-cylinder engine.

Drought

"Drought as a natural disaster is more subtle than a tornado or flood. It comes on slowly. People tend to postpone the reality. Finally, they react in disbelief dismay and, sometimes despondency. The end of a tornado or flood is usually definite and recognizable. The end of a drought, though, can be stretched through a whole succession of false signals and misplace hopes (*Nebraska No Place Quite Like It!*, Harold Hamil, pg.119)."

Nebraska natives are no strangers to drought or other hard times associated with unusual weather patterns. One of the meanest droughts ever recorded in state history is said to have occurred in 1859-60 when many of the state's creeks and rivers completely dried up. The 1894-95 drought is legendary, while other so called "short crop" years occurred in 1874, 1901, 1913, and 1918. During the

The Way It Was

1894-95 drought many discouraged farmers left the state seeking friendlier places to farm. The "dirty thirties" drought was probably no worse than many earlier droughts with the exception that it lasted eight to ten years rather than the normal one or two years.

The July 30, 1894 edition of the *Milford Nebraskan* newspaper carried this news item: "It is now 50 days since we have had any rain and 35 days since we had the devastating hot winds that turned everything brown. Yesterday a string of nine teams passed through Milford heading back east."

The Milford community experienced good crop yields in 1932-33, while some northern counties experienced drought as early as 1931. Although crops were good in those years, prices were more or less on the sick side. The "great" drought hit the Milford community in the fall of 1933 and the spring of 1934 and lasted until 1940. Where corn production was concerned, 1934 and 1936 were by far the worst.

Statewide, the 1934 corn crop averaged 3.2 bushels per acre, while the 1936 crop was a close second with 3.5 bushels; 1894 would come in third at 7.5 bushels; 1934, 1936, and 1894 still hold most of the records for the least average rainfall statewide of about 13-14 inches (Crop data from *History of Nebraska,* James Olson and Ronald Naugle, pp. 412-413).

Compare this with the 45 inches that fell in the Milford-Lincoln area in 1965. The year 1936 also holds a good share of the heat records, with 41 days edging above 100 degrees, including the hottest day ever recorded on July 25. But weather records varied from community to community. If I remember correctly, it reached 114-115 degrees in Milford and Lincoln and 118 degrees in Grand Island on July 25. That year (1936) also holds the record for the coldest February ever recorded.

So far we have said little about the "dirty" part of the ten-year drought known as the "dirty thirties." I just assume it was referred to as the "dust bowl years" because of the tremendous amount of dirt traveling through mid-western skies. The total picture of these trying years are exemplified in Steinbeck's book *Grapes of Wrath*. Evidently Milford lucked out by not suffering dust storms as recorded by counties farther west. While I don't recall storms as dirty as some of those reported in Kansas, Oklahoma, Texas, or Eastern Colorado, I do remember waking up one morning to find mother's good furniture all covered with a layer of fine red Oklahoma dirt.

Born and raised about eighty miles southwest of Milford in southern Adams County, my wife Eileen recalls some of the horrific dust storms in the Roseland vicinity. During bad storms, they were forced to wear wet rags across their faces to filter the air before breathing (even in the house). She also remembered dust in the middle of the day that completely blotted out the sun.

The editor of the *Hastings Tribune*, Harold Hamil tells the "whole dusty story" as he remembered experiencing it in Adams County, only 80 miles west of Milford, in 1935:

"The summer of 1934 at Hastings—and throughout the region—was the hottest and driest on record. To this writing no summer like it. For that single season the vast farmlands of Nebraska and neighboring states were condemned to the kind of climate that explains the Sonora Desert in Arizona. Rainfall at Hastings for the first eight months of 1934 was comparable too that of Tucson. The temperature exceeded 100 degrees on an average of almost every second day between mid May and mid August. Crops withered and died in the field. The most defiant of weeds were reduced to naked stems that shivered in the fiery winds. Dust clouds skipped across virgin pastureland with the slightest breeze. Farmers and their wives carried water to trees that had gone unaided through the rigors of 50 previous summers. The earth and all that rested upon it seemed to store heat from the searing daytime sun and released it at night. Tired and sleepless humans deserted stifling bedrooms to seek relief in basements, doorways or on any kind of hard ground outside where a slight breeze might be stirring. Old timers who have lived here for over sixty years, claim they have never witnessed a dust storm equal to that Friday evening. Dust banks piled several feet along country roads in some places. One family scooped 17 bushels of dust from an enclosed porch. Persons caught in their autos were nearly suffocated with dust (*Nebraska No Place Quite Like it!*, Harold Hamil, p. 119).

The Way It Was

Confessions of a Survivor

Considering the fact that most farmers were still under the influence of the Great Depression at the time, it is amazing how many were able to survive. No mature corn was raised in Seward County in 1934 or 1936 with the exception of some grown in the low, river bottom or swampland. Much of the corn that was raised in 1935-37-38-39 was cut for fodder (some reached only several feet tall). Few had the facilities at this time to irrigate, most of that being introduced about 1955-56 during another dry cycle.

Thanks to pigs, cows, and chickens most Milford area farmers managed to feed their families. I can still see (and sometimes smell) the five- and ten-gallon milk cans filled with sour cream sitting, and occasionally standing in the hot sun, at the railroad depot waiting for a ride to Lakeville, Minnesota, or Omaha. Others were content to sell their cream and eggs to one of the half-dozen produce houses in town. For many a family, eggs and cream provided most of the grocery money. By the way, try asking your granddaughter or grandson what a "produce house" was or how many dozen eggs it takes to fill one egg case, or what is considered a good butterfat test?

With very little income how did farmers survive financially? We just did without many of the things we feel are so important today. No eating out, no skiing trips to Colorado, no television sets or other fancy electronic gadgets; no dishwashers, no bicycles, or other types of toys children enjoy today. Although we did have telephones available, many neighbors removed their phones to save the $1.00 to $1.50 per month service charge. Several neighbors came to our house to use the phone. Somehow my parents did manage to pay the yearly rent. As for food, we lived on whatever was available. Believe it or not—casserole meals were not even invented at this time. This meant living on lots of potatoes, home-butchered meat, home-baked bread, and loads of navy beans and home grown vegetables. Since we were fortunate enough to have our own apple trees, we made about 20-25 gallons of apple butter every fall, which resulted in numerous meals of apple butter and bread. Wheat was usually taken to the Crete Mills for processing into white flour. Bread, meat, eggs, homemade cheese, and home-canned vegetables provided good, but cheap eating. Store-bought bread costing 9 or 11 cents a loaf was usually considered a double sin—spending money foolishly and eating an inferior product.

Many young people were forced to leave home and look for work where conditions were somewhat better. At this time, many Milford community residents had farm sales and moved to other states where today, some may even be millionaires. Contrary to today's child-rearing philosophy, we were not paid for working at home, nor were we allowed to keep our earnings. Instead, we were always expected to share it for the support of the family.

My first earning job in 1937 consisted of carrying water for the threshing crew for which I was paid a whopping 15 cents an hour. In 1933, skilled carpenters were paid from 20 to 25 cents an hour, while ordinary laborers were usually paid by the day or month. In 1937, my dad employed an excellent, 25-year-old man, paying him $30 per month. But, hired girls were only worth from two to four dollars a week. The depression of the dirty thirties, which lasted from 1929 to 1941, came to a screeching halt soon after United States entered World War II. Those of us older than seventy who did survive all ten years are not quite sure if we should be bragging or complaining.

It often appears that many of we "older citizens" see things just a wee bit differently, especially in our money spending habits. I guess in many respects some of us are still considered just a little *old fashioned* in many of our tastes and habits. At least, I know some have hinted that I could be classed as slightly conservative, while some have even suggested that I may be more than one generation behind the modern "let the good times roll, spend your money now, max out your credit card, and pay when they catch you" philosophy.

For example, I have always believed it made sense to pay as you go by not obligating yourself to long term debts. In other words, if the money was not on hand, we often decided we really didn't need it. Second, I am still old fashioned enough to believe that electric lights should be turned off in the daytime, at least when the sun is shining. In fact, many from the present generation argue that paying for the power is no big deal and it makes more sense to save wear and tear on the light switches. Also, have you ever observed some of the "yuppie generation" eating at a fixed-price cafeteria? I often wonder if the garbage cans aren't the ones who should be asking for Alka Seltzer. Due to the scarcity of money, as well as the conservative philosophy of our parents, we were often "forced" to clean our plates before being allowed to eat dessert.

Now I hesitate to use the word "force," especially in referring to child/parent relationships. According to modern-day apostles of Sigmund Freud and Dr. Spock, this would be considered a "nasty yard stick" to use in training children. Remember, repressed, emotionally disturbing childhood experiences have been known to cause all kinds of weird and unusual types of behavior in otherwise healthy adults. I guess what I am trying to say is that maybe some of my weird hang-ups, like insisting on turning out lights, being tight in my spending habits, and feeling guilty when I see good food tossed in today's bloated garbage cans could be blamed on the severe parental discipline my generation was subjected to during these trying years.

But then, on second thought, I think we 1920s generation are entitled to do some bragging for even being as normal as most of us are, especially after having survived the Depression.

An "Old Fashioned Winter"

Nebraska natives who cannot remember back to 1949 may not agree with me when I suggest that in their short lifetimes they have never really experienced an "old fashioned winter."

While the winters of 1983, 1975, and 2000-01 were "ugly" I know from personal experience that they did not compare to some I remember from the "good old days." No, I am not going to bore you by relating tired old stories about the long miles we walked to country school—always in sub-zero weather and usually through knee deep snow—just to earn an eighth-grade diploma. Today, weather experts and environmentalists continue to debate what role, if any, our modern-day civilization plays in changing global weather patterns by what is known as the greenhouse effect. Knowing little about the subject, I will let the experts slug it out while I tell you about some early, nasty snowstorms. According to Seward County historians, the winter of 1866-67 would probably win all awards as one of the worst winters ever recorded in our county. Tradition hints at more snow in the winter of 1856, but we have no documented records to prove amounts, at least in Seward County. In the winter of 1866, it began to snow on the first day of December. From that day until April 1, a rapid succession of nasty storms blasted the county. By April, the snow was deep enough to cut off all communication between scattered settlers, shutting off all possibility of securing provisions that may have been available elsewhere. Livestock and people were both hard hit by diminishing food stocks. Livestock was especially hard hit, and many were nothing but skin and bones before spring. Most of the wild game perished as well. Two days of heavy rain in April precipitated a sudden thaw. Water rampaged down local steams and caused the Blue River's worst flooding that history records.

When I lived in the Beaver Crossing vicinity, old timers often talked about an old settler/Indian tradition telling of a time when the West Fork of the Blue stretched from "hill to hill" and covering the entire valley floor. Water levels were even higher than the record setting 1950 flood. According to Seward County historian, W.W. Cox, many settlers living in the vicinity of Ruby were forced to flee to higher ground.

Having barely recovered from the devastating winter of 1867, a new and more deadly storm clobbered early settlers in 1873. Spring came early in that year, at least that is what most people thought. The weather had been fair and warm. Gardens were planted and many of the winter livestock shelters had already been allowed to deteriorate. In fact, all precautions taken to protect man and beast for the winter had long been forgotten.

But on April 10, rain commenced to fall with a light wind blowing mildly from the southeast. Intermittent rain continued to fall until April 12, when dark clouds accompanied by lightning and thunder heralded an approaching storm. During the night, settlers were awakened by an unusual roaring of the wind. They soon realized the wind carried snow so fiercely, it blinded all visibility. Veering to the northwest, it blew with such force it reminded one of a small tornado. The blizzard continued for three days and three nights with no interruption. One eye witness said during this 72-hour period, "No object of any dimension could be discerned more than ten steps distant and two minutes of exposure was about all any man could take."

Some saved livestock including horses, cows, pigs or chickens by bringing them into their sod shanties. One settler living in L Precinct kept his horses in a dugout stable located at the foot of a hill. The storm's severity prevented him from attending to the horses for three days. After the storm, he opened the door to find the interior packed solidly with snow, but not one sign of the horses. After digging for a while, he discovered both horses standing, the snow so solid around them they could not lay down. Because their body heat had melted enough snow to provide them with sufficient breathing room, they were both alive. Why was this called the 1873 "Easter Snowstorm?" Starting on the 10th of April as a normal rain, the storm raged through the 12th, 13th, 14th and 15th of April, the 15th being Easter Day. Strange as it may seem, witnesses said the temperature never fell below 28 degrees throughout the entire storm.

Few incidents of suffering have ever been recorded and preserved like the 1888 snowstorm. When I was a small boy, I still remember old timers, many of whom were either eyewitnesses or had heard the story from their parents, debate which storm (1873 or 1888) did the most damage in Seward County. But it appeared to me the majority would have chosen the 1873 Easter Day Storm as the official yardstick to be used in measuring Seward County snowstorms.

Although early settlers had already suffered two mean storms by 1875, Mother Nature was not quite finished. The winter of 1879-80 also proved nasty. Throughout the entire winter, settlers were forced to use sleds rather then wheeled vehicles. About mid-December, several inches of wet, watery snow and sleet fell quickly and froze into a solid mass of ice. Later, a 12-inch snowfall covered this ice sheet, catching many farmers with part of their corn crop still in the field. On the night of December 23, the wind rose to a force of at least sixty miles an hour, sweeping the snow into drifts up to fifteen feet. Although the drifts were hard enough to support cows and horses, it would not support the weight of wagon wheels. As a result, most rural communities were isolated.

One old settler said, "The greatest suffering in our community was due to the fact that nearly every man used tobacco and all had been stretching their plugs to make them reach to the end of corn picking season. They were out of 'the weed,' when the roads became blocked. And if there is ever a time when a man who uses tobacco cannot get along without, it is when he is snowed in."

Eldon Hostetler

The Blizzard of 1888

Less than ten years later, on Jan. 12, 1888, Nebraska settlers were faced with yet another nasty snowstorm. In fact, it was one of the worst blizzards ever recorded in the state. It is often called the school childrens' storm, because it arrived in Seward County about the time children were starting home form school. This storm also caught most settlers unaware. The morning had been very pleasant. In fact, a warm breeze blowing from the south allowing children to wear light clothing as they frolicked to school. Some men even worked in their shirtsleeves.

Although large flakes of snow had been falling all morning, the warm south breeze hinted more at a "January thaw" than a savage winter blizzard. Not being forewarned by the type of weather forecasts available today, few people could have realized what was about to happen. However, some older, more experienced observers recognized the possibility of what they called a brewing "weather breeder."

Traveling about 45 miles an hour, the storm had passed through western Nebraska by mid-morning and reached Seward County around 3:30 P.M. By late afternoon, the storm engulfed the entire state. The only advanced warning appeared to be a low, dark, fast-moving cloud accompanied by a thunderous roar. Driven by an avalanche of blinding snow propelled by terrific winds from the northwest, the storm appeared with astonishing quickness. Temperatures fell dramatically while flour-like snow whipped through the air and cut visibility to practically zero. One witness said the storm shook his wooden frame buildings like a tidal wave. Another said it felt like his house had been hit by a train. The storm caught many children on their way home from school with little protection. Restricting visibility to a few feet, one settler said it was like trying to see with his face pushed in a snowdrift. Those caught in the storm were forced to follow fence lines, corn rows, railroad tracks, or a rut in the trail. Some found refuge when accidentally bumping into a building, a fence line, or a neighbor's home. One girl caught hold of a milk cow's tail, since the animal appeared to know its way home. Others sought refuge in road culverts and hay stacks. Some drivers turned over their wagons and sought shelter under the boxes. Many simply loosened the reins and let their animals find their own way home. Even people who were safely inside their homes when the storm struck suffered hardships. In some homes where fuel was short, settlers were forced to burn their furniture, while teachers and pupils caught in school houses sacrificed the school desks and chairs.

Although the storm lasted only one day, temperatures as low as 30 degrees below zero followed, exposing unsheltered people to frostbite or permanently discolored skin. It has been estimated that close to one hundred lives were lost in the storm statewide. Livestock losses were heavy in some parts of the state. One rancher in northeastern Nebraska reported that he lost 265 out of 300 yearling steers, while another reported, "In one day the Great Blizzard destroyed more livestock on the range than any winter storm, before or since." One early settler said she could see dead livestock scattered over the prairie for months.

A returned soldier forced to spend the night in the blizzard said, "I faced shell shock for four years in the Civil War; but I never passed such a night at this in my life." Eleven-year-old Lena Woebbecke, who lived near Pleasant Dale at the time, was forced to remain outdoors all night. Rescued the following morning, Lena survived but suffered the amputation of one leg due to frostbite. Seward County native, Miss Etta Shattuck, who was teaching school in Holt County near O'Neill, sought shelter in a haystack. Although her pupils arrived home safely, Etta lost her way when she tried to reach the home of a board member to have a warrant signed. Seeking refuge in a haystack, she was found seventy-two hours later in a weakened condition barely able to move. Etta eventually died from the experience.

According to W. W. Cox, livestock loss was low in Seward County, probably because by 1888 the county was fairly well settled and many farmers had already erected good livestock shelters. While many heroic survivor stories were reported from the Milford community, the majority appeared to have a happy ending. One old survivor said, "For a number of years it was not all that unusual to meet people who had parts of their ears, fingers or toes missing." This storm is said to have changed the minds of many potential immigrants, while a few natives simply packed their bags and returned home. One Illinois visitor said, "The West! Never again for me." Comparing notes from Seward County historians and newspaper editors with those from other parts of the state, it would appear the storm was not as severe in Seward County as experienced in northern and western parts the state, where settlements were less developed.

Several days after the storm, the *Nebraska State Journal* stated, "Returns from all parts of the northwest show that the storm of last Thursday was the most calamitous that has ever visited the country since it was settled by the white man." But this was before 1949!

I will long remember other nasty snowstorms during the "dirty thirties." Although rainfall was always short during the summer months, winter snowstorms appeared to be a dime a dozen. Nasty snowstorms in 1935 and 1937 blocked country roads for days. One of the worst two-day storms that I ever witnessed blasted Seward County in January and February of 1940. Drifts too deep for road maintainers were scooped open by "money starved" farmers using heavy steel scoops. Seward County paid the whopping sum of 25 cents an hour for what was hard, back-breaking work. But most farmers were thrilled to get the work. How many over seventy remember the nasty month of February, 1936? No, not bad snow, just old-fashioned "make a polar bear happy" type weather and a nightmare for farmers with livestock. And then there was the winter of 1948-49! While not as well known and famous as the 1873 and 1888 storms, it is now referred to by many as the worst winter ever experienced in the state.

While the 1949 storm claimed only seventy-six lives and the blizzard of 1888 cost two hundred, the death toll would have been astronomical had the same conditions prevailed in 1949. By 1949, America was living in the machine, radio, and airplane age—a far cry from the primitive conditions prevailing in 1888. The first snowstorm struck in the middle of November just about the time most farmers were hurrying around to finish their corn harvest. It started snowing in the late afternoon about suppertime and reached a peak during the early morning. Lightning and thunder, accompanied by heavy wind and blowing snow continued until about midnight. This all happened before the blizzard hit, a storm that blew for two days straight without interruption. I remember waking up the following morning staring directly at a snowdrift on the foot end of our bed. A second and larger drift smiled at me from its home under the north door.

Just before Christmas, a second storm dumped more snow on the state bringing the 1948 total to a record 65 inches (the total for Lincoln). By New Years day, most of the roads were cleared and the

The Way It Was

sun shown brightly giving one the idea that spring must be just around the corner. But on January 2nd and 3rd it started snowing again, this time accompanied by winds up to sixty miles an hour. By January 4th, nearly every road as well as many railroads were blocked. The storm was also severe in the Dakotas, Wyoming, Colorado, Utah, Montana, Idaho, and Northern Arizona. Rail and auto traffic came to a complete standstill in many parts of the state. Western Nebraska appeared to be the hardest hit.

Newspaper headlines on Jan. 4th reported, "WESTERN NEBRASKA SWEPT BY ONE OF THE WORST BLIZZARDS IN HISTORY. Nebraska was gripped Tuesday afternoon in the second day of a driving snowstorm, which has marooned hundreds, blocked all roads and was taking its toll on countless thousands of head of livestock. Mountainous drifts of snow ranging upwards to 20 feet formed gigantic roadblocks choking off all lifelines to hundreds of small western communities. Chadron's 40 inches of snow was the deepest fall as 55 mile per hour winds whipped the snow into impassable drifts. Old timers called this the worst storm in Western Nebraska's history (*Lincoln Star*, Jan. 4, 1949)."

As storms continued to hammer the region, ranchers did their best to feed their livestock, but were losing the battle. Hundreds of thousands of head of cattle and sheep died. Hogs suffocated in barns completely buried in snow. On January 24, President Harry Truman coaxed $500,000 from Congress and launched "Operation Snowbound." Troops under the direction of General Lewis A. Pick mobilized and launched an armada of C-82 "Flying Boxcars" that delivered hay to stranded animals. Military snowmobiles, known as weasels, delivered food, medicine, and other needed supplies to stranded people. Within eleven days, the Fifth Army, under General Pick, had opened 32,000 miles of roads, providing access to 69,000 people and one and one half million head of livestock, though some ranchers were not freed until late February. Finishing his job by the first of March, General Pick estimated that 76 people had died, while overall losses totaled 190 million dollars. More than 2.5 million head of cattle and 2.8 million head of sheep died or were severely injured by the storm (combined losses from all the states affected).

Traffic on our road in Seward County was limited to either walking, or bypassing the road with team and wagon. A 20-foot high cut west of our house was completely plugged with snow, the first time in memory according to people who had lived in the neighborhood since 1900. Ten days later the county finally opened our road with a small track-type bulldozer one layer at a time. When the snow started to melt we were stranded again—this time in the mud. Although not as bad as in the Panhandle, even in Seward County, the winter of 1948-49 was a *real doozie*. Again I say it. "If you were born after 1950, maybe you hain't never even experienced a real Nebraska winter!"

"The Big One?"

Milford residents are no strangers to hard times and tragedies, the majority having been associated with accidents, sickness, fire, drought or other weather-related incidents. A destructive fire on November 2, 1882 completely destroyed the original flour and saw mill erected by J. L. Davison in 1867. In 1891, what was probably the worst fire in the town's history completely destroyed Milford's new two-story 140- x 50-foot brick livery barn and armory building. This fire killed fourteen horses, seriously injured several people, and destroyed valuable equipment belonging to Cavalry Troop A.

A devastating fire in 1899 destroyed five Milford business houses, including the Saratoga Hotel. Other notable fires destroyed several large ice storage sheds and the Milford High School. Fires in 1927 and 1934 did considerable damage to the Milford Corn Mills, at which point the mill was closed.

In 1888, a tornado destroyed several farmsteads three miles west of Milford, while the earliest recorded windstorm did considerable damage to the northeast edge of town in June of 1877. The first tornado I remember, destroyed the Sterling Stauffer farmstead eight miles west of Milford in 1945. A second storm destroyed the Jonas Bontrager farmstead located two miles south of the Highway 6 corner west of town around 1947. Many local residents may still remember the most recent tornado (June 15, 1992) that struck south of Milford near the state recreation grounds. After every disaster, Milford citizens rose to the occasion and offered support to those in need and the tragedy was quickly forgotten.

The Way It Was

The Milford school building built in 1882 burned on November 14, 1916. A new schoolhouse was dedicated in 1918.

    I will never forget what happened on Thursday, April 25, 1957—a day that will long be remembered by those living in Milford. It was one of those days you would have called about perfect. It was warm, with a gentle southern breeze carrying fleecy white, blue-edged clouds northward. That morning I remember exchanging small talk about the possibility of rain with the boys at Milford Farmland while we waited for my anhydrous tank to fill. From my place (nine miles southwest of town), the mid-afternoon sky gave indications that something unusual was about to happen, especially in the southwest. Shortly after six o'clock, restless, angry-looking clouds all seemed to melt into one dark blue center, quickly forming an ugly black cloud slightly south of my place. A few claps of thunder preceded scattered hailstones, some larger than golf balls. For a few seconds we could see an ugly looking funnel cloud which was quickly obliterated by a larger, dark blue-green cloud. To those viewing the storm from the west and north it appeared to be an ordinary summertime hail and wind storm. But those living east and south of the cloud said they could see a huge, angry looking tail.

    Ed Stapowich, chief meteorologist at the Omaha Weather Bureau, said the stormfront developed when warm moist air from the

Eldon Hostetler

gulf clashed with cold air moving in from the west. At 4:14 P.M., the Omaha office forecast the possibility of severe thunderstorms for southeast Nebraska. At 5:06 P.M. the Weather Bureau reported that a strong line of thunderstorms had developed in central Nebraska and could now be expected to produce tornadoes sixty miles on either side of a line stretching along a 120-mile line from North Platte to Omaha. The tornado first touched down in southeastern Clay County near Edgar and Ong. Six sets of farm buildings were either leveled or severely damaged in Clay County. From there, the storm roared northeast through Fillmore County passing about two miles north of Geneva where it hit at least seven sets of farm buildings doing considerable damage. About 6 P.M. the storm passed through Saline County two miles north of Friend where several more sets of farm buildings were damaged.

Some Friend residents reported that they saw two funnels pass north of town, the second one following the same path a short while later. I remember watching the storm form again and reorganize east of Friend, just south of my place, and head for Milford. Thanks to a cooperative effort by many watchful eyes, Milford residents were not caught unaware. Two state patrolmen driving on Highway 6 near Friend, Ben Molcyk and Lawrence Hanus, are credited with saving many lives. Seeing the tornado form shortly before 6 P.M., they radioed patrol headquarters in Lincoln, which quickly relayed the warning to Milford residents via Lincoln radio and television stations as well as telephone. Mrs. Eirene Brandhorst, who was manning the night fire department phone, was the first one to receive this warning relayed by the operator at the Lincoln Air Force Base, "A tornado is believed to be heading your way."

Mrs. Branhorst activated the city siren before phoning Milford Chief of Police, Bill Rumler. He tore through town with his police cruiser, warning people to take cover. Lincoln radio and television stations continued to urge local residents to take cover, relaying the warnings received from the state patrol. Spotters using a radarscope at the Lincoln air force base tracked four funnels at one time. The storm pounced on the city of Milford at exactly 6:24 P.M.

Had the storm occurred in the middle of the night, without any advance warning, the death toll could have been much higher. One eyewitness watching the storm approach from a safe distance said it appeared to him to be about one-quarter mile wide and black as coal.

The Way It Was

What was left of the Clarence Stauffer home. This two-story house was completely obliterated by the same tornado that devastated Hebron, NE in 1953. Larry and Roger Stauffer who were sleeping in the first floor bedroom lived to tell of their experiences.

He said, "It just didn't look like a tornado—it didn't spiral like the pictures you see, just a wide boiling mass of dark clouds." At the time, the storm was deemed the third most powerful to ever hit the state, at least up to that date. It was surpassed only by the 1913 Omaha tornado, which killed 94 people and injured hundreds more, and the 1953 Hebron storm that did an estimated $2,000,000 in damage and injured 69 people including five who later died from their injuries.

Milford residents might remember the May 9, 1953 Hebron tornado as the same storm that wiped out the Clarence Stauffer farmstead four miles west of Milford later that night.

What probably seemed like an eternity to those caught outside a safe shelter on that fateful day in 1957 actually lasted only a few minutes. Several witnesses reported the usual "tornado roar" as well as hailstones crashing through the south and west windows—some the size of baseballs. During the height of the storm, most of the 300 Trade School students and their families plus dozens of others huddled in complete safety in the heating tunnels that connected the buildings.

Eldon Hostetler

Others were not so fortunate. Sixty-nine-year-old Paul Wittmuss was caught in a small shed connecting his kitchen and garage when the storm struck. The structure fell on Mr. Wittmuss, crushing his chest and breaking his left leg in two places. The next day, Mr. Wittmuss was reported in critical condition in the Seward hospital. His two daughters, Juanita and Leta, survived the storm by huddling in the southwest corner of the house. One daughter reported that she heard the familiar roar of the tornado as it struck their home. Hailstones accompanying the storm smashed windows and blew food off the dinner table.

Herman Heinz and his wife missed sudden death by reaching their basement just seconds before the tornado ripped off the south wall of their bedroom. After the storm had passed, Mr. Heinz helped save the life of Alvin Stolz. A 2 x 4 with a nail plunged through Stoltz's car window and pierced his neck. Heinz removed the board and helped Stoltz find medical assistance. Milford Trade School student Don Kruger, along with his wife and two small children, also suffered a narrow escape. Thinking the siren meant a fire at the trade school, Don quickly returned home to get his family to shelter in the basement. The storm struck just as they were attempting to enter the basement.

Tornado damage from the 1957 storm that hit Milford.

The Way It Was

Kruger said, "I had my hand on the cellar door, but couldn't hold it; everything was hitting it. I saw my home demolished before my eyes. It hit with such force that my wife's shoes were blown from her feet. The next thing I knew, the wind had blown my wife and kids about five feet across the ground. It is a miracle we that we weren't hurt seriously." The Krugers escaped with only minor cuts and bruises.

Another close call took place at the northwest end of Southeast Community's parking lot, in a house owned at that time by Mary Gardner. This story is rather unusual because Mary's body was waiting for burial the following day. Seventeen relatives and friends, mostly from Illinois and California, were staying in the house waiting for the funeral. Fourteen of the 17 managed to escape to the basement seconds before the storm hit. But three of the men were a mite too slow and rode out the storm on the kitchen floor. Although the roof was partially torn off, the only injuries they suffered were from flying glass. Alvin Saltzman from Upland California said, "Right before it hit, the hailstones were as big as baseballs. They shattered all of the porch windows and sprayed us with glass. This has been quite a week for me. I had my first plane ride and now I survived a Nebraska tornado."

On Friday morning, April 26, 1957, Milford people rolled up their sleeves and prepared for action. News headlines in the *Lincoln Journal* read, "One Dead, Eighteen Injured and more than 200 Homeless; Milford Begins Huge Recovery Task With Help of Neighbors." City officials geared up for action by appointing a three-man committee consisting of Everett Yost, Wesley Matzke, and Vester TeSell to survey the damages. They initially reported forty-nine houses were totally destroyed, the homeless taken in by neighbors and friends. Four businesses were gone and three badly damaged. Many homes and business places suffered broken windows from the large hail and high wind. More than one hundred window glasses were broken in Milford school buildings. Milford's trade school lost the automotive shop roof, along with the roofs of several housing units. Four trailer homes were destroyed and many windows broken.

Senator Roman Hruska's office in Washington informed Milford officials that Seward County had been declared a disaster area by the Small Business Administration. Among the eighteen people injured were Paul, Juanita and Leta Wittmuss, Alvin Stolz, Mr. and Mrs. Don Kruger, Larry Kruger, Mr. and Mrs. Leonard Kolterman, O. V.

Eldon Hostetler

Anderson, Mr. and Mrs. Seth Huges, Fred Welsh, Debra Olson, and Mrs. Ethel Hall. The body of seventy-three-year-old Paul Cast was found in the wreckage of his house about 3 A.M. on Friday morning by Seward County R.E.A. workers looking for downed power lines. Paul lived alone in his big farm home located about ten miles southwest of Milford in N Precinct along Johnson Creek. Mr. Cast died in a second storm that hit west of town about midnight.

Damage statistics were later revised. It was found eighteen homes were completely demolished, including those owned by Wilton Stauffer, Dr. Frans, Neil Wurst, Leo Stauffer, Dan Weaver, Fred Welsh, O. V. Anderson, Norman Roll, John True, W.A. Bennet, Dale Anderson, Dick Patton, Wilbur Schweitzer, Don Kruger, Gladys Dewey, Ezra Stauffer, Ed Beckler, and Paul Cast. Approximately thirty homes were severely damaged while an additional forty homes suffered lesser damage. Farm places suffering severe damage included those owned by Wallace Stauffer, Clayton Beckler, Floyd Burkey, Lester Burkey, Louis Brose, John Ficke, Beryl Conner, Danny Sutter, Leonard Kolterman, Fred Ficke, Hank Ficke, Eugene Fougeron, Conrad Dankers, and August Luebbe.

Considerable damage was also done as far east as the Lincoln Air Force Base where the roof of a medical supply building was blown off. Hail, high winds, and heavy rain was reported as far east as Ceresco and Raymond. Many Omaha natives sought shelter as threatening storm clouds passed over the city's downtown district.

Milford businesses completely destroyed included Subway Motors, owned and operated by Derold Eicher and Ralph Eigsti; Texaco Service Station, owned and operated by Stanley Eicher; Newtons Café, owned and operated by Frank, Lee, and Carl Newton; Jaegers Sinclair Station, owned and operated by Mrs. Jaeger; Heyens Garage, owned and operated by Leo Heyen; Standard Oil Service, owned by Edgar Hershberger and operated by Roy Hershberger; Conoco Service, operated by John Hershberger; and Milford Dairy Sweet, owned and operated by H.R. Phanasteil.

Since the storm hit only the southeast tip of the city, water service was not seriously interrupted, although one pump house was destroyed. All electrical service, except in the damaged area, was restored by Friday afternoon. Milford Trade School Director, Lowell Welsh said it would be necessary to find temporary facilities for the auto mechanics class and that glass damage alone amounted to $900.

The Way It Was

Total damage to the school was $43,424.00. All emergency repairs were financed through the school's current budget.

The carpentry class at the school worked through Thursday night repairing damaged roofs. Sightseers were warned by the media to stay away, saying, "There are two types of visitors to a tornado-stricken town—volunteer workers and sightseers. The former are gratefully welcomed. But Milford requests no sightseers today. The possibility of a large influx of Sunday drivers brought fears that cleanup operations would be hampered." Preliminary estimates of the total damage was pegged at between one and 1.5 million dollars.

The Seward National Guard (the first unit to arrive) and the state patrol took care of Highway 6 traffic through Milford until Monday morning, keeping out all sightseers. From then on the 119th Tank Battalion of the Nebraska National Guard shared duty with the Seward unit. Men from the Crete Volunteer Fire Department were on the scene by 7 P.M., while members of their Municipal Electric System were standing by to assist if needed. A disaster committee headquarters, located in the city hall and headed by acting mayor George Phipps, was organized to coordinate all restoration efforts. The committee began operating by Friday. Others serving on the committee included Evert Yost, chairman of tornado damage; Leonard Kuhre, feeding chairman; Fred Matzke, shelter chairman; Don Wilsey, welfare chairman; and G. A. Dunlap, chairman of volunteer emergency workers. Salvation Army volunteers, including a mobile canteen, provided lunch around the clock for victims and volunteer workers. They also provide two trucks to move furniture and other belongings.

Red Cross representatives operated from the high school cafeteria and were available to provide emergency shelter and other welfare needs. A Red Cross spokesman reported all housing needs had been met by relatives and friends, although they did have numerous requests for trailers to house families near their shattered dwellings. National Guard units were on duty arranging for a collection point for valuable articles found in the cleanup. Workers arrived from Lincoln, York, Seward, Crete, Beaver Crossing, Dorchester, Hebron, Shelby, Tecumseh, Omaha, and Hastings as well as smaller groups from many other towns. Students from Doane College in Crete and three Mennonite Colleges in Kansas made their appearance ready and willing to work. Seven relay teams of 12 to 25 men, one for each block in the hardest hit areas, made short work of the initial cleanup. Dozens of Boy Scouts from Hebron, Seward, and Milford cleaned up small debris with garden rakes.

It was estimated that 800 to 1000 workers with trucks, chain saws, and heavy equipment were on hand Saturday morning to assist in the cleanup. Twelve combination dump trucks with heavy lifting units were provided by the city of Lincoln. G.A. Dunlap, temporary chairman of the local disaster committee said, "They were just what we needed and they really made the difference Saturday." Able Construction Co. of Lincoln brought 33 men to Milford Saturday along with trucks and chain saws. Twenty men from Able Construction showed up for work on Sunday morning. The Lincoln Public School System furnished an emergency generator to provide power for Milford High School. The city of Hastings donated the use of four dump trucks, two chain saws, and seven men for the Saturday cleanup. Mennonite Disaster Service workers from across the United States, as well as some from as far away as British Columbia arrived to help clean up and rebuild, a process that lasted for several weeks.

Sunday's *Lincoln Journal and Star* organized the "Hand of Help For Milford" fund, organized to assist tornado-stricken Milford. By Saturday morning the fund totaled $4,700, later reaching more than $10,000. The *Journal* and *Star* kicked off the fund by contributing $3,000. Contributing $500 or more was the Veterans of Foreign Wars of U.S., Lincoln Lodge No. 80 B.P.O.E, Miller and Paine, and the Sesostris Temple. Many smaller gifts were received from sympathetic individuals and Sunday School classes. Eight-year-old Susan Lee Zimmer of Lincoln, gave from her allowance, money she had been saving for a trip to Coney Island. Susan gave 35 cents out of her $2.00 "nest egg." Her mother said, "Susan was terribly concerned that the tornado might hit Lincoln, then when it hit Milford she felt sorry for them."

A twelve-man advisory committee was organized to supervise the disposition of this fund with Mayor George Phipps being the only Milford native. Out of town members on the committee included Mayor Bennet Martin, Jack Hart, and Bill Dobler, all of Lincoln, Henry Mead of Seward and ex-Mayor Ralph Hawkins of Hebron. Mayor George Phipps designated Sunday May 4, as Milford Appreciation Day. Badly damaged areas were roped off. All interested persons were invited to come and see the destruction of a tornado firsthand and then rejoice together in Thanksgiving to God for kind, loving neighbors and friends who so kindly assisted the town in her hour of tragedy.

The Clash of Two Cultures

"Dad (John) Welsh had reasons to dislike Indians. About two years before, near Fort Robinson on the Wounded Knee battleground, his cousin's wife and two blonde daughters aged eight and ten were attacked, lashed to the wagon and scalped. All of the victims were then burned. The hired man who accompanied them was out of sight at the time rounding up the horses for an early start in the cool morning. Seeing the smoke he crawled to the brim of a hill just in time to see the Indians hurrying away. Riding bareback to Denver, which was nearly one hundred miles away, the hired man met in a saloon a group of discharged U.S. Cavalry men. When he told his story, the ex-colonel asked for twenty volunteers to return to the scene. Rightly or wrongly, they followed the Indians' trail and killed them. [Author's Note: The John Welsh family arrived in Milford in 1868.) ("Reminiscence," *History of Milford*, Dr. J. Stanley Welsh).

"In the summer of 1864, the whole west was very easily excited over the horrible massacre in Minnesota. Wild rumors were afloat continually and the scattered settlements were harassed with fears throughout the summer and fall. The most trifling circumstances were magnified as they were related by the panic stricken people, into general massacres or wholesale slaughters of some neighboring settlement. The impression prevailed that the rebel government in Richmond was inciting the red skins to a merciless warfare all along the frontier. Tomahawks and scalping knives of the red devils were vividly pictured in all our dreams. We knew this much, that the dark hours of the war presented a grand opportunity for them to clean us out, root and branch. We also knew that they were in no friendly mood, or in other words, we were sure they were thirsting for our blood, and all that kept them back was their fear of terrible retribution. There were people murdered in Nebraska by them and not a few. At Plum Creek of the west, on Turkey Creek and on the Little Blue and at some other points there were murders diabolical as the devil ever engineered (*Revised History of Seward County*, W. W. Cox)."

Who were these so-called "diabolical red-skinned, Satan-inspired killers" the early settlers learned to fear and hate? Were they really as bloodthirsty and uncivilized as they are often portrayed in American history books, John Wayne movies, Western novels and T.V. dramas, or were they just normal human beings fighting for survival? One of the first settlers to arrive in N Precinct near West Mills in 1865, Israel M. K. Johnson, evidently had mixed feelings and said, "The Otoes and the Omahas frequently brought their whole village of tents and would camp for weeks at a time near the mill and run all the game out of the county so that we would not be able to kill any for our own use. We then, as now, thought the only 'good Indian' was a dead one. But for all that, we believe they were no worse thieves than the same number of whites (*History of Seward County*, W.W. Cox)."

"The European conquest of the Western Hemisphere could be considered as one of the darkest chapters in our history. No one will ever know how many Indians were enslaved, tortured, debauched and killed before the Western Hemisphere came fully under white domination to allow moderation and enlightenment to ameliorate between the races. The newcomers—equipped, armed and supported by more advanced technology—conceived of themselves as a super race. To them Indians were Indians and they regarded the Natives as a single group, disagreeing among themselves only over the extent to which Natives differed from, or were inferior to themselves (*Colliers Encyclopedia,* Vol. 12, p. 671)."

"There is no reason to regard the North American Indian as an inferior race. Backwards in many respects he was, but he proved to have every potential common to other human beings. Some who have taken the time to live with them and understand their ways, find them inferior to none, and superior to many in firmness and integrity of character. As children of nature who 'take no thought for the morrow' and give their last bread to an unknown guest, the Indian followed the New Testament better than many who profess and call themselves Christians (The *Oxford History of the American People*, p. 15)."

Ever since I can remember, I have been intrigued by stories pertaining to Native Americans, the people who owned and lived on the land before it was taken over by our European ancestors. While we of European descent celebrated our 500th anniversary of the

The Way It Was

discovery of America, we quickly forgot how another so-called "lesser civilization" would forever remember it as the beginning of great sorrows. Most American history textbooks have done a good job of concealing the truth regarding the treatment of these so-called "uncivilized savages." I am continually haunted by the cruelty inflicted by our government on the peaceful Ponca Indians in 1877, the year they appeared in Milford to set the stage for the famous Prairie Flower story.

Although the phrase "Manifest Destiny" is recorded in most good dictionaries, few Americans have ever heard the word used or know what it means. My Random House *Webster's College Dictionary* describes it as, "The 19th century belief that it was inevitable for the U.S. to expand to the Pacific coast." Other works I consulted expanded on the usage to, "Vast territories of land inhabited by Indians that the whites had to have to fulfill their 'Manifest Destiny' as allotted by Divine Providence."

One historian summed it up saying, "It mattered little what precautions the Indians took to preserve their lands, what alliances they formed, what concessions they made, what solemn treaties they secured from the whites; the story was always the same. Whenever the whites moved west he displaced the Indians by force of arms, by destroying his hunting grounds or by fraudulent treaties in which the uncomprehending red man often exchanged his patrimony for glittering trinkets (*Reader's Digest, Story of America* pg. 82)."

The meaning of the phrase could best be illustrated by an episode that happened in Lancaster County, Pennsylvania, in 1763. When white settlers first arrived in Pennsylvania, messengers from the Conestoga Indian tribe met them with open arms, bringing gifts of badly need food and other provisions. The entire tribe entered into a treaty of friendship with William Penn in 1722, a treaty they were assured would be in effect "as long as the sun shines and the waters run in the rivers."

By 1763, mostly due to extreme cruelty, only twenty Conestoga Indians remained, including seven men, five women and eight children. On December 14, 1763 their camp was attacked by a group of white men. Luckily only six out of the twenty were at home at the time, three men, two women, and one boy. All six were stabbed and hatcheted; some in their beds and their bodies horribly mutilated before their huts were set on fire. The magistrates of Lancaster, shocked at the frightful barbarity, took steps to protect the remaining fourteen Indians by lodging them in the local jail for safekeeping. Two weeks later the mob returned, broke down the jail doors and killed the fourteen remaining Conestoga Indians.

One eyewitness said, "When the poor wretches saw they had no protection nigh, nor could possibly escape, and being without weapons, they divided their families, the children clinging to their parents. They fell on their faces, protesting their innocence and declared their love for the English and that in their whole lives they had never done them any injury. In this posture they all received the hatchet, men women and children murdered in cold blood. The barbarous men who committed the atrocious deed mounted their horses and 'huzzahed' in triumph as if they had gained a victory and rode off unmolested—in spite of the fact that a regiment of Highlanders was quartered in the town barracks."

The real meaning of the words Manifest Destiny several hundred years ago, could best be explained by the reactions of Lancaster, Pennsylvania, residents at the event: One local clergyman wrote a letter in the newspaper vindicating the killers by saying, "We have scripture to prove that it is right to destroy the heathen." Another writer said, "The Presbyterians think they have good justification— nothing less than the Word of God." Commenting on the massacre, a friend of the Indians wrote, "With the scripture in their hands and mouths they can set at naught that express command Thou shalt do no murder and justify their wickedness by the command given to Joshua to destroy the heathen *(A Century of Dishonor*, Helen Jackson, 1882, pg. 307)."

In April 1787, an aged Moravian missionary heard Delaware Chief Pachgantachilias addressing a group of Indians that had been converted to Christianity by white missionaries. Recapitulating many of the past events since the white man came to America, he concluded with these words:

"I admit that there are good white men, but they bare no proportion to the bad; the bad must be the strongest, for they rule. They do whatever they please. They enslave those who are not of their color, although created by the same Great Spirit who created them. They would make slaves of us if they could; but as they cannot do it, they kill us. There is no faith to be placed in their word. They are not like the Indians, who are only enemies while at war, and are friends in peace. They will say to an Indian, 'My friend; my brother' and take him by the hand, and, at the same moment destroy him. And so you will be treated by them before long. Remember that this day I have warned you to beware of such friends as these. I know the 'Long Knives', they are not to be trusted."

Did the old Chief's prophecy come true?

In 1791 the Cherokee nation signed a treaty with the new American government, a treaty they thought would guarantee them independence forever. But the state of Georgia had different ideas. Defying the federal agreement, the state declared the treaty obsolete. Discovery of gold in Cherokee land in 1828 brought the controversy to a head as well as a flock of white settlers to the spot. In 1838, regular Army troops, under the command of Winfield Scott, rounded up the stubborn Cherokees and started them on the long trail to Indian Territory in Oklahoma, a move that cost them one-fourth of their total population. One U.S. soldier reported, "I saw the helpless Cherokees arrested and dragged from their homes and driven by bayonet points into the stockade. In the chill rain I saw them loaded like cattle and start for the west."

In 1830, Congress passed a bill known as the Indian Removal Act. This law was designed to move all of the Eastern Indians to any part of the new Louisiana Territory purchased from France in 1803. By the time the Kansas and Nebraska Act was passed in 1854, few Indians were living east of the Mississippi River.

By 1871, 370 Indian treaties had been signed, although the majority had at one time or another been broken, usually by the U.S. government. Yes, the American Indians did have some friends who were horrified at the way they were being treated. Henry B. Hipple, Episcopal Bishop of Minnesota, was alarmed at what he saw happening and called on Americans "to rise up with one voice and demand reform of an atrocious Indian system which has always garnered the same fruit of anguish and blood."

In contrast, many in high places appeared to have no sympathy. James M. Cavnaugh, congressional representative from the Montana

Territory, said, "I have never in my life seen a good Indian; except when I have seen a dead one." William T. Sherman had this viewpoint: "The more we kill this year, the less we will have to kill next year. They all have to be killed, or be maintained as a species of paupers." General Custer said, "When the soil he has hunted on is claimed by white civilization, there is no appeal. He must yield or it will roll over him destroying him as it advances (*Reader's Digest, Story of America*, pgs. 83-84.)."

By 1880, more than thirty tribes had already been removed to "Indian" territory in Oklahoma, a land they had been assured would be theirs forever, mostly because they assumed white Americans would never want it. However, by 1880, adventure-seeking whites sometimes known as "Boomers," many hired by railroad people anxious to cash in on land sales, helped to generate a public outcry against leaving Oklahoma in the hands of "shiftless" Indians.

One more time public opinion overruled years of Indian treaties and a humane outcome. The first wild race for Indian land took place in 1893 when "Cherokee Outlet" was opened for white settlement. The biggest rush took place on April 22, 1899, when approximately 15,000 settlers were waiting on the border for an opening gunshot to signal a rush in to stake claims. Those who arrived that day for the first time found out that earlier "eager beavers" had beaten them to the punch days before. Those who jumped the gun were quickly known as "Sooners." Now you know why Oklahoma's football team is sometimes known as "The Boomer Sooners."

When Hendric Hudson anchored the *Half Moon* off New York Island in 1609, friendly Indians were on hand to greet him, exclaiming, "Behold! The Gods have come to visit us." These so-called "friendly" Indians were the Lenni Lenape Tribe, or the" Original People," often known as the "people of the rising sun." For some unknown reason, early English settlers renamed the tribe the "Delaware" after Englishman Lord De La Warre. Objecting to the name at first, they were told they should be proud to be named after a "great English brave" as well as a big river.

During William Penn's humane administration, the Delawares were some of his most devoted friends. Responding to his unusual kindness they called him *Elder Brother*. Needless to say, after Penn's death, friendly relationships quickly deteriorated, often prodded by British or French influence during the French and Indian War. The

United States signed a treaty with the tribe, guaranteeing the Delaware people "all territorial rights in the fullest and most ample manner as quarantined by all former treaties, and should it be of mutual interests of both parties to invite other tribes who have been friends of United States to form a state, where the Delaware nation shall be the head, it shall be done; and the new Nation shall be entitled to send a representative to congress." This was only the first of many treaties signed with the Delaware people. A second treaty signed a few years later guaranteed that, "any other person not an Indian attempting to settle on any lands allotted to the Delaware Nation in this treaty, the Indians may punish him as they so please."

You probably know the rest of the story—a brutal and sad commentary on 18th century American/Indian diplomacy. They were allowed to live in peace—as long as the land was not wanted by the new white settlers. In the late 1700s the president wrote this memo to the governor of the northwestern Ohio territory: "The treaties which have been made may be examined, but must not be departed from, unless a change of boundary beneficial to United States can be obtained. You will not neglect any opportunity that may offer of extinguishing the Indian's rights as far as the Mississippi."

At this time no one even dreamed that white settlers would covet land as far west as the Mississippi. Delaware Indian sorrows were only beginning. In 1794 they were defeated by General Wayne, their homes and cornfields burned, forcing them to sign a new treaty.

This time they were told, "The heart of General Washington, the Great American Chief, wishes nothing so much as peace and brotherly love, that such is the justice and liberality of the United States, and that he is acting the part of a 'tender father' to them and their children in thus providing for them not only at present, but forever." Additional treaties were signed in 1813, 1814, 1817, 1818, and 1829. In 1829 the Delaware Indians were told they would be moved to eastern Kansas, "where the Government will give them as their permanent residence the quiet and peaceable and undisturbed enjoyment of the same against the claims and assaults of all and every other people whatsoever."

Here the Delawares built a thriving farming community only to be cheated out of their farms by new treaties and advancing settlers, as well as greedy railroad people. White settlers stole their property and livestock, big lumber companies cut down their forests, forcing the tribe to move to poorer land in Oklahoma.

By 1862, one hundred seventy Delaware males had volunteered to serve their country during the Civil War, this out of a total population of only two hundred males between the ages of eighteen and forty-five. Arriving in Oklahoma about 1870, they discovered their "tender father" had mistakenly given part of their land to other tribes and had already transferred their funds to the Cherokee Nation. Eventually the Delawares were forced to disband and join other scattered Indian Tribes (*A Century of Dishonor*, Helen Jackson and *Reader's Digest, The Story of America*).

From the hundreds of different Indian tribes living in America when the Europeans arrived, I have a personal reason for telling the sad story of the Delaware Tribe. In 1738, Jacob Hochstetler, (my ancestor seven generations ago) arrived in America and settled in Berks County, Pennsylvania. Having thousands of descendants today, Jacob could be considered as the progenitor of all the Hochstetlers (Hostetlers) found in the community, and since his only daughter, Barbara married Christian Stutzman, most of the Stutzman relatives as well.

By 1757, Jacob and his family were living near the edge of the white settlements south of the Blue Mountains near Shartlesville. On the night of September 19, 1757 the Hochstetler family was surprised by a party of eight to ten Delaware warriors who, after setting fire to their cabin, killed mother Hochstetler and two of the smaller children. Tradition says that one Delaware brave, in the process of tomahawking the youngest son Christian, noticed his beautiful blue, pleading eyes and spared his life. Father Jacob and the two older boys, Joseph and Christian, were taken captive. Marched to northwestern Pennsylvania they were all adopted as members of the tribe.

Three years later, Jacob managed to escape and returned to his family, while Joseph and Christian were held until 1764, at which time the Delawares signed a new peace treaty forcing them to release all white captives. All three reported they had been treated kindly by their captors and it was reported that Joseph appeared to have a difficult time adjusting to white civilization (*The Jacob Hochstetler Story*, Dr. Harvey Hostetler, 1912).

While many early European settlers treated American Indians with disrespect, early Seward County residents appeared to have little trouble with the natives, although records disagree somewhat on early Indian and settler relationships. One record mentions that two early settlers were killed south of Seward in the late 1850s, while according to W. W. Cox, early white settlers killed two Indians near Ruby about the same time. The first family to settle in southern Seward County, Tommy West, had several narrow escapes before his kindness and generosity won them over. Until he died in 1880, the Indians appeared to be his good friends. It would appear that many of the early settlers possessed the same attitudes concerning their rights to "Manifest Destiny." Quoting from an editorial published in the *Seward Advocate* newspaper in 1879:

"We can imagine many feats of valor performed by the noble Red Man, how he went forth to conquer, his capture of the beaver, the bear and the bison, how he wooed and won the dusky maiden; but he left no footprints in the sands of time. To chase the game that roamed the prairie, and watch the prairie fire was his calling. No progress marked his years, he built no cities, opened no farms, he planted no vineyards. If he occupied the land for a thousand generations, he left it as he found it in its primeval condition. When in the fullness of time it was necessary that a better and nobler race should have the possession of the heathens for an inheritance, the way was opened in 1858 for the settlement of the county."

Sounds more or less like a third or fourth stanza of the same old song sung by eastern forefathers in 1700. Does it not echo some of the identical sentiments expressed by many modern day environmentalists and conservationists? It was very difficult for our early ancestors to grasp the attitudes Native Americans held towards the land and its use, nor could white settlers comprehend the Indian attitudes concerning the ownership of land, while the Indian had trouble understanding the white man's concept of private ownership.

Shawnee Chief Tecumseh argued that a man could not sell the land any more than he could sell the sea or the air he breathed. Apparently many of the Indians did not realize that when they accepted gifts for granting the right for using parts of their tribal domain, they also gave up their own rights to use it forever.

The cost of accepting the white man's culture was unusually high. The newcomers introduced diseases to which the Indian had low resistance. Epidemics of small pox, tuberculosis, dysentery, and measles wiped out hundreds. Warring European powers enlisted

Eldon Hostetler

Indian allies who were soon dependent on white man's goods, causing tribes to war against each other to the ultimate benefit of the white man. Fur traders and other business entrepreneurs offered whiskey and other goods that eventually disrupted and destroyed the Indian's culture, leaving them in a helpless and demoralized condition. Famous American Indian painter and writer, George Catlin, interviewed Ponca Indian Chief Shoo-de-ga-cha in the mid-1830s. Shoo-de-ga-cha reported the demoralized condition of his tribe at that time:

"He related to me with great coolness and frankness the poverty and distress of his nation...Poor, noble chief, who was equal and worthy of a great empire! He sat on the deck of the steamer, overlooking the little cluster of his wigwams mingled among the trees, and like Caius Marius weeping over the ruins of Carthage, shed tears as he was descanting on the poverty of his ill fated community, which he told me had 'once been powerful and happy,' and that the buffaloes which the great spirit had given them for food, and which formerly spread all over the green prairies, had all been killed or driven out by the white men, who wanted their skins; that their country was now entirely destitute of game and food; and that his young men, penetrating the countries of their enemies for buffaloes, which they were obliged to do, were cut to pieces in great numbers. That his people had foolishly become fond of firewater, and had given away everything in their country for it; that it had destroyed many of his warriors, and would soon destroy the rest; that his tribe was too small; that they were met and killed by the Sioux on the north, by the Pawnees on the west, by the Osages and Konzas on the south, and still more alarmed from the constant advance of the pale faces from the east with their whisky and small pox, which had already destroyed four-fifths of his tribe, and would soon impoverish and at last destroy the remainder of them *(A Century of Dishonor*, Helen Jackson, pg. 187)."

Most of us are quite familiar with our family roots and backgrounds. We also have a comprehensive history of any land we own by having access to recorded papers and other government documents that are carefully filed away for safe keeping. As an example, I can trace my Hostetler family ancestry back to Switzerland some three hundred years ago. However, for many Native Americans who kept no written records, it was a different story. Consequently little is known about the background of many of the Indians living in the Milford community in the late 1850s when the earliest settlers arrived. Most historians would agree the Indians living in the community were relative newcomers, some having arrived in Nebraska about the time Columbus set foot on the shores, most having been driven out of their original homelands by stronger tribes further east or south.

Although many different tribes traveled through and used Seward County for hunting purposes, no one tribe ever claimed Seward County as its permanent home. Probably the nearest tribe claiming permanent homes would have been the Otoes living in the Ashland area. By 1854, the Otoes and the Missouri had ceded all of their land to the U.S. Government and were no longer a threat to new settlers. Other tribes using Seward County at one time included the Kansa, Omahas, and Pawnees. The Kansa Indians living south of Seward County gave up their land as early as 1825, while the Omaha Tribe living northeast of Milford had given up the bulk of their land by 1865. The Pawnees, who lived west of Milford and claimed the lion's share of Central Nebraska, had given up everything south of the Platte River by 1833.

By 1875 the Pawnee Indians were even forced to give up their reservation land along the Loup River and move to Indian Territory. The Sioux, although a threat at times in the Milford vicinity, kept pretty much to their land in the northern and western parts of the state where they threatened settlers as late as 1890. The Ponca, although famous for their short stay in Milford in 1877, lived along the mouth of the Niobrara River and played no further role in Seward County history.

Stories shared by early Milford community settlers usually portray wandering Native Americans as more of a nuisance than a threat. Local newspaper accounts report numerous Indians circulating in the Milford community, one party as late as 1886. While they did not appear to cause any trouble with the early settlers, it may have been more like a forced truce since they had already been "whipped into submission" by earlier defeats as well as white man's diseases and scarcity of buffalo.

Many settler-Indian encounters were fueled by starving Indians who usually took it for granted that if it was growing on "God's earth," it was meant for whoever needed it. In the early 1870s large groups would arrive in the Milford and Beaver Crossing communities to spend the winter, where the men trapped for beaver and other fur-bearing animals found along Seward County streams. During extra cold winters, it was reported that many died from the extreme cold and lack of nourishing food.

The following was recorded in the Feb. 10, 1871 issue of the *Milford Blue Valley Record*.

"A large party of Omaha Indians have just returned home from their annual buffalo hunt along the Republican River country camped along the Blue near Beaver Crossing and are saying, 'low not much plenty of buffalo'." The editor noted that many were dying from the severe cold.

Since Milford was on the route used by many eastern Nebraska tribes traveling west and south to the Republican River Valley (one of the few places they could still be found by 1870), friendly Indians were often seen on Milford streets. It would appear they were usually half starved, always looking and asking for meat or fresh-baked bread, or "just one chaw" of chewing tobacco. In my younger days, I talked to older residents who remembered when traveling Indians would come begging. They would first ask for good food, and if refused, they would take anything edible, even dead farm animals, including cows, dogs, and chickens.

One of the saddest examples was told by the James E. and Elmina Jones family. James and Elmina emigrated to Nebraska from Wisconsin in 1874 and purchased land three miles west of Dorchester. The following account is published in the *Centennial History of Dorchester and Pleasant Hill* (pp. 22-23).

"Jones had some hogs die of cholera and hauled them out in a field to a ditch where he was going to bury them. Some Indians came along and asked if they could have them. Jones told them they were not good for food having died of Cholera, but the Indians loaded them in their wagon and drove away. They seemed glad to get them. An older resident told the Joneses that they once had poisoned some coyotes, and the Indians came along and found them. They cooked the coyote meat in a big kettle with some pumpkins and ate them. When they were told that the coyotes had been poisoned, the Indians said, 'No hurt Indian'. As settlers became more numerous, the lot of the Indians became poorer, and they often resorted to begging. Usually they had a letter written by the Agent at the reservation saying to help these people, as they were good Indians."

The Way It Was

The following excerpt was taken from "Reminiscence" in the *History of Milford*. Dr. Stanley Welsh was the son of early Milford settler John Welsh who arrived in Milford in 1868. The Welsh family donated land for Camp Easter Seal and Welsh Ball Field.

"One day an Indian chief and two bucks came to the barnyard near our two-room house. A group of Indians were camped near Shogo Springs near the present trade school area. They were to have a wedding feast and wanted two fat pigs for which they were willing to pay five dollars each. The two bucks and dad's hired man entered the muddy pigpen and tied a rope to the hind leg of each pig so they could be driven to camp. When it came time to pay, the old chief handed dad a five dollar bill and said; 'All poor Indian got.' Dad demanded the ten dollars. In the ensuing argument, the pigs were thrown back into the pigpen, the Indians shoved back towards camp, and the chief got a kick in the buckskin."

The following story appeared in the Aug. 19, 1937 edition of the *Seward Independent*. The Berneckers arrived in Seward County in 1873 and lived four miles south of Seward.

"The young folks here should stop to think of some of the hardships we early settlers had to endure. The Indians which camped right here were very friendly. They would come through as we were eating and beg us for food. One morning they saw us eating pancakes and mother and I were busy the rest of the morning making pancakes for them. In the middle of October, the Pawnees were at war with the Sioux. About 200 Indians and their captain wanted a load of corn for their ponies so they helped hitch the horses to the wagon. The men left their rifles but kept their revolvers and knives in their belts and with the ten men drove in the field and all I had to do was hold the lines and drive the horses while the Indians picked the corn."

Lillian (Wright) Cromwell arrived in Seward County in 1879. The family lived several miles northeast of where Goehner is now located. Cromwell offered the following in the *Seward Independent*.

"Indian tribes were often seen as they came through the county in the spring and again in the fall. They hunted buffalo along the Republican River during the winter, trailing through the county single file. Mrs. Cromwell does not recall being afraid of them and remembers helping small Indian children hunt feathers. However, a scare did grip the area one spring. A tribe held a council of war and threatened to scalp the settlers for burying the body of a tribesman left in a treetop, according to Indian burial customs. Burial was contrary to the Indians method of arriving at the Happy Hunting Grounds. During this time Mrs. Cromwell remembers her mother taking her children to the cornfield where they lay between the rows awaiting a safe time to venture forth. She recalls another encounter when an Indian, finding the family seated at the table eating, seated himself and ate until he was satisfied."

Henry H. Smith contributed the following in *Early Days in Seward County*. The Bishop family arrived in Seward County in 1870 and lived in the Pleasant Dale vicinity.

"We were frequently visited by Indians who would approach the house with their stealthy tread, and often times one would be seen standing in the kitchen unannounced. Great beggars, Mr. Indian always wanted two things, tobacco and meat. Mrs. Indian usually had a sick papoose and was greatly in need of sugar and flour. In the very northwest corner of the southeast quarter of section 3, one or more Indians are buried. As a boy I witnessed them camp on this spot. The squaws carried the wood from the timber nearby, the property of C. D. Ficke at the present time."

Joe Winsor of near Beaver Crossing recounted the following in the *Seward Independent*. Winsor arrived with his parents in 1869 and lived in K precinct.

"There are some things I remember as a small boy, and one of them was the Indians. When they were moving them from Omaha to Indian Territory I stood on the old sod house and watched a string of Indians coming across the country from the northeast in single file with tent poles fastened to the sides of the ponies with a kind of basket or swing fastened to the pole behind the ponies with two or three small children riding, and a papoose strapped on the back of the squaw. The squaws walked having charge of the procession. The Chiefs and braves rode ponies in pairs."

The Way It Was

The Prairie Flower Story: Which Version?

In 1856 the U.S. Government signed a treaty guaranteeing the Ponca Indians 96,000 acres of land along the Niobrara River. They also agreed to protect them from their bitter enemies—the Sioux. At this time, the tribe numbered nearly 800 people. Due to a spotless behavioral record they were known as one of the most gentle and peaceful tribes in all of the United States. Living in two small villages in 160 permanent houses they boasted of five hundred acres of growing crops and appeared to be happy and contented. Due to the fact that The Methodist Episcopal Church had established a mission school complex in the village some time earlier, they were well acquainted with modern civilization. In December of 1863, one Ponca camp was ravaged by a party of American soldiers, and in 1868 their territory was mistakenly given to the Sioux when the government signed a new treaty with that tribe. It was said the two tribes reached a compromise on how the land should be divided, but Uncle Sam failed to act and payed slight attention to their plight. When the government insisted the tribe move to Oklahoma, Ponca leaders were marched to Oklahoma against their will to view the new country. Although Ponca leaders utterly rejected the land, the entire tribe was forced to leave their ancestral homes along the Niobrara, forced by bayonet wielding U.S. Soldiers. Ponca Chief Standing Bear tells the story:

"Then the inspectors told them: 'Tomorrow you must be ready to move. If you are not ready you will be shot.' Then the soldiers came to the doors with their bayonets, and ten families were frightened...The soldiers brought wagons, they put their things in and were carried away. The rest of the tribe would not move. Then, when he found out that we would not go, he wrote for more soldiers. Then the soldiers came and we locked our doors, and the women and children hid in the woods. Then the soldiers drove all the people to the other side of the river, all but my brother Big Snake and I. We did not go; and the soldiers took us and carried us away to a fort and put us in jail...And they took wagons and went around and broke open the houses. They took our reapers, mowers, hay-rakes, spades, ploughs, bedsteads, stoves, cupboards and everything we had on our farm, and put them in one large building. We told them we would rather die than leave our land; but we could not help ourselves…When we came back from the Council, we found our women and children surrounded by a guard of soldiers…They took us down (to Oklahoma) many died on the road. Two of my children died. After we reached the new land, all my horses died. The water was very bad. All my cattle died; not one was left. I stayed until one hundred and fifty eight of my people died (*Native American Testimony,* p. 168-169)."

Starting for Oklahoma on May 21, 1877, the party of about 700 Poncas lead by Indian Agent E. A. Howard driven by soldiers reached Milford on June 3, where Chief Standing Bear's daughter, Prairie Flower died of consumption at 2 o'clock. The story of the Ponca Indians, as well as their experiences when they arrived in Milford in 1877 appears to have several different versions. Like other early happenings various versions of the same event usually disagree on several points, and this story is no exception. The book *Removal of The Ponca Indians* published in 1882 is a record of the official congressional hearings which followed several years after the Poncas arrived in Oklahoma. On page 449 we have Howard's own version of some events as they happened during the 500 mile journey in the spring of 1877. This letter was addressed to the Federal Indian Commissioner and was written by Howard as the Ponca party was nearing Beatrice.

"The rain storms have been most terrific, both as to the amount of water fall and velocity of wind, many times continuing with unabated fury for hours and completely flooding the whole country. In consequences of these extraordinary storms small creeks have been suddenly swollen to the magnitude to raging rivers, carrying away bridges and rendering the fording of them almost impossible; and altogether the roads have been rendered to the worst condition possible for the elements to make them, causing great hindrance and delay for the Indian Train. The continuous storms have also caused much annoyance and no little suffering to the Indians, especially to the women and children who were poorly prepared to meet such a condition of the elements. As indicated by my telegram of the 9th instant, the storm most damaging and fatal to my train occurred on the evening of the 6th instant, while in camp on the Blue River near Milford. It came upon us suddenly at about five o'clock, accompanied by sharp, incessant lightning, almost deafening thunder, and a very deluge of rain, continuing with unabated fury for nearly four hours.

The Way It Was

The wind blew a fearful tornado, demolishing every teepee and tent in the camp, and rendering many of them into shreds; overturning wagons, and hurling wagon boxes, supplies and camp equipage through the air in every direction like straws. Some of the people were picked up by the wind and carried as much as 300 yards without touching the ground. Quite a number of the Indians were injured, and one child died the next day from injuries received and was given a Christian burial at Milford. The cries of the people, mingled with the terrific thunder and tumult of the storm made "confusion worse confounded" and I earnestly hope to be spared any similar experience in the future. I had the injured removed to Milford and caused medical attention and assistance to be furnished them. Besides the injuries received by the people, this storm was disastrous in this, in that it caused a delay of several days for repairs and quite a heavy expenditure in connection therewith. It has also had a depressing and bad influence on the hearts and minds of the Indians, which on account of their superstitious nature, is hard to dispel. During the journey several of the Indians have been seriously ill, and in consequence of the bad conditions of the roads it has been extremely difficult to move them with any degree of comfort; but I have done all within my power to make their conditions as comfortable as possible. The prevailing diseases of a dangerous character have been and are consumption and scrofulous complaints, of which quite a number are now sick. Since leaving Columbus there have been four deaths; two of consumption - both adults; one of fits, and one from injuries received in the storm in Milford, both children. All of these deceased persons were members of the families of chiefs or headmen of the tribe. I caused each to be given a Christian burial, at an average expense of about fifteen dollars. The care that I bestowed upon them before and after their death, and

Ponca Chief Standing Bear visited Milford in 1877.

especially the manner in which they were buried, had a very great effect for good upon the hearts of the relatives and friends of the deceased, which they openly expressed. Standing Bear, one of the chiefs, expressed himself at the grave of his daughter as desirous of leaving off the ways of the Indian and adopting those of the white man. There are several sick in the tribe, but none in immediate danger. I am doing all within my power to improve the sanitary condition of the tribe, but cannot hope to do much in that direction until I arrive with them upon the reservation and secure the services of a competent physician—"

Another version of the Milford-Ponca Indian story is told by Seward County historian Cox. His version of the story is copied from his Revised work published in 1905:

"A scene of wild excitement occurred in the summer of 1878 [Author's Note: According to all other versions, Mr. Cox is incorrect on the year, other records say 1877.] when the Ponca Indians were journeying from their old home in the northern part of our state to their new home in Indian territory. Under the command of Major Howard, the Ponca tribe, about five hundred strong, were passing through this county. As they passed through Seward all seemed cheerful and happy. We recollect that the tribe was well provided with excellent teams, new wagons, and all the necessaries of life, but were under current of dissatisfaction at having to leave their old home. Shortly after leaving Seward, one of the teamsters had an accident which started trouble. His wagon overturned and a child was killed. That was a bad omen to the mind of the Indians, at the same time a Chief's daughter was very sick and was carried on a litter. Later in the day the band arrived at the proposed camping ground near the bridge, and just at this time the young squaw died. This was another bad omen, and the Indians were becoming excited thinking the Great Spirit was angry with them. The Major saw there was a great spirit of discontent, and he promised them a week of rest. The teepees were placed and the campfires were started, just then a serious storm broke in upon them. One squaw had a kettle of boiling water suspended on a tripod over the fire. Some children were playing near the fire when an awful gust of wind overturned tents and threw the camp into dire confusion, and the huge kettle scalded one child to death and another was seriously burned by being thrown into the fire. Confusion ruled the hour, and pandemonium broke loose. Fortunately the Bucks had just finished shooting beeves and had used up all the ammunition at hand. Major Howard sent a messenger post haste up town for a doctor. Dr. Brandon quickly responded, little thinking that he was to "walk into the jaws of death" into the mouth of hell. Darkness soon began to veil the sky, and peal on peal of dreadful thunder with a ghastly scene only illuminated by the flashes of lurid lightning and the whole camp in wild revelry of a war dance and ready to wreak vengeance upon the pale face. Major Howard had under his command about thirty white teamsters with the doctor in their midst. A hollow square was formed and the men with revolvers were given strict orders to fire to kill, provided the ferocious savages made an onslaught with raised scalping knives and tomahawks. The doctor of course was brave, but somehow his hat raised a foot or more. Thirty white men had to coolly face five hundred infuriated savages. The moment was awful in the extreme. The Indians were so frantic with rage that it was with great difficulty that a parley was effected, but finally a truce was made when the poor creatures could be made to understand that it was the medicine man come to their relief, when they quieted down. The people of Milford knew nothing of the trouble or danger until it was all over. If a blow had been struck or a shot fired, there would probably have been one of the bloody tragedies of history to relate for the village would only have been awakened when the work of death and destruction had commenced."

A third version is told by former Milford resident Dr. Stanley Welsh. His parents, John and Mary Welsh were early settlers in the Milford community:

"Nearly 500 displaced Ponca Indian migrated from north of Omaha on the Missouri River toward more dry acres south in the Indian Territories. These Poncas camped for a while on the horse shoe bend timber strip where they could find shelter, fire wood, water and food. The Indians were usually well treated at Milford, and with a familiar camping spot on the timber land we learned to know more of them. On one visit a daughter of a friendly Chief was known to be dying from tuberculosis. The accompanying Indian Agents compelled the tribe to move along until they reached Camden, where beautiful Prairie Flower died. Upon the death of the Chief's daughter the Indians insisted on returning to Milford to bury her. My mother (Mrs. John Welsh, Mary) made a new dress to clothe her, and Mrs. Borden prepared the body for burial. One of the Milford carpenters made her a new coffin (From later news notes we know that Mr. Borden was a carpenter.) (*Reminiscence*, Dr. J. Stanley Welsh)."

An article printed in the *Milford Review* in 1967 gives this account of her burial:

"The Christian ladies of Milford came to help. They prepared the princess for burial...They remained near the Council Oak in the northwest part of Milford three days so their wagons and tents could be repaired. On June 9th the journey began again. It began to rain soon and after making about seven miles they made camp. While there a small niece of Prairie Flower died. They fashioned a wooden coffin and returned the body to bury it beside her aunt, in the cemetery located where the Jay Dunlap and Mrs. Branhorst house now stand. Before this time the Tribal custom of burial was to place the body on a wooden platform in a tree with food and water, then leave it there. Thus the ladies of Milford really did make a contribution to help civilize the Indians (From *Out Of Old Nebraska* submitted by the Nebraska State Historical Society; Author's name is not given)."

This version somewhat contradicts the record given by Mr. Howard who wrote: "Remained in camp all day, for the purpose of obtaining supplies. Prairie Flower, wife of Shines White and daughter of Standing Bear, who died yesterday, was here given Christian burial, her remains being deposited in the cemetery at Milford, Nebraska, a small village on the Blue River (from his June 6th entry)."

Milford residents have long speculated where Prairie Flower and her young niece are buried. While some say somewhere in the north part of Milford, I would rather agree with Howard's account that she was buried in the Milford Cemetery, the one used by Milford residents of that day. We have no indications that a white, or Indian cemetery ever existed in the northwest corner of Milford, with the exception of the tree platforms mentioned. From a letter written in 1870s, one writer mentioned that Milford's earliest cemetery was located somewhere north of Milford. Blue Mound was not purchased from the railroad until 1879. Another early letter mentions the fact that the Ponca Indians camped on the east side of the river, or the spot where Grover is located today. Quenchauqua dam water as well as high water on the river at that time would have prevented the Indians from coming into Milford during their stay.

My theory is that Prairie Flower and her niece were buried in the only cemetery located north of Milford—Mound Prairie. Cemetery records show burials as early as 1863, at least ten years before any in Blue Mound. Written on the cemetery records is this notation: "several Indians are buried in the 'pauper's' field."

Now for the "rest" of the story: About two years later, Standing Bear returned to Nebraska to bury his son's bones along the Niobrara. Arrested for leaving the reservation, in a land mark trial held in Omaha a federal judge ruled that "an Indian is a person within the meaning of the law, and should be entitled to the same freedoms as white Americans." While we may never know which version of this story is correct, the Ponca story continues to be an important part of Milford's historical heritage.

Will the Real "Council Oak" Please Stand Up?

"COUNTY LANDMARK WILL BE ON DISPLAY IN SEWARD." These headlines from the November 30, 1977 *Seward Independent* newspaper would retell the story of a famous historical incident that had taken place in the Milford community in 1932.

"About one hundred years ago some of the early settlers in Seward county met with the Indians in the area at the base of a large oak tree southeast of Milford. Because of these meetings, the tree soon became known as the Council Oak, the place where the Indians and pioneers met and held council. Perhaps that was the tree chosen for that purpose because of the fact there was a spring below its base" In the 1930s (1932) the Daughters of the American Revolution (D.A.R.) of Crete placed a large boulder with a bronze plaque near the tree to identify the location of the landmark. Now a large cross section off the Burr Oak is on display in Seward before being taken to a permanent home in the Seward County Historical Society museum near Goehner.

According to the number of rings found at the base of the tree, the acorn which produced it sprouted and began growing in the 1740s. In May of 1974 the roots of the big oak which were holding it to the top of a high creek bank broke after a heavy rain (four inches) and the tree slid down the bank into the channel of the creek, standing upright all the way. Some time later when Seward County road machinery was in the vicinity of the tree which is on land farmed by Frederick Andelt, the dead trunk was pushed and pulled out of the creek channel. Hughes Brothers of Seward donated men and equipment to saw cross sections of the tree and at a height of fifteen feet the trunk was sound throughout and the section which was on exhibit was obtained. Dave Tuma, a carpenter and contractor in Seward volunteered his time and equipment to saw the cross section To uniform width and sand it to a smooth finish (*Seward Independent,* Nov. 30, 1977)."

A story and picture published in the *Crete News* in the spring of 1951 tells more on the famous tree: "Rev. J. F. Balzer took a *Crete News* photographer with him when he measured the Old Council Oak tree located on the Vance farm northwest of here on the road between Crete and Milford. The oak measured 14 feet and eight inches and so Rev. Balzer claims it to be the biggest Burr Oak in the state." For over seventy years, most Milford residents (including myself) have accepted these so-called facts regarding this tree's claim to fame. The bronze marker mounted on a native rock read: "This tree and spring are on an old trail used by the Pawnee Indians between 1870 and 1880, where many councils were held. On the farm of the late Mr. and Mrs. Alex Vance. Erected by the Crete chapter D.A.R. June 14, 1932. (The bronze marker was removed by vandals in the 1940s.)

This tree was said to be the Council Oak Tree by the women of the Crete D.A.R. in 1932.
Photo from Jan Stehlik, courtesy *Crete News.*

Dedicatory speaker, Mary (Vance) Johnson, told the assembled group the following story. [Author's Note: This is only about one third of her speech.]

"...But I must tell you how this old tree became known as the 'Council Oak' Back in the years between the 1870s and 1880s, and for how many years before, we know not—the Pawnee Indians, who were a friendly tribe, trapped the beaver and hunted and fished up and down the Blue River, as far from the forks as the 'Council Oak,' on the small creek called then Wolf Creek. At the foot of the oak was a small spring of clear water, sweet water, which was found and used by the Indians. It became a habit when they wished to hold a pow-wow or council, to come up to the spring and hold it under the oak tree. As soon as they were all assembled the chief took his seat on a ledge on the bank under the tree, the rest sitting around in a circle on the little island across the creek we can see today. The Chief filled his pipe, lighted it, and after he had smoked, would hand it to the one near him and they all smoked round by round, until the council was over. This was a custom to denote that their council was one of peace and friendliness. So from that time on this tree has been known as Council Oak. ...This marker we are dedicating today will be a safeguard for the old tree, for it will never be cut down while this farm is owned by the Vance family, this marker will still guard the tree when the farm passes to strangers."

Is this the "authentic" Milford Council Oak Tree mentioned by early Nebraska historians? This tree would meet most specifications of the old Connecticut Charter Oak tree. Located at 111 Oneida Street in Milford, the tree now belongs to Terry Rediger.

Most Milford natives have long accepted this version of the Council Oak story as reported in the July, 7, 1932 *Crete News*. However, a second version is recorded in what is now considered some of the first recorded history of Seward County. Written in the early 1880s, this book known as *Andreas History of the State of Nebraska* tells a conflicting story. Based in

Chicago, Andrea's writers gathered information and early facts in each community by inter- viewing older settlers well acquainted with the history of the area. His writers tell the Council Oak story this way:

"The village of Milford is situated on a high plain inclining to the east bordered by the high banks of the Big Blue River on the north. The first authentic knowledge of this lovely site was given by some early hunters, who found it occupied by some 5,000 Indians, comprising the Pawnees, Otoes and Omahas, who had rendezvoused here when resisting the whites' encroachment of the Sioux territory. Traditional history makes it a favorite camping ground of the Pawnee and a rendezvous of the Otoes, and Omahas when joining their united bands to defeat and protect themselves from the inroads of the their bitter enemies, the murderous Sioux. A gigantic oak tree standing alone on the prairie near the bluffs is pointed out as the traditional 'Council Oak' Tree, where many a compact has been sealed for exterminating the white man and saving the lives of the squaws and papooses."

The "bluffs" referred to by Andrea's writers are located south of the river near the site of Davison's first mill north of the present elevator. He also mentions that the tree was standing alone on the prairie, allowing the branches to spread low and wide, which according to early paintings was the exact shape of the famous Connecticut Charter Oak. In 1639, Hartford and New Haven joined together to form the Connecticut Colony adopting a charter known as the Fundamental Orders, said to be the first written constitution to create a government by the governed. In 1662, John Winthrop Jr., governor of the colony, persuaded King Charles of England to grant him a charter, thereby placing the King's approval on the system. The new Colony jealously guarded their new independence granted in the charter. However, when King Charles was succeeded by King James, he adopted a different policy and attempted to organize New England under one central government.

When the King's new governor, Sir Edmund Andros, came to Hartford to seize the Charter, it mysteriously disappeared in a darkened meeting room after the candles were suddenly extinguished. Capt. Joseph Wadworth was accused of hiding it in a huge, hollow oak tree. Blown down by a storm in 1856, today the spot of the now famous "Charter Oak" is marked by a granite boulder. An article

The Way It Was

published in the Milford Review in 1967, retelling in some detail the Ponca visit and Prairie Flower burial in June of 1877, also mentions the Milford Council Oak:

"The Christian ladies of Milford came to help. They prepared the Princess for burial... They remained near the 'Council Oak' in the northwest part of Milford three days so their wagons and tents could be repaired... Thus the ladies of Milford really did make a contribution to help civilize the Indians. This 'Council Oak' still grows on the property of Jay Dunlap. It was named Council Oak because of its resemblance to the famous Charter Oak of Hartford, Conn." ("Out of Old Nebraska," submitted by the Nebraska State Historical Society, author's name not mentioned) One additional fact I remember reading is contained in a letter written by an early Milford resident, who mentions, that in 1880 this tree measured 13 feet in circumference.

Today, the tree Andrea's writers called the Milford "Council Oak" is still standing strong and tall south of the bluffs on Oneida Street in the yard of the former Jay Dunlap home, now owned by Terry and Peggy Rediger. Although many of the lower branches were cut to make room for the Dunlap residence, the remaining branches were reinforced with steel cables. Today the tree measures nearly 14 feet in circumference. A painting of the original Connecticut tree matches the shape of the Milford tree, while a photo taken of the south tree in 1951 shows a tall, straight trunk with no low spreading branches. Today the North tree measures approximately the same circumference as the south tree did in 1951. Mary Vance also mentioned that "the Indians trapped beaver and hunted and fished up and down the Blue River from the forks," as far as the "Council Oak" on the small creek called then "Wolf Creek." Most Milford natives know that Wolf Creek is located one mile north of town and empties into the Blue on the north side of the river close to Riverside. She also mentions that the Chief sat on a ledge under the tree, while the Braves sat on a little island across the creek during meetings. To me, this would seem a rather awkward arrangement to pass a pipe, started by the Chief from person to person if some were seated on the north side of the creek. Tradition also mention that the south tree was struck by lightning, which damage was very much in evidence. Recent examination of the Milford tree also shows evidence of severe lightning damage at one time.

While we may never know for sure which tree is, or was the authentic "Milford Council Oak," taking a cue from the old television program popular in the 1950s known as "What's My Line?" I do hope, some day, the spirit of the "real Council Oak" tree will rise to its feet and announce his presence.

Early Milford Industry

Today we would probably not consider Milford a city of industry, in fact you would have a difficult time naming one product produced in the community for the outside consumer market. Around 1874, many dreamed of Milford becoming a great industrial metropolis. Some citizens realized the potential of a slumbering village with all the natural advantages Milford had to offer

Making bricks at Sample Brothers Brick Yard. This yard was located near the present railroad underpass. The yard was for sale for several years before being abandoned in 1899.

and took steps to catalog and advertise them. A news note in the August 19, 1875 *Seward Reporter* declared, "the manufacturing interests are looking up in Milford. Her unsurpassed water power and natural advantages are already the attention of the eastern capitalists."

By October 27 it was announced, "A Company is being organized and articles of incorporation have been drawn up to utilize the fine water power on the Blue. Its object is to manufacture flour and to erect woolen and oil mills. Gen. Amansa Cobb is interested in the venture, and it promises much success." Several weeks later it was announced the shares had all been sold.

In an 1876 newspaper editorial, the editor wrote: "A large number of visitors from the east are now visiting Milford, who were attracted by the extensive advertisements it is now rumored that a couple of eastern capitalists have bought interest in the Milford Mills and water power, and will put in an appearance soon."

Part of this vision was fulfilled when Johnson and Perry bought the Mills from Davison and Culver in 1880. Many were sure Milford was now on its way to industrial fame and fortune, especially after the burned mill was replaced with an even larger mill. About this time the Burlington Railroad signed a long-term contract with a Lincoln firm to furnish the bulk of the ice needed for their refrigerator cars, ice was readily available every winter in Lake Quenchauqua. Thousands of tons of ice was cut and shipped out of Milford each winter, some going as far as St. Louis and Denver.

While the woolen and oil mills were never built, several small industries did spring to life contributing to the well being of the town. One of the earliest industries mentioned was the existence of a brick yard in 1866 located four miles southeast of town. The editor of the *Seward Reporter* noted that many of the large early chimneys in Lincoln were built from bricks hauled from Milford. Another yard was founded in Milford by M. R. Hamilton in 1880. By June 2, the editor announced he was ready to "burn" his first kiln of 70,000 bricks. Evidently Mr. Hamilton sold out to Davidson and Culver in a few years. A notice in the October 31, 1884 *Milford Ozone* announced "that the foreman, Mr. Shaffer, was burning a kiln of 555,000 bricks." Many of these were used for the large brick building erected in Milford about this time. This brick yard was located directly east of the old Yost Brothers Lumber Yard building, now used by Dorchester Co-op.

263

The Way It Was

By 1894 the yard was owned by the Sample family who made both bricks and drain tile for about four years. Sometime before 1900 the yard was closed, and in July of that year it was announced that David Boshart would take over the yard, clean it up, and resume making bricks in the city. One week later Mr. Boshart said he had given up on his plans to restore the brick yard. Records would indicate the last bricks manufactured in the city were made around 1898. [Author's Note: The bricks on Milford streets laid in 1919 were not made in Milford. They may have come from Seward, since they had a booming brick factory at this time.]

Other early factories in Milford included an oak tub factory operated in Grover by Jacob Culver, a broom factory first started by J. W. Barnes and later owned by John Schifferman. The local *Milford Nebraskan* newspaper editor reported Mr. Schifferman bought broomcorn in northern Kansas, and shipped out several loads of brooms in 1900. A pickle factory was also operated in the city for several years. Few details are available on the pickle or oak tub factories. In 1886, Mr. Schamp and J. M. T. Miller formed a partnership to manufacture picket fences, an enterprise that only lasted for several years.

Cheese was first manufactured by Jacob D. Stutzman, who opened a plant at his farm located two miles west of town in 1888. Jacob used his milk as well as some purchased from his neighbors. Jacob announced he would decide how much to pay for the milk after he sold the cheese.

Sensing dairy profits in the air, Milford businessmen assisted the Seiler Butter and Cheese Company in building a new plant on Park Street in 1891. What some predicted would be a "big economic transfusion" for the city failed to fly. In July of 1891, they were buying 15,000 pounds of milk per day and the future looked rosy. Evidently something went wrong and the plant only lasted two years. Several years later the plant was bought by the newly organized Fairmont Creamery Company who used it for two years. This was the plant used by the Roberts Dairy Company from 1913 to 1924.

In June 24, 1915, the *Milford Review* editor reported, "Roberts dairy and cream is a booming business for the city from a financial standpoint. They are now going forward to put their product in other cities. Milford was successful in having them locate in the city the only cheese factory in the state. Increased residence among us will be

A broom factory was started in Grover in 1894 and was still operating in 1904. No date on photo. Photo courtesy Keith Boshart family.

sought by respectable families and we will soon outrun Seward. For the week ending Wednesday, the factory shipped 2,800 pounds of cheese, and our merchants are now handling the cheese. Dan Roth now has it on sale in his store." This summary of the business is given in the August 10, 1916 *Review*. "Roberts cheese shows a large increase in production. Milford merchants alone have sold 3,500 pounds. In the months of April, May and June, the grand total of milk bought was 333,709 pounds, and 35,956 pounds of cheese was made. The price now paid for the milk is 1.50 per hundred." In March of 1924 this branch of the Roberts Dairy Company moved to Lincoln.

Hoping to cash in on the dairy action, on October 5, 1892, thirty-two area farmers met in a Milford lawyer's office to sign a historic document, agreeing to build a cooperative butter and cheese plant. While some lived directly west of Milford, others lived closer to Dorchester or Beaver Crossing. This group met with the purpose of organizing a company to manufacture and market cheese and other related dairy products. After much discussion, the group decided to build and operate their own milk and cheese processing plant. Many of these farmers lived too far to market their milk at one of the commercial cheese factories already established in Milford and Goehner. Many probably felt this would be a good, long-term investment. From the list of thirty-two original signers, twenty-nine different family names are represented, the majority of names now being extinct in the Milford community.

A processing plant was built six miles west of Milford on land now owned by Vilas Steckley, in that day owned by Daniel R. Eicher. Little additional information is available concerning the operations of the plant, although one news note in the January, 10, 1893 *Milford Nebraskan* reported, "Stockholders of the Pleasant View Butter and Cheese Company were in town to haul their yearly supply of ice for the business. It was difficult to determine just how many teams were involved." Apparently the plant closed down after several years, probably around 1896. Since the plant was located on land owned by her father, the late Mary Schlegel remembered playing in the abandoned ice house, although she never realized that at one time cheese was manufactured on the spot. One later news item reported that J. M. T. Miller was treasurer of the company.

Another good business in the early Milford community was the manufacture of sorghum syrup. In 1885, Abraham Stutzman advertised "that he would put his syrup-making experience learned in Ohio to good use by crushing your cane and boiling your syrup." Joseph Gascho also had a mill and usually raised 20 acres of cane. One year he produced 1,400 gallons of sorghum syrup from 25 acres of cane. In 1892 J. M. T. Miller bought the very latest in cider mills for use on the 200 apple trees in his orchard.

In 1906 brothers Dave and Jake Boshart were making cement building blocks in the city. In 1906 they had already made 5,000 and could not keep up with the demand and were considering investing in another machine. By 1909 they were making cement bricks from various molds, and also added a second mixing machine. By 1916 Al Unzincker had purchased the business and was operating it by himself.

The November 25, 1916 *Milford Review* tells us about another industry located in Milford about that time: "There is now a new metal toy factory in our community. Such toys were exclusively made in Germany, but the supply has been cut off by the war. Mr. C. R.

Eldon Hostetler

Vaughan has taken the matter up and is now making as good an article as can be shipped from Germany. He has already secured a market in the East to which place all the toys he can make are shipped."

In 1874, one unusual area craftsman living in the Pleasant Dale community, Charles Armstrong, was busy cutting mill stones from native rock. The *Seward Reporter* editor commented, "they are nearly as good as the "celebrated" French stones."

Milford also had one cigar maker. This announcement appeared in the September 1, 1906 *Milford Nebraskan*: "The gentleman who is going to start a cigar factory in the Norton building is moving his equipment in and are preparing for business." About one week later this ad appeared in the same paper: "Wanted a boy about 14 to 18 to strip tobacco, and learn the cigar makers trade. H. W. Stahl"

Other not so famous capitalistic entrepreneurs in the community included Isaac Whitman, who lived near West Mills. Mr. Whitman was caught making 50 cent pieces from powdered pewter and ground glass. And then there was said to be a man over in N Precinct, "who was for a fact running a brewery." In 1886 the editor also reported "It is said there are two professional gamblers located in N Township." On May 20, 1935, federal agents made a surprise raid in the city of Milford and arrested a local citizen for 'being in the wrong kind of manufacturing business.' He was fined $200 and costs for having in his possession twenty gallons of 'mash' and sixteen quarts of beer. From stories I have heard from older citizens, wine making was quite common in the Milford community around 1900. In spite of some irregularities in the business ethics of a few of the local "big time" industrialists, the editor of the *Milford Nebraskan* could still write in the August 24, 1894 edition, "Milford can boast of the finest springs, the prettiest location of any burg in the state. Then in an everyday sort of way, with 'ego' clear down to zero, we will also mention that we also have the largest flouring mills in the state, as well as the best ice fields, and some of the best opportunity for investment in the state."

The Way It Was

KLAY KRAFT POTTERY

now located at "Dahle, NE"
(unincorporated, population 23)
EXIT 382 ON I-80

Across from the world's Largest Covered Wagon.

1984 advertisement.

Milford's Klay Kraft Pottery

    Most Milford natives may still remember when the business complex known as "Westward Ho Campgrounds and Motel" was doing a booming business on the northeast corner of the Milford interchange. A sign in the driveway informed visitors that you are now entering "Dahle City Nebraska— population 42." In addition to the campground, the complex included a 32-room motel, a café, a pottery manufacturing and retail outlet, two service stations, and a trailer court. The pottery business, known as the "Klay Kraft" pottery was housed in an old-fashioned red farm barn. The motel, café, and east side service station was operated in partnership with Roger and Claridy Stauffer. Stauffer's Café, featuring home style cooking, was a favorite stopping place for weary I-80 travelers as well as hungry natives. On the west side of Highway 15, a service station, housed in huge replica of an old prairie schooner, Conestoga style freight wagon dispensed Phillips 66 products.

Eldon Hostetler

Visitors were invited to visit an old country church, an old one room country schoolhouse, and an old water tower said to have belonged to Williams Jennings Bryan at one time. The entire complex was the brainchild of Milford businessman Kenneth Dahle. The huge Conestoga shaped service station sporting 24 foot authentic-looking wooden spoke wagon wheels attracted enough publicity to put Milford on the national road map. Although Kenneth and Marie Dahle were the designers and owners of the I-80 complex including the Red Barn Pottery, they were not the founders of the original Milford pottery.

While more "mature" Milford natives may remember when the concrete block building opposite the new Jones National bank building located on Highway 6 was used to manufacture pottery, younger residents may remember it as only as an automobile agency. The pottery's early history goes back to 1943. This news note from the March 4, 1943 *Milford Review* tells the genesis of the now abandoned Milford pottery building. "Virgil Stutzman was severely burned last Thursday when he came in contact with an electric power line near Syracuse. He was helping to move a house and was on top of the roof taking care of wires when he raised up and the back of his head came in contact with a hot wire. He was knocked unconscious, rolled off the roof and was caught by Charles Miller before he fell to the ground. He

Photo courtesy Marie Dahle.

was taken to Lincoln General Hospital where he is recovering." Although Virgil eventually recovered from his burns, the healing process was slow and painful, leaving Virgil considerably handicapped. Realizing he would never again be capable of performing the types of work he had been involved in before the accident, Virgil and his wife (the former Julia Ann Erb) moved to Illinois. Here they gained pottery making experience while working in a pottery located in Morton, a small rural town near Peoria.

A second news item from the May 23, 1946 *Milford Review* tells more: "A lump settlement of $10,000 has been agreed upon between Virgil Stutzman and Floyd Roll, doing business as Milford Ice and Cold Storage. The settlement has been approved by the District Court Judge and was awarded for total and permanent injuries. Stutzman is 23 years old."

While this may have looked like a lot of money in 1946, today it would be considered "peanuts" compared to the million dollar judgments awarded modern-day injury victims. However, in that day it was enough to fulfill the young couple's dream of supporting themselves by building and owning their own business enterprise. Several weeks later the *Milford Review* editor reported more: "Virgil Stutzmans have purchased the Emanuel Hauder lots west of the Phillips 66 station on Highway 6 and are now erecting a building suitable for installing equipment for a pottery. They hope to have the pottery in operation in 30 to 60 days and will make novelties, vases, and lamps of all kinds. Virgil and Julia Ann learned the trade in Morton, Illinois where they were both employed in the business for three years. They have recently returned from Illinois where they spent several days at the place. The new establishment will be known as "Virg's Pottery."

Erected in the summer of 1946, a severe summer windstorm forced a partial rebuilding of several concrete block walls. The Stutzmans, with the assistance of four hired helpers molded, glazed, fired and painted assorted pieces of pottery. Finished pottery was either sold on the site or transported to other retail outlets. Few of those associated with the founding of the pottery business remember why the Stutzmans sold the business within one year. The Federal Aid Highway Act passed by Congress in 1956 may have helped to change Milford's image in the 1960s, in fact as much or more than the arrival of Highway 6 in the early 1930s. Known for years as a sleepy, isolated little country village, the arrival of a paved highway in 1932 put

Eldon Hostetler

Photo courtesy Marie Dahle.

Milford on the national road map. A personal visit from the Governor in 1930 convinced skeptical Milford residents it would be to their advantage to reroute Highway 6 traffic to the south edge of Milford rather than funneling it through Main Street.

The Federal Aid Highway Act provided the needed funds to construct an interstate highway system through Nebraska. The bill was designed to fulfill a pressing need at the time: "to insure a properly articulated highway system that will solve the problem of speed, safe continental travel, interstate transportation, access highways, farm to market movement, metropolitan area congestion, bottlenecks and parking." Rewritten in 1959, the act provided for a 41,000 mile national system of interstate and defense highways connecting 209 cities in all 48 states. It was estimated at the time that the cost of the entire system would be about 28 billion. With the federal treasury picking up approximately 90 percent of the total cost, most Milford citizens gave the act scant attention. However, I do remember the suspense, as well as the shouts of victory, when it was announced that the road would come within three miles of Milford. While the majority of our citizens may have been "sleeping at the switch," Kenneth and

The Way It Was

Marie Dahl, owners of Milford's Klay Kraft Craft Pottery since June 1, 1947, were ever alert to new and innovative business opportunities.

Hearing the new road would eventually reach Milford, the Dahles could hear "opportunity" knocking. A recent recipient of a degree in Mechanical Engineering from Iowa State College, Kenneth Dahle realized the advantages of doing business on a busy coast to coast highway. Having forsaken a boring desk job in Omaha, Kenneth Dahle was now ready to pursue new and exciting challenges. His long-range vision, plus faith in his own capabilities convinced the Dahles to either purchase or lease ground on both sides of Stanley Matzke Memorial Highway north of the exit. When the Interstate finally arrived in 1964, the Dahles were ready to try new and innovative ideas in retailing. Interested in preserving and conveying that old time "Oregon Trail" type western heritage associated with the settlement of the west, the Dahles designed their new business around an old fashioned pioneer motif. Their Milford pottery business was moved to the Interstate corner in 1966, the Camp Ground featuring the Indian teepee shaped bath room building was opened in 1967. The thirty-two room motel was completed and opened in 1969. The west side service station housed in a replica of an old Conestoga wagon was operated by the Dahle family until 1997.

Beginning in 1966, souvenir pottery items were made and sold in the "Red Barn." Mr. Dahle designed the majority of the molds, featuring different plate designs for all 48 states, while Mrs. Dahle handled the financial and bookkeeping chores. The old pottery building located in Milford, on the north side of the street opposite Dairy Queen, at one time remodeled and enlarged by the Dahles, was purchased by former employee, Milton Erb. Erb designed and built concrete yard ornaments under the brand name "Craft Ware." Milton sold the business to a Lincoln buyer in 1973. Today, the covered wagon is being used to house a motorcycle business, while the service station and Café located north of the pottery barn is used as a storage depot.

One exciting moment in the history of complex happened on June 19, 1978, when, without advance notice, Charles Kurault and his traveling entourage stopped at the station. Fascinated by the unique and authentic design of the covered wagon service station, they took numerous photographs and later featured the story on one of his radio programs. The unique building was also featured in advertisements sponsored by several large companies and published in several prominent magazines. The DuPont Carpet Company sponsored advertisements published in both *Time* and *Newsweek* featuring the wagon. To show their appreciation for the privilege of using the picture, DuPont carpeted the station office free of charge.

During his spare time, Mr. Dahle loved to tinker with and fly airplanes. Kenneth Dahle assembled two airplanes, the first one from a kit. In 1988, he built a plane from his own design, a plane he named the *Blue Sky*. After passing several short test flights, the plane was partially destroyed by high winds at the Seward Airport on July 8. 1993. Kenneth Dahle was feeling the deteriorating effects of the cancer that eventually took his life in August of 1993 when friends from the Experimental Air Craft Association restored the plane. The *Blue Sky*, minus the engine, is now on display in the Seward County Historical Museum in Goehner. This plane, along with numerous surviving pieces of Milford Klay Kraft Pottery offered for sale over the Internet, continues to remind us of a brilliant and multi-talented individual, who although his life was cut short by cancer, helped to put Milford on the "National Business and Highway Map."

Milford Role Models

Remember the anxiety, the disbelief, and confusion triggered by the sudden rash of school shootings several years ago? School authorities, law enforcement personnel, and other professional people were dumbfounded by the realization that American school children could be capable of such senseless violence. Law enforcement officials, the press, school authorities, as well as the general public were quick to join in the finger pointing, explaining how "middle class have it all" school children could commit such dastardly deeds. Contributing factors mentioned by some included a constant diet of violent movies, television, and video game shows. Others insisted it was because of America's love affair with killer firearms. Conservatives blamed it on the erosion of American family values, saying, "we are now reaping the harvest produced by an abundance of single parent families. Deterioration of the family unit has resulted in children growing up in homes lacking positive, hero type role models."

Most authorities would agree that "hero-type" role models play an important part in child development. Webster defines a hero as, "A man of distinguished courage admired for his brave deeds and noble qualities; or any person who has heroic qualities or has performed a heroic act and is regarded as a model or ideal."

If you were fortunate enough to have grown up in a loving, two-parent family environment, a home where both parents showed high moral values, your parents were probably your earliest role models. Remember those early Sunday school days where great Bible characters were portrayed as role models and objects of hero worship?

Today, most people would agree these Bible heroes have been crowded out by other lesser contemporary role models. If you were lucky enough to have attended an old single room, rural country school, you may remember the two famous "hero" portraits present in every school room. George Washington and Abraham Lincoln seemed to watch more than our every move as if to say, "You had better practice honesty in everything you do, or you will have us to answer to." Now any boy honest enough to admit that he was the one who chopped down the cherry tree, or saintly enough to walk all night to return a borrowed book just had to be a great role model. A total stranger arriving in our land for the first time would soon discover the reality of modern-day American hero worship.

Unlike my school day heroes seventy years ago, the majority of the so called "heroes" of today would probably not be involved in government, teaching, medicine, or even in mission or church work. Most modern-day heroes are found in professional sports, big business, or in the entertainment and music industry. Witness the salaries we Americans are willing to pay these present-day heroes. President Bush receives a much smaller salary than most popular "Rap" singers, or great sports heroes, or Hollywood movie stars. On second thought, after listening to some of the modern-day, celebrity heroes "bare their souls" on Barbara Walters Specials, would you still want them as role models for your children?

Contrary to the practice of many neighboring cities, Milford streets are not named after early local celebrities although, Southeast Community College has honored many of their "heroes." Stanley

Matzke, Lowell Welsh, Robert Eicher, and Alan Dunlap will long be remembered by the new buildings dedicated in their honor. On the west end of town, Milford's great ball park is rightly named to honor the generosity of the Welch family. While we cannot boast of a Johnny Carson celebrity in our Milford's heritage, many outstanding families have made generous contributions to the city's history. Included are J. D. Davison, Jacob Culver, F. S. Johnson, Dr. George Brandon, and Allen Dunlap to name just a few. Similar to the dilemma faced by *Time* Magazine each year, it would be difficult to select one outstanding man in Milford's history.

His name remembered by only a few, my vote would go to Jacob Culver. It is interesting to note that *Time* Magazine chose three ladies as their choice for the "2002 Man of the Year" Award. For the "Outstanding Woman of Milford History" Award, my vote would go to the majority of Milford's early pioneer women, most whose stories have never been told.

Earning Respect the "Old-Fashioned Way"

"My address is now West Mills, Seward County Nebraska. On January 3rd, 1878, with my family and the family of Joseph Stauffer we left our homes in Illinois and came over the B&M Railroad to the new Seward County Mennonite settlement." This letter published in the February, 1878 *Herald of Truth* magazine introduces us to what was at that time a Seward County Post Office. Founded by the West family in June of 1859, most Seward County historians agree that this was probably the first permanent settlement in Seward County. Located in the southwest corner of O Precinct, today all that remains is a small cemetery to remind us that at one time this community was a beehive of activity. Born in New Jersey, Thomas West married Catherine Hufmaster while living in Maryland. In 1845, the Wests left Maryland and moved to Iowa where their six children Isabella, Cornelius, Thomas, John, James, and Charles were born.

Like others in that day, they were quickly caught up in the excitement generated by the discovery of gold in California in 1848. Crossing the Missouri River at Plattsmouth, they met large groups of very discouraged fortune seekers returning home empty handed. While debating their next move, the family decided to explore the vast, unsettled wilderness area known as the "Blue River Country." Traveling from north to south through what is now Seward County they were pleasantly surprised with the land surrounding the spot where the West Blue and North Blue Rivers join. Building a small log cabin and breaking sod for a garden they decided to stay and seek their fortune panning for "Nebraska farmer gold." Living for some time on the provisions they brought for the trip, they planted a garden and broke ground for a small patch of sod corn. At this time the closest source of supplies was located at Nebraska City, some seventy-five miles to the east. Harassed unmercifully by the natives, they decided to make friends. The first year their cabin, along with most of their worldly goods was burned by Omaha Indians disguised as Sioux.

On one occasion Mr. West was tied to a large elm tree and abandoned by his tormentors. The following summer the Indians stole most of the families garden produce and destroyed their corn crop, although they were gradually learning to respect and trust the West family. In 1864 he built the first dam in Seward County, erected a saw and grist mill, and established a small store.

Once a month Tommy would send an ox team to Nebraska City for needed supplies. His honest dealings with visiting Indians and surrounding neighbors earned him great respect. To his Indian friends he was known as "Good Thomas" and to his white neighbors as "Uncle Tommy." Thomas acquired this reputation the old fashioned way "he earned it." In 1862, the family buried their son John on a hillside near the mill in what is now known as the "West Mills" cemetery; which some say was the first white child buried in Seward County. One neighbor who remembered Tommy West had this to say:

"He is remembered by all the old settlers as a genial, kind-hearted man. The latch string of his cabin door was always out, and no one in want ever called him in vain. By his energy a post office was established in 1868 at the mill and store. He was also elected as the first county clerk at the organization of Seward County in 1865. When he died in 1880, he was buried beside his son being followed to the grave by his old neighbors as mourners of one they had grown to love and respect. His widow followed him to the tomb in the winter of 1885. These dear old people have gone to the better world, leaving very many sad hearts at their departure. "Uncle Tommy" acted his part well in the development of this new land, and for the many acts of kindness shown he will ever be remembered by all the earlier settlers (*History of Seward County*, W.W. Cox, from a letter written by I. M. K. Johnson)."

"Uncle Tommy West died of typhoid fever in 1880 after a few days of illness. His body was laid to rest near the earlier graves, about a quarter mile from the site of his first log house. He died in January, and in the fall the Indians came to trap along the river. When they came to the store, they missed seeing Mr. West. His daughter, Isabella Johnson, happened to be visiting her mother that morning and she talked with the red men, while her daughter hid behind her skirts. They wanted 'Good Thomas' and she told them 'He slept.' 'Where did he sleep?' they asked with emotion, and she pointed up the hill to the cemetery. The Indians held a little powwow amongst themselves, then started up the hill on a trot, their blankets over their heads. On reaching the cemetery, they formed a circle around the grave. The leader produced a peace pipe, lit it, and breathed some smoke down to the ground and stamped his feet on it. A whiff of smoke was blown to the west, one north, one south, and one east, then one straight up. Each Indian present went through this ceremony, which is similar to other Pawnee peace pipe ceremonies that recognized the spirits of nature- of the earth, the sky and the four winds. Thus the Indians paid their respects to the man who had led white settlers into their 'West Blue River Valley,' and in doing so had touched off a series of events that changed their lands and lives. Then covering their heads with their blankets again, they came howling down the hill to the home (*Centennial History of Dorchester and Pleasant Hill*, p. 13)."

Why They Give a Red Rose

Probably no one living in Milford today remembers for sure what the weather was like on the morning of Friday, Jan 12, 1968, although I suppose we could just assume that business was going on as usual. For those who had gathered in the local cafés for fellowship and coffee that morning, I'm sure the hot topic of conversation was the latest death in the Milford community, that of William J. Webermeir. Community residents had long speculated on the financial status of this middle-aged bachelor and farmer. He had lived west of town since anyone could remember. Most Milford residents had just assumed he was somewhat different. In fact, he had often been labeled as "Milford's most eligible eccentric."

While local residents had occasionally gossiped about the eventual disposition of his estate after he died, few in that day realized the extent of his holdings, or his potential generosity to the Milford community. For reasons unknown today, the local paper, the *Milford Times*, did not even mention his death, or print his obituary.

The first mention of his death in the local newspaper is mentioned in the February 8th edition:

"A public hearing was held at 10 am Friday, Feb 2, in the Seward County Court to determine the validity of the last will and testament of William J. Webermeir. Mr. Webermeir, who farmed west of Milford, passed away Jan. 12, 1968. County Judge Fred Bruns presided at the hearing and read the will. His will stated that all of his farm ground, including the choice 320 acre farm located five miles west of Milford would go to his nephew, Mr. Richard Cast. Eight other persons, some relatives and others former employees shared a total of forty five thousand dollars. After the satisfaction of all debts and previous devices and bequests, the will allocates $100,000 to the Village of Milford for a community hall with library, or if such a building is under construction, the amount of the indebtedness not to exceed $100,000. A second residue provision is for a trust fund income to be used to help Milford High School graduates attain a college education, and be known as Webermeir Scholars. It is also Mr. Webermeir's desire that beneficiaries place a flower on his grave and that of his mother, each year on May 30."

Mr. Webermeir's desires were carried out by the City of Milford several years after his death. The building we all know today as the Webermeir Memorial Building was dedicated on April 23, 1972, using approximately $115,000 of Mr. Webermeir's money. When Mr. Webermeir first approached the Milford City Council in June of 1966, he insisted that his bequest be kept a well-guarded secret until after his death. He also requested that the building be erected in the Milford City Square.

Eldon Hostetler

Twenty-eight years later, most Milford residents are well aware of the huge benefits local residents continue to share, courtesy of his generosity, but few living in the Milford community today are familiar with the Webermeir family story.

Bill Webermeir, son of Herman and Minnie (Seieber) Webermeir was born near Milford in 1893 and spent his entire life on the Webermeir family farm located five miles west of town (where Dan and Nicole Stauffer live today).

Bill Webermeir's father, Herman Webermeir, emigrated from Germany to Wisconsin and settled near Tamora. Around 1879, the Webermeirs moved to the Milford vicinity. This news note published in the July 31, 1891 edition of the *Milford Nebraskan* newspaper gives us one good clue as to the source of Mr. Webermeir's fortune: "Herman Webermeir, who lives five miles west of Milford, suffered quite a loss. While at church Sunday, someone broke into his house and extricated $195 in gold coin. He had $600 more in money hidden in bags in various spots in the house, which was not found." Twelve years later, on July 25, 1903, Herman was killed while cutting wheat with a grain binder. Seward County historian and Beaver Crossing newspaper editor, John Waterman, reported the details:

"He was running a harvester and something got out of order with the harness on one of the horses and he stepped out on the tongue between the horses to fix it, which frightened them and they ran away, he falling to the ground in front of the machine which passed over his body. Mr. Webermeir was a resident of N Precinct, where he owned a large farm and was a progressive and prosperous farmer."

A second account from the *Tamora Weekly Register* reported that little William, who would have been nine or ten years old at the time, was a witness to the tragedy and the first to summon help.

On August 7, 1893, this announcement also appeared in the *Tamora Weekly Register*: "The estate, it is said, is worth between $2,000 and $14,000, but the deceased, it seems, kept his family in ignorance of his financial affairs. It was thought by them that he had considerable money at the time, but none could be found until finally $350 was located under a false bottom under which a hen was sitting. Neighbors of the deceased had borrowed money from him, but the notes are nowhere to be found, and it is probable they are hidden away in places just as odd as where this money was found."

The Way It Was

Little additional information is recorded about the Webermeir family until the 1930s. Bill attended the old Pilot Knolb District 23 rural school, graduated from high school, and attended the University of Nebraska College of Agriculture for two years. Bill continued to live with his mother, plus other assorted relatives including one girl from Germany. Nephews Howard and Fred Sieber also lived with the family at various times from 1930-40. William had one sister, Ida, as well as several other siblings who died as small children. Ida was married to a Lincoln chiropractor, Gotthlieb Cast. The Casts were the parents of one son, Richard Webermeir-Cast, the nephew named in the will to receive the bulk of the Webermeir estate.

During his farming days, William relied on hired men to help with the farming as well as hired girls to do his housework and cooking. Many of these are still living, and some have volunteered bits and pieces of information regarding the personal life of Mr. Webermeir. Most agreed Bill made no attempt to hide the fact that he made his money by wise investments when stocks and other funds were "dirt cheap." He often told his hired men that for him, farming was just a hobby, since he really didn't need the money. All agreed that Bill had one outstanding characteristic—frugality in his money spending habits. Although he usually bought the best, he was always very cautious as to how his dollars were spent, saving money any time he could. One hired girl told me he showed her how to grease a hot pan used for frying eggs by rubbing it on a waxed bread wrapper, thereby saving lard. Another reported he always allowed one piece of meat for each thresher or corn sheller. In other words, if they had twelve men to feed, she was ordered to buy just enough meat to cut into twelve equal pieces.

Several said he usually paid hired help the going wage, no more or no less. Others said he would often say, "It is really not necessary to use both butter and jelly on your bread." Most agreed he was very easy to work for, if you did it his way and didn't disagree. One former hired man reported he demanded a smaller and cheaper tractor than most of his neighbors were using at the time in order to save money as well as fuel. Several said he wore the same suit for 20 years—although it was a good one.

While most of his neighbors were driving cheaper cars, Bill usually drove a Buick. Bill also loved to feed cattle—good cattle—and he always fed them the old-fashioned way, by wheelbarrow and scoop shovel. He loved to ride with neighbors and friends to the Sandhills on cattle-buying trips. Bill always bought the finest calves and usually insisted on eating at the best place in town. One hired man told me he worked for days straightening out used nails from a salvaged building—nails that were probably never used again.

Although quite frugal in many respects, in other instances Bill could be very generous. One person told me recently that Bill was one of the few people, who, after he had suffered a tremendous loss, demonstrated his sympathy by presenting him with a generous check. One person said he also helped struggling churches build new buildings, and often paid the school tuition for deserving youth in the community.

In 1964, he designed and built what was at that time one of the finest houses in the community. During one stay in the hospital, he invited the nursing staff to come out to his farm and see his wonderful new house. Part of the trim is solid walnut, sawed from logs he had collected for more than forty years. For several years he lived in the basement for fear of scratching his new house. While some may have imagined his new house was built to attract a wife his only try at marriage, somewhat late in life, was short lived.

Mr. Webermeir also enjoyed good, classical music, occasionally inviting guests to hear music from his personal record collection played on his new hi-fi set. One neighbor who remembered said he would spend hours listening to opera music, his favorite singer being Lily Pons.

For years the Webermeir family attended the Salem Methodist Country Church, although one hired man told me he rarely attended, at least while he worked for him. Others said he would often attend other neighborhood churches, especially in his later years. Bill truly enjoyed flowers, particularly red roses. During the summer months he would insist that a fresh flower be placed on the table at mealtime. To him, flowers were to be treated just like you would treat the finest butter. Bill told one of his neighbors, that he loved roses best, mostly because he could watch their growth and enjoy them on Sunday afternoons, the time of the week when his days were probably long and lonely. Since Bill's death in 1968, hundreds of local residents have benefited, and many more will continue to reap the benefits of one generous local resident who many viewed as eccentric.

Maybe, at least in the Milford community, frugality should be reclassified as a virtue and not as an eccentricity, like many natives seem to think today. Most of the old retired farmers and businessmen who just happened to be "hanging around" in Dinna Rediger's Hardware Store in 1972, said it this way, when asked how they would evaluate "Milford's old eccentric Bill." He was a conservative with a zealous belief in education." Could it be that the current definition of 'frugality' is only in the eye of the beholder?

A Joy to Sacrifice for His Sake

Alice Troyer prior to leaving for China.

Alice Troyer was born April 3, 1871 in Clinton Township, Indiana, the eighth of eleven children born to John D. and Catherine (Egli) Troyer. Her father was born in Holmes County, Ohio, in 1833, her mother in Stark County, Ohio, in 1837. Both moved to Indiana with their parents and were married there in 1859. After their marriage, they moved to Michigan. Other children born to the Troyers included Daniel J., Mary, Emma, Anna, Lydia, Joseph E., David F., Ella, Mattie, and John E.

In March of 1888 John and Catherine, along with their four youngest children, moved to Nebraska. The couple settled near Plattsmouth for the summer, but before winter moved to Milford. There, they joined the East Fairview Amish Mennonite Church. Both parents are buried in the East Fairview Church Cemetery. The first news we hear of Alice is a note from the *Milford Nebraskan* dated Feb. 12, 1892, telling us that as a high school senior, she would be playing the role of the "Quaker Lady" in the school play. Other news notes confirmed she was very active in school, church, and community plays. After attending Normal School for one summer, she received her teacher's certificate that fall. By 1894 she was living in Lincoln and in 1895 was attending Gospel Union Bible Institute at Abilene, Kansas. Other members of her family moved to Nebraska's Custer County, 150 miles west of Milford. Alice is not mentioned again until April of 1896: "Milford is proud of Alice Troyer, our fine missionary lady in China. A letter from her will follow soon." The letter mentioned was published in the December 16, 1896 issue of the *Milford Nebraskan*.

Alice arrived in China about January 30, 1896 sponsored by the "China Inland Mission," an interdenominational mission effort pioneered by Englishman J. Hudson Taylor. The first missionaries were sent in 1865 and by 1914 over 1,000 missionaries were in the field. As the name indicates, they sought to reach interior regions untouched by other organizations. Willing, skillful workers were accepted regardless of their denomination. No fixed salaries were promised, their mottoes being, "Hitherto hath the Lord helped us" and "The Lord will provide."

After Alice arrived in China, she had only six weeks of language training before being assigned to a station at Lu-an in Shan-si in northern China. From March 16 to April 17, she traveled to her first assignment and wrote vividly of her experiences. Her last letter is dated about two weeks before her death.

After the publication of a long letter in the December, 1896 *Milford Nebraskan* we hear little about Alice in her hometown paper until 1900. We have several sources recalling what happened to Alice at this time. One is from information found in a short history of Milford, probably written from information published in newspapers of that day:

"News of the death of Mrs. Alice (Troyer) Young and her husband has been received by her parents Mr. and Mrs. John D. Troyer of this place. They were murdered near Peking, China by the Boxers on July 16. Five years ago Miss Troyer left here and entered the mission work in China. About one year ago (in the spring of 1899) she married Mr. Young, a Scottish missionary. She was murdered at Kio-Chow, fifty miles south of Pekin. She was cut to pieces after being beheaded and was 29 years old. Other information says the bodies were thrown in the Yellow River. [Author's Note: The Boxers were intent on eradicating all foreigners from China.]

A second version of her death is recorded in her father's death notice found in the December 11, 1911 *Milford Review*:

"John D. Troyer was the father of Alice (Troyer) Young, the missionary to China. Alice entered the mission service for the China Inland Mission, and was sent to the interior of China. During the Boxer Rebellion they were seized and her husband was lashed to a tree and literally cut to pieces before her eyes before she suffered an even worse fate."

Her father's death notice reads as follows: "John D. Troyer drowned Sunday afternoon in the Blue River two miles south of Milford. He was camped near the river trapping, and had attempted to cross on ice made rotten by the warm weather. He was discovered by Jake Boshart's boy who realized something was wrong when he found his rifle laying on the ice and soon gathered a group of men who retrieved his body in 16 feet of water."

Catherine died at her home in Milford on December 19, 1925 at the age of 88. This branch of the Troyer family is now extinct in the Milford community. The following excerpts from letters written by Alice may help us to better understand her motivation and character.

"This letter is not very personal, because it will be duplicated and sent to other than home people. This is the second time for me to go out alone and on Wednesday I took my first Bible class among outsiders. Carrie was ill, so I went alone to Jang N - Touany Village where we have a company of Christians. The Lord gave me much liberty in speaking on sin and the believer and he was in our midst to convert some. One dear woman, who was once a dear Christian, but now is away from the Lord, wept during the meeting and the Lord surely spoke to her, for he has promised it shall not return unto him void. Though he may not be able to use our words, He does use His own, and for that reason can connect and explain my own. It is not pleasant to be alone, but then we did come to China for a purpose and it is a joy to sacrifice for his sake, who not only became lonely for our sake, but suffered unto death."

Following is an excerpt taken from a letter written to the Mennonite Board of Missions:

"Dear brother Hartzler: Ever since I gave my life to the Lord for any work he may have for me, I have had it in my mind to write you about it and tell you that never through all these years has the Lord allowed me to forget Romans 12:1,2 from which you preached a few evenings before my conversion. I am certain the Lord then wanted this work done, that is, my body presented as a living sacrifice to him. But it was not done; I fought against it, the flesh was too strong. It gained the victory… All these years this text has clung to me, and now at last I have yielded and I am willing, yes more than willing to be separated from the world unto Himself, and only for His glory would I live henceforth. Only to be a broken and empty vessel at the Masters feet, that His life may flow freely through me to these poor 'blinded' by 'Satan' people. I wish I could tell you something of the joy, peace and quite of soul, I have had since coming to China, just resting in his love, just in knowing that the battle is the Lord's and not mine…I trust the Lord will speak through His word, and give me as many words as will be for His glory to be spoken by me. Will you not pray for China and me? It is a great help to know that friends are praying for me."

Early Milford Missionaries

In 1902, two young Milford ladies, Katie and Lydia Burkey, daughters of Christian and Catherine Burkey, lived with their parents on a farm several miles south of Milford. The family attended the old "Defenseless Mennonite Church" located one mile west of East Fairview on the spot now home to the Pleasant View Cemetery. From 1915 to 1921, the church was known as the Seward County Pentecostal Church, and from 1921 as "Silas Miller's Church." In late 1902, both girls volunteered for mission work in China. One news article printed in the March 4, 1904 *Milford Nebraskan* is about all the information available concerning their short missionary careers.

"Word has reached here of the death of Misses Katie and Lydia Burkey in north China. These young ladies, daughters of Mr. and Mrs. Chris Burkey, left here for the foreign mission field one and one half years ago. They spent the winter in California and left for China in February. During the course of their labors they became separated and Miss Katie, located in Tal-Nein-Fu and Miss Lydia in Wei-Hesin, being about 60 miles apart. Both were taken sick with small pox, from which neither recovered. Lydia died on Jan. 20 and Katie on Jan. 23.

Their parents had been hearing regularly ever since they were sick and the news of their death here Wednesday evening was quite a shock."

Evidently it took from Jan. 20 to March to receive the news in Milford.

The early deaths of the two young sisters did not stop other members of the family from serving as missionaries. Another sister of Lydia and Katie, Amelia Burkey, married John C. Birkey from Illinois. Together they sailed for China in 1913 established a mission station in northern China where three to four hundred people would gather every Sunday morning. In 1927, the Birkeys returned to Milford due to Mrs. Birkey's ill health.

John served as pastor of the Mennonite Brethren In Christ congregation (now Missionary) for some time. Later, he was appointed as District Superintendent of the Missionary Church Association. At one time in his life he was supporting three overseas pastors, one each in China, India and Africa. It was said at the time of his death in 1952, that he had read through the Bible sixty times during his lifetime. Their daughter Ina who married Paul Bartel and her brother John, also served as missionaries in China for many years.

The next Milford lady to volunteer for mission work was Lydia Rediger, daughter of Joseph C. Rediger, pastor of the Pleasant View Church. We first hear of her in 1916 when she took a job in Akron, Ohio with "down and out girls." By 1920 Lydia had graduated from Moody Bible Institute, as well as Beulah Heights Bible School of New Jersey and was said to be proficient in both German and English. Later in 1920, this information was reported in the *Milford Review*: "Miss Lydia Rediger has finished her training for a missionary and now has her permit from the ruler of India to at once engage in that line of work. She will soon go on a western journey to India."

But, a short while later we read this news note: "Mr. Joseph Rediger of Lankerisham, California is visiting family and friends. He formerly resided five miles southwest of Milford. His daughter, Lydia, is en route to China to do mission work." No reason is given as to why the switch was made from India to China.

Another young lady from the Milford community, Miss Phoebe Yeackley, a member of East Fairview Church, put her faith into action in 1917 when working as a nurse in a Chicago City Mission. By 1924, she was working in the Mennonite Children's Home in Kansas City.

A second missionary from the Pentecostal church was Miss Amanda Rediger, cousin to Lydia who sailed for China as a missionary on April 10, 1924. Amanda was the daughter of Dave Rediger, who served as Deacon of the church. The only other information I could find regarding Ms. Rediger was a note in the 1930 paper saying she was returning to China to resume her missionary work.

Erma Miller, daughter of Silas Miller, (co-pastor of the Pentecostal church) left for mission work in Brazil in 1932. This news announcement from the August 5, 1937 *Milford Review* shares more:

"Mildred Eigsti, who spent nine months in mission work in Minnesota, said she will be going to Liberia, Africa as a missionary for the Full Gospel Assembly Church. Mildred sailed for Liberia on December 15, 1938, sponsored by the Full Gospel Assembly Church of Friend. Her good friend, Lillian Swanson, of Duluth, Minnesota will be accompanying her."

One man from this community was also involved in overseas mission work prior to 1940. This information is from the August 9, 1928 *Milford Review*:

"Dr. Ed Stahly has accepted a call to the Indian mission field at Bengal Province, 200 miles northwest of Calcutta. He will be the first white doctor to practice in the vicinity. The Mennonite Brethren in Christ Church has a mission station at Rangatith. Dr. Stahly is a graduate of the U.N. Medical School in 1927. His wife Agnes was an instructor of nurses at Bryan Hospital in Lincoln. The Stahlys will stop over in London for a five-week study of tropical diseases, and leave for India September 6, 1928."

The Stahlys were forced home in 1932 because of health problems. Dr. Stahly was a brother to the late John Stahly. A long letter from the Stahlys was published in one edition of the 1932 *Milford Review*. Several other Milford residents served in overseas mission work after 1940. [Author's Note: the names Birky - Burkey, are all from the same family.]

The Way It Was

Milford's Number One Family

From the hundreds of families who have migrated to Milford since 1864, the Jacob Culver family stands out for their outstanding contribution to the growth and progress of the city. At one time the most respected and influential family in the city, today no members of this particular Culver family remain in the community.

"He is one of the most widely known of our citizens, and is most untiring in his efforts to build up his town and country. His zeal knows no bounds. Milford owes very much to him for her prosperity, for by his bulldog determination the great mill was secured, and in no small degree he helped to secure the A&N Railroad, and the Sanitarium owes its existence to him. Also the Industrial Home. Mr. Culver is a man of pronounced views on all questions of public importance, a strong Republican in politics, and a radical temperance man, a man of out- standing social qualities, he has many friends and of course some bitter enemies (*Milford Nebraskan*, 1905 N/A)."

Although one Culver family is presently listed in the Milford phone directory, no famous land marks, no city streets, or no Blue Mound tombstones are dedicated to the memory of the Culver family name. Today, the only reminder we have of this family is the name given to one small section of town known as the "Davison and Culver's addition to Milford."

Mrs. Robert (Charlotte) Moomey, third-generation spokesperson and guardian of the family history, said it like this: "It would seem that considering the strong characters of some of the Culvers, and Grandma's Aurilla's (Jacob's oldest sister) penchant for telling family stories, we should have more complete data, but we do not. There were a lot of 'Culver' stories around Milford, and I wish we knew them now. They would be mainly of Jacob, a go-getter."

Although widely known in the state for his military accomplishments, Mrs. Moomey said, "The Adjutant General's Office reported to me that a thorough search of our records did not reveal any records on a veteran by that name." Forced to search for information pertaining to the family following a request from the Culver City, California Historical Society in 1997, my version of the family story is compiled mostly from assorted bits and pieces of information gathered from old Milford histories and county newspapers; consequently, it may not agree in every detail with older versions of the family story as told by earlier writers. Jacob and his four sons, Culver family members who created history in Milford, were not the only Culvers to move to Nebraska. Jacob's parents, Lewis and Mary Culver, also moved to Seward County shortly after Jacob arrived in late 1869. Living in Milford for some time, they later moved to the Sutton area. His father, Lewis, died while living with Jacob's sister, Bula (Culver) Ball in York and is buried in the York Greenwood Cemetery.

Milford's all-time number one citizen, J.D. Culver.

Jacob's oldest sister, Aurilla, married Hugo Lubben in 1856 and in 1885 were living on a farm two miles northwest of Pleasant Dale bordering Highway 6. Hugo and Aurilla are buried in Wyuka Cemetery in Lincoln. Their oldest daughter Mary, married Curtis Beach and lived on the adjoining 160 acres to the west. Curtis and Mary Beach are buried in Blue Mound Cemetery. Hugo and Aurilla (Culver) Luebbens youngest son, Ummo Luebbens, was born in Wisconsin in 1867, grew up in the Milford and Pleasant Dale vicinity and attended the University of Nebraska where he studied mechanical drawing. Failing to make money on a so-called "rough hilly" farm near Pleasant Dale, he moved to Lincoln where he worked as a machinist, mechanic and lathe operator.

Although Ummo Luebben was very good at his job, he spent hours tinkering with inventions, including the round hay baler. In 1903, he exhibited his first model at the 1907 Nebraska State Fair. Clinging to the theory that round bales would cure better than rectangular ones, he eventually sold his patent to Allis Chalmers on a royalty basis. By the time he died in 1953, he had paid off all of his old debts and had accumulated a sizable estate. Today, one of Ummo's early hay balers is on display at Harold Warp's Pioneer Village in Minden.

Hugo and Aurilla's son, Melchoir, lived in the Sutton area for some time before moving to California. Like his brother, he too tinkered with inventions. He was said to have invented the first successful two-roller knife sharpener as well as the first roll down edge can opener. Jacob's sister, Priscilla, born in 1843, married F.B. Plopper and lived in Brown County, Nebraska. His oldest brother, Jasper, born in 1839, married Helen Davenport in 1867, came to Milford in 1870 and later moved to the Grafton, Nebraska community (All early Information on Culver family history from the Culver and Lubben family story as told by Mrs. Robert Moomey in *The Seward County Nebraska Book*, pgs. 77, 240 -241).

Jacob Culver was born in Mercer County Ohio in 1845, the seventh child of Lewis and Mary (Hazel) Culver. Married in Champaign County, Ohio in 1833, in 1847 the Culver family moved to Sheboygan County, Wisconsin where Jacob's father made his living by operating a sawmill near Sheyboygan Falls. (Sheyboygan County is located about half-way between Milwaukee and Green Bay.) Three of the children qualified as school teachers, while three of the sons and three sons-in-laws served in the Union Army during the Civil War. Jacob enlisted in Company K of the First Wisconsin Infantry, serving as drummer boy. One eyewitness reported the story: "After the flag bearer was killed at the battle of Perryville, Jacob dropped his drum and grabbed the flag bearing it aloft in triumph, a job he held until the end of the war."

Jacob served in battles at Chaplain Hills, Chickamauga, Mission Ridge, Lookout Mountain, Chattanooga and the Atlanta Campaign. Returning home from the war in 1866, Jacob entered the University of Wisconsin where he was a member of the University Cadets of Wisconsin. Later he was elected and served one term as Engrossing Clerk for the Wisconsin State Senate. Hearing of the great opportunities available in the west, Jacob left home in late 1869 destined for Milford, Nebraska.

No stranger to hard work or opportunity, by Christmas day of 1871, Jacob had already made his mark in the young community by meeting and marrying Ada Davison, daughter of the founder of Milford, by helping to organize a new Congregational church, and by being appointed as Milford postmaster.

During his first tenure as postmaster in 1871, a much-needed money order office was established. He also served a second term as postmaster from 1889 to 1894. Mr. Culver was the organizer of Winslow Post No. 56 of the G.A.R. chartered on September 1, 1888 and was chosen as its first commander. He also served as the state commander in 1882. Jacob was an active participant in the Good Templars Organization, one of the first nationwide organizations designed to discourage liquor use. Always ready to speak his sentiments on any issue, it was said by someone who knew him well, "He refused to pander to the liquor trade." In company with H. G. Parsons, he published the first newspaper ever printed in Milford (second in the county) known as the *Blue Valley Record*. The first edition hit the streets on December 29, 1870, the last edition on April 10, 1873. In his first edition, Mr. Culver laid his goals and values on the table: "Morally we shall labor for the best interests of the Republican party, not in a partisan spirit, but in a firm belief that it is the true party of progress and reform." Jacob spared no words to uphold the viewpoint he felt was good for the southern half of the county, especially during the early railroad bond battles. While Milford lost the first struggle for an early rail connection, Culver continued to lead the fight that resulted in a rail connection to Milford by 1879. Early Seward County historian, W. W. Cox said, "We have looked through every page of the *Record* files from first to last, and it is our pleasure to say that the paper was a credit to the county and the state."

Consolidating the paper with the *Lincoln Daily Leader*, Jacob moved to Lincoln for several years where he continued in the newspaper business. Several years later, he sold his interest in the *Leader* and bought one half interest in his father-in-law's milling business, where he served as manager of sales. During his tenure, the mill was enlarged and improved several times. Under enormous pressure, fighting several lawsuits due to the heavy indebtedness carried by the mill, Davison and Culver were forced to relinquish control of the mill to the newly-arrived Johnson family from New York. On October 9, 1879, Jacob sold his half interest in the mill to Mr. Webster for $18,000, thereby severing all connections with the milling business. At this time Jacob and his father-in-law sold part of Davison's original homestead for town lots, the section now know as Davison and Culvers addition to Milford. One newspaper article reported he also owned part interest in the Morris Lock Factory in Seward, serving at one time as vice president. In 1882, he purchased the brickyards built by Mr. Hamilton in 1880 at that time located on the northeast edge of town. Operating this yard for a short time, he made many of the bricks used in Milford's oldest brick buildings. Several years later he sold the yard to Mr. Sample. For several years we hear very little of Jacob's activities. One newspaper story would suggest that Jacob homesteaded government land in Washington County, Colorado, and tried his luck at "suit case" farming.

Others from the Milford community also homesteaded vast tracts of land in northeastern Colorado about this time (1885-87). As many soon discovered, it proved to be a "financial disaster." At least the editor mentioned that, "Mr. Culver was very happy to be back in the Milford community." In 1884 Culver persuaded the Nebraska State Game Commission to stock lake Quenchauqua with thousands of German Carp, a move the editor agreed "would soon make Milford one of the best fishing spots in the state." Other activities included selling coal and operating a farm.

The September 2, 1899 edition of the *Milford Nebraskan* announced that Jacob would be disposing of his farm equipment by public auction, selling 14 "milch" cows. Jacob had already disposed of one 80-acre farm in October of 1885, selling it to Jake Stutzman for $1,600.00. Jacob also had a hand in organizing the Seward County "Old Settlers Reunion." The first meeting was held in Seward in 1884. In 1886, old settlers from a four county area met in Seward with a huge crowd present. At this meeting Jacob was elected president for two terms. He was also active in all state and county G.A.R. organizations, usually taking a lead role in the conventions. Although he was active in various pursuits, Jacob's first love was the Military. He was instrumental in organizing National Guard Cavalry Troop A, Northwest Quad on July 22, 1887.

This unit, consisting of from 45 to 70 men including many from Milford and Beaver Crossing, chose Culver as their Commander and regularly trained in Milford's new brick 140' x 50' two-story Armory Building. While some early historians report that Jacob and his men saw action in the Indian rebellion of 1891, this account released from the *Omaha World Herald* tells a different story. "A news dispatch from Milford says that Cavalry Troop A, Northwest Quad, Captain Culver commanding will be mustered into action to help out in the northwestern Indian Campaign. The Cavalry Unit, forty-five strong, is ready to move to the front to aid in annihilation of the Indians. Troop A is composed of as gallant a company of soldiers as ever rode cavalry horses, and should they ever have the opportunity of engaging in battle, their bravery will be fully demonstrated and their friends will have more cause than ever to feel proud of the boys from Seward

County who were the first to respond to their countries' call (*Seward Independent*, May 5, 1891)."

Later this news note appeared in the *Milford Nebraskan*: "Troop A.N.N.G. were mustered out of service Wednesday and will not leave to fight the Indians, but they want it understood, twenty-four hours is all the time they would need to prepare for action." In other words, this war was practically over before it started. On January 8, 1891, Milford's new brick armory building, built in 1887 and used for Troop A headquarters, burned to the ground, destroying $1,800 worth of Troop A equipment—including most of their rifles and saddles. Captain Culver not only suffered a personal loss of over $1,000, he was also severely burned while attempting to rescue equipment. It was said it took him ten weeks to get back to normal. Thirteen members of Troop A were from Milford, including three of Culver's sons. Several years later, Troop A was disbanded without having ever engaged in actual combat.

One account from the *Lincoln Journal* sums up Captain Culver's ability as a military leader: "Captain Culver was a practical soldier and believed in instructing his men in a manner they would be compelled to live in time of war. Each year they would march to wherever they were holding maneuvers. One year in Hastings, one year in Grand Island and many times in Burlington Beach (Capitol Beach) in Lincoln. His boys showed good training, this compliments of Captain Culver, and he was just as proud of their appearance."

In 1887, Jacob spearheaded the fight to secure the State Industrial Home for the city. Although few details are given, the complex was built on 40 acres of land homesteaded by his father-in- law, J. L. Davison, who by this time had moved on to the Las Cruces, New Mexico area. Jerusha Davison died on June 21, 1898 and Jonathan on May 28, while living in Los Angeles.

Before the Industrial Home was finished, Jacob was determined to take advantage of Milford's magic water by erecting a Health Spa similar to the famous "Queen of the Spas," a 3,000 capacity unit located in Sartoga Springs, New York.

With his military-centered mind, Culver dreamed of a Soldiers Home in the Milford community, one to take advantage of Shogo Springs healing water. In 1884, he traveled to Dayton, Ohio, in an attempt to persuade the Veterans Administration to locate a proposed facility in Milford. Losing out to a town in Missouri, Culver did not give up. By December 6, 1886 this announcement in the *Milford Nebraskan* thrilled local residents: "It's a go! Milford will have a new Sanitarium costing $11,500."

Five wealthy Milford businessmen formed a corporation, purchased forty acres of land from Mr. Culver and proceeded to build. Before the building could be finished, hard financial times brought construction to a standstill. Partially finished and mostly empty, Mr. Culver decided this might be the time to act. Somehow, he convinced the state legislature to open a home for old soldiers using his unfinished building. Persuaded by his military savvy and political clout, the Legislature voted to open a branch of the Grand Island Veterans Home in Milford. Leased for several years at $800 per year, in June of 1899 the state paid the builders $13,000 for the building, and the rest of the story is "Milford history." Culver was chosen as first commandant with his son Elwin, serving as adjutant without salary. When Jacob resigned several years later, Elwin took charge of the home for several years. This note from the *Milford Nebraskan* reports the mood of the Culver family in early 1898 during the height of the controversy with Spain: "Captain J. H. Culver of Milford served three years in the war for the Union, and if war is declared against Spain he will again enlist and his four sons will go with him. This will make a record for the family, such as few families can attain, and which will be referred to with pride by descendants in generations yet to come."

In 1898, he offered his services and was mustered into the 3rd Volunteer Cavalry, serving in one of the "Rough Rider Regiments" camped at Chickamauga. These successors to Troop A were often known as "The Seward County Cowboys," or as "Grigsby's Rough Riders." Consisting of 82 volunteers, 40 of them from Seward County, training camp was established north of the Soldiers Home on April 26.

Mustered into active service on May 14, 1898, his company marched to Lincoln and embarked via the Missouri Pacific Railroad for Chickamauga Park, Georgia, reaching their destination on May 23. In spite of giving a good account of themselves in training exercises, by mid-July the war was practically over and much to the disappointment of the "cowboys," Troop A never did see real action and the unit was mustered out of service on September 11, 1898.

From this point on, Culver's military exploits are difficult to trace. In August of 1892, Jacob was chosen by the city of Lincoln to greet and welcome the Governor of Ohio, William McKinley, who was also known as a great Civil War hero. The *Milford Nebraskan* newspaper editor said, "This was indeed an honor others might envy." In 1903, he was asked to serve as State Adjutant General, a position he held until he asked for permission to resign on July 1, 1907. On October 14, 1898 he was invited to testify before an investigating committee in Washington D.C. about, "what he knows about food and water for soldiers at camp." In the spring of 1899, at the age of 54, Culver was asked to accompany the U.S. 32nd Cavalry for service in the Philippine Islands. Selling his livestock and farming equipment, he took additional training at Fort Leavenworth, Kansas, before leaving for the Philippines on September 10, 1899. He was accompanied to the Philippines by his wife and daughter Lulu, as well as two of his sons. Arriving in the Islands in November of 1899, he served in several campaigns in Central Luzon. Injured during a scouting expedition on March 30, 1900, Captain Culver, his wife and daughter returned home for what the editor said "was a two-month furlough." Returning to the Philippines after recovery, he served as Provost Marshal, Post Commander, and superintended the establishment of American schools in his province.

The original Shogo Bottling Works erected by J. D. Culver in 1905 was closed about 1916 when the plant moved to Lincoln. Mose Schweitzer tore down the plant in 1921 using the salvage material for his business buildings uptown.

The Way It Was

Returning home in 1902, he was awarded an increase in his pension, now said to be $18 per week. From this time on, it would appear the entire Culver family lived in Lincoln.

By 1905, Jacob Culver had already celebrated his 60th birthday and may have been ready to tone down any strenuous military activity. On July 1, 1907, he resigned from all connections with the military as well as any responsibility at the Soldiers Home and turned his attention to Shogo Springs. On May 14, 1906, Jacob and his sons, plus three other wealthy friends, met in a lawyers office in Lincoln and signed this agreement: "We, the undersigned, do hereby associate ourselves together for the purpose of forming a Corporation under the laws of the State of Nebraska and do adopt the following Articles of Incorporation..."

Articles one, two, and three explain what it was all about: "The name of the corporation shall be called Shogo-Lithia Spring Company. The principal place of business shall be in Milford. The object for which this corporation is formed is to purchase, own and operate the Shogo Lithia Springs, park, and Hotel grounds near Milford Nebraska; to erect bottling works, sell the spring water, and generally develop the resources of the property." Signing the papers were: J. H. Culver, H. H. Culver, E. E. Culver, E. C. Babcock, W. R. Smith and Archabald G. Evans.

The Culver family was now organized for action and a new industry was launched in the city of Milford. Jacob quickly gathered his boys to join him in the family business. Harry Culver quit his job in Detroit, Elwin resigned his job as assistant cashier of the Sutton National Bank to supervise the project and a new three-story brick building was erected. By April of 1906 the *Milford Nebraskan* editor reported, "The development of the Springs means considerable to Milford, and a certain pride should be taken in them by the public."

By May the editor could report, "The Shogo Lithia Springs will soon be ready to send healing waters to the people, and the rest of the world will have the chance to live as healthy as the Comrades here."

Later the *Nebraskan* editor reported more progress: "The output of Shogo Lithia water has increased to such an extent the company found it necessary to increase the size of their plant. Manager H. H. Culver reports the business is developing rapidly."

Although it appeared the project was apparently booming, for some unknown reason the Culver family sold the company to a group of Lincoln investors in February of 1907. The newly formed Shogo Lithia Company took over the business with great expectations in the spring of 1909, but were soon forced into bankruptcy. At the bankruptcy sale, the company was bought by a Mr. Trumen from Lincoln for $6,000, leaving a total debt of $25,000. From this time on, the business was mostly operated from an office and bottling plant in Lincoln.

Yes, the city of Milford did recognize Jacob's contribution to the growth and development of Milford. In June of 1906, they awarded him a gold headed cane presented in a special ceremony. The editor of the *Seward Blue Valley Blade* said, "The people of Milford ought to appreciate the efforts of Captain Culver to secure for that place the new Soldiers Home. Culver has done more for them than ten men, and there should be nothing too good for him that the people can do." An earlier writer of the *Milford Ozone* echoed the same opinion: "Jacob was one of the proprietors of the town site, and to his energy and ability the success of Milford may be largely attributed." Jacob died in East San Diego, California, on August 19, 1921 at the age of 76 years, having reached the rank of Brigadier General.

Ada Davison, wife of Jacob Culver, was born on April 13, 1853 in Wisconsin and married Jacob Culver on July, 2, 1870. Ada was the daughter of Milford founder J. L. and Jerusha A. (Weeks) Davison. Ada's father, Jonathan, was born near Limetown, Conn., received his education in Bloomfield, Conn., after which he attended Genesee Wesleyan Seminary. Married to Miss Jerusha Weeks in 1842, they moved to Dodge County, Wisconsin, where he farmed until 1857 at which time they came to Nebraska settling on a Salt Creek claim ten miles south of Lincoln.

In 1862 he moved his ranch to Seward County, locating about one mile west of the new town of Camden. In 1862 he was appointed by the Territorial Legislature as one of those commissioned to blaze a new trail from Nebraska City to Ft. Kearny, the trail often known as the "Old Territorial Road." Later, he was asked to help stake out the new Steam Wagon Road using the old limestone Indian ford to cross the Blue. Evidently Jonathan sensed changes prompting him to move six miles north to the limestone ford. In April of 1864 he staked a second claim on ground that is now the city of Milford.

The Way It Was

The rest of the Davison family story is Milford history. Jonathan not only surveyed and laid out the foundations for the city of Milford, he was also chosen as the first Probate Judge of Seward County.

We hear little of the Davisons after 1886, probably because the family moved to Las Cruces, New Mexico where he was said to have operated a cattle ranch. Later the family moved to California.

Jacob and Ada were the parents of five children: Clarence, born on Dec.25, 1872; Elwin, born Jan.1, 1875; Harry, born Jan. 22, 1880; Fred, born Aug. 20, 1882 and Lula, born March 13, 1887. Jerusha died in Los Angeles on June 21, 1898 and Jonathan died on May 28, 1908. All five children were born in Milford.

Clarence is listed as one of the first four pupils to graduate from Milford's first high school in 1888, a class that only went to the tenth grade. From 1891 to 1896 he attended the University of Nebraska, and was especially active in the military classes offered by the University. In 1887, he is listed as being a member of Troop A.N.N.G., the unit captained by his father. After finishing his work at the university, Clarence worked as a cashier for a meat packing firm in Denver. In 1898, he resigned his position, returned to Milford and enlisted in father's troop, serving as Quartermaster Sergeant. After mustering out of the regiment he was sent to Washington D.C. and later to Camp Mead in Pennsylvania. In July of 1899, he was ordered to the Philippines where he served as Division Quartermaster Clerk for General Lawton's division serving through several campaigns in North Central Luzon. He was later ordered to Manila where he was commissioned as 1st Lieutenant Volunteer, and authorized to organize a Troop of Philippine Scouts.

After spending four and one half years in the Philippines, Clarence returned to the states in December of 1903, and was sent to Fort Meyers, Virginia. There, he was promoted to 1st lieutenant and was then transferred to the 3rd U.S. Cavalry, stationed at Fort Assinniboine, Montana. He served as Post Commissary Engineer and Signal Officer, and Post Exchange Officer. By 1910, one year after the U.S. Army Signal Corps bought their first airplane, he was one of the first to become involved in the development of aviation radio.

By 1915, he was the Chief Aviation engineer in the office of the Chief Signal Officer. In late 1915, he took charge of the San Diego Radio School, the school at the center of most aviation radio research at the time. He served as the meteorological and communications officer. During World War I, he traveled to France to learn more about the latest in radio aircraft technologies. After his return in 1918, he was chosen to head what was later known as the communications division of the Army Air service.

In 1925, Clarence Culver became Post Commander of Kelly Air Field in Texas, as well as the commandment of the Air Service's advanced flying school. In 1926, he was serving as commander of Langley Air Field in Virginia. In 1929 he was promoted to chief of the Air Section in the war department headquarters in Washington D.C. He was awarded the highest military non-combat honor for distinguished service in pioneer electronics. Clarence Culver was buried in the Arlington National Cemetery.

Elwin, the second son of Jacob and Ada Culver, was born in Milford on January 1, 1875. Although he attended school in Milford, he is not listed as an alumni of Milford High School. After attending the University of Nebraska for two years, he enlisted in Troop A.N.N.G. when he was thirteen years old and served as trumpeter. By 1897, he had risen to the rank of 2nd lieutenant and was mustered into service with Troop K of the 3rd U.S. Volunteer Cavalry where he often took charge of the troops during the absence of his father. Returning to Milford at the close of the Spanish War, he enlisted as a private in Company L, 32nd U.S. Infantry, where he was quickly promoted to corporal, then quartermaster sergeant and 1st sergeant. Serving with his regiment in the Philippine insurrection he was actively engaged in several battles. Returning home after his unit was mustered out of service he served as assistant cashier at the First National Bank of Sutton. He eventually resigned when he was called by his father to help with the Shogo water business. He was also the quartermaster of the 2nd Regiment, Nebraska National Guard, holding the rank of captain. Elwin died in Culver City, California on April 25, 1962.

Harry Culver was born in Milford on January 22, 1880 and attended grade school in Milford and like his older brother is not listed as graduating from Milford High School. He also attended Doane College, and the University of Nebraska before enlisting in the National Guard Troop commanded by his father at a young age, serving as trumpeter. He was mustered into service with the unit during the Spanish-American War and sent to Georgia, where he was promoted to squadron sergeant major. Near the end of his term he was stricken with typhoid fever, and nearly died on Lookout Mountain where he was taken to benefit from the high altitude. Recovering, he returned home and enrolled in the University of Nebraska to finish his schooling.

In the summer of 1899 Harry took his famous bicycle trip. Leaving Milford with a companion, when they reached Galveston, Texas, his partner took sick and dropped out of the trip. Harry continued on alone, traveling 4,000 miles, as far south as Florida and north to New York City averaging 77 miles a day. One report said he traveled through 15 states, shot 53 dogs, was held up one time and lost 17 pounds. His "Wheel," covered with badges and ribbons, was put on display in the Lincoln "Scycle" store.

In 1901 he left for the Philippines, where he engaged in the mercantile business before taking a job as a news reporter for the *Manila Times* newspaper. Later, he was appointed as a special agent for the Customs Department of the Philippines. Returning home because of his wife's ill health, he was assigned to special duty in U.S. Customs Service in St. Louis. We are not sure when Harry Culver moved to California (probably about 1910) but he soon became a successful land and real estate developer. In 1914, he founded the city now bearing his name and in 1927, University City. In 1922, he founded Pacific Military Academy in honor of his father. Anticipating a real estate boom in Southern California, about 1915-16 Harry took options on ordinary farmland at "farmland" prices. Using all kinds of ingenious promotion methods, Harry convinced people to buy lots in his sub-division later known as Culver City. One news report mentioned the fact that he was soon worth 20 million and later married a motion picture star. The rest is history.

On June 28, 1928, he received a telegram from President Hoover congratulating him for being elected as president of the National Association of Realtors. Promoting Culver City as site for motion picture production, it was at one time home of MGM and Hal Roach Studios and now Sony Entertainment (where "Jeopardy," "Wheel of Fortune" and other television shows are taped). Milford, Nebraska history was reunited with Culver City history in 1997 when the Culver City Historical Society produced a documentary entitled *Reel Life In Culver City* which dealt with the 80-year history of the film industry in Culver City. Wanting to connect Harry Culver with his Milford roots, Culver City historians contacted Southeast Community College asking for information on Culver family roots in Nebraska. Accepting the challenge, I offered what information I had available at the time. Later, I received a personal invitation from the Culver City Society to attend the first showing of this reel. Many famous, old-time Hollywood movie stars were invited to attend including Ted Turner, Rita Heyworth, Mickey Rooney, and other Hollywood celebrities.

Fred Culver, youngest son of Jacob and Ada Culver, was born in Milford on August 20, 1882. He attended Milford public schools, although he is not listed as graduating from Milford High. Following the example of his older brothers, he enlisted in Troop A.N.N.G. at fourteen years of age and was serving in that capacity when the Spanish-American War broke out. Following the troop to Chickamanauga, Georgia, he served for a short time as chief trumpeter and as a cornetist after the mounted band was organized. After the war he returned to Milford, but became restless when his father and brothers left for Philippine service. Only sixteen years old at the time, he begged to join them, and was given special permission to by the Secretary of War to enlist. Joining the Regimental Band he served throughout the Philippine campaign until he was struck down with malaria, and discharged two months before his regiment's time had expired.

After several years in California, he returned to the University of Nebraska to finish his education and later assisted his father in the Adjutant General's office. After moving to California, Fred became a writer and died while still in his forties.

Early Seward County Liquor Struggles

Writing about 1888, Seward County historian, W. W. Cox had this to say about a certain Seward County town: "Tamora is a beautiful village with a good trade, and a very desirable place in which to live. The people are universally intelligent and wide awake. Having always been free from the contagion of saloons, they say they have never had any need for saloons and they throw their surplus energy into beautifying their homes and maintaining their schools and churches. Anyone desiring a neat, quiet home, with excellent churches and school facilities, where they are within a few minutes of the city and where they are free from the influence of the saloon, we cheerfully recommend Tamora (*History of Seward County*, W.W. Cox, p. 113)."

Cox wrote more concerning the start and progress of early temperance work in Seward County:

"Temperance work commenced at a very early day in the history of Seward County. As early as 1869 a lodge of Good Templars was organized in the old school-house, and flourished for a number of years, exerting a wide and salutary influence, especially on younger people. About the same date there was a lodge instituted at Milford. In 1874, a Women's crusade was made, and created a wide interest. Many of the best Christian ladies of the day united in their efforts to suppress the liquor traffic, by visiting daily the saloons and earnestly pleading with the saloon keepers and their customers. These ladies would fervently pray with these abandoned men, and implore them in the name of the divine Master to abandon their ungodly ways, and lead better lives…In 1872, after a night's carousal on the part of a number of men, they were suddenly awakened by a sense of their own shame, and they agreed with one another that the night's debauch should be their last, and bound themselves by a most solemn oath, in which they pledged not only their sacred honor but their solemn oath that they would forever abstain from the use of intoxicating drinks as a beverage (*History of Seward County*, W.W. Cox, p.160)."

Records regarding the issuance of the earliest liquor license in the town of Milford are just not available, although all indications would point to about 1884. This news note from the *Milford Ozone* newspaper in the fall of 1884 could give one the idea that it may have been a long and hard fought campaign. "Well! at last, Milford has two saloons. But no one has seen that it puts more money in our merchants pockets. It has been said 'he who comes to town to buy beer seldom buys anything but beer, and if he has any money left, he just buys more beer!'"

There is no mention of liquor sales in the town before this time, one reason could be due to the fact that Milford founder J. L. Davison, as well as his son-in-law J. H. Culver were strong supporters of prohibition. From 1884 on, several incidents involving alcohol use are recorded giving one the idea that alcohol was legal for several years, voted out for a time, voted in again until 1899 when it was said "even the saloon fixtures have been removed." By 1904, Milford was said to be "dry" until the end of prohibition.

Eldon Hostetler

Although Milford was famous for its great entertainment complex known as "Shogo Island," liquor is never mentioned as being a part of the celebrations, since alcohol was usually considered a threat to family centered entertainment.

Not able to blame the town's women for the decline in town morality, the *Milford Nebraskan* editor put on his "righteous robes" and said this: "If any small town in the country needs a temperance rally, Beaver Crossing certainly does." Turning his head south this time, he opened his mouth once more: "One man from Dorchester balked at paying a five dollar fine for drunkenness. He said: 'In Dorchester I could get drunk for one dollar' (*Milford Nebraskan*, 1888)."

In 1868 the Good Templars Blue Mound Lodge Number 22 was chartered with only one purpose in mind—to encourage alcohol abstinence. It was the first lodge organized in the city. Every member was required to pledge himself to abstain from all intoxicating drinks, work for the prohibition in manufacturing and sale of all alcoholic beverages, and to aid in the election of public officials pledged to enact and enforce such a law. The fact that the organizational meeting was held in the home of Milford's founder J. L. Davison would indicate he, as well as his son-in-law J. H. Culver, were supporters of alcohol abstinence.

In 1885, the *Milford Ozone* editor aired some of his personal opinions on hoodlum activity in the city when he reported, "Something should be done to prevent any more disgraceful rows; they are becoming too common. Either the whiskey is bad lately, or the roughs are permitted to drink more. A change is demanded." This note from the July 9, 1880 *Milford Nebraskan* would suggest that interest in complete prohibition was high in the 1880s: "Nine cars of excursionists spent the weekend in Milford, they were mostly Temperance people. A special train was run from Seward."

By 1892, many local citizens were angry enough to vote the saloon out of town. However, this solution appeared to be very short lived. In fact, by 1894 the town boasted of two saloons, evoking this sarcastic comment from the *Milford Nebraskan* editor: "At last Milford has two saloons. Now according to some people, we will have a big business boom, and yet we will not suffer any worse from drunken men on the street, or more liquor sold to minors."

For several years it must have been a real struggle between the "wets" and the "drys." By 1898, the *Milford Nebraskan* editor could issue this triumphal report to his "dry" minded readers: "Suddenly, our saloon's furniture has all been removed and our town still has substantial business and it has been quiet all week. Not one drunken man has graced our streets all week."

The 1898 vote was not the final answer. The issue was not really settled until 1904, at which time dry forces succeeded in closing down the last saloon. From 1904, until national prohibition was repealed in 1933, Milford was without a legal liquor outlet. Without a saloon in the town, the *Milford Review* editor could report in 1917: "There was no need for a town Marshal during the city picnic, as John Barley Corn was not once in evidence."

While some continued to enjoy "illegal" drinks, stressing moderation, others continued the fight for total prohibition. In March of 1911, M.S. Paulson, Supt. of the Anti-Saloon League, appeared in town and spoke in five different churches as well as the Old Soldiers Home. Just like today, some were convinced the lack of a liquor outlet in Milford could shut the town down causing great financial hardship to Milford merchants. Others boldly proclaimed that alcohol was the father of everything "sinful or corrupt" in the community. Early news notes would suggest that many times the struggle appeared to be "us against them," meaning the women against the men.

Evidently the local evangelical pastor joined in on the anti-alcohol crusade as well. "Rev. Plunkett preached a sermon to his congregation entitled "the Black Horse of Intemperance." He preached about the danger of using liquor, playing cards, dancing and the use of tobacco. All Milford should have heard this sermon (Milford Review, August 15, 1918)."

In 1935, a Milford resident filed a complaint against his neighbors, insisting they had threatened him while drunk. Two people were arrested and taken to the county jail after the sheriff found a small distillery in their home. In 1932, three Milford men were accused of "boot legging"—a charge they vehemently denied. Apparently, Milford citizens who craved alcohol were usually well supplied with drink, regardless of existing liquor laws. Even several years after prohibition ended, federal liquor agents raided a Milford home and arrested the owner, charging him with operating a distillery. Twenty-five gallons of homemade brew was seized as evidence.

By 1932, Milford dry forces were already gearing up for the expected repeal of the Prohibition Amendment. In October, a Union

Young People's Temperance Rally was held in the Milford Methodist Church. In April of 1933, three Milford churches (Methodist, Evangelical (E.U.B.) and M.B.I.C (now Missionary), organized to register a protest against the "beer bill" before the state legislature. Local citizens were urged to put pressure on Milford's State Senator Andy Welsh, to vote against the bill.

After the repeal of prohibition in 1933, a petition to prevent the Milford Village Board from issuing a license to sell beer was circulated. On August 10, 1933 Milford church members, determined to keep the town dry, presented a petition containing 290 signatures. From this total 62 were in favor of granting a license, while 228 were against. The Village Board voted to reject the petition because of "improper wording." This setback did not deter Milford's dry forces. The following week, another signed petition was presented to the Board, this time with an even greater majority in favor of keeping the town dry. Once more the petition was rejected on the grounds that a number of the signers had failed to vote at the last election. Within one week Milford was home to a new saloon—the first since 1904.

While some older than eighty may remember when the nation adopted the 18th Amendment to our Constitution (often known as prohibition), few remember why it was adopted, or how it impacted American life. A word rarely used by Americans today, Webster defines the word prohibition as "the legal prohibiting of the manufacture, sale and transportation of alcoholic beverages." Passed by Congress in 1917, ratified by the required thirty-six states by January 16, 1919, the Act went into effect on January 16, 1920. Hailed by American Temperance Organizations, the Anti-Saloon League declared it was, "the beginning of an era of clear thinking an clean living."

But Congress repealed Prohibition within the first 100 days of President Roosevelt's administration in 1933, and many American historians would now deem it as the noble experiment that failed. This is the story of an exercise in futility—a moment in American history that many think failed miserably and will probably never be repeated. News items from modern day newspapers could convince one that the misuse of alcoholic beverages has not changed all that much since 1920—and, perhaps the past 3,000 years.

"If asked what they consider the biggest drug problem, most Americans would probably say cocaine," said drug czar William

Bennett in Omaha, as he urged the members of a national Commission on Drug Free Schools not to lead off their report with concerns about cocaine. "Liquor may not be upsetting most Americans, but liquor is the drug killing many Americans. Take a look at the drug body count, and you'll see that the legal killers lead the list. Nicotine is at the top. One in four smokers will die directly from smoking. Alcohol is second. In fact it is responsible for more than an estimated 100,000 deaths a year, according to federal health officials. These are the big killers: emphysema, lung cancer, and cirrhosis of the liver, car accidents. You won't find many coke addicts in local graveyards (*Lincoln Journal Star*, 2003)."

One role already mentioned was the use of alcohol as a medicine or tonic. Remember the days when many Nebraska farmers kept a bottle of their favorite bourbon hidden away in their barn for "medicinal" purposes only? Several widely advertised medicines such as Hostetters Bitters and Lydia E. Pinkham's Vegetable Compound for Women carried large percentages of alcohol.

Advertisements sponsored by the Liesey Brothers Brewery of Peoria, Illinois, trumpeted the medicinal value of their product in the 1880s: "The Ideal Family Beverage: more and more people are learning the advantages of having beer in the home. As a tonic for run down and nervous systems, Malt-Ease will produce remarkable results. Ask your druggist for Malt Ease. It is the one tonic that you can be sure will do you some good. It is a healthful tonic that is recommended by physicians generally. If your system is tired and run down, order a few bottles, or take a case. Take a glass before meals, and before retiring, and you will be surprised at the results. Malt Ease is good for men, women and children. It's a tonic for both brain and body. It is also a valuable nutrient for nursing mothers and a concentrated food for convalescent."

Eldon Hostetler

The Methodist Church Tried

For those who usually assumed Christians of yesterday were better behaved than the generations of today, may need a refresher course in American church history:
"Incredible quantities of whiskey were consumed, everybody, women and preachers included, drank the fiery liquid. A bottle was in every cabin to offer it was the first gesture of welcome, to refuse unpardonable incivility. All used tobacco, chewing, smoking, snuffing, and corn cob pipes in the mouths of women were not an uncommon sight. Men were quick to fight and combats were brutal. Profanity was general and emphatic. Everybody came to the General store on Saturdays to trade, gossip, wrestle, raffle, pitch horseshoe, run races, get drunk, maul one another with their fists, and indulge generally, in frontier happiness, as a relief from the weeks monotonous drudgery on the raw and difficult farms. (*Flames On The Plains—History of the Nebraska Methodist Church*, Don W. Holter, Albert J. Beveridge, writing about the time Abraham Lincoln was practicing law in Illinois.))

Peter Cartwright, famous circuit rider and presiding Elder of the Methodist church wrote, "From my earliest recollections drinking drams (small drinks) in family and social circles, was considered harmless and allowable. It was almost universally the custom for preachers, in common with all others, to take drams; and if a man would not have it in his family, his house raising, his harvest, his log rollings, weddings, and so on, he was considered parsimonious and unsociable; and many, even professors of Christianity, would not help a man if he did not have spirits to treat the company" (*Autobiography of Peter Cartwright,* page 145).

As early as 1743, John Wesley was extremely concerned about the shortage of food in his native England. He wrote, "Why is food so dear? The grand cause is because such immense quantities of corn are continually consumed by distilling. Add all the distillers through England, and have we not reason to believe that little less than half the wheat produced in the Kingdom is every year consumed, not in so harmless a way as throwing it into the sea, but converting it into a deadly poison, that naturally destroys not only the strength and life, but also the morals of our countrymen."

The Way It Was

In one year, Wesley excluded seventeen members from one of his societies for drinking or retailing spirituous liquors Article 11 of the 1814, Discipline of the United Brethren Church stated, "Every member shall abstain from strong drink, and use it only on necessity as medicine." The 1839 Discipline went even further when it stated, "Should any exhorted, minister or Elder be engaged in the distillation or vending of ardent spirits and continue after admonition and warning, he should for the time not be considered a member of the church (*Flames On The Plains—History of the Nebraska Methodist Church*, Don W. Holter, pgs. 144-145)."

In 1856, the Kansas and Nebraska Conference approved this resolution, "That we give king alcohol no quarters without our bounds." Is it any wonder that Martin Luther decided it would be impossible to "dry up" church people, and that "only the second coming of Jesus Christ would root out the evil."

In 1857 tobacco came in for condemnation as: "…a baneful poison unnatural to the human system, destructive to the health and often to life…we hereby recommend to all members and probationers of the conference to desist from the use of it (*Flames On The Plains—History of the Nebraska Methodist Church*, Don W. Holter)."

In 1858, this action was approved; "that our efforts among the people shall be directed to the passage and sustaining of prohibition liquor laws in our territories, and in regard to tobacco, we cannot but regret that any of our ministers or lay members should indulge in the use of this poisonous weed." In 1870 the Methodist Conference said this about tobacco: "The use of tobacco is a filthy habit…costing consumers on an average of $20.00 per year. We affirm that we will not receive into full connection any man who persists in the use of tobacco (*Flames on the Plains*, Don W. Holter, pgs 144-145)."

During the Civil War years the consumption of alcohol actually increased from $28.5 million in 1860 to more than $450 million in 1900. Old temperance organizations gained new members, while new ones were being formed in an attempt to stem the increasing toll of wrecked lives from alcoholic abuse. In 1868, the General Conference of the Methodist Church passed this resolution: "We hail every legal measure to effectually restrain and extirpate this chief crime against society, and trust the law of prohibition may yet be the enactment of every state, and of the National Congress and be successfully executed throughout our republic."

Eldon Hostetler

The first Nebraska territorial legislature held in Omaha in 1855 passed a prohibition liquor amendment. It was sponsored by Taylor G. Goodwell, a loyal Methodist from Omaha. The law, said to be patterned after one in Iowa, prohibited the manufacture, sale, or consumption of all alcoholic beverages. Three years later the law was repealed, and a license law was substituted, probably because the law was impossible to enforce. In the first session of the Nebraska Methodist Conference the body adopted this resolution: "First, that if it was ever necessary to oppose an unbroken front to this evil, now is the time. Second, that a prohibition law would give force and vigor, edge and point to moral Suasion. Third, that at each of our appointments during the Conference year we will preach at least once on the subject."

Each year the conference urged that the question be submitted to the people for a vote. In 1871 the state's voters defeated the question of prohibition. Evidently this did not discourage the Methodist conference. In 1873 the Conference persisted and resolved: "To petition the Hon. Governor Furnas that an extra session of the Legislature shall be called, and he will embody in the call a necessity of a change in the liquor laws of the state, so that the people may have some chance for protection against the extensive sale of intoxicating drinks, the greatest curse to Nebraska has to contend with, which is eating out our substance, depraving our young men, demoralizing whole communities, filling the land with vagrants, paupers and criminals. It also being the cause of three fourth of our murders, and other crime in the state, and making the streets of our town and our cities a pandemonium of obscenity, blasphemy and staggering debauchery; causing a heavy burden of taxation to fall upon the industrious and innocent classes, and being the direct cause of more misery than any other influence known in the land."

One more time the voters of the state turned down the petition, and the problem remained. In 1889, the United Brethren Church passed a resolution stating, "…that temperance in all things is taught in the word of God and is to be practiced by all Christians; while intemperance, especially in the use of intoxicating drinks, is the greatest curse of our times. That, as ministers, we favor the absolute prohibition of manufacture and sale of every liquid that will intoxicate."

The Way It Was

In a bitter election held in 1890, the prohibition amendment was defeated once more. By this time Iowa and Kansas had already enacted prohibition legislation, Kansas as early as 1880. It would appear that John Wesley and the Methodist people were one century ahead of most churches in realizing the dangers of the unrestrained use of strong drink, and were attempting to take some action.

The Methodist Church was not alone in the fight for prohibition. Neal Dow, a prominent Maine businessman, was campaigning against "demon rum" as early as the 1820s. By 1857, thirteen states had already enacted prohibition laws, while Maine included prohibition in the state constitution by 1884.

The big push for nationwide prohibition came after 1850 and was often associated with the women's rights movement. Carrie Chapman Catt and Susan B. Anthony joined forces with the prohibition movement towards the end of the century. The Women's Temperance Union founded by Frances Willard, and the Anti-Saloon League led by Wayne B. Wheeler, determined to make the country dry. Assisted by a few American churches, twenty-seven states were bone dry by 1917, while other counties or municipalities voted themselves dry even if the majority of the state stayed wet. This was the option chosen by Milford voters in 1904. During World War I, dry states complained they could not enforce prohibition while adjacent states were wet. The Anti-Saloon League printed over 100 million flyers, posters and pamphlets furthering the idea that alcohol was mainly responsible for the poverty, insanity and most of the degeneracy found in the world. The league held prohibition would empty the jails, the asylums and the poorhouses. Wanting to model a true American "spirit of sacrifice" for the war effort, many citizens succumbed to the spirit of the times and by 1917, nation-wide prohibition was a reality.

In October of 1919, Congress passed the "Volstead Act" defining prohibited intoxicating liquors as any beverage containing more than .5 percent of one-percent alcohol. The said law to be enforced after January 1, 1920. This act gave the government authority to set up whatever machinery was needed to enforce the new liquor laws. Under its terms, federal agents were empowered to raid "speakeasies" (the new term for illegal saloons) smashing barrels of booze as well as searching for the bootleggers supplying the now illegal product. Touted by the Anti-Saloon League of America and other temperance groups, the act was seen as the cure for practically everything that ailed the American people.

But they were in for an unpleasant surprise. While it did cut down on per capita alcohol consumption other, more serious problems, loomed in the horizon. Bootlegging, so named after the practice of Civil War soldiers who hid booze in their boot tops, quickly sprang up to quench the public thirst.

In ten years the federal government made more than 500,000 arrests for breaking the Volstead Act, securing more than 300,000 convictions. Still, smuggling only increased. Canadian and Mexican borders were full of leaks. Boats ran cargoes from Cuba into Florida and other Gulf ports. Mountain "moonshiners" multiplied; vineyards in California and New York conveniently supplied kegs of grape juice to those capable of emulating the miracle performed by Jesus at the wedding feast in Cana. Carloads of grapes were sold to Italian and Greek Americans experienced in the art of old fashioned wine making.

Ocean-going vessels loaded with every variety of wine and liquor known to man waited for the opportune time to unload their cargoes. Millions of gallons of industrial alcohol, manufacture of which was permitted, were converted into bootleg whisky or gin and bottled under counterfeit labels. Poisonous wood alcohol, sometimes inexpertly converted, caused numerous deaths. Liquor and wine imported under license for "medical purposes only" ended up in many "healthy' stomachs and speakeasies became a normal fixture in most cities. In defiant states like Rhode Island which refused to ratify or enforce the amendment, one could buy a good bottle of British gin right off the grocery shelf if willing to pay the price.

Those who did not care to challenge the law, made their own "bathtub" brew at home. Enforcement of prohibition proved very difficult. From 1924 to 1925, 20 million gallons of moonshine was seized and destroyed. While 77,000 people were arrested, just 38,000 were convicted.

Some think the bravado associated with committing illegal acts encouraged many rebellious teenagers to drink. Needless to say this atmosphere encouraged law breaking in the masses and created political hypocrisy. A criminal class comparable to today's drug trade was created.

This was the heyday of Al Capone and George (Bugs) Moran, a relationship that climaxed in the Valentine's Day Massacre in 1929. In one four-year period, Chicago recorded 215 unsolved murders. In 1927, Mr. Capone's income was said to have exceeded 104 million dollars, the largest personal, taxable income up to that date. Much of it was derived from illegal liquor trafficking.

In May of 1930, the U.S. Supreme Court ruled that buying illegal liquor did not violate the Constitution, a ruling that helped to take the teeth out of law enforcement. Both political parties blinked at the issue for one decade. The Republicans, strongest in rural communities and middle classes, stood behind President Hoover who called it "an experiment noble in motive and far reaching in purpose." Democrats were torn between Southern constituencies which were dry because prohibition was supposed to help keep Black Americans in order.

When President Hoover appointed a commission to investigate the success of how the law was being enforced, they brought back this confused report: "Federal Prohibition is unenforceable but should be enforced—that it is a failure—but should be retained." By 1932, many admitted the "noble experiment" was a complete failure. Even the Republicans favored a revision of the Amendment while the Democrats demanded outright repeal. Prohibition did have some effect on American drinking habits. In 1934, per capita consumption of pure alcohol for those 15 years and up was less than one gallon, a figure which rose to over two gallons ten years later.

Miscellaneous Short Stories

Earning an Oyster Supper

Most Milford natives have every right to be proud of the achievements of their recent high school football teams. Few sports teams in the school's history have duplicated the feats of the football teams of the past ten years. Although the town of Milford has been around for more than 135 years, high school football was added just 63 years ago in 1937. Prior to 1937, Milford football was more or less the type we would classify today as the "sand lot" variety, organized and played by super energetic teenage boys.

One local newspaper editor mentioned a game of this type being played with Dorchester in 1918. What some have designated as Milford's first noteworthy team was organized by some of the community's better known young male citizens in about 1900. Few, if any records are available to tell us who, when or where the games were played. While high school sponsored basketball is mentioned in Milford newspapers as early as 1917, Milford High School sponsored football is never mentioned prior to 1937.

One of the better basketball teams of the early 1900s included D. Eicher, K. Eicher, M. True, M. Lux, D. Buettgenbach, O. Williams, and D. Busboom. That group had enjoyed a terrific season. Evidently, many felt 1937 was the year to introduce another choice of sports for those not playing basketball, may be a sport designed more for the brawnier-type boys.

The Way It Was

This news note in the Sept. 9,1937, *Milford Review* must have thrilled Milford football lovers: "Football, newly added to the Milford athletic program got started Tuesday P.M. when 24 candidates donned their uniforms and went through a brief drill under coaches Baldwin and Williams. Some of the lads with plenty of size and weight are: Donald Conklin, Duane Findley, Roland Roberts, Keith Kenney, James Austin, Max Buettgenbach, Charles Gingerich, Robert Vogel, Leo Heyen, Gale Summers, Merle Ebers, Gerald Stutzman, Dale Conrad, and Earl Hutchinson. Others, who are smaller, but the fast type are: Carleton Casteel, Don Wilsey, Richard Aggen, Claude Trimble, Harley Danner, Boyd Heyen, Melvin Williams, Robert Bonn. Orville Wyman, and Glen Weaver. The schedule for this year will include: Friend, Cortland, Wilber, and Ulysses. Games with Seward Concordia Academy, College View and Lincoln High reserves may be added."

One week later we read more on the team's progress: "Friday night Oct. 1, a practice scrimmage was held under the flood lights on the local field with the Crete reserves. After a very ineffective first half, the local lads finally 'got their sea legs' and picked up the momentum—until two touchdowns were scored. The probable starting lineup for the Friend game will be: Conklin at left end, Buettengbach at left tackle, Austin at left guard, Summers at center, L. Heyen at right guard, Vogel at right tackle, Wilsey at quarterback, Roberts at left back, Casteel at right back and Findley at full back."

Hearing that Friend had several very talented players, the Milford coaches came up with a bold game plan: "We hope to put up an aerial as well as a powerful ground offense which will completely baffle the Friend team. We also hope to put up a stonewall defense."

The game proved to be a hard-fought contest. In the third quarter, Friend was able to score one touchdown and finally won the game 7-0. One interesting sidelight to Milford's first football game was the fact that Milford's senior physician, Dr. Wertman, suffered a stroke while watching the game. Wertman's right side was partially paralyzed, a disability from which he never completely recovered. The second game scheduled with Cortland was canceled because of a muddy field and rainy weather.

Meanwhile, the coaches made changes in the starting lineup for the next game with Concordia Academy. Roberts was shifted to fullback, Boyd Heyen was moved to half back, Conklin to left tackle and

Eldon Hostetler

Buettengbach to left end, while Leo Heyen and Austin were moved to guards. Concordia won the game by the score of 13-8.

Several times during the first season, the Milford team scrimmaged with the Crete High reserves on Wednesday evenings. The third game played with Wilber was a tough one, especially since no opponent had crossed Wilber's goal line up to this point. Wilber won the game 27-0. In the next game, Milford managed a 6-6 tie with the Beatrice reserves. College View also had a good team that season and beat Milford 34-6.

The second to the last game of the season was against a so-called "tough" Ulysses team that had lost only one game all season. Again Milford lost 0-6. The final game of the season against Bethany, (now part of Lincoln Northeast High School) proved too much for the inexperienced Milford players to handle. Bethany won 33-0.

Like all good sportswriters are supposed to do, the 1937 *Milford Review* sports editor summed up Milford's first-ever football season trying to sound optimistic in spite of a rather dismal record: "The first year of football has been completed and 17 players stuck with the program. Seniors lost for next year are: Aggen, Austin, Buettegnbach, Casteel, Conklin, Conrad, Leo Heyen, Kenny, Roberts, Stutzman and Vogel. Returning will be: Ebers, Findley, Summers, Wilsey and Boyd Heyen." (By the way, all games played at Milford were free admission.)

One year later in 1938, the team, now under the direction of new Head Coach Tonkin, started off with a bang by beating Friend 2-0 and Fairmont 12-0. The team appeared to go downhill from there, losing its third game to Eagle. Once more, the time came to challenge the "big, bad-boy type football neighbors" to the south in Wilber. Again the inexperienced Milford team was humiliated to the tune of 0-59. Milford also lost its fifth game of the season, 6-34 to a good College View team.

At this point in the season, it must have taken tremendous courage to tackle long-time neighbor and enemy to the north, Seward. Sure enough, the Milford eleven put up a terrific scrap before finally succumbing 0-25. In 1938, six boys played their final game: Gale Summers, Don Wilsey, Duane Findley, Merle Bender, Merle Ebers, and Boyd Heyen.

While I have no record of the 1939 season, the 1940 team lost their first game of the season to Exeter by a score of 6-0, again giving some indication they could be in for a losing season. After the defeat suffered at Exeter, Coach Harold Reeves was said to have made this promise: "Win the remaining games on our schedule, and I will treat you to a delicious oyster supper."

Maybe because this was in the days before pizza, or because they actually loved oysters, the team excepted the challenge. For whatever reason, they proceeded to win the next four games, allowing only one team to cross their goal line. By early November, the only obstacle standing in the way of their oyster supper was an Armistice Day game scheduled with a big, physical Seward team. Due to the deadly Armistice Day snow and sleet storm, the game was postponed to Thanksgiving Day.

The game proved to be one, huge defensive struggle, the majority of the game being played on Seward's half of the field. Recovering a fumble on the Seward five-yard line, Milford required three downs to punch the ball over the Seward goal line. This was to be the only score of the game. The *Milford Review* editor reported, "Although much the smaller team, Milford came out ahead by virtue of their fast, heads up football and their ability to make and cash in on the breaks."

Several weeks later this paid notice appeared in the *Milford Review*: "To the Milford Eagles: Congratulations Milford; You fought hard, and you won, You came to Seward with the cards staked against you. You were out-manned and you were out-weighed. You had to depend on your speed, and the field was slick, but you won. Some say you got the breaks. You did, but you made them. You played hard, fighting relentlessly, fighting doggedly, always fighting, and you won. You were pointing for this game and you worked hard to win. You had never beaten Seward, but this time you won. This is the third of what we hope will be a long series of well played games. This year the victory is yours. Next year who can tell. Maybe there will be a lasting friendship between our schools. We'll be seeing you on Armistice day in 1941: Your friendly opponents; The Blue Jays."

One week later, the Milford Eagles answered their friendly opponents with this notice: "Dear Opponents; We wish to thank you for your letter. We admire the sportsmanship the letter displays. Thank You; We'll see you at the Seward-Milford basketball game on Jan. 31, 1941- Milford Eagles."

Now hear the "rest of the story." On Jan. 31, 1941, the Eagles defeated the Seward basketball team 33 to 32. On Armistice day in

1941, the Milford football team defeated the Seward Blue Jay football team one more time.

The Milford boys truly earned—and enjoyed—their oyster supper.

Naughty Boys, Good Boys & Watermelons

Most Americans are familiar with the old cliché "Idleness is the devil's workshop." Nine times out of ten, whoever was responsible for authoring this statement was referring to energetic teenaged boys. It seems like society just assumes that whenever a group of normal, idle teenage boys get together to more or less just "hang- around," one or two will usually hatch up some new and devilish way to express and release this stored up energy. While this is just considered normal, it is not always released in a constructive fashion. The city of Lincoln recorded sixty plus acts of vandalism in the six days from January 3-9 of 2001. Court records in most cities report all-time highs in this crime, the majority being attributed to teenaged boys. Local and county court records would indicate that Milford area boys may be far above the national norm in their ability to keep out of trouble. In fact, it would appear they may be even more "angelic" than their counterparts of 50 to 115 years ago.

Now of course if you listen to Grandpa or Great-Grandpa tell his side of the story, you could get the idea that their generations consisted of all "good boys." However, early newspaper editors tell a somewhat different story. Now please—don't blame them for trying to hold back "questionable" details. Actually they may just have forgotten many of the smaller details associated with being naughty in their boyhood years. As early as 1884, the *Milford Ozone* editor was concerned that Milford boys were careless in the use of their slingshots. "They should be prohibited from our city, steps should be taken by the law."

Another complaint in the 1885 paper reported, "The parents of a certain bunch of boys better take heed, or I shall have to enforce the village ordinance as they are making a great deal of disturbance in public places (no other details are mentioned)."

Seems like the gals joined in on the "fun and naughtiness" in 1909: "We wonder if the young ladies and gentlemen going home from church and acting like hoodlums would like to have their names published and have their parents find out about their conduct. They should remember that darkness does not always hide their identity (*Milford Nebraskan*, 1904)."

This note published in the 1917 *Milford Review* not only reported a nasty incident, but it also revealed the editor's innermost attitudes and feelings: "Friday night some young fellows went to William Cars place and tore up his watermelon patch. The old fellow has put many hours of hard work in this project. Now these fellows deserve to have the 'cat' (ugly leather whip) applied to their backs, and salt rubbed into the wounds."

Yes, local teenaged boys have always had trouble with the sensible use of the so-called "sparkling, frothy beverage." One of the saddest incidents occurred in the Goehner community in 1894, when a seventeen-year-old boy died after being forced by companions to indulge.

But, Milford men dominated by far the news pertaining to the misuse of alcohol. Halloween pranks by local lads are also mentioned. One prank in 1931 resulted in five Milford boys spending one night in the Seward County jail. In my youthful days, "outhouse tipping" was the rage. If you are unfamiliar with the joys and challenges involved in this sport, please ask your grandpa for more details.

One "ornery boy story" recorded in 1931 has been passed down for nearly seventy years in the Hostetler family. My grandfather, Nathaniel Hostetler lived on a small acreage nine miles southwest of Milford, where he loved to garden and grow watermelons. One day in late August, a group of idle Milford boys who just happened to be "hanging around" in Cleave Tremble's Cigar Store hatched up what they thought would be real fun, mischievous plot. Older people tell me the store was located near the spot where Hackbarts Chiropractic Center stands today. Here local boys would gather for food, fun, fellowship, and various types of games.

This August day, one young blade suggested they stir up some excitement by raiding Nat Hostetler's watermelon patch. About six "naughty" Milford and Grover boys agreed to the idea and plans were made to do this exciting, fun job that night. As so often happens, they overlooked one small detail. The late Willie Hauder had somehow gotten wind of the proposed "naughtiness." Willie refused to join the party, but made a few plans of his own. Willie, and his younger brother, Harry, gathered up several friends, including one of Nathaniel's grandsons and together they, with the old family double barrel 12 gauge shotgun, were laying in wait when the "naughty" boys arrived at the melon patch.

Hiding behind the chicken house the "good" guys could hear the "naughty" boys coming. Since Grandpa was already in bed, they just assumed they were in control of the situation. About the time they were ready to enter the garden gate, Willie jumped up and fired two shots in the direction of the moon, being about eight feet away from the lead "bad boy" at the time. What happened next proved to be the real excitement of the evening. One "bad boy" fell flat on his face, while several ran straight for a gooey, mud bottom creek bed, plunging in up to their hips. Who knows what happened to the rest. Next day in Milford, one of the bad boys was heard to say over and over, "Boy! That old Nat Hostetler came so close to killing me. In fact, he only missed me by several feet." As for the rest of the story, grandpa, awakened by the shotgun blasts, came out and offered the "good boys" all the cold watermelon they could eat. (Author's Note: This story may not be correct in every detail. This version is as remembered by two of the eye witnesses on the occasion, Oliver Roth and Harry Hauder.)

What Happened to Herbert?

To most Milford natives, mention of the "dirty thirties" would trigger little emotion, while to others, it may bring back a flood of memories. To members of the Pete Oswald family, most of whom are now living in Illinois, mention of the 1930s may bring back some very sad and unpleasant memories, remembrances of a tragedy that has haunted the family for 64 years. The years from 1934 to 1940, often said to be the longest drought period in recorded history probably reshaped economic and living patterns for many older Milford residents. The year 1936 was very memorable for several reasons. Not only was it the driest year ever recorded, (about one half of normal rainfall) it also holds the record for the highest temperature ever recorded (115 degrees on July 25). Just for good measure, February of 1936 also proved to be one of the coldest months ever recorded. Since 1934 and 1935 were just as bad, Milford community farmers were experiencing financial difficulties probably not seen since the 1890s. While many farmers were still reeling from the low prices experienced after the 1929-33 stock market crash, the drought proved to be a double whammy to area farmers and business men alike. Few jobs outside of agriculture were available, consequently, those with large families to support were left with few financial resources. Many were forced to look to other states for jobs. Those who had relatives living in states where conditions were somewhat better were considered quite fortunate. Although most of the work available was seasonal, or migrant harvest jobs like threshing grain, husking corn, topping sugar beets, or picking up potatoes—it was work. Young people were just expected to go wherever work was available, returning with cash to help support their younger brothers and sisters.

By 1936, the Peter J. and Mary Ellen Oswald family was feeling the full effects of the two-year drought. At first the family lived on a farm five and one half miles south of Goehner, later moving to a farm seven miles west of Milford on Van Dorn Road. In March of 1936, twenty-one-year old Herbert Oswald traveled to near Amenia, North Dakota where he worked for his sister and brother-in-law (Ethel and Ben Roth). In early September, soon after finishing wheat harvest in North Dakota, Herbert and a friend named Isaac Mast heard that there might be work available in the sugar beet and potato fields near Glendive, Montana. Since little money was available, they decided to "hop" the freight train to Montana. Here they spent about one week searching for work that was evidently not available. Herbert wrote a letter to his parents telling them that since they were unable to find work in Montana, he would soon start for home, stopping in North Dakota for one week before returning to Nebraska.

About the time his parents received the letter in Nebraska, Isaac returned to his home in North Dakota and reported; "I lost Herb somewhere in Montana." He reported that when they were attempting to board the train he asked: "Herb are you on?" and thought he had heard Herb answer "Yes." What actually happened at the time of this boarding has remained a troubling mystery for sixty-four years. Herbert Oswald was never seen or heard from again. It has been said that Herbert was carrying $60 in cash (about two months wages in that day) which he had intended to give to his parents. He was not reported missing to police until his parents (who were now living on a farm near Dorchester) arrived in North Dakota. For many years the Oswald family prayed, searched, waited, and hoped for their son to return.

In 1937, the four older children moved to Illinois and found employment near Hopedale. In 1940, Pete, Mary, and the younger children said good-bye to their Nebraska friends and relatives and joined their older children in the Hopedale community, the same place where Pete was born in 1886. Pete Oswald died in 1957, and Mary Ellen in 1987 without ever knowing what happened to their son Herbert.

Herbert was born within one mile of my birth place in the Beaver Crossing community. I remember Herbert well and attended country school with several of his younger sisters. Two of Herbert's first cousins, Dale and Ron Oswald, are well known in the Milford community. My thanks to eighty-four-year-old Don Oswald, (younger brother of Herbert) for furnishing me with some little known facts regarding this story. Don and his wife Bernice are presently living in Morton, Illinois.

Beautiful—But Deadly

Early visitors were much impressed with the scenic beauty surrounding Milford, especially the clear water in the Blue River. Years of dirty silt generated by careless use of farm ground helped to change the character of the river. A news note in the 1875 *Seward Reporter* said, "The stereoscopic views taken by Mr. Young embracing many beautiful scenes along the Blue River are finding ready sales."

Early Milford historian Maude Wertman realized the river scenery was pretty, but also agreed it did pose a threat. Wertman said, "For many years we have enjoyed our beautiful Blue River. Many of us remember moonlit boat rides, skating and swimming parties, and also long walks along the shady banks. But there is a gloomy side, since many of us remember when this beautiful river became vicious and claimed the lives of our children."

The fact that the river has not claimed any lives recently may be attributed to two factors. First, the river itself has changed and, second, it is no longer used extensively for fishing and recreational purposes.

The first Blue River dam, built in 1866-67, was replaced by a higher dam in 1883. This dam raised the water level fourteen feet, backing up water for three miles and creating Lake Quenchauqua. One of the best boating, fishing and swimming lakes around, it was used by many Lincoln people. In 1885 the water was said to be eight feet deep for more than one half mile.

When the 1883 dam washed out in 1901, it was replaced by the concrete dam still partially visible north of Milford's grain elevator. This eight foot channel prompted wealthy investors to purchase a little steam ship known as the *Laura M.* One Hastings visitor visited the town in 1888 and said, "Bathing facilities are excellent, children and adults indulging in daily baths, there sometimes being fifty or more persons in the river at once."

Today, no ordinary citizen would even think of swimming in the Blue, especially if you had a choice of using the town swimming pool. Nor would you feel comfortable using Blue River water for your quarterly or annual bath—like many did in the "good old days."

The first recorded drowning occurred in December of 1874. "On Wednesday afternoon about 4 p.m., shortly after being released from school, Walter Haverstock, age 10, Charlie Haverstock age 8, and Oliver Maston age 8, attempted to cross the ice on the Mill Pond on their way home. Walter and Charlie both drowned while Oliver was rescued and survived. The following Sunday, the Congregational church, the largest church in town, was not able to hold all who attended the funeral services." The Haverstock brothers' tombstone may be seen in Blue Mound Cemetery, one of the oldest stones in the cemetery.

The next recorded drowning occurred in the West Blue near West Mills in 1881. This drowning also involved an eight year old boy. "Nicholas, the eight-year-old son of Joseph Burkey, drowned in the West Blue River on December 18, 1881. The young boy had stayed in the home of his brother-in-law, Joseph Gascho, over night. On the morning of the 18th, he, along with Gascho's son started for home one and one-half miles distant. Before starting, Gascho had warned the boys to use the bridge in crossing the Blue but young Burkey was determined to use a boat. When they were near the shore they determined the boat was about to sink and young Burkey jumped out and drowned. After a search of 28 hours the body was recovered. Services were held in the Amish church conducted by P. P. Hershberger and Joseph Schlegel. The Burkey family had just moved to Nebraska from Illinois in August (*The Herald of Truth,* January 15, 1882)." This drowning took place near the spot where Don and Linda Burkey live today. Nicholas was my mother's uncle.

The third recorded drowning also occurred in the West Blue somewhere in the same vicinity in August of 1882. The details concerning this drowning were recorded by J. R. Stauffer, and published in an August issue of the *Herald of Truth* magazine. "A serious accident occurred on the Fourth of July in that one of our brethren was unexpectedly called home to eternity. Several brethren went to the West Blue to fish. Joseph Beckler got into deep water and he sank and rose no more. He was not found until death had set her seal. The doctor said he had suffered a paralytic stroke of the heart. This is a sad occurrence for the family as he leaves a wife and six children. The church also lost a useful member, since he had just been chosen as Sunday school superintendent."

Used by hundreds of people for boating, swimming and fishing from 1874 to the time when the Salt Creek Watershed dams were finished, you might think more people would have drowned in the Blue Rivers. Compiled from several sources, mostly newspapers and early history books, this list does not include the age and date, or give details in all cases. The next victim of which we have a detailed story is recorded in the December 11, 1911 *Milford Nebraskan.* "Seventy-eight year old John D. Troyer drowned Sunday afternoon in the Blue River two miles south of Milford. He was camped near the river trapping, and had attempted to cross the river on ice made rotten by the warm weather. He was discovered by Jake Boshart's boy who noticed his rifle laying on the ice and soon gathered a group of men who retrieved the body in sixteen feet of water."

Several old soldiers living at Milford's Soldiers Home were drowned about this time. James Arnell died on Sunday afternoon April

The Way It Was

13, 1913, and John Cavanaugh on December 3, 1913. Another young boy, Tim Lacker, fell in the river near Milford while fishing on June 15, 1901 and drowned. Several other drowning victims are mentioned by Maud Wertman, although dates are not given.

"Little Nellie Trimble, three-year-old daughter of Mr. and Mrs. Trimble, who wandered too near the banks, fell in and gave up her life," Wertman said. The second child she mentions is the small daughter of Mr. and Mrs. Kearns, who wandered away from home, came too close to the river and drowned. In 1902, the ten-year-old son of F. S. Johnson, owner of the Milford Mill and Milford Bank drowned while skating on thin ice. Wertman also mentions another near drowning that must have taken place around 1900. "Another small boy, Guy Pumphery, fell into the river near the mill dam. He, too, would have drowned had it not been for a mill hand, Mr. John Wright, brother of Riley Wright, who saw what happened from a window. John ran fully clothed and jumped into the water after him. After a very strenuous workout he was able to revive the boy and the child was spared." Mr. Pumphery was in charge of the Milford railroad depot for many years. Wriley Wright owned one of the first jewelry stores in Milford. My guess would be that these deaths took place from 1890-1900.

Two additional tragedies occurred in the West Blue near dam number seven located about seven miles southwest of Milford. Thirty-four-year-old Charles Mills of Lincoln drowned on July 9, 1936, and Alexander Schufeldt from the Friend area drowned on July 21, 1938. Fifty-three-year-old Walter Sulfine, who lived in a cabin south of town drowned in August of 1946 when he accidentally stepped in a deep hole while searching for clams.

Those drowning in the West Blue in the Beaver Crossing vicinity would include: Emil Martsen, said to be a "young man" on June 19, 1898; Clifford Heizart, age 15 in August of 1899; William T. Jarks age 17, a resident of Dunbury, Nebraska on July 7, 1911; Leonard Weibly, age 34 from Cordova on July 8, 1893; Carl Mortenson and Clayton Larson from Cordova, who were spearing carp two miles west of town on June 2, 1918. Six-year-old Merwin Tucker, son of Mr. and Mrs. C. B. Tucker, drowned when he slipped down a bank while the family was picnicking west of Beaver Crossing on July 19, 1914.

One drowning I will never forget happened west of Beaver Crossing on May 12, 1942, when Raymond Paul Trojan, thirteen-year-old son of John and Rose Trojan, drowned in a flooded creek during high water on the West Blue. The last drowning recorded in the West Blue happened about eighteen years ago when two men from the Friend area drowned west of town during high water.

One of the last drownings to be recorded in the Milford area took place on July 12, 1933, just below the Mill Dam, probably during high water. Marvin C. Johnson, his three-and-one-half year son Dicky, John Morrow, Kenneth Schriner, and Henry Rank all of Lincoln were boating on the river. They were rowing up the river to satisfy the whim of little Dicky, who wanted to see the water tumbling over the dam at close range. Having just turned around to go back, their boat hit a submerged log, causing it capsize and throw all five in the water. John Morrow, a Nebraska Wesleyan freshman and an excellent swimmer who had recently passed the Red Cross life saving test, was able to save Schriner and little Richard Johnson, but was unable to rescue Henry Rank and Marvin Johnson because of exhaustion and lack of time. An eyewitness to these drownings told me recently that several men from the Milford community helped to rescue the small boy. A call for help brought the Crete Lifesaving Corps and all their equipment to the scene, although they were already too late. The bodies were not recovered until late the following day. While local people still drown in the vicinity, most deaths occur in artificial lakes or farm ponds.

Early Hunting & Fishing Stories

"Oscar Ragan, another of the first businessmen of Utica, settled on Lincoln Creek as early as 1867. We must tell a little story of him that demonstrates the hardships of pioneer life. Mr. Ragan was very poor when he located on his homestead, as were all his neighbors. Often the entire settlement would get very short of provisions and at times the family would be without meat for long periods. The elk and antelope had all taken their departure, but Oscar thought he must have meat, and so he went hunting. A long day's tramp and nothing could be found except a chicken hawk. Oscar said to himself, 'We're out of meat. Now I don't know how hawk will taste, but I have heard of politicians eating crow. Guess it will be all right.' So he takes the hawk home and prepares it for the next day's dinner. A nice hawk pie was prepared, and, since Oscar was a generous soul, some of his neighbors were invited to the feast. His good wife had made all things ready, and the guests were seated, with Oscar at his place at the head of the table. Each person was served with a plate of the dainty dish, and all commenced eating at the same time. One mouthful partially swallowed, and Oscar, with a heaving breast, found it necessary to find his way to the door. The hawk showed great discontent in his stomach. Oscar was quickly followed by his guests, but they were not going to see what was the matter with Oscar. They each had serious business of their own to look after. Oscar has always, since that dinner experience, wondered how it can be that men can eat crow without wincing, as so many politicians have to do. He is quite sure that he will never again hanker after a hawk pie (*History of Seward County*, W. W. Cox, pg. 56)."

This "king-sized" fish tale was recorded in the 1887 *Milford Nebraskan* as told by the Beaver Crossing correspondent. "Last week the Pearl Mill wheel was not working properly. Mr. Powell shut the water out of the race to examine the wheel to see if he could discover the trouble. He found no less than 407 turtles and about as many catfish caught in the wheel. After their removal, the wheel worked fine again."

"William Brokaw killed an elk with his pocket knife; It was tired out from running in the deep snow (*Blue Valley Record*, Dec. 1871)."

"Twenty-one year old Valentine Springer, who lived north of Milford, was found dead in the Blue River near his home. He had gone duck hunting and had been riding in a boat. The opinion was that he had lain his gun down, and on picking it up to leave the boat, it accidentally discharged striking him in the face (*Milford Review*, Oct. 3, 1915)."

"Our bankers a hunting did go and about two miles above town tried to cross the Blue on the ice. Banker George Sallidin broke through, and the river bottom foreclosed on his shot-gun (*Milford Nebraskan*, April 17, 1899)."

"Riley Wright lugged up three big carp from the river one day last week weighing about 13 pounds each (*Milford Nebraskan*, June 2, 1899)."

Eldon Hostetler

"John Logan, who lives near Utica, comes to town once in a while to show the local boys how to fish. Last week he caught a pickerel weighing in at nine pounds (from the Beaver Crossing correspondent, printed in the *Milford Nebraskan*, Sept 17, 1886)."

Changes in Community Mores

"Most of southeast Nebraska and the whole state west of Lincoln, was open range in 1871, but about 1876, a whole flock of settlers took over the country. There were other people besides cowboys in the state in the seventies, but not the kind that could influence a boy. The settlers were very religious and narrow-minded. I remember once when me and Harry went fishing on Sunday, we caught a big catfish. One neighbor saw us and had us arrested, and father had to pay a five-dollar fine *(We Pointed Them North*, Abbot and North, pgs. 49 - 54)."

If you are under seventy-five, you probably have no idea how community mores have changed in the past seventy-five years. Webster defines the word mores as "folk ways of central importance accepted without question and embodying the fundamental moral views of a social group." He defines moral as "pertaining to, or concerned with the principles of right conduct or the distinction between right and wrong."

This little episode, taken from the April 17, 1899 *Milford Nebraskan*, not only reflects community mores in vogue one hundred years ago, it also serves as an introduction to our topic.

"A farmer living near Seward erred in his reckoning and drove into Milford on Sunday morning with his hayrack to buy feed. He soon returned home with downcast conscience and it was a big joke on him, but, it also shows Milford is a civilized and Christianized community." Was the editor trying to say Milford citizens were just a little more civilized and Christianized because its businessmen closed down their stores on Sunday?

In the February 16, 1900 edition of the *Milford Nebraskan*, one prominent citizen questioned this assumption. "Is it right? Can a Christian conscientiously say while using tobacco, 'God bless me'?

The Way It Was

Would Jesus indulge in the filthy habit? Is it right to spend more for tobacco than for saving the heathen?"

In 1900, just like today, everyone had his own opinion as to what true morality is, or how Sunday (known today as the weekend) should, or should not be spent. Sunday could be described as a day set apart by most Christian denominations similar to the seventh day Sabbath observed by Old Testament Jews. Rules governing Sunday observance were formulated as early as A.D. 330 when Emperor Constantine issued a decree warning Christian people to rest from their ordinary vocations on Sunday. He did, however, exempt farmers.

During Queen Elizabeth's reign in England, Sunday church attendance was made obligatory with the decree, "Every person shall report to his parish church on Sunday on pain that each person so offending shall forfeit for every offense 12 pence to be levied by the church warden for every offense to be used for the poor of the same parish." This law was not repealed until 1846.

The first Sabbath law in America was passed by the Virginia Colony in 1617. Anyone failing to attend church on the Lord's Day was subjected to a fine payable in tobacco. A Connecticut law passed about the same time stated that no person could leave his residence on the Lord's Day unless going to or from church.

As you might suspect, early New England Puritan forefathers had it all figured out. Strict standards of decorum were set for almost every situation in life, including Sabbath observance. Householders were also encouraged to spy on their neighbors and report any breach of conduct to church elders. A body of stern "Blue Laws" banned both labor and "frivolity" on the Sabbath. These laws probably reached their zenith in 1656 when a Boston sailor was forced to spend two hours in the public stocks. His big transgression occurred after returning from a three-year absence at sea and kissing his wife in a public place on the Sabbath. Early Milford citizens were encouraged by county and city rules-expected to be enforced by the law—to keep the Sabbath holy. In 1883, for example, Milford city fathers were rather "crabby" concerning the types of recreational activities allowed on Sunday, stating, "We will not allow any recreational activities or excursions to be held on Shogo Island picnic grounds on Sunday (*Milford Ozone*,1884)." A news item in the June 1913, *Milford Review* mentions another problem solved: "The matter of Sunday baseball was brought before the County Board of Supervisors. By a vote of 5 to

1, the privilege of playing baseball on Sunday was granted only if an officer of the law was present."

Changes in Milford community mores in the past hundred years regarding Sunday observance might translate to something like the tobacco ads aimed at American women in the 1950s: "You have come a long way baby, you are now liberated, so go ahead, puff away on your extra slim, specially made for women cigarettes—whenever and wherever you wish!"

Parable of the Tobacco Seed

The recent "tobacco controversy" resulting in billions of dollars being awarded to the states by the courts is not really new, since tobacco use has been suspect for many years. First discovered by our European ancestors when Columbus met up with the "fire brand smoking" Carib Indians of Cuba, its popularity spread rapidly throughout the so-called "civilized" world. Used at first for religious ceremonies, the Spaniards named it after the Tobago pipe, a Y-shaped hollow cane used by the Natives to snuff powdered tobacco up their nostrils. Following the example of Native Americans who used a variety of roots and herbs for healing purposes, Europeans were anxious to experiment with the newly discovered herb. English physician John Josselyn, who made several trips to America to explore tobacco's medicinal value said, "The virtues of tobacco are these: It helps digestion, the gout, toothaches and infections... It heats the cold and cools them that sweat, feedeth the hungry, restoreth the spirit, purgeth the stomach and killeth nits and lice (*Story of America, Reader's Digest*)."

At the suggestion of her Ambassador to Portugal Jean Nicat, Catherine deMedicia, Queen of France, popularized the use of tobacco for health purposes in 1561. It's chief active chemical component known by the Spanish as "nicatiana" was named after Mr. Nicat. Today, what we now know as nicotine is said "to be good for its depressant action on vital nerve centers and is effectively used in the destruction of insect pests." Those of you over seventy may remember the poisonous tobacco product known as *Black Leaf Forty* we used to kill the ticks and mites that insisted on living in chicken houses.

First grown in Virginia around 1612, tobacco proved to be America's number one agricultural export for 150 years. Used for chewing and snuff for many years, after the Civil War cigars, cigarettes, and pipes became popular. Although tobacco use spread quickly worldwide, some countries fought its introduction for many years—one country as late as 1895. Several countries enacted stiff penalties, one as severe as death for the third offense. Contrary to what many "old-timers" told me about the days when nearly everyone used the weed, tobacco use was considered a health threat—as well as a public nuisance—for many years. This little essay printed in a 1907 Church paper tells the story (author unknown).

"Them shall the Kingdom of Satan be likened to a tobacco seed, which, though exceedingly small, being cast into the ground became a great plant and spread it's leaves rank and broad, so that huge vile worms formed an habitation thereon. And it came to pass, in the course of time, that the sons of men looked upon it and thought it beautiful to look upon and much to be desired to make lads look big and manly. So they did put forth their hands and did chew thereof. And some it made sick and others to vomit most filthy. And it further came to pass that those who chewed it became weak and unmanly and said; 'We are now enslaved and cannot cease chewing it.' And the mouths of those who used it became foul, and they were seized with violent spitting; and they did even spit in the ladies' parlors and in the house of the Lord, and the saints of the Most High were greatly plagued thereby. And in the course of time it came to pass that others snuffed it and they were taken suddenly with fits, and they did sneeze a great and mighty sneeze, inasmuch that their eyes were filled with tears and they did look exceedingly silly. And others cunningly wrought the leaves into rolls and did set fire to the one end thereof, and did suck vehemently at the other end and did look very silly and calf-like, and the smoke of their torment ascended up like a fog. And the cultivation thereof became a great and mighty business in the earth and the merchants waxed rich by the commerce thereof. And it came to pass that the professed saints of the Most High defiled themselves therewith; even the poor, who could not buy shoes, nor bread, nor books for their little ones, spent their money for it. And the Lord was greatly displeased therewith and said; 'Be ye clean that bear the vessels of the Lord.' Let us cleanse ourselves from all filthiness of the flesh. Wherefore come ye out from among them and be ye separate, saith the Lord, and touch not the unclean thing, and I will receive you. But with one accord they exclaimed; 'We cannot cease from chewing, puffing, and snuffing."

In 1899, the editor of the *Milford Nebraskan* wrote, "Please do not smoke in our office, as it is very offensive to those at work and those visiting here."

Deadly World Plagues

Advanced medical science and miracle drugs invented in the last fifty years may have caused many to forget the life and death struggles faced by our forefathers. One of the most tragic diseases to ever hit the United States exploded in 1918-19, or about the time World War I was winding down. This disease, known as the Spanish Flu, was short lived but deadly. Lasting less than three years, is said to have killed more people in a shorter period of time than any other documented plague in history. Five thousand Nebraska natives died in this epidemic, most in the fall of 1918 and early winter of 1919.

Disastrous, plague-type diseases have always been considered a part of man's lot on earth, one of the deadliest being the Plague of Justinian. This plague, which peaked from A.D. 542-558, raged for over one hundred fifty years. Named after the great Byzantine emperor Justinian who was reigning in Constantinople at the time, this plague is said to have killed more than 100 million people before finally subsiding. During the height of the epidemic one early historian reported that 5,000 people died every day in the city of Constantinople, eventually killing half of the city's population.

Another plague, often referred to as Black Death is said to have been the most virulent bubonic and pneumonic disease ever recorded in human history. Arriving from Asia about 1347, the disease had completed its sweep through Europe by 1350. Successive waves continued to haunt Europe until 1398. It has been estimated that about 67 percent of those living in the civilized world at that time were stricken, causing an estimated 25 million deaths. Those that didn't perish were often left wretched cripples.

While the above two plagues are the best known, other lesser known plagues devastated parts of the world. One plague hitting China around 1880 caused an estimated 13 million deaths, while as late as 1896 to 1933 at least 12 million died from a similar plague in India. In the year 1907 alone, 1.3 million died.

Hampered by medical ignorance and handicapped by years of religious and superstitious traditions, medical help was practically nonexistent and complete recovery was rare. The most deadly of the early plagues, the highly contagious pneumonic type, was characterized by high fever, spitting of blood, followed by death within three days. At this time, the medical profession was not aware the disease was being spread from country to country by the common household rat, along with their friendly fleas. Unable to find a cause or a cure for the disease, some even blamed the Jewish people for the cause of their misery.

For several hundred years following the Black Death, the United States and Europe appeared to be relatively free from serious, prolonged plagues. In an average year, 20,000 Americans are expected to succumb to some type of influenza-related disease. The earlier mentioned worldwide epidemic of 1918-19 is said to have killed an estimated 21 million people worldwide—550,000 in United States alone. The disease called the Spanish Flu is thought to have originated in Spain.

The first reported cases of Spanish Flu surfaced March 1918 at the Fort Riley Army Base in Kansas. Additional cases were soon reported in many other military camps and the disease quickly followed American troops to Europe. By August the disease was reported in most countries of the world. By late September the disease reached Nebraska, the first victim being a University of Nebraska student from Omaha.

October proved to be deadly month in many Nebraska communities. Omaha authorities closed all schools and theaters, banned public gatherings and ordered that caskets of all victims be sealed. Many other communities and cities soon followed, while a statewide ban on public gatherings was imposed on October 21. Wyuka cemetery in Lincoln was forced to declare a one day holiday, needed to give gravediggers a chance to catch up.

Eldon Hostetler

The new flu came on victims suddenly. Starting with a high fever of up to 105 degrees, sore throat, runny noses, and severe headaches, those unfortunate enough to develop pneumonia usually died.

One indication of the flu's devastation in Seward County could be determined by analyzing causality figures during World War I. From a total of twenty-six Seward County causalities, seven were killed in action, two died from wounds, one from an accident and sixteen from disease. Milford suffered three wartime causalities—all from disease (*Early Days in Seward County*, W. M. H. Smith).

While many families escaped without deaths, others were devastated. A most tragic story was reported from the Wood River community as experienced by a family who had recently moved there from Milford. This death notice printed in the February 20, 1919 *Gospel Herald* tells the sad story: "32-year-old Joseph Schweitzer was born near Milford, Nebraska on Nov. 18, 1887 and died in his home located near Wood River, Nebraska on Jan. 24, 1919. His wife, Minerva (Stutzman) Schweitzer (age 30) died on Jan. 11, their son, Ervan, (age 9) died on Jan. 13, his brother, Peter, (age 22 and still living with the family) died on Jan. 12, and his sister Angie, (age 20) died on Jan. 30. All died from the same disease—influenza followed by pneumonia. The above were laid to rest in the Wood River Mennonite cemetery, but on account of the disease and the fact that others in the family and many of the relatives had the same disease, services were not held until February 2, 1919."

Now, wouldn't it be great if we could just sweep several thousand years of history under the rug and numb ourselves into believing it could not happen again? Modern day demographers tell us that by 2016, seven billion people will be jockeying for less and less world resources, especially fresh water. While plagues like smallpox, diphtheria, typhus, polio, tuberculosis and Spanish Influenza are now under control, (at least in America) how many really want to hear the "rest of the story?"

The Way It Was
Before Bathroom Plumbing

Remember the last time your grandchildren stayed at your house for the night...how they seemed to tax your shower and bath facilities? Remember how they ran the hot water for what seemed to you like an eternity, or until you thought you could hear your poor old water heater groaning and begging for mercy? Now, that was just before they retired for the night. Do you recall the words you muttered to grandma the following morning when they repeated the same procedure? "Just how did they get so dirty over night? I vividly remember seeing you change the sheets yesterday." And then you reminded her one more time about life in the "good old days" and how you always managed to get by on 50 kilowatt hours of electricity per month. Maybe our grandchildren are just trying to make up for the baths their grandparents never had, or are they really more dedicated to cleanliness? Or maybe we were just a wee bit lax in personal grooming habits?

Few children of the so called "Yuppie" generation realize how and why personal grooming habits have changed in the past seventy years. B. P. (before plumbing) few homes enjoyed anything that even looked like a bathtub, especially farm homes, since few had electricity before the early 1940s. Some farm families fortunate enough to be living near town may have had power before 1920.

Now it has been said that good old Grandpa Schrock never used a bathtub in all of his ninety years, although he did bathe in a wash basin. This appeared to be the standard procedure for most children before 1940. The older generation may remember the old Saturday night "wash tub" ritual. Saturday night was always bath time, need it or not. For many families the same galvanized tub used to mix the pork sausage at butchering time was also the family bathtub. Why Saturday night? From way back I somehow caught the message that Sunday was the day to meet and mingle with strangers. Consequently your mother always wanted you to look and smell your very best.

For the benefit of the younger, more squeamish readers—no, the water was not changed after each bath, which usually set in motion a mad dash to be first. Now, of course, in the winter you did your very best to skip the colder months, especially if the water reservoir in the cook stove was covered with ice. Even if you skipped several weeks, it was no big deal. After all, English historians tell us that one queen of England did not bathe for five years. She just greased her skin with bear tallow. Most medical experts in that day considered bathing very harmful, since they felt it washed away essential, friendly skin oils and bacteria. Not to change the subject but, did you ever smell a bear up close, or even non-refrigerated bear tallow?

Now if you think my generation may have been just a mite lax in grooming habits, history tells us that several generations before they may have been even less concerned about their personal appearance. A news note in the 1886 *Milford Nebraskan* carried this advice from the editor: "Well we see that Barber, J. A. Kolar has again filled up the bathtub in his shop. Down in the deep recesses of our heart, we hope, we trust, and we pray that certain individuals will go in and at least wash their feet."

Some even used Blue River water to clean up for the Saturday night dance or that special Saturday night date. This note from the 1895 Beaver Crossing paper reported a narrow escape. "Miss Alta Eager, and Abbie Maul (girls from two of the town's wealthiest families) along with several other girls were bathing in the Blue River Saturday. They wandered too far away into deep water and had a very close call indeed."

During my teenaged years one of the favorite spots to clean up after threshing was located on the Jake Erb farm (now owned by Ken Chab) about a half-mile from my place. Here a dirty, smelly bunch of tired threshers often gathered to clean up. I remember one gent who always appeared with a bar of soap and a clean towel. And scrub his body he did, probably assuming he went home "hygienically" clean. Well, maybe he did and maybe he didn't. After all, the West Fork of the Blue carried some very "used" tired water from several questionable sources, like the sewer systems of Hastings, Harvard, York, Sutton, McCool Junction, and Beaver Crossing as well as several smaller towns.

For those without bathtubs and not blessed with Blue River water like I was, one more option was always available. This was to rent the bathtub in the local barbershop. Now this arrangement worked out pretty well, since you usually needed a haircut about every four to five weeks. Of course, if you were getting married or wanted to celebrate some other special occasion you probably needed to break your rhythm. While I well remember the days when most barber shops had a sign offering baths for 20 cents, I really don't ever remember seeing anyone taking advantage of the tub. One reason may have been the money. For years and years the price of a haircut at Jake Hubertus's three chair Barbershop in Beaver Crossing was 20 cents. Now, during the "dirty thirties" who in the world would have had the 20 cents to "blow" on a questionably needed bath, especially since it could just as well be postponed until the next hair cut? After all, in that day, I'm sure many subscribed to the philosophy, that a neat haircut is always quite noticeable, while a decision not to spend 20 cents for a bath not really needed could only be detected by a smell, shall we say kind'a like "rancid bear tallow."

Folk Medicine and Faith Healing

Webster defines folk medicine as, "Health practices arising from cultural traditions, from empirical use of native remedies, especially food substances, or from superstition." While we like to think of the sophisticated, medical-wise generation of today as far removed from cultural tradition or superstition, you may be surprised to learn how folk medicine and family tradition has helped to shape ideas about medicine and health care.

Now speaking just to the old timers—remember how grandmother warned you about stepping outside in the cold air with wet hair or without something on you head, or with bare feet, or how quickly you could die if you continued to eat green apples? Did your family observe the old traditional practice that *everybody's* bowels need a good "purging" at least once a week?

An advertisement in the May 20, 1919 *Milford Review* helped to affirm the credibility of this time tested tradition: "Cools the stomach, washes out the bowels, drives out impurities, helps the liver, it's Hollister Rocky Mountain Tea; take it once a week and see how happy and contented you will be." And that's the final answer!

Or this gem of wisdom from a July 1877, newspaper widely read in the Milford community. "For diphtheria the following is a good cure, is cheap and easily obtained: Take gum phosphorus and yellow sulfur of each a teaspoon full and mix with sufficient honey to make a

Eldon Hostetler

paste to swab the throat. If you should swallow some it will do no injury; then take red pepper tea and gargle the throat. This is said to have cured cases given up by doctors."

How many remember being told peppermint or sassafras tea was great to purify the blood, in fact practically a necessity, especially after a long hard winter? I will never forget the day my grandmother insisted I sit down at her table and eat a half-pound box of comb honey, because she said "it's the best cure for a cold." Most of us might be surprised to know how attitudes toward medicine have been shaped by old folk medicine cures, or family traditions handed down from generation to generation.

Another very controversial method of so-called healing practiced in the Milford community by some early Amish Mennonite settlers was a system of incantations or sometimes incorrectly called powwowing; the correct term in Pennsylvania Dutch being "Braucherei." The formulae used was supposed to possess some magical qualities, to promote faith healing. The practice is thought to have originated in medieval Europe, possibly before the Reformation. References to the Virgin, saints, archangels, and the use of an abundance of Latin words would suggest an early Catholic origin. According to the theory, this "healing gift" was handed down from a male to a female and then in turn to another male. Visiting evangelists holding meetings in the community often "blasted" local church members across the pulpit for indulging in the practice. Although the practice was discouraged by many in the Mennonite Church, some older people would probably attest to authentic cures.

The April 24, 1930 edition of the *Milford Review* carried this news story. "Much interest is shown in the work of Mr. and Mrs. Harry Peterson who are supposed to be miraculously endowed with the power of healing. Since locating in Beaver Crossing numbers of testimonials from people who have been treated by them recommend them highly. The Peterson's will be in Milford April 25, to May 3, and will take care of any who may require their services at the home of E. M. Bender." (The Benders owned and operated a Boarding House.)

Later, this ad appeared in the local paper: "'Christian Healing.' Come and be healed by the laying on of hands. We treat any sickness, or disease. Harry and Enola Peterson; Beaver Crossing."

This type of healing was actually "old hat" in the Milford community. From 1905-25 special evangelistic and camp meetings often featuring speakers dedicated to the art of healing were held in the community. Some meetings lasted more than six weeks.

Around 1910, some "Egli" Mennonites (now Missionary, or Assembly of God) decided they no longer needed doctors basing their decision on a literal interpretation of James 5:14. A few literally suffered the consequences of death for loved ones, rather than violate their conscience by calling for the aid of a physician in times of sickness.

A Tribute to Pioneer Women

by W. W. Cox

"The mothers and wives of the pioneers are justly entitled to kind remembrance. They were devoted and self-sacrificing beyond measure. The labor they performed and the hardships they endured should live in the hearts of the people to the remotest generation. Here is a picture of the overdrawn; A young bride of twenty has left her father's home of comfort and luxury in the East, and with her young husband has turned her face towards the setting sun, with the determination to assist him in hewing out a new home in the wildness of the West. With no capital except a strong resolution to win and a strong faith in the future, they bid adieu to friends and kindred, and with a steady eye fixed upon the star of empire they penetrate the wilderness. A little log cabin or a sod house or a dugout has been hastily built for shelter. A parlor, sitting room, kitchen and bedroom are all combined in one. The bare walls of this crude home brought in contrast in the mind he young wife with the beautiful home of her childhood, but in her young breast 'hope is like an anchor to the soul.'

"When the first Sabbath dawns she may listen in vain for the sweet chimes of the church-going bell, but looking out on the broad prairie, all is solitary. Sometimes with heaviness of heart she labors on, and cheers the heart of her faltering husband in his endeavors. The little means they have brought are rapidly melting away before any return for their labor is in sight. The beautiful garments of her youth are fading and become tattered. By and by she becomes a mother, and while the beautiful gift from heaven may bring joy and gladness, yet in the same train it brings anxieties and sorrows, a constant care by day and by night.

"The young father must sometimes go long distances from home, to be gone for days at a time, to a mill fifty or a hundred miles away, or to a city far away, and the young mother and her darling must stay weary days and long nights in the lonely home with no protector but her God. And now comes a strolling band of hungry Indians to frighten and annoy her, and while her child is screaming with fright she must stand in the door and face these strangers. She must frequently leave her child to cry, while she goes long distances after the cows, or to a distant spring for water, or carry the baby on her arm and a heavy bucket of water. Then again harvest time comes or something else occurs when several work hands must be provided for, when, with scanty means at command she must carry the babe upon her arm and with the other do the work of cooking for the hands. And again when night comes she must divide her bed and make beds for the men on the cabin floor as her husband keeps a 'free' hotel for all strangers, she must deny herself and little ones ease and comfort to wait upon strangers, and frequently makes her children wait at meal time, while strangers eat their bread, mother and the children make their meal from the scraps.

"This is no fancy sketch, it has occurred ten thousand times, of which there are plenty of living witnesses. Oh! who but a mother can tell of the weariness of a mother's life on the frontier; so often struggling to keep the wolf from the door, so often beset with dangers, so often overworked with slavish labor, and so often overwrought with anxious care. No wonder that untimely gray hair appear, and that her cheeks are furrowed while she should yet be in the prime of her womanly strength and beauty. Young men and maidens of Nebraska, you that have such pleasant homes today, will you please remember what it cost your mothers in years gone by to prepare those homes for you. In your grateful hearts will you In a becoming manner reverence and love them? If you can fully realize what they have done for you, in your imagination it will surround their gray heads with grace and beauty, intermingled with a halo of holy light (*History of Seward County*, W. W. Cox, pp. 166-167).

The Way It Was

Prose or Poetry

While a handful of Seward county citizens may enjoy opera or classical music, others enjoy country western, rock, jazz, or you name it. The same may be true regarding the form of literature that "turns you on." Comparing prose and poetry, Webster says that "prose is the ordinary form of spoken or written language often dull, or commonplace, without metrical structure," while poetry is described as "literary work in metrical form characterized by a highly developed form of and the use of heightened language and rhythm." Remember how we old timers were encouraged to learn some of the so called old "classic" poems by memory when we were in grade school? In fact, I can still quote several of these classics by memory. Throughout my life time I have had little desire to express myself through the medium of poetry. However, I may be changing my mind regarding the natural beauty of poetry. Recently, I began to notice some of the poetry written more than a hundred years ago. Several poems impressed me to the point where I feel they are worthy of reprinting for the enjoyment of the present generation. Although these poems would not be considered "great poetry" by today's standard, they do portray the conditions and the mood of the day.

School Days

In eighteen hundred and seventy two, not having all that much to do, and dreading to remain a fool, I buckled up and went to school.

In a sod house with a dirt floor, with a deep set window and a pine board door;

It was warm in winter, in summer cool, now this was my Nebraska school.

I studied arithmetic, geography and grammar, and practiced the use of a saw and hammer.

I stood six feet above the ground, my weight being one hundred and eighty pounds;

I was large enough to be a man, but my school mates called me "Little Dan.

Written by Daniel Brown. (The Brown family settled in L Precinct in 1871)

Eldon Hostetler

It Ain't What it Used to Be

It was a sweet and restful place, the barbershop of old;
where a man could bring his hairy face, and have it scraped and rolled;
And while the barber did the job, he spoke of Rumler, Ruth and Cobb.
of Monte, Schalk and all the mob of athletes brave and bold.
It was a place where all could hear a story rich and quaint,
or talk of horses, fights and beer, without the least restraint.
A place where men could rave and shout, and criticize a wrestling bout,
and bawl the lowly umpire out, it was but now it ain't.
The barber toils with solemn face; his merry voice is still.
The genial tales that filled the place are rendered void and nil.
For maidens fair with shingled hair have parked themselves in every chair,
while menfolks wait in dumb despair, and all is cold and chill.
This poem appeared in a 1927 newspaper. Author's name not given.

Census Taker

It was the first day of the census, and all through the land;
The pollster was ready—a black book in his hand.
He mounted his horse for a long dusty ride,
his book and some quills tucked close by his side.
A long winding ride down a road barely there
towards the smell of fresh bread wafting up through the air.
The woman was tired, with lines on her face,
and wisps of brown hair she tucked back in place.
She gave him some water…as they sat at the table,
and she answered his questions the best she was able.
He asked of her children…yes she had quite a few.
The oldest was twenty, the youngest not two,
She held up a toddler with cheeks round and red;
Her sister she whispered is napping in bed.
She noted the persons who lived there with pride;
and felt the faint stirrings of the we one inside.
He noted the sex, the color the age,

The marks of his quill soon filled up the page.
At the number of children she nodded her head,
and felt her lips quiver for the three that were dead.
The place of their birth she nearly forgot.
Was it Kansas or Utah, or Oregon, or not.
They came from Scotland, of that she was sure;
and she quickly remembered they'd always been poor.
They spoke of employment, of schooling and such;
they could read and write some…though not very much.
When the questions were answered, his job there was done;
so he mounted his horse and he rode towards the sun.
We can almost imagine his voice, so loud and so clear;
"May God bless you all for another ten years."
(Taken from an old Genealogical Magazine, no date or author given.)

The Corset Curse

    Much like the automobile industry that normally introduces new models every three or four years, the clothing business also depends on change and planned obsolescence. It may come as no surprise that the fashion business has also had its share of "Edsels," including the "zoot suit" in the early 1940s; the "bubble" in the late 1950s; the "Nehru jacket" in the late 1960s; and "hot pants" in the early 1970s. In recent history, a basic fashion, with some variations, has lasted an average of seven to ten years. From 1840 to 1870, wealthy American women imitated the so-called "crinoline craze," better known to many as "hoop skirts." Then came twenty years of more conservative dress known as the "Victorian period," named after Queen Victoria of England. From 1890-1910, the rage appeared to be the "Gibson Girl look (sometimes better known as the "hour glass" look)." The majority of the Milford community wedding pictures taken around 1900-10 show that many local brides were indulging in the Gibson Girl fashion, which depended more or less on tightly laced foundations to achieve the end results.

Eldon Hostetler

Just like many mother-daughter disagreements on proper attire today, this mother, appealing to the editor of the *Gospel Herald* magazine appeared to be having a difficult time selecting clothes for her teenage daughters in 1909:

Brother Editor- I have two young girls who are just in that age when they think they must dress like many of the big girls dress. They want to wear corsets, bringing the plea that many other girls in the church wear them. I am convinced by sad personal experience that corset wearing is ruinous to the health of anyone. Would it be out of place to make a plea through the church paper against such evils? From a concerned Mother.

Answer: When we read 1 Corinthians 6:19-20, and are convinced that health is impaired by its use, we believe it is perfectly right to discuss this subject here. I will give quotations from several able writers. Alice B. Stockman, in *A Book for Every Woman* states: "If women had common sense instead of fashion sense, corsets would not exist. The corset, more than any other one thing, is responsible for women being the victims of disease and doctors. Who can prophesy the untold and manifold sufferings for which a factory of corsets must be responsible? I am a Temperance Woman. No one can realize more than I do the devastation and ruin alcohol in its many forms has brought to the human family. Still I solemnly believe that in weakness and deterioration of health, the corset has more to answer for than intoxicating drinks."

Professor N. H. Flower, in *Fashion and Deformity*, states: "The true form of the human body is familiar to us from classic models. It is, however, quite possible that some of us may think the present fashionable shape the more beautiful of the two. The fact is that in admiring such a distorted form as the constricted waist, we are opposing the Maker of our bodies. We are taking fashion and nothing better, higher or truer, for our guide. Tight lacing is the chief cause of infantile mortality. By girting the lungs, stomach, heart and diaphragm, it cripples every one of the life manufacturing functions, impairs circulation, prevents muscular action and is thereby very injurious to good health. Christian fathers, mothers, sisters and brothers, come let us with one accord unite in presenting a frowning face to this race-ruining practice. May we all desire to glorify God with our bodies in the form he has created us."

The Way It Was

One hundred years ago, one newspaper editor spoke his mind concerning the latest in women's fashions; but, contrary to today's trend, apparently designed to wear as little as possible, it appeared to be a problem of wearing too much: "Our Village daddies must wake up or York will 'distance us.' An ordinance has been introduced in York preventing all persons from wearing at public gatherings—felt, broad, slouch, sailor, derby, or any other kind of hat or cap, bonnet, plumes, or any trimming or ornamentation, false hair, false teeth, bangs scrambled or unscrambled, in such fashion in such a way as to obstruct the view or prevent the diffusion or transmission of ideas. Nor shall persons wear sleeves fluted, frilled, scalloped, puffed, balloon, ballot, short, long, round, elbow, jointed coat or any other kind unless they are rolled up parallel with the ears. It might go pretty hard with milliners and dressmakers, but more money could be saved for tobacco and people could sure see much better (*Pleasant Dale Quizz,* March 27, 1897)."

Why one city passed an ordinance forbidding the wearing of hats at public gatherings. Mrs. D.F. Todd, Milford public school teacher. Circa 1895.

Eldon Hostetler

Bibliography

While the lions' share of the information concerning Milford and Seward County history was taken from Local newspapers and old county histories, other stories dealing with topics concerning world and American history were written largely from information taken from Collier's Encyclopedia, published by the Crowell-Collier Education Corporation (1970). Other works consulted include:

America's Fascinating Indian Heritage, Reader's Digest Association, 1978.
Dick, Everett. "Conquering the Great American Desert." Nebraska State Historical Society.
Hamil, Harold, *Nebraska No Place Quite Like It*. Lowell Press, 1985.
Holter, Donald W., *Flames on the Plains*. Parthenon Press, 1983.
Jackson, Helen, *A Century of Dishonor*. Indian Head Books.
Lass, William E. *From the Missouri to the Great Salt Lake*. Nebraska State Historical Society, 1972.
Latourette, Kenneth Scott, *A History of Christianity*. Harper Brothers.
Lee, Wayne C., *Wild Towns of Nebraska*, Caxton Press, 1992.
Mattes, Merrill J., "The Great Platte River Road," Nebraska State Historical Society, 1969.
Morrison, Samuel, *The Oxford History of the American People*. Oxford Press, 1965.
Moulton, Candy, *Roadside History of Nebraska*. Mountain Press, 1997.
Nabokow, Peter, *Native American Testimony*, Penguin Books.
Olson, James C. And Naugle, Ronald C., *History of Nebraska*, Third Edition. University of Nebraska Press, 1997.
The *Peoples Almanac #2*, edited by David Wallechinsky and Irvin Wallace, 1987.
The Story of America, Reader's Digest Association.
Where the Roses Grow Wild, Roseland Centennial Committee, 1987.
World Almanac and Book of Facts, World Almanac Books, 2003.